MODERN SOUTHEAST ASIA SER.

Stephen F. Maxner, *General Editor*

Also in the series

UPHILL BATTLE

Reflections on Viet Nam Counterinsurgency

Frank Scotton

Texas Tech University Press

This book is typeset in Minion Pro. The paper used in this book meets the minimum
requirements of ANSI/NISO Z39.48-1992 (R1997). ∞

Designed by Kasey McBeath
Cover designed by David Deal

Library of Congress Cataloging-in-Publication Data

Scotton, Frank, author.
  Uphill battle : reflections on Viet Nam counterinsurgency / Frank Scotton.
    pages cm — (Modern Southeast Asia series)
  Includes bibliographical references and index.
  ISBN 978-0-89672-869-1 (hardcover : alk. paper) — ISBN 978-0-89672-867-7
(pbk. : alk. paper) — ISBN 978-0-89672-868-4 (e-book) 1. Vietnam War, 1961-
1975—Personal narratives, American. 2. Counterinsurgency—Vietnam. I. Title. II.
Series: Modern Southeast Asia series.
  DS559.5.S395 2014
  959.704'34—dc23   2014003526

14 15 16 17 18 19 20 21 22 / 9 8 7 6 5 4 3 2 1

Texas Tech University Press
Box 41037 | Lubbock, Texas 79409-1037 USA
800.832.4042 | ttup@ttu.edu | www.ttupress.org

Contents

Illustrations

Preface

cclivity is ascending terrain. On maps the proximity of topographical lines indicates relative steepness. For the United States of America, and especially for us serving in Viet Nam from 1960 through 1975, the conflict had a certain "uphill battle" aspect throughout the war. Struggling through the early advisory period, we thought well-intentioned Americans deploying resources could tutor counterpart Vietnamese to a level of competence that would match the competition. Disappointment at our failure to reach the summit argued for increasing numbers of advisors. When that did not work as anticipated, then introduction of regular combat units was thought (by some) to be what might carry American policy to the crest. However, the mountain was so precipitous that increasing the number of deployed units never fully satisfied MACV's expressed need.

Our notional strategy was so flawed as to be incomprehensible in retrospect. Americans spoke of the war and "the other war," while the Viet Nam Communist Party conducted one war. Attrition worked both ways. When America began falling back, political will exhausted, from commitment in Viet Nam, some officials hoped that a pacification regimen supporting an authoritarian regime might still secure what foreign advisors and brigades had failed to obtain. But ARVN could not fill the space vacated by foreign divisions on the game board,[1] and the American pacification structure and practice were unsuccessful grafts on the Republic of Viet Nam. Perpetuating the war was expedient for some politicians in America but tragic in consequence for those who bore the burden. Failure of the illusion that pacification could substitute for political dynamic in the Republic of Viet Nam was made obvious by rapid erosion and collapse in 1975.

I was an ordinary young man with an opportunity to serve in an extraordinary, challenging environment. I was counseled and encouraged by an uncommon supervisor who overlooked my raw ignorance and encouraged me to seek knowledge and share risk with Vietnamese friends. Ev Bumgardner provided guidance, unmistakably, but allowed me flexibility in carrying out directions. My account is also in part his story. He was a sponsor while introducing me to others, especially John Vann and Howard Walters, in 1962. Other "elder brothers" who extended friendship were Jack Gibney, Robert Kelly, John Bennett, and Bob Montague.

Vietnamese friends—Nguyen Be, Nguyen Duy Be, Ha Thuc Can, Tran Ngoc Chau, Jusiu, Nay Luette, Phan Manh Luong, Do Minh Nhat, Tran Van Phien, Touneh Ton, Tran Huu Tri, Nguyen Tuy, Nguyen thi Kim Vui, and many others— shared adventures and insights into the history and sociology of their country. Vietnamese in hamlets, local militia units, province and district towns, churches, and pagodas and even prisoners were approachable and shared thoughts about their country. Some government ministers and senior military officers were also responsive. I think that was because of my trying to speak their language, even when I didn't speak it well; showing trust by keeping conversations private; and never insulting them by suggesting payment for information or that our relationship would be exploited for my benefit. When I thought a conversation drew information of immediate interest to the US mission, I would ask permission to report what was shared. Often a discussant would prefer that the information or opinion remain private, and I would honor that preference but find another way to weave it, unattributed, into discussion with other Americans.[2] I never betrayed a confidence.[3]

David Engel, Dick Holbrooke, Jerry Dodson, Jim Nach, Phil Werbiski, and Jean Sauvageot are representative of other young Americans who were learning about Viet Nam at the same time with me. Looking over the literature of American involvement in Viet Nam, I feel there is little recognition of the unofficial candid exchange of information and policy discussion among us in person or by letters. My observations, documented to the extent that I can, will fill only part of that vacuum.

The reader may be surprised that a civilian worked with military and paramilitary units. When I arrived in Viet Nam during 1962 there was (relative to what came later) absence of doctrine, organizational rigidity, and placement within boxes from which there could be no escape. Moreover, my immediate supervisor, Ev Bumgardner, put no limit on my horizons and in fact set expectations that kept me reaching. Had I been first assigned in 1966 or later, I would have been hobbled by increased structural discipline.

When going to central Viet Nam to be eyes, ears, and pair of hands for Ev Bumgardner, I tried to meet as many people, Vietnamese and American, as possible and then to follow up over time with those we could usefully support. In one province the most knowledgeable and approachable discussant might be the USOM provincial representative, and in another the MAAG (later MACV) sector advisor or a Vietnamese administrator or army officer. I cannot reproduce all the conversations, but every one contributed to my education and understanding. I felt year by year there was always more for me to learn. Even during return travel on orders in 1996 and 1997, I sought to increase my personal level of understanding.

Although I was twice ill with dengue fever and hepatitis, and survived exchanges of fire and a helicopter crash, this narrative is not one of courage controlling fear. Brave men and women on every side risked all in battle or political struggle, over and over, and suffered for their belief or unit loyalty. My occasional moments of daring do not bear comparison with their prolonged exposure and sacrifice. I will instead describe a Viet Nam education and portray field problems with approaches developed for their resolution. While not intending to write a chronology of any part of Viet Nam's thirty-year war (1945–75), I do mention some circumstances and events (often as footnotes) in order to place observations, decisions, and project involvement in context. Especially during the period 1962–66 I was only vaguely aware of Washington debate, developing policy, and leading personalities. Much of the description in the first several chapters is like the view from a hamlet's deep well located in Binh Dinh, Long An, Quang Ngai, Chau Doc, or some other province; I looked upward from time to time but was most familiar with my immediate surroundings.

From 1970 onward I was more cognizant of the Saigon and Washington dimension of the war, although without concomitant expectation of success. For those years as well, commentary is derived from the particulars of what I personally observed or was reliably informed. No one volume, or perhaps even set of volumes under one editor, can fully account for the Vietnamese-American relationship from 1945 through 1975. Even two officers in the same organization will see Viet Nam differently. When Barry Zorthian speaks or writes about his JUSPAO stewardship, he understandably focuses on mission press policy, media operations, and mission council activity, whereas for me that was his distant infield while I played outfield.

I call this beautiful country Viet Nam, whereas much of the literature spells it Vietnam. Either is acceptable, but I believe spelling as two separate words provides a more accurate sense for the pronunciation and is consistent with common abbreviations such as ARVN, RVN, VNCH, PAVN, and so on. Personal force of habit causes me to write some place names as one word, Saigon or Danang, rather than two syllables; likewise, for most tribal place names I usually run syllables together. I can not seem to refrain from that inconsistency. My spelling of Vietnamese names, places, and phrasing is without diacritical marks, but I think Vietnamese readers will understand from context and compensate for the omission. Here and there I provide a Vietnamese word or phrase. Faulty memory might produce error. I also acknowledge regional differences and even generational change for some Vietnamese expressions and slang.[4] It is a marvelously expressive and happy language, and I smile whenever I hear it spoken. There is a strongly felt Vietnamese belief that no one can understand Vietnamese people as well as Vietnamese understand themselves. Khong ai hieu nguoi Viet bang nguoi Viet. I endeavored to be a partial exception.

For the most part (but not always) I provide names without rank. This is because over the years rank changed (as Maj. Nguyen Be became a lieutenant colonel and, ultimately, colonel), but the person stayed the same.

The narrative flow proceeds from year to year, but I provide three reflective intermissions to summarize and consider matters that were on my mind in early 1965, later in mid-1967, and again in mid-1973.

I do my best, from memory, to restore conversation that captures the personality of a friend or the dynamic of a particular event. Except in a couple of instances when a friend asked that his name be withheld, sources are identified. When I cite a reference, it will be available either as part of a well-known research collection or from my papers, memoranda, and collected documents (Ngo Van Binh Collection). There is no shortage of footnotes, and that is because writing early in the twenty-first century requires placing pitons for following climbers not familiar with the terrain. The opinions and feelings expressed are based on my personal involvement. I will be, as long as compos mentis, responsive to researchers whose curiosity is piqued by this text.

I stored boxes of maps, correspondence, books, and other research material, but, despite requests, I never motivated myself to develop a written account of events to be shared with other people.[5] My reluctance was due to continuing assignments in the Foreign Service and consequent lack of time to examine the past. Several years ago, after realizing my son and daughter did not have a research curiosity for ancient and contemporary Viet Nam, I provided everything to Ngo Van Binh. When I reference something from those materials, I will note it as being in the Binh Collection. I finally decided to share Viet Nam memories for three reasons. First, much of what I read is mistaken, so I want to provide an accurate account of what I observed and tried to do.[6] Second, conveying a sense of what happened in Viet Nam should prove that every national environment (historic political culture) is unique. Third, I ought to express appreciation for my association with unforgettable Vietnamese and Americans who accepted and carried out their duty.

Do not suppose that my text is shaped to make it appear as though I was more perceptive than at the time and on the spot. It is not difficult to evaluate a situation and scale probability versus possibility. One need only understand the environment, make dispassionate analysis of the operative factors in a situation, gauge relative intensity and form of interaction, and then make a prediction.[7] The difficulty is that analysis and estimate may provide a conclusion that hierarchal others are loath to receive. You will read that I did not foresee the emergence of Nguyen Van Thieu, but once he attained power I did perceive he would be tragically inadequate to the challenge posed by Viet Nam's Communist Party.

Frequency of the first-person pronoun should not be misconstrued as reflecting an egotistical sense that I was more than a minor figure in the Vietnamese-American drama. It is simply a consequence of portraying what I was personally involved in or personally observed or a matter of which I had well-informed knowledge. I mean to serve as no more than a lens through which some aspects of Viet Nam from 1962 through 1975 can be viewed. What may seem excessive attention to myself is just background for evaluating reasoning and conclusions. Descriptions of others and judgment of their performance may read as severe. William Colby noted that propensity forty years ago in Viet Nam.[8] I do not, personally or professionally, spare myself.

Finally, believing government service provided opportunity to work with admirable people of Vietnamese and American nationality, and that many of them died in the course of duty or subsequently as the actuarial factor operated, it would be dishonorable to profit from their memory and the work that we did together. Moreover, it is ethically questionable for retired officials to profit from their own accounts of service for which they have already been compensated. Therefore all proceeds from sales of this book will be specifically to the publisher, Texas Tech University, in appreciation for the university's maintaining the Vietnam Center and Archive.

Chung ta khong bao gio quen duoc nhung nguoi da hi sinh vi dat
nuoc Viet Nam than yeu.

Frank Scotton

UPHILL BATTLE

1
Initiation

We all get two kinds of toilet training. The first is applied by parents and accomplished (maybe with difficulty) at such an early age we have no memory of it when having our turn with the next generation. The second, what Ev Bumgardner called "adult toilet training," is while we are on our first real job with a supervisor and we are instructed in how to perform without embarrassing ourselves.

I was a recently appointed officer in the foreign service of the United States Information Agency (USIA) when my wife and I arrived in Saigon in 1962.[1] Junior officer training in Washington had been pedestrian at best. I had made my own arrangements for orientation at Fort Bragg and had argued (successfully) for some study of Vietnamese.[2] Everet Bumgardner met us on arrival and brought tired travelers to lunch with him and his family. He would coordinate the junior officer trainee phase of my assignment, which would include spending time with each of the USIS sections before finally getting attached to one of them for the remainder of my tour of duty.[3] He advised me to expect considerable time with him, the USIS field operations officer, because he was increasing activity in selected provinces.

During and after lunch he briefly described the Information Section (including media relations, publications, and motion pictures); the Cultural Section (including English teaching, the Vietnamese American Association and Library, visiting scholars, and occasional visual or performing artists); the Research Office, just beginning to collect and analyze SVNLF (South Viet Nam Liberation Front)[4] material; and his own nascent

Field Operations Office. He told us the Field Operations Office consisted, right then, of himself and a Vietnamese assistant, Ung Van Luong, but he had agreement with the Directorate General of Information to place a USIS Vietnamese employee with the Vietnamese Information Service (VIS) in each province.[5] The purpose of VIS was to support Republic of Viet Nam communication with citizens, especially in rural areas. But, Everet said, for support to be effective, we need to know what is happening in each province. So he required biweekly reporting from the provincial representatives. The impetus for the program was amplification of his USIS experience in Laos. He also did field liaison with the USIS branch public affairs officers (located in Hue, Dalat, and Can Tho), who conducted USIS programs in each of their regions at the direction of the country public affairs officer, John Mecklin.

After registering in the Continental Hotel annex, we reported to USIS and were processed there and then once more by the embassy administrative section. Late in the day Everet introduced me to John Mecklin. John had worked with Time-Life until he entered government service a year earlier. He had significant experience as a journalist in Viet Nam, was with photographer Robert Capa when Capa was killed in 1954 in North Viet Nam, and was respected by many who had an Indo-China baptism during that period. John welcomed me into the USIS family and said there could not be a better guide than Ev Bumgardner. "But Ev is persuasive, and he will try to pull you into field operations long term. Don't make a commitment until you spend time with the other sections."

The man who would provide my "adult toilet training" just smiled. I think he sensed that he already had me. Everet Franklin Bumgardner was born in western Virginia and grew up hunting squirrels and playing pranks with other family members. As a youth he was an amateur boxer in tank towns along the East Coast.[6] He enlisted in the US Navy during World War II as soon as he was of age. When the war was over, he attended George Washington University to study photography. He took employment with USIA as a photojournalist for *Free World* magazine. Most of his assignments, beginning with the Korean War, were in Asia. Moving in and out of Indo-China, he met, courted, and married a young woman from a Mekong Delta family who was educated in Dalat and worked for the Viet Nam national airline. He was the field operations officer in Laos before assignment to Viet Nam. Like John Mecklin, he was acquainted with many people who had previous assignments (with mixed results) in the region. Everet was twelve years older than I, shorter, muscled, wiry, and balding. (In one photograph his wife showed me from the Laos years, he was heavier, bearded, and looked a bit like the performer Burl Ives. Everet was not amused when I suggested some similarity.) As we left John Mecklin's office, my appointed "guide" told me I ought to just call him Ev, since everyone else did.

The Field Operations Office for USIS was located on the lower floor of the Rex Building, adjacent to the movie theatre of the same name. USIS rented three floors in what was previously a French commercial building. Ev Bumgardner's work area was next to the garage space by the vehicle side entrance off Le Loi Street. I was allowed a few days to poke around Saigon, settle with my wife in a small house rented by the embassy from Nguyen Van Y (National Police director) on an alley off Ngo Dinh Khoi Street,[7] and familiarize myself with the Bumgardner files of folders, maps, and reports beginning to come in from the first Vietnamese employees assigned to the provinces. Ev promised travel to a couple of provinces as a necessary tutorial for me.[8]

Our first pedagogical trip was to Kien Hoa. We drove down Route 4 over the Ben Luc Bridge and through Long An, then to My Tho, and took the ferry across one of the Mekong branches on our way to Ben Tre.[9] We were bringing a USIS Vietnamese employee to work in the Kien Hoa office of the Vietnamese Information Service. Ev's practice was to have an American officer personally introduce each new representative to province officials. He said this was absolutely necessary because, even though there was agreement between the Directorate General of Information and USIS, Saigon was remote (in every way) from the provinces. He taught that every new project needed a recognizable face, because before anyone buys into your program, they have to buy into you. Ev would say: "First you sell yourself, and then you can sell the program."

As we drove, Ev required me to be observant and to prepare for discussion during return travel; meanwhile, he distracted me with running commentary on what he had witnessed during the previous several years. His method was to assert a conclusion, provide reasoning, and expect a reaction. If none was drawn forth (and I was too much a rookie for intelligent questions, much less opinions), then he would provide further instruction. I realized months later that from the beginning he was torn between loving argumentation and a need for me to comprehend and digest his cram course.

The French, he said, paternalistically preserved Laos from Thai encroachment, revived Cambodia distinct from Thailand and Viet Nam, divided Viet Nam from within (the better to maintain control), and wherever possible exploited all three countries while brutally suppressing any movement for independence. He elaborated by describing the colonial period division of Viet Nam into three regions with different forms of government and then separation of the Central Highlands (supposedly for protecting tribespeople) to provide exclusive exploitation by French enterprises and settlers. Opportunity for Laotians, Cambodians, and Vietnamese in education, local government, and police auxiliaries often depended on conversion to Catholicism, signaling acceptance of a *demi-francaise* role. I asked whether achieving independence in 1955 had not made irrelevant the colonial history that he summarized.

"Not at all," Ev responded. "Well, in the North, colonial baggage might just be for the history books all right, because they won, and won big. They not only took the North, but they won big chunks of the Center and South too, and then had to settle 'temporary until elections' for less than earned from 1945 to 1955." More important, Ev told me, the 1954 Geneva Agreement recognized the independence of Viet Nam but did not establish a separate national territory for the South. The Republic of Viet Nam, he said, has to create conditions for independence from the North, win support from the population, and then fight to maintain its own identity. Ev went on to describe anticolonial President Diem as a man of good character but aloof personality and so disconnected that on assumption of the prime ministry (and later the presidency), he relied on the same civil service clerks, constabulary, and police personnel that previously served French masters.

Furthermore, he said, President Diem is not comfortable with his own people. Ev described a visit to Phu Yen province when Ngo Dinh Diem was introducing himself as the new national leader.[10] Ev said that he witnessed an enthusiastic reaction from local people, and President Diem appeared excited in response. But thereafter, and especially following an assassination attempt in 1957 at Banmethuot, he retracted back into the security of family and palace. Ev actually laughed and said that even the palace was not as safe as Diem expected, since paratroopers surrounded the grounds in 1960, and recently two air force planes had dropped bombs on it.[11]

A fundamental mistake, Ev continued, was that beginning in 1956 and intensifying in 1957, the government conducted a countrywide campaign to identify everyone who had fought against the French, had supported anti-French activity, or had relatives involved with the Viet Minh.[12] More than anything else, this operation and inherent abuse of police power made it easier to resuscitate the residual communist apparatus in the South. So the December 1960 announcement of the Liberation Front for South Viet Nam was a step the Viet Nam Communist Party would have eventually taken anyway, but was made more plausible by government stumblebumming.[13]

Approaching the line at the ferry landing, Ev drove right to the head of the line, passing vehicles that were already waiting their turn. When we took lunch at a kiosk by the side of a small lake in Ben Tre, I asked him if it were not contradictory for us to advocate a different way for government to relate to citizens and then take our own advantage by seizing the head of line at a ferry landing. Ev bristled. The Vietnamese employee who we were escorting to Kien Hoa answered for him by saying, "If we lived in Kien Hoa, Ong Buom would certainly wait, but he has to hurry so that he can have you home again tonight."[14] Ev sulked for a bit, and I thought perhaps my asperity would mean a long, silent ride back to Saigon. But pretty soon his need to educate overcame his irritation. Ev spoke, while we ate, of Kien Hoa during the French war period, when the province was under command of Colonel Leroy, a French/Vietnamese officer who armed Catholic militia and suppressed Viet Minh activity but unintentionally so fractured the province that it was now a seed bed for communist expansion.

We met briefly with the Kien Hoa province chief, Tran Ngoc Chau, and spent more time with the head of the Vietnamese Information Service (VIS). Ev described our representative in the VIS office as a link intended to improve USIS support to information work in the provinces. Nothing was said about our representative link reporting to us on provincial conditions and developments.

Departing Ben Tre, once again we went to the head of the line at the ferry landing. Ev kept looking in my direction, checking reaction. I simply said, "I know, you have to get me home tonight." He grunted affirmation, not particularly in good humor, adding, "And we are going to make a short stop outside My Tho." Returning to his tutorial mode, he spoke admiringly of Province Chief Tran Ngoc Chau. He described Chau, a former Viet Minh officer, as one of the few independent thinkers not hounded into detention or irrelevance by the Diem family. Strangely, he added, the previous Kien Hoa province chief was also former Viet Minh,[15] but his being Catholic might have afforded some protection, whereas Chau was Buddhist. Ev continued by saying that although the past province chief had a reputation for honesty and was now assigned strategic hamlet responsibilities, Chau developed an approach to governance that could have applicability in other provinces. Ev explained that Chau's way depended on respect for the people, identifying their grievances, and taking steps to resolve problems. I thought that seemed pretty basic, but Ev informed me that in almost every respect Chau was exceptional.

The province files that he assigned for reading were impressive by detail and volume, and I asked Ev how he acquired so much information. I told him that half the time the sense of what he conveyed seemed far from what I was told in Washington just a few weeks earlier. Ev smiled rather grimly and responded that it did not surprise him that I barely knew anything about Viet Nam, or that what I thought I knew was irrelevant or just plain wrong. He said the important question was whether I would make a consistent effort to learn, to really learn. He went on to say that nobody would ever know as much about Viet Nam and the Vietnamese as they knew about each other; second, everything he knew was taught by Vietnamese; and third, he would always need to keep learning.

A short drive from the Dinh Tuong province side of the ferry crossing brought us to an American advisory detachment north of My Tho. Ev said this compound, originally built as a Catholic seminary facility, was the location of the advisory team for the ARVN 7th Infantry Division. "If we're lucky, we might catch the senior advisor, John Vann."

We were lucky, although I did not think so on first acquaintance. One could not expect another person who would appear even more pugnacious than Everet Bumgardner. I was tired, and not yet simpatico with Ev, so their rapid exchange of derogative greetings was confusing. That rooster of a colonel grabbed my hand and, while pumping it furiously, said with great enthusiasm, "Stick with old Ev here, and he'll get you killed for sure!" Nor was I pleased to hear Ev respond, "Naw, he's so ignorant, he'll manage that on his own." Only later, when I found out they both had western Virginia roots, did I figure that was just good old country boy humor. Ev and

John ("Call me John," he said, "as long as you're here with Ev, and save the rank for when there're others around.") got into some discussion about the past failure of something called "agrovilles," problems with newer strategic hamlets, and John's difficulty getting performance from his counterpart.[16]

Later, driving back through Long An toward Saigon, Ev asked what I learned during the day. I responded that it seemed from what he told me, and what I had observed, that this was a late innings ball game, and I'm thrown in not knowing the other players or even the rules.

"Well," he said, "it's more like a fight, wrestling or boxing, and here you are in the ring, and there really aren't rules. Except that the other guys can win by knockout or points, and we can only win on points."

"Why can't we win by knockout?"

"Because," he said patiently, "the fight is here in the South, not in the North. So they can go for the knockout and we can't."

"Then who judges points?"

"Okay," Ev answered, "good question. We can't be sure yet. Could be the Vietnamese people, or could be the American voter. One side will out-last the other, retain support of its base, and then 'enough will be enough' for the loser."

I was almost asleep as we approached Phu Lam at the edge of Saigon. But Ev was not finished. "How many Viet Cong did you see today?"

I told him that I didn't suppose I saw any. He asked whether I would know one. I guessed out loud, for his benefit, that there wouldn't be any way of knowing. He then asked whether any Viet Cong might have seen us. I acknowledged that could have happened.

"So," Ev concluded, "today you found out that you don't know very much. I hope now you'll bear down and learn all you can. It's the key to being useful, and maybe the key to survival."

Back in Saigon, Ev instructed me to have a local print shop do some business cards. He suggested that the cards simply have my name, the office address, and a translation of "United States Information Service," all on one side. He advised me not to print the phone number on the card, but to write it on the back if I decided to provide the number to someone. Ev said with that card one could gain admittance to any office in the country, because few would know what USIS meant, but, being curious, they would want to find out. He urged me, when not temporarily in another section for orientation or traveling with or for him, to be constantly learn-ing, and the best way was to get away from Americans and meet Vietnamese. He applied only one restriction: avoid politically active personalities. A mistake could result in expulsion and reflect poorly on him.

Since there was mention in My Tho of agrovilles and strategic hamlets, I decided to read into those subjects. Ev's files were crisp and informative. The agroville concept had been a 1958 to 1961 initiative designed to separate the population from SVNLF activity, while at the same time providing improved social, medical, and agricultural services. I deduced from my reading that whatever the theoretical benefits might have been, implementation failed for three reasons. First, agrovilles were placed at the very beginning in some of the toughest areas.[17] Second, condensing what had been a dispersed population into a concentrated location for defense was a major inconvenience and point of resentment. Third, resources necessary for improved government services were inadequate relative to need. The strategic hamlet vision, in contrast (as it seemed to me from descriptive papers), appeared more modest in that it would deal with a smaller basic community, there should be less dislocation, and slow, deliberate implementation could allow for corrections. I decided to look up Pham Ngoc Thao, previously Kien Hoa province chief and now inspector for strategic hamlets.

Colonel Thao was a fascinating, almost mesmerizing, character, but simultaneously somewhat Mephistophelian. Whereas I had thought strategic hamlets would be created with some caution, Colonel Thao informed me that speed was critical to success, and mistakes could be corrected later. He let me know, pretty early in our meeting, that he had many American friends, had been active ("very active," he said) with the Viet Minh, was Catholic, and was a good friend of Archbishop Ngo Dinh Thuc. He also told me that he had a brother in the Hanoi government. He asked what I thought of that. When I replied it was a common circumstance in civil wars, and we had experienced that during our own history, he replied, "Exactement!" Our conversation was a mix of Vietnamese, English, and French. Although he complimented me for trying to speak Vietnamese, his striving to be a persuasive conversationalist did not allow the time required to patch together my meaning from tortuous attempts to express myself in his language. It seemed as though he treated me to a practiced performance, but I was also convinced that I needed to take a look at real strategic hamlets.

Ev told me that the closest strategic hamlet high-priority national campaign area was in Ben Cat just north of Saigon. USIS even produced a single-sheet news periodical, *Kien quoc*, in a special Binh Duong edition for that strategic hamlet priority zone. Ev said he could give me a carbine for "noise making comfort," and I could drive up there the next morning and return in the afternoon. "Not too late in the afternoon," he cautioned. He asked that I check in with local officials, any American advisor who might be around, and then look up the VIS office for assistance in visiting a hamlet information reading room.

The next morning when I departed from the office, other than the M1 folding-stock carbine,[18] Ev also insisted on providing me with an experienced driver. "A precaution," he said. "Don't want you winding up in Cambodia." Off we went. Did I know what I was doing? Not at all.

We went through the suburb of Gia Dinh, itself capital of the province by the same name that wrapped around Saigon. We reached Route 13 and drove north through some visually pleasing countryside, with more roll to the terrain than the simpler flatness of rice fields interrupted by distant tree lines seen during travel to Kien Hoa. We paused in Thu Dau Mot, a pleasant, well-treed small town with interesting shops and small restaurants. I immediately wished this were our destination, but we pressed onward another twenty-five kilometers to reach Ben Cat. This place had a grubby appearance, and I wondered whether it was just a simple market-town convenience for nearby rubber plantations. We found the local VIS office. They were surprised that we had driven up from Saigon with no advance notification,[19] but everyone in the office was friendly and seemed glad to have visitors. After tea, and I already learned that tea would be a constant part of the Vietnamese diet, a couple of VIS employees took their vehicle, an old Willys station wagon,[20] and drove away on a side road from town. We followed, soon pulled up behind them, and shortly passed through a crude gateway and entered a cluster of rural houses. We were within a mixed palisade–barbed wire enclosure that stretched away from the gate until it disappeared in the foliage that also sheltered additional homes a distance from those immediately before us. A sign just inside the gate, artistically painted to include a flaming torch emblem, proclaimed, "Ap Chien Luoc bao dam An Ninh, xay dung Xa Hoi Moi." We agreed, as I puzzled it out, that the meaning was, "Strategic hamlets guarantee security and build a new society."

Sitting in the hamlet reading room, actually a small shack, I noticed bundles of *Kien quoc* and so enquired as to their usefulness. The answer was that all publications were very popular, and usually the reading room was crowded. When pointing out that the bundled material, including some copies of *The gioi tu do* (Free World) magazine, could also be distributed within the hamlet, there was embarrassed silence. I added that USIS could even provide additional copies. Finally one of the two who had guided us to the hamlet explained that it was better not to bother people in their homes, and then he added that it was "safer to let people come to the reading room when they had time." Gradually, as we conversed, it was apparent that not everyone in this strategic hamlet was content with the new society experience. Several families (at least) had been relocated to within the perimeter fence, and in fact they often returned to their previous homes. Both men acknowledged that at night security around the hamlet was inconsistent. When asked about security within the hamlet, the answer was "cung vay" (also same). As we made farewells and departed, our two friends were carefully locking the reading room to preserve the precious material within.

I was exhilarated: a trip with driver, on our own, and learning—not entirely comfortable with all that was learned, but learning. A short distance from Ben Cat, transiting an area of rubber trees not far from the road, our USIS jeep wagon was the target of a couple of rounds. With primeval survival instinct, the driver hunched lower over the steering wheel and accelerated. I had not expected anything like that, but the driver assured me there was nothing unusual about warning shots around rubber plantations. "Everybody in there Viet Minh," he confided. Later, over a bowl of soup in Thu Dau Mot, I swore him to secrecy. My concern was that if Ev was informed of the ballistic incident, he might forbid further road travel. I didn't yet understand Ev Bumgardner as I would in the months and years to come. Proud of my persuasiveness, I also failed to realize that, of course, the driver would faithfully report everything to Ev, because he was the *ong chu* (boss).

Ev did seem pleased with my report and safe return. He said he expected, while hoping to be wrong, that strategic hamlets would be folly on a grander scale than agrovilles. "Anyone who cites Malaya as a case in favor of strategic hamlets does not understand the demographic difference between that country and Viet Nam." And he believed the program would be pushed too quickly. When told that Pham Ngoc Thao thought mistakes could be corrected later, Ev was doubtful. "In this country mistakes are never corrected, they just accumulate and fester."

I asked why rubber plantations seemed to be Viet Minh land. He replied that thirty years earlier, during the world depression, desperate Vietnamese, especially from the north, were contracted to work on the expanding French plantations in the south. They were worked like slaves, came to hate the French lords, and so were an important source of manpower and support for the Viet Minh. Now, he said, we were into a second generation that supports the SVNLF almost instinctively.

After two weeks of orientation in the Cultural Section, my next trip was to An Loc, the capital of Binh Long province. Ev wanted me to bring posters and publications to the Military Assistance Advisory Group (MAAG) team. He told me this trip, an overnight one, would have to be by air, because road travel to An Loc was excessively risky. He explained that visitors from Saigon were always an imposition on the hospitality and good humor of a remote team, and the best way to win acceptance was to bring a couple of containers of ice cream. Good advice!

I prepared all the necessary travel gear and, with dry ice packed around the ice cream and wrapped in thick toweling, got dropped off at Tan Son Nhut so early the next morning that there was opportunity to speak with the pilot about a small course diversion.

Several days earlier, when talking with Ev about special difficulties in the plantation zone north of Saigon, he told me that a year before my arrival a communist force of a few hundred had briefly seized Phuoc Vinh (capital of Phuoc Thanh province), executed the province chief, fought off government reinforcements, and then disappeared back into the forests of what he called Zone D. I hated to be constantly asking questions that taxed him and revealed my ignorance. It should be possible to just find out on my own what Zone D was all about. As we stood before the large wall map in his office, it looked like Phuoc Vinh was somewhat northward from Saigon, probably not more than sixty kilometers distant and maybe only thirty from Ben Cat, where I had been just weeks earlier.

So, when planning my short visit to An Loc, I thought of seeing, at least from the air, what Phuoc Thanh province looked like. That morning the pilot, after glancing at his chart, was agreeable to a slight alteration of flight plan. We flew generally north, following Route 13, then approaching Ben Cat slipped slightly north-northeast. In a few minutes the pilot told me that we were over Phuoc Vinh and would circle. I could not have imagined such a modest-appearing province capital, nor expected the extent to which plantation and forest growth enveloped the small town. There were low hills to the north, and the Central Highlands were northeast on the distant horizon. Now I could visualize, as not possible on the Saigon map, how a sizable force could mass unseen, strike, and afterward submerge back into the forests and rubber plantations.

From the airspace over Phuoc Vinh we flew west-northwest until we sighted Highway 13, then turned toward An Loc. The sky was clear, and this light aircraft was a high-wing, single-engine Cessna type, if not an actual Cessna, so the view was unobstructed. The pilot was conversational, telling me he was previously an air force officer, and he expected to return to air force duty within a few months. He tolerated, with good humor, my effort to speak Vietnamese and offered helpful corrections. I asked him why the area that we flew over was called Zone D.[21] He replied that he only knew it was an old Viet Minh term for the area that was now included in Phuoc Thanh province.[22] He added that there was also a Zone C to the west in upper Tay Ninh province, but that he had never heard of a Zone A or B. We parted on the runway in An Loc. We did not meet again, and I regret not remembering his name.

The American military advisory team welcomed me as a young strap-hanging visitor and willingly, or at least kindly, set up a cot and mosquito net. I am positive the Bumgardner ticket, two gallons of ice cream, was persuasive. An NCO drove me downtown to meet the VIS chief for the province.[23] He just dropped me off so that I could make my own way back. The VIS office was a small building with little equipment. Two other employees were present when I paid my call. They seemed glad to have a visitor and welcomed the few bundles of publications I brought along. When asked what would be done with the material, the chief told me it was difficult to make any distribution outside An Loc. He said rubber plantation management (still French for the most part) did not welcome government reach into the plantations. "They are neutralists," he claimed, "and pay taxes to the communists." There was another glimpse of complex Vietnamese reality. It had not occurred to naïve me that enterprises were paying taxes to both sides. He went on to say there was a VIS branch office in Loc Ninh, and he could send some material to that town by bus.

One of the employees graciously offered to show me around town. It took little time, even though there was definitely more to An Loc than what was seen of Phuoc Vinh from the air. I suspected this, like Ben Cat, was primarily a center for all the surrounding plantations. The market sold basic necessities but did not have the variety of goods that could be found in the larger towns of My Tho and Ben Tre. I noticed a small hospital on a slight rise and asked to take a look. My escort was obliging, but embarrassed by what we found. Although not as grim as accounts of the Crimean War, the place was pretty bleak, lacking in equipment, and filthy. There were seven patients, five civilians and two soldiers, but no staff on duty. Asking whether there were other medical facilities in An Loc, I was told there were first aid stations on plantations, and military were usually brought to Bien Hoa. When I wondered out loud whether the province chief was aware of the situation, the reply was, "Ah, the province chief, he is very busy." With an appreciation for Vietnamese tact, I understood that meant the province chief did not trouble with the hospital.

The next day the same VIS employee took me along while he made a rare visit to a nearby rubber plantation. He brought some USIS periodicals for placement at the reading room. That small building was locked (to preserve the reading material, he told me), and as usual (I learned over time), finding the person with the key took awhile. When the keeper of the key finally appeared, he had a sour disposition, as if our visit was a burden. And maybe it was. If what I was told about residual Viet Minh influence on plantations was true, perhaps the key keeper would have to do some explaining after our departure.

My enduring impression, persisting even today, is how chilling a rubber plantation is when you are in the middle of one. The trees are all planted in even rows. If you look in one direction your view is limited to twenty yards, but if you glance at a different angle, down the parallel rows, it seems that you can see all the way to Cambodia. From one direction you are concealed, but from another, completely exposed. Gordon Huddleston, an older experienced Special Forces officer, in 1965 once remarked that the safest way to enter rubber plantations "is on your stomach, very slowly."

Late in the afternoon another aircraft flew into An Loc and returned me to Saigon. I didn't return to Binh Long province until 1973 as a member of a prisoner recovery team.

Ev continued to schedule orientation with other USIS sections, but he also encouraged me to get around Saigon, using the business cards, to meet interesting people. I already knew an office director in the Ministry of Education. We had met in 1960 when he was in Hawaii for a training program. I called on him at his office, and a few days later he organized a lunch with three of his friends. One of them was Nguyen Luu Vien, another interesting former Viet Minh. During lunch Vien told me that, like other patriots, he had joined Vanguard Youth as a young man and later served as a medical officer with the Viet Minh in the north.[24] He said that he left the Viet Minh because of disagreement with one-party control of the national independence movement. As we continued talking, I was unwittingly in violation of Ev's stricture to avoid political personalities, because after mentioning his work as president of the Viet Nam Red Cross Association, Vien began to explain how he happened to draft the Cara-velle Petition in 1960.[25] And, as a result, Vien told me, he had spent a few months in prison the previous year.

When I returned to the office later in the afternoon and told Ev about the interesting lunch and Nguyen Luu Vien, he flinched. He asked me to prepare a brief, repeat brief, memorandum describing lunch with the official of the Ministry of Education whom I knew before arrival in Saigon. "Mention attendance of a former Red Cross Association president. I will tuck that memo deep in our files. If any question is raised about the lunch, then with the memorandum I have you covered. If there aren't any questions, then the memo will eventually be lost. But remember, I would rather have you meet military people, especially those active in psychological and pacification operations. In the end, maybe everything is political in some sense, but try to avoid obvious labels. I don't want to lose you on a misunderstanding."

So, having seen something, even just a small slice, of Ben Cat and An Loc, and following that reminder from Ev, I decided to introduce myself at 5th Division headquarters in Bien Hoa. Vietnamese were always, in my experience, amazingly receptive when strangers introduced themselves. The basic business card that Ev suggested was probably an icebreaker, but I also came to believe that the Vietnamese are innately hospitable. The commanding officer of the 5th Division was Nguyen Duc Thang, but at division headquarters I was told that he had been recently transferred. Fortunately, the chief of staff, Pham Quoc Thuan, was available. Thuan was about thirty-five and (by accent) of northern origin. He told me that he was Catholic, hated communists, and was a 1952 graduate of the military academy in Dalat. Just a couple of months earlier he had returned from a course at Fort Leavenworth. He inquired as to my background and reason for visiting the division. I explained being recently assigned in Viet Nam and hoping to provide information to the provinces that would assist government programs. My bona fides somewhat established, Thuan visibly relaxed, walked over to a large map of the 5th Division area, and began what seemed a candid description of operations and problems. When asked a couple of questions in sketchy Vietnamese, he was patient and good-humored in response.

Basically, Thuan said the 5th Division's principal difficulty was responsibility for an extensive area, much of it forested and with a history of sheltering communists. He said the greatest need was for expansion of ARVN, with at least one more division assigned north of Saigon. I asked about strategic hamlets and government information programs. He said that he did not know much about the latter, but as for strategic hamlets, it seemed to him that it would take a long time for the program to be effective. He said hamlets were supposed to have their own self-defense force that could raise an alarm, resist, and hold out until the district or province sent assistance. However, he explained, there were not always enough young men in a hamlet. Some had disappeared (he looked at me and nodded, supposing that I read his meaning: disappeared to the other side), and those remaining lacked adequate weapons and were fearful. He also cited communication as a major difficulty: How to inform a district or province that an enemy was attacking a hamlet? "Often we do not know until the next morning, and then we have to take care to avoid an ambush as we approach the hamlet."

As we sipped tea, I thanked Thuan for his kindness and explanation of the situation in the 5th Division area of responsibility. I asked how problems might be solved. He replied that for him, everything began with expansion of military strength. As far as strategic hamlets were concerned, he suggested a visit to III Corps headquarters. He referred me to Hoang Van Lac, who was director of pacification planning, and Pham Van Dong, the deputy commander of III Corps and inspector of strategic hamlets.

Up to late 1962, the III Corps area was enormous. It covered the provinces around Saigon and all those within the Mekong Delta.[26] When I called on III Corps headquarters, there was an atmosphere of impending change. Hoang Van Lac was not available. It was explained he would soon be named chief of secretariat for a new interministerial committee coordinating strategic hamlets. Fortunately, I had the opportunity to talk with Pham Van Dong. He told me that working as inspector for strategic hamlets in III Corps was increasingly difficult because there were more and more of them. "And," he grimaced, "when the inspector finds problems, there is much unhappiness."

Pham Van Dong was a colonel whose father had been a sergeant in French forces before World War II. As with many others, I picked up his northern accent, but he made a point of telling me that his place of birth was in Son Tay, a tribal area, and that he was a Buddhist. He said that after partition (the Geneva Conference demarcation of North and South, pending elections and reunification), he commanded the 3rd Field Division at Song Mao before it was reorganized as the 5th Division and relocated to Bien Hoa.[27] He was, he told me, also a 1958 graduate of Fort Leavenworth. I found Dong both voluble and believable. He convinced me that the pace of strategic hamlet expansion should be slowed, with renewed emphasis placed on quality.

I asked Dong why, if that was his conclusion, the program could not at least be altered in III Corps. "Many reasons," he replied. "First of all, I have to be careful how I make my reports. The president believes that we are in a race with the communists to take control of the countryside, and so province chiefs are competing with each other for most strategic hamlets completed." Dong departed for a meeting, but told me that he would always be available for discussion. We did not meet again for a couple of years. Returning to USIS, I felt sure that what had been shared with me would not dispel Ev's sense of foreboding.

A few days later, Ev suggested I drive back to My Tho and spend a couple of days with John Vann. He said that time with Vann would not be wasted. When I arrived, Lieutenant Colonel Vann was about to meet with some of his battalion advisors. Toward the end of the session he invited me to ask some questions. I enquired about experience with strategic hamlets. The reaction was general skepticism. "Potemkin Hamlets" would be more like it, said one lieutenant. They all agreed that the government was satisfied with numbers rather than substance. "The difference between a regular hamlet and a strategic hamlet is a lot of barbed wire," commented another advisor. A captain in the room suggested that Kien Hoa might be an exception. Vann interjected, "That's because Chau has his own ideas."

These young officers were heading back to counterpart battalions, but one lingered to have a soft drink. He was Philip Werbiski, and, by memory, I think he was the advisor to the 1st Battalion of the 10th Regiment. In Bien Hoa I had been told that the principal problem was insufficient ARVN forces. I remember asking Phil what the fundamental difficulty was in the area where he worked. His answer was dramatically different from what I expected. He said the biggest problem was that ARVN plundered the rural population, so they were even more disliked than the communists. I asked him how that could happen. He believed the reasons were that ARVN troops were poorly supplied in the field and not local to the area where they operated, and their officers seldom applied true command and control. Phil and I parted, but a couple of years later we worked together and became good friends.

John Vann allowed time for me, I think as a courtesy to Ev. He felt a major difficulty was lack of knowledge as to what was really happening in the countryside. "Hell, I don't even know what is going on across the river at night. They only tell us what they think we should be allowed to know, and something is always held back." I told him that in my limited experience, I was favorably impressed with how candid Vietnamese officers could be while discussing problems. Vann shook his head, not convinced, and said, "Let's go see my counterpart, then tell me what you think."

Huynh Van Cao was absent. We were told that he had been called to Saigon ("A frequent f——ing occurrence lately," said Vann), but Bui Dinh Dam was ready to meet us. Dam was previously the 7th Division chief of staff and now was deputy division commander.[28] John was good enough, although it strained his patience, to allow me to run through my social introduction in Vietnamese. By now I was sufficiently practiced to explain who I was, my interest in Viet Nam, and inquire politely as to the background of someone met for the first time. Dam, I could tell by his accent, was another senior officer from the north, and he volunteered that he was "a loyal Catholic."[29] He, like others of his age and grade, was a graduate of a course at Fort Leavenworth.

I asked Dam how he felt operations and strategic hamlets were proceeding in the Upper Mekong Delta. He responded that everything was perfect. I wasn't sure that I had adequately communicated in Vietnamese, so I asked again. Yes, he said, "hoan toan" and more colloquially, "tat ca tot dep." I knew rudimentary ability in Vietnamese could not provide for nuance, but I had not previously been offered such complete affirmation of the absence of difficulty.

On the way back to the seminary compound, John wryly asked how candid I thought that conversation had been. I told him that maybe he just happened to be in an area where everything was looking good. "Yeah," he said, "I'm a lucky guy, 'tot dep,' whatever that means!"

I went to the room assigned to me as an overnight guest, tossed a towel, pistol, and camera into my shoulder bag, walked to the gate, and caught a short ride to the ferry landing. There being just a short line for pedestrians, it was easy to catch the next ferry to the opposite side. As simple as that, I was in Kien Hoa. There were two rows of shops and dwellings along the sides of a road that ran from the ferry landing to Ben Tre. I spent a couple of hours strolling through shops, striking up conversations with people who seemed approachable, and drinking lots of tea. After a while I had urgent need to locate a urinal facility.[30] A shop owner indicated a spot just behind his premises. When I returned, he reminded me that long shadows of late afternoon were becoming dusk. He suggested I ought to either get on my way to Ben Tre, about ten or twelve kilometers onward, or find a safe place for the night. He said that since I was a journalist (assumed from my snapping photos and asking questions), I might safely stay overnight, but maybe best with the local police.

He walked me over to the post, which, since it lacked the appearance of a strong defensive position, was inconspicuous. Every one of the men in the small, low-mud-walled enclosure was friendly. They made space for me on one of the communal plank beds. That night we had tea (of course) and lively conversation. They complained about low pay, talked frankly about asking shop owners and travelers for "tea money," and told me that supervisors seldom inspected or even visited. One of the youngest claimed it was safer on the My Tho side. That provided a natural opening for me to inquire about security at the landing. I wondered if communists would ever attack. "Of course not, they need the ferry too!"[31] They glanced among themselves and then said that even though the area around the ferry was all right, it was better to stay with them. Continuing, all agreed that they didn't have problems with communists, "because they only come by night. And they don't come every night. And when they do come, it's

only to talk with people. We don't bother them and they don't bother us."
With confidence born of that guarantee, I slept soundly. The next morning
all were relieved it had been a quiet night. After the entrance barricade
of barbed wire on a wood frame (not much of an obstacle) was dragged
aside, in a noisy group we all trooped out, and I treated my hosts to a
breakfast bowl of soup before catching the ferry back to My Tho.

At the seminary, while I was having a shower, irate John Paul Vann
accosted me. "Where the hell were you last night?" I grabbed a towel to
wrap around me while he yelled about telling Bumgardner that I was irresponsible, probably chasing women in My Tho, and one stupid son of a
bitch. "You won't be staying here again!"

When he paused for breath I quickly interjected, "You said you didn't
know what went on across the river at night, so I went over to take a look."

Long pause. He was obviously surprised. But quickly, "Ev was right;
you are dumb enough to get killed on your own." Then, to the point,
"What did you find out?"

While explaining the previous evening's observed situation, John
calmed down. I told him it seemed there were advantages for both sides at
the ferry site. The SVNLF did not impede citizen and government use of
the ferry because it was important for them, too. They did not attack the
post, such as it was, because the police stayed out of their way. The government could claim the landing was a secure area because in fact there were
no reported incidents. But there was no guarantee this equilibrium would
be permanent. John provided me with a cup of coffee and a couple of My
Tho croissants, and then I was on the road to Saigon.

Back in the office Ev shot calculating looks while I busied myself reading reports from our Vietnamese provincial field representatives. Finally,
he said that we needed to have a coffee, his signal for serious discussion.
He told me that I would be of little use to him, or anyone else, if a mis-
guided appetite for adventure wound up with me floating in a rice paddy.
He said Vann called last night, and then again just before my return to the
office. John wanted me assigned to work with him. "I'm not going to do
that. Going off alone at night is foolish. You and Vann together would be
a bad combination. No restraint."

Ev continued in his teaching mode. "Risk has to be balanced against
return." He was not sure I made that calculation. "I am not holding you
back," he said. "Take my guidance and then be forceful depending on your

read of a situation, but there's no license for being irresponsible." While attempting to explain basically sitting around talking with policemen the previous night, Ev interrupted. He was not deflected: "Be daring, but not stupid."[32]

The next few days were spent with the Information Section. I was shown how to operate a 16mm Bolex movie camera, sent out to shoot some background scenes for the weekly newsreel USIS produced for RVN theaters, and taught how to thread film in a projector.[33] The people in the Information Section were all friendly and professionally able, and I could have been comfortable assigned with them, if I had not already been infected by Ev's more exciting field operations.

My next Bumgardner test (realizing he let me out on a short leash and then pulled me back for discussion) was to central Viet Nam. One of his friends, George Taylor, piloted the Air America twin-engined Piper Apache that had previously been the property of Tom Dooley in Laos.[34] The first flight with George was to Phan Rang in Ninh Thuan province. We landed on a field outside of town, and George had to buzz the grass strip to frighten off grazing cattle.[35] My task was to discuss placing a USIS employee with the province VIS. I met with the province chief first, and later the VIS chief. They were both agreeable. After meeting with the VIS chief, he asked an assistant to drive me west to Thap Cham to let me see something of the countryside.[36] From that Cham site he brought me a short distance up Highway 1 to visit an area of Catholic hamlets with an almost baronial church and residence at the center. My guide told me that he was Catholic, and his family had converted two generations earlier. I asked if he knew why his grandparents adopted a new religion. He gave two reasons for the family change. Buddhism, he said, was superstitious and lacked discipline and focus.[37] "And," he continued, "becoming Catholic brought advantage for the family."

I thought to myself that an originally pragmatic decision for family benefit echoes through generations, with eventual political impact. Based on a few discussions with Vietnamese in which religion was mentioned, I understood that this identity marker was also a significant fault line within the nation.[38]

Another flight to central Viet Nam with George, maybe a week later, brought us to Tuy Hoa in Phu Yen province.[39] This was the same airfield south of the city where Ev saw President Ngo Dinh Diem greeted by enthusiastic crowds in 1955. Americans much later established a large air-base with an extended runway, but in 1962 it was just a vast coastal plain. George left me on the rough tarmac, saying that he would fly south to Nha Trang, top off fuel, and return to pick me up at 1500.

As he taxied away for takeoff, a lone vehicle appeared from the distant and unmanned entrance to the airfield. This was another of the jeep wagons ubiquitous in 1962 because so many had been provided earlier by USOM. The province VIS chief was driving, and our USIS representative was with him. I was in Tuy Hoa because Ev had told me that he had feedback from the Directorate General of Information reporting friction between our representative, Ba, and the VIS chief.[40]

We drove north a few kilometers over a long iron bridge, much repaired but originally constructed by the Eiffel Company (of Eiffel Tower fame), crossing the Song Ba. Part of the morning we spent talking at the VIS office. I spoke as though unaware of the friction and conveyed the Bumgardner philosophy, that we approach problems from different backgrounds and therefore with different ideas about how to solve them. It is most important to keep in mind that sometimes we need to compromise in order to keep our team together. We in USIS believe open discussion and good will is an important part of our support to government programs. That is kind of a nail head summary, but the two men appeared relieved and pledged to resolve differences and work together.

Ba and I took lunch in a small restaurant on a dirt road in the direction of the old city. I impressed upon Ba my belief that he was basically a guest in the province, our representative, and so the burden for compromise and making the greater effort was his. Ba acknowledged the guidance and then drove me on a tour of the old city that was destroyed during the 1945–55 war against France.

Major Dong, province chief, was not available. Ba suggested that we visit the liaison office for the 47th Regiment.[41] Pham Anh was the regimental commander. We exchanged some pleasantries, and then Anh asked Ba to wait outside. Once we were alone, the conversational exchange began to resemble interrogation. He wanted to know the purpose of my travel to Phu Yen, how old I was, how long I had been in Viet Nam, and whether I had any experience before arriving in his country. These questions cut close to the bone. They were ones I had successfully evaded in other conversations but that I could not duck with him. I explained the nature of our help in provinces, where we placed USIS representatives to expedite USIS support to the VIS. He questioned why assistance could not simply be requested from VIS through the Vietnamese government, with USIS assistance provided at that level. I responded that requests through the Directorate General of Information might be treated slowly, because it was a big ministry-sized organization with many responsibilities. USIS was small and could react more quickly.

He asked again how old I was. I replied that I was twenty-four and had been in Viet Nam only a few months. I explained that I had been trying to learn the language and history of Viet Nam, and then I ventured that some might think him young, but he had the regiment and considerable influence in Phu Yen. Anh smiled a bit and replied that he was ten years older than I and had much more experience.[42] Then he offered that, "although I am from Hue, my wife is originally from Phu Yen, and so I must care for the people here as I do for her and our children." (At this point I thought to myself, at last we begin a conversation.) I continued by expressing appreciation for the opportunity to meet him and respond to his questions. And I confessed that the only way I could learn about Viet Nam was by conversation with people who would answer questions as honestly as I tried to answer his. So, in that spirit, I asked him what he thought were the principal problems in Phu Yen.

He explained that during the Viet Minh period, 1945–55, the region from Phu Yen, "where we are right now," north almost to Danang was occupied and governed by communists. After Geneva, he said, thousands of Viet Minh from this region that communists called Lien Khu Nam (Inter-Zone V) grouped to move north of the demarcation line on ships from Qui Nhon. But, he added, some remained, and of course families and others who supported the Viet Minh are still here. "So," he continued, "my regiment can conduct operations, but the communists must be rooted out." The rooting out, he said, requires information from the people, but few are willing to betray friends and family members. "So this is going to take a long time. I know the difficulty because I was with the Viet Minh for two years."[43]

Glancing at my watch, I saw that we were almost at George Taylor's 1500 hours appointed time. I asked, as politely as I could, for permission to leave, caught Ba outside the modest office, and off we went to the airfield. As we drove, I wondered if Ba, knowing Anh to be a tough character, had sandbagged me. But anyway, it was another productive conversation. Once past an awkward beginning, Anh's Vietnamese civility took precedence over my obvious inexperience.

We crossed the long Eiffel Bridge and headed toward the Tuy Hoa South airfield. As we approached the gate, the Apache was just taking off. Ba angled parallel to the runway, and we raced along, hoping to be noticed. The plane climbed, then banked, circuited the field, and landed. I grabbed my bag and ran to climb on the wing and board before George changed his mind. As we rolled toward the end of the runway for takeoff, George shot me an angry glance. "Don't you ever agree to a time for pick-up and come late. That is a no-show in my book. We have flight plans, and no pilot wants to be left waiting on an empty airstrip anytime, anywhere. God damn it!"

At least he hadn't quite god damned me. But the lesson was clear and the reprimand deserved. During the next several years when a rendezvous point or time could not be met, I always made sure the other party was informed. That didn't mean I was not myself twice left waiting for a lift that failed to arrive, once in Long Xuyen on an abandoned strip and once at Thuan Hoa in Quang Ngai. But twice over several years is not bad.

Another Bumgardner task a few weeks later sent me to Quang Ngai with the USIS information officer to participate in drafting a psychological operations annex to the 25th Division's 1963 campaign plan.[44] I told Ev, when he first raised this with me, that I had no, literally no, idea how to prepare a psychological operations annex. He responded that it would only require being clear-headed to set down on paper what needed to be done. "Tolerate the senior officer traveling with you, he won't spend more than a day or two; and by the way, I sent a message to Capt. Howard Walters, advisor to the 4th Psychological Operations Company in Qui Nhon, asking him to meet you in Quang Ngai. He will be a big help."

Howard Walters and I became good friends. I learned a lot about ARVN field organization and Quang Ngai province. I met a young, impressive division commander, Lu Lan, and some province officials, and I worked closely with the G-5 advisor, Maj. Bob Kelly, who became another close friend and elder brother.

The end of the year, end of tutelage, was also the time for decision. Ev wanted me to work with him in field operations, and he had in mind an assignment to open a small field post in Qui Nhon as a base to cover northern II Corps. He told me to wait until John Mecklin presented other options. In the meantime, he wanted me to take Do Minh Nhat to Xuan Loc and introduce him as our representative in Long Khanh province. I wanted, as usual, to drive, but Ev had already scheduled a small plane to take us to a rubber plantation airstrip just outside Xuan Loc. Nhat and I, after our one shared adventure in Kien Hoa at the ferry landing, thought we were going to be at almost opposite ends of the country and did not know when we would meet again.

While I was learning from Ev's orientation, from exposure to Viet Nam realities, and while becoming infatuated with Viet Nam, my wife was adrift more than ought to have happened in a responsible relationship. She befriended families of Vietnamese we had met in Washington and worked to understand our new environment. She was supportive of my wanting a field post—not a field administrative post,[45] but a bare-bones field base that would allow getting into the country, finding problems, and seeking solutions.

John Mecklin spoke with me at a USIS social event and asked whether I would be interested in working with the research officer evaluating communist documents. I remember telling Mecklin something like I preferred to catch VD, because it's treatable.[46] He replied, "Well, you really do have the Bumgardner facility of expression."

And that is how the decision was made for my placement in Binh Dinh. In January, Marv McClure (USIS executive officer), Pham Ngoc Quang (McClure's assistant), Ev, and I flew to Qui Nhon to locate a place for rent that would have space for living and a small office. We found a two-story, shop-style house with a sliding steel grill across the front at 49 Vo Tanh Street, next door to a small villa leased by the New Zealand humanitarian surgical team. The landlord, Cao Dan, was a trader in livestock who lived with his family in a smaller house just behind the one that he was willing to rent. Contract signed, we returned to Saigon. Shortly afterward, my wife flew back to Qui Nhon with me. We stayed temporarily in a small hotel near the bus station while some modifications (installing a shower and hot water) were made to the rented property.

I was ready to begin and went in search of Capt. Howard Walters.

2
An Lao Valley

Ev placed me in Qui Nhon with the mission to travel throughout Quang Ngai, Binh Dinh, Phu Yen, and (when I could) Kontum and Pleiku. He said the USIS branch post in Dalat occasionally looked into southern II Corps but never got north of Nha Trang, and the consulate in Hue seldom reached as far south as Binh Dinh. With two divisions (the 9th and the 25th) recently raised and trained in Binh Dinh and Quang Ngai, security had generally improved. He did not anticipate difficulty with road travel on major highways. A USIS field representative, Le Quang Tuyen, was already in Qui Nhon, and he would be my assistant. Ev described him as a clever operator who spoke good English and worked effectively with local officials.

Ev's instruction was for me to become knowledgeable, find good people, make myself useful, and keep him informed. "Perceive, engage, report," was his summary directive. He elaborated by encouraging me to learn everything possible, explaining that no piece of information lacked value. He allowed that I could take measured risk, and he urged me to continue speaking Vietnamese. He counseled that people would see me as young and inexperienced, but if his principles were applied, the Vietnamese would eventually take me seriously. "The knowledge you accumulate will build respect and potentially some influence."

Captain Walters was in Phu Thanh, the training area southwest of Qui Nhon where the 9th Division was organized and maintained headquarters. Howard Walters had entered the US Army at the end of World War II, observed the Trieste problem in 1945–46, and fought in the Korean

War.[1] He had an advanced degree in psychology and had studied psychological warfare beginning with the writings of Paul M. A. Linebarger. Howard told me that the unit he advised, the 4th Psychological Operations Company, was recently withdrawn from operations in Phu Yen province because the company commander fiercely criticized provincial corruption. He expected the future area of operations would be primarily in Binh Dinh.

He described the 4th Psychological Operations Company and its commander, Capt. Nguyen Tuy. He said Captain Tuy had received special operations training at Fort Bragg, and when he returned to Viet Nam had asked for command of a psychological operations company. Partially because of Fort Bragg exposure, and partly because of his own perception of need, Captain Tuy ran the company like a politically enhanced special operations force. His vision was to compete politically with the Viet Cong in the countryside. He wanted to spread a message within ARVN that every military move had political consequence, so the political, or psychological, as he called it, must be planned. The problem, Walters explained further, was that Tuy didn't have the rank necessary to promote a new concept, and as he advocated political competition with communists, he needed to avoid sounding like one. Tuy was in Pleiku for a meeting, he said, but we would all get together as soon as he returned.

That connection was accomplished two days later. Tuy and the deputy company commander, Captain Jusiu, who was Jarai,[2] were my friends from first handshake. Just as I was trying to speak Vietnamese, Tuy was learning Jarai so that he could communicate with Jarai soldiers. Tuy believed psychological operations should not be only about encouraging enemy surrender or publicizing government programs. He wanted to promote political development by encouraging rural self-sufficiency, including administrative independence through local elections. I thought his vision dynamic but somewhat in advance of government policy. He explained that the government did not entirely understand what needed to be done, and he acknowledged recent failure in Phu Yen because of a corrupt province chief.

My first long drive out of Qui Nhon would be to Pleiku. I had blanket travel orders, so my schedule was my own. I asked our provincial representative, Tuyen, about the roads between provinces. He informed me that they were all dangerous, and the two worst were Route 19 to Pleiku and

Highway 1 to Quang Ngai, especially at the provincial border. When asked how he could be so sure, he replied that everyone knew. Then Tuyen said that Province Chief Bui Thuc Duyen would be uncomfortable if I were driving out of the province, because he might be blamed if something happened to me. I pointed out that our boss (Ev) expected me to move between provinces and not roost in one. "But everyone else flies," Tuyen replied. It was obvious that I was pumping a dry hole, so it seemed smarter to check with someone who did travel in his own vehicle, an old truck.

The next morning I went behind our house to search out Cao Dan, our landlord. He often drove interprovincial roads as well as the four national routes in the region: Highway 19 through An Khe to Pleiku, 14 from Pleiku to Banmethuot, 21 from Banmethuot to Ninh Hoa, and 1 along the coast from Ninh Hoa through Tuy Hoa back into Binh Dinh and home to Qui Nhon. He bought and sold livestock from market to market and occasionally (just behind his house) slaughtered a pig for sale in the Qui Nhon market.[3] We talked about road travel. It was obvious, by his animated commentary, that he loved the open road—a Vietnamese Dean Moriarty. He described hotels that were good, and why, and which ones ought to be avoided. He knew where the usual risk points were for each route. He explained why his old *xe camnhong* was painted blue.[4] He said that "the other people" understood from the color blue that "road tax" had been paid to them. He offered to have our jeep painted blue and to let one of his old friends know that I was working with him on a study of Vietnamese livestock. Two days later our jeep was blue.

I was ready to get on the road, but travel was delayed because Ev sent a message telling me that Ken Bunce, the USIA assistant director for East Asia, was arriving in Viet Nam for briefings. The USIS deputy director, David Sheppard, and Ev would bring Bunce to Qui Nhon for a look at our low-budget, one-man field post. Ev asked that the stop in Binh Dinh also include a quick trip in the countryside beyond Qui Nhon. I asked Tuyen to arrange a meeting with the VIS chief and coordinate with him for visiting a hamlet in Tuy Phuoc or An Nhon.

Bunce was a distinguished gentleman, something of a scholar (Korean studies, Ev told me), and Dave Sheppard was an enthusiastic proponent of the one-man, low-overhead field post concept. We had a short meeting in the office area of my house. I explained (with Ev smiling) that the plan was to provide supervision and support for the USIS Vietnamese employees in each province of the region. I would accomplish this by almost constant movement among the provinces, and I intended to make much of the travel by road. Ev added that an important byproduct would be identification of opportunities for USIS programs.

Tuyen drove Bunce and Sheppard to the VIS office for a presentation by the VIS chief. I took Ev in my jeep, and this was the opportunity to share first impressions of Binh Dinh. The provincial government had the lid on a pot that could boil over. The heat was generated by popular dissatisfaction in the hamlets (Tuy's view), and the lid was the recently formed 9th Infantry Division.[5] Fail to address hamlet issues, remove the 9th, and the pot would boil over.

The VIS chief, Mr. Tram, showed us a photo exhibit of strategic hamlets in Binh Dinh, gave a short summary of government information activity in the province, and expressed appreciation for USIS support facilitated by assigning Tuyen to Qui Nhon. He told us, through Tuyen interpreting, that the overall government position in Binh Dinh was strong and improving *hang ngay* (day-by-day). In 1962, he acknowledged, there were setbacks in Vinh Thanh and An Lao districts, but the province, with support from the army, was planning to recover the initiative in 1963. He concluded by saying that we would visit a strategic hamlet information reading room about twenty-five kilometers distant, "a beautiful drive."

We proceeded in three vehicles from Qui Nhon past two thirteenth-century Cham towers, took a local side road, stopping to take photos of a beautiful small pagoda situated against a small hill, then passed through Tuy Phuoc town. This road connected with Highway 1 at the intersection with Route 19, which was overlooked by three Cham structures on a hill. From there we remained on Highway 1 just past An Nhon town (where the Binh Dinh citadel was located until destroyed by the Viet Minh in 1946) and soon turned east on a dirt road that led to Go Boi. This side road passed through a hamlet set back from the highway, and that was our destination. We parked our vehicles just inside the wooden gate, and as we strolled to the hamlet information reading room, Mr. Tram told us that this strategic hamlet had been completed six months earlier. He said we would find our publications and VIS posters in the reading room, with benches for people's convenience.[6]

Tram was therefore disconcerted to find that the information station was empty, not only of publications and posters, but of benches as well.

Tram said that he would find someone who could provide an explanation. As we turned to leave, I saw a couple of small, notebook-sized pieces of paper discarded in a rear corner. I picked them up, glanced at what was printed on them, and saw that they were leaflets from the Binh Dinh Liberation Forces. After showing them to Ev, I tucked both into my pocket. Now it was obvious what had happened to the benches and reading material.

What occurred next, while a shock for Mr. Tram, was a sort of epiphany for me.[7] As we walked just a bit farther along the dirt road bisecting this strategic hamlet, we discovered the fencing along the far sides and rear of the hamlet was gone. While Tram was immobilized, trying to process the absence of fencing, we were suddenly approached by a husky, middle-aged man in dark purple farmer's clothing (pajamalike) who almost belligerently asked who we were and what we wanted.[8] I was not sorry that folding-stock carbine, slung from my shoulder and almost invisible beneath my jacket, was with me and not back with the vehicles.

Mr. Tram stammered and replied that he was a province official bringing American guests to visit the hamlet. The man, virtually snorting audiovisual distaste, sarcastically snarled, "Khach My! [American guests!] You should bring them back to Qui Nhon before there is a problem." Tram had no argument against that advice, and we retraced our steps to the vehicles and returned to Qui Nhon.

We parted with Tram and Tuyen at the VIS office and returned to my home work space for discussion before the visitors flew back to Saigon. Ev asked what I thought of the confrontation in the hamlet. I told them it was an important revelation of the real situation as opposed to that portrayed by the government. I showed the two small leaflets I had found, roughly translated them, and gave one to Bunce. I expressed my feeling that in some areas strategic hamlets were not keeping communists out, but instead enclosed hamlets that were already communist controlled or at least in which the communists were ascendant. If the man we met in that hamlet was not a member of the "liberation forces," he was certainly a supporter.

I described what Pham Anh told me concerning Viet Minh presence in this part of the country from 1945 through much of 1955. If there was hamlet governance, a school, a health station, and postal service, it was all managed by the Viet Minh, so now less than eight years later, President

Diem's forces and officials are seen by some people as illegitimate, not the Viet Cong.[9] I told Dr. Bunce and Dave Sheppard that even so, it could be possible for the government to gear itself for the long haul, and by providing service to people and political opportunity in hamlet elections, over time it could make Viet Minh history irrelevant. Ev, to the rear, nodded agreement.

I had been in Viet Nam less than a year. What did I really know? Not much, but I was learning (from Vietnamese) and beginning to focus on hamlets as the critical level of conflict.

A couple of days later I headed toward the highlands. After the hill surmounted by Cham remnant towers, Highway 19 rose gradually on the coastal plain toward Mang Pass. On the way I paused at Phu Phong, where there was a handicraft industry working a beautiful two-hued local wood on pedal-powered lathes to produce cups, bowls, and other items for sale in Qui Nhon. Beyond Phu Phong a branch road led north into the Vinh Thanh valley.[10] Just after that, Route 19 bore to the left and began an abrupt climb to the An Khe plateau. This was Deo Mang, sometimes called Deo An Khe, because the pass (*deo*) led travelers to An Khe.[11] This was in 1963 a pleasant highlands town with a short laterite airstrip next to an abandoned French plantation house. Curious, I asked the district chief if he knew the history of that building and what had been cultivated on the plantation. He did not know. But he reassured me concerning Route 19 security from An Khe to Pleiku. He said daytime travel was not a problem. He simply advised going between ten in the morning and four in the afternoon. He suggested checking with the British advisory team, because they had twice made the drive. I was surprised. "British advisory team?" I had not heard one mentioned in Qui Nhon. The district chief explained that I could find them just outside town in the old road construction compound.[12]

I found the compound, and on entering noticed that the visible personnel were not Vietnamese or American. I was invited to wait in one of the buildings while the team leader was located. Shortly two British officers appeared and introduced themselves as Dick Noone and Norman Herboldt. They seemed as surprised to find a lone American driving to Pleiku as I was to learn of their team in An Khe. Dick Noone, the taller and leaner, told me that they were with the British Military Advisory Mission, and having experience against communist terrorists in Malaya, their service was made available to the South Viet Nam government. He described the Senoi Praaq program in Malaya and his family background with the Senoi and spoke of the difficulty working cross-culturally in a guerrilla war. Norman Herboldt, a shorter, fit, but chunkier man, had also been with the Senoi Praaq. All of the other team members were serving Malayans.[13]

They asked what sort of USIS program would be available in the highlands, and, other than surprising them as I drove to Pleiku, what could I hope to accomplish. This was reasonable curiosity on their part, but a little disconcerting for me, since I really wasn't sure how to respond. The easy part was letting them know we could provide print support in the form of Vietnamese language leaflets and publications, and we could reproduce their instructional material. I gave them a couple of copies of *Nguoi linh chien* (Combat soldier) as an example of what could be available.[14] I told them about Ev Bumgardner and summarized his guidance as: "Get out, get educated, get involved, support good people." I explained that our connection within provinces was VIS, but Ev expected to reach beyond the obvious. I was accordingly developing friendships in ARVN and thought the 9th Division was essential as a screen for political development in Binh Dinh. It just seemed a more aggressive attitude was required.

Herboldt told me that, from what he had seen, VIS seemed a weak link, and the government as a whole excelled at obstruction. Dick Noone commented that Ev Bumgardner must be a most unusual supervisor, but probably the sort that was needed in Viet Nam. Judging by my youthful appearance and estimating my inexperience (he told me a few years later), he said that as far as aggressive attitude is concerned, "It is easy for those who have not walked the jungle to insist that others do." I winced, if not visibly then certainly within. I left with handshakes and a conviction that I would never ask another to do what I had not.[15]

Pleiku and Kontum might have been on a different continent from Qui Nhon, so great was the difference from the coastal plain where most ethnic Vietnamese resided. Pleiku was a sprawling, dusty intersection of market and military camps astride north-south Highway 14 and east-west Highway 19. If there was an attractive aspect to Pleiku, it escaped me then and during the next dozen years. Kontum was very different—a smaller town with an abundance of red-flowering flame trees. The VIS was actually working to carry information about government policy to tribal communities. In fact, the VIS chief had developed a Bahnar language primer and had some interesting ideas. He told me that collecting tribes in fixed locations and training them to operate from camps (Special Forces) was, in his opinion, a mistake. In the long run tribal societies would not be comfortable, and meanwhile the mobile communist forces would always know where the hostile (from their point of view) camps were and could easily avoid them. He also speculated that communist propaganda would portray camps as a scheme to concentrate tribal people so that their land would be available for use by others. He had a sympathetic understanding of the ethnic minorities' situation unique among Vietnamese officials.

Just three months earlier I had visited the Special Forces camp at Dam Pao on the interprovincial dirt road between Lien Khuong airfield and Phey Srunh.[16] Like most visitors to Special Forces camps, I was deeply impressed by the appearance of the camp, the dedication and quality of assigned personnel, and the informative briefing. Now there was a different point of view to consider.

The forested and brush-covered margins of the road between Pleiku and Kontum were cut back about a hundred meters or more. Most of the traffic on this part of Highway 14 was civil government or military. The reason for cutting back was to prevent communist forces from creeping to the edge of the road to spring ambushes. That seemed logical, but at the same time it also provided a broad field of fire for those ambushers who might be just as comfortable a hundred meters distant.

Highway 14 south to Banmethuot seemed more consistently used by commercial traffic. Although I would not say there was heavy flow, I did pass a number of buses and trucks. The land was beautifully undeveloped, the road traversing areas of forest that could (and years later would) conceal thousands of combatants. Not long after departing Pleiku city, Highway 19 branched westward toward Cambodia, but that portion of 19 was not improved to the standard of the An Khe–Pleiku stretch. Just a bit farther south, Provincial Road 6C led southwest, made a great arc, and then rejoined Route 14 near Phu Nhon district. Interprovincial Road 7B forked off southeast to Cheo Reo. One of Tuy's ARVN friends in Pleiku had warned against accidentally or intentionally traveling on any of those other roads. I followed that advice. Highway 14 ran generally south to the Buon Ho area and then southwest to Banmethuot. This was a long drive.

The VIS chief for Darlac province was away, but his assistant seemed glad to have a visitor and an opportunity to describe information activity. He helped me find a hotel, and we agreed to meet mid-morning the next day for a visit to a Rhade community.[17] Following a long drive, it was not hard to sleep soundly even after the cold-water shower typical of provincial hotels. The next morning I walked around the market area and found a small café frequented by local French residents. Assuming any foreigner was French, they hailed me and invited me to join their group. I made myself understood with barely adequate French, and they, being a jovial group, made allowance. I asked about security on local roads. They responded that even for travel to and from plantations there was no difficulty. "Mais pour vouz, peutetre beaucoup des problemes."[18] Everyone but me seemed amused.

My VIS host drove his vehicle southwest from Banmethuot on Route 14. We passed a large community that he mentioned was a resettlement village. He told me the people there were Vietnamese, mostly resettled from the north in 1956 and 1957. He said the land was made available by the government. When I asked whose it had been before the government provided the location to settlers, he said that it had all been just empty. "Some 'moi' complained, but they have to learn to share land with people who need it."[19] When we arrived at Buon M'Bre I was relieved there was no artificial welcoming ceremony for a visiting foreigner.[20] We were able to stroll around the small community. The long-house architecture was impressive. There was an atmosphere of lassitude, but at the same time everything was clean. We conversed, in mixed French and Vietnamese, with some older men who seemed friendly. The small information station actually had publications available, but no readers while we were there.

My guide chattered on about how eventually all the highland tribes would live in small, clean houses "like Vietnamese," cultivate nearby fields, and stop roaming around. The highlands will develop, he believed, when there is social control. I was listening carefully and began to feel that whichever Vietnamese party won, consequences for the hill tribes would be grim.

Changing the subject, he mentioned a remnant Cham tower north of Banmethuot, and he wondered if I would like to see it the next day.[21] I was very interested but thought it too great a diversion. I supposed there would be the same opportunity in the future. No fortune-teller was I. Much later in 1967 there was opportunity to fly over the location in a 4th

Division helicopter, but by that time it was too insecure for an amateur archeologist-historian. In 1971, while briefly in Banmethuot with Ngo Khac Tinh, minister of information, I suggested taking a look, but no one else in the party shared my interest.

The next day, like Kerouac, I was on the road again, this time heading east on Highway 21 toward the coast and the town of Ninh Hoa. The road is at first across the plateau with less forest cover than what was seen between Pleiku and Banmethuot. Almost at the rim of the plateau was a large Rhade settlement, Buon M'Drak. I paused there, parked my jeep, and entered among the longhouses. Communicating with people in rudimentary French (mine rudimentary, theirs better) was not difficult. Very hospitably they showed me around their dwellings, asked lots of questions (some personal, but with an innocent, guileless manner), and responded to queries about the surrounding area. They told me they had been in the same general location "forever," previously had good relations with the French, and had always traded with Vietnamese coming from Ninh Hoa. Among the longhouses they had an extensive collection of jars and gongs. I was shown a beautiful blue and white jar with a dragon design, about a foot high, and with educated hindsight I believe it was early Ming or Yuan.

I inquired about local security. They were sure the road to the coast was completely safe, but a provincial road not far from M'Drak leading north to the river (this must have been the Song Ba in Phu Yen) was closed, "ferme." When I asked why the road was closed, they responded, "Viet Minh." These people were so friendly anyone could have comfortably stayed a day or two. However this was my first circuit of upper II Corps, and I felt it best to keep moving.

Route 21 dropped from the plateau through a mountainous defile and emerged on the coastal plain west of a ranger training camp at Duc My. I stopped to inquire whether USIS could provide assistance in the form of publications for reading rooms, or possibly assist with training material. I still had copies of *Nguoi linh chien*, and although the intended audience was in basic training, the ranger center commander said they would like to have as many copies as possible. I assured him our representative in Nha Trang would make delivery in a few days. After a generous lunch with some of the training staff, I drove on to Ninh Hoa. It was tempting to go south to Nha Trang, but then later it would be necessary to backtrack in order to reach Qui Nhon. The effect of several days on the road seemed to point me like a compass toward the north. I found a small hotel, as usual near the bus station, and stayed the night.[22]

Going toward Phu Yen province from Ninh Hoa on Highway 1 provides the traveler with spectacular coastal views. I paused for coffee at Dai Lanh, a small fishing hamlet located within a sheltered bay. The beautiful beach there, with hills just west of the community, seemed an ideal location for a resort when peace was won. Passing Vung Ro, a deep-water, narrow bay geologically resembling a fiord, I was soon on the South Tuy Hoa Plain. Our USIS representative, Mr. Ba, was in his room at the provincial VIS and visibly shocked to see me unannounced before his desk. He recovered quickly and asked what I would like to do while in Phu Yen. I told him that my preference would be to go along the Song Ba as far as Son Hoa and Phu Duc districts. Ba advised that the road, Interprovincial 7, was in very poor condition, but that he would make inquiries while I settled in a hotel. The hotel was *phong ngu* class, but you could have a decent bowl of noodles across the street. So with nourishment I waited for Ba to reappear. He had good news. The USOM representative was going to the two districts with his assistant the next day, and we could tag along. Meanwhile, for the remainder of the afternoon he suggested looking at a Cham tower just outside town and then later visiting the prison for discussion with the director about communists in detention. I was all for going straight to the prison, but Ba explained that just after lunch the director would be resting, not available.

The Cham tower, brick as usual, was on a small hill. There was considerable erosion of the tower and hill itself that I attributed to centuries of weather. Ba explained that local people used to remove some brick and laterite for their own building material. The evidence, rubble strewn down the slope, was persuasive. I could not see, even high on the tower, any remaining statuary.[23] When asked about that, Ba responded that before World War II the French senior administrative officer in the province removed statuary and some excavated items.

Poking around the site absorbed enough time before the hour for visiting the prison. It was also located outside town but in a different direction, to the north close to Chop Chai hillock and adjacent to a small airstrip. Once inside the fence, and then another fence, and within the walls, we were escorted to the director's office. If one could estimate moral temperament by appearance, then you would not want to be in that man's custody.[24]

We had tea and then a tour of the facility. The director surprised us by asking whether I would like to meet some of the prisoners. Of course!

I anticipated being face to face with hardened SVNLF combatants and revolutionaries. But on entering a room where several people sat on benches, I saw these were mostly older men and women, grandparents by appearance. As we entered, they rose and sang the Republic national anthem, followed by chanting "Ngo Tong Thong Muon Nam! Ngo Tong Thong Muon Nam!"[25] I wondered what incentive, what encouragement, inspired the choral group—and what punishment there might be for lack of performance. Before leaving we had still more tea with the director. We asked him about the people in the prison. "All communists," he replied. I asked how to know who was a communist. He smiled at my ignorance, "Because the police have information and proof of past support for the Viet Minh, some have sons who followed the Viet Minh, others have relatives or friends who disappeared more recently. And these are all people who speak against the government, even while here." I left with some depression. It was just one visit to a place of detention, not a broad sample of the category, but I was not comfortable.

The next morning Ba picked me up at the hotel, and we went to meet Bob Burns, the USOM rural affairs representative in Phu Yen. Bob Burns worked in Laos before being hired for USOM Viet Nam, and he knew, and was known by, many who worked out of Vientiane before relocating to Saigon. He was a doppelganger for Broderick Crawford of the popular television program *Highway Patrol*, and I couldn't help wanting to call out "ten-four" at some point to see whether he made the connection.[26] Driving west on Interprovincial Route 7, at first an impressive canal was on our right. The road at a couple of spots was by the river but usually farther off, traversing scrub growth and more low hills than I had expected. We left Route 7 and took a smaller provincial road to descend back to the river at Son Hoa, also called Cung Son.

The district chief revealed this was where Nguyen Huu Tho was held in detention until he escaped when communists raided the town in 1961. I asked how that happened, but he replied it took place before his assignment and he did not know more of the story. However he seemed strangely proud of this local history, as if somehow it provided Cung Son and himself, derivatively, with importance not otherwise possible.[27]

We crossed the Song Ba in a small boat and arrived at Phu Duc district, where we were met by an ever-smiling captain who was district chief. At first I thought he might be nervous (smiling in Southeast Asia sometimes indicates anxiety), but I soon realized he was genuinely glad to have company. "Nobody comes to Phu Duc" was his lament.

The district was a lonely outpost for the Republic of Viet Nam. USOM had previously provided some cement and other durables. A small market was being built. A nearby tribal cluster of small huts was clean, but obviously a relocation. The district chief confirmed these people had been brought closer to the river for safety. They did not look happy. I could only make out that they were Jarai, not Rhade. One had the feeling that everything in Phu Duc was made of tissue paper, and a brisk wind would fling it all away. Bob Burns was much more substantial, a rough diamond with a sarcastic sense of humor. I thought USOM fortunate to have him in Phu Yen.

The next day I drove back to Qui Nhon, passing through another beautiful coastal community with beach and palm trees. Absent war, one could live contentedly in Song Cau.

Home again, I decided that during the next few weeks I ought to make two or three forest walks in response to what was definitely the Noone-Herboldt challenge. Procrastination would prevail unless I organized a hike right away. Cao Dan was my collaborator and supporter.[28] I told him that I needed to make some long walks, overnight, in forested parts of the province. After some discussion, he agreed to carry me in his truck to a point along Route 19, where I could choose to be dropped off. From there I would be on my own. His only request was that I absolutely not tell another person, not even our wives, what he was doing. So I understood he wanted to be sure government agents and SVNLF sympathizers would not learn of his help. Cao Dan suggested carrying only cooked rice (which he provided as wrapped rice balls) and nuoc mam. He learned long ago that it was better to travel alertly hungry than satisfied on a full stomach. This prompted me to ask an overdue question. Had he spent time with the Viet Minh? "In Binh Dinh," he replied, "we were all Viet Minh."

On the first excursion, Cao Dan, on his way to Pleiku, carried me in his truck up Route 19, through An Khe, and then farther west about twenty-five kilometers. Well short of Deo Mang Yang, I signaled. He slowed to a stop, and then I was out the door with grim determination and maybe not much common sense. I dashed across to the southern side of the road, went into some bushes, and took stock. I had a small rucksack bought in the Qui Nhon market, two extra pair of socks, a couple of dark brown T-shirts, a first aid kit, some mosquito netting (originally white, but dyed dark brown by a friend of Cao Dan), a compass, rice balls and nuoc mam, a canteen, my Bumgardner Special (folding-stock M1 carbine), ammunition, and a map.[29] I wore loose-fitting long trousers, a dark brown T-shirt, a floppy khaki hat with brim, and canvas boots (hard to find in my size) purchased in the market.

My plan was to go southeast about fifteen or twenty (at the most) kilometers toward the Special Forces camp at Plei Ta Nang Le. I thought it best not to go all the way and risk being shot by friendly forces. But moving in that direction meant, supposedly, traveling in a relatively secure area. I was definitely not looking for "liberation gentlemen" (may ong giai phong), but just wanted to experience the forest on my own and then get back out.

Another friend knew what I had in mind, but not in detail. Capt. Nguyen Tuy insisted that travel on my own was not a good idea. First, Tuy suggested talking with Captain Walters. I replied that the more people I spoke with, the more would oppose my plan. Then he thought it perhaps best to accompany a patrol from the Special Forces camp at Van Canh. But I felt strongly that would not be the same as going alone. Finally acquiescent, he urged moving off-trail as much as possible. "Slow and quiet, not quick and loud. When in doubt, stop, even for an hour." He advised when on any trail, or approaching a trail, to stop often—often—and listen. "Listen for noise, listen for absence of noise."

That morning, truly on my own, I was so keyed up that I was practically listening to me listening. For the first time in my life I was conscious of how loud was the sound of my own breathing. I moved so carefully that it felt like walking underwater or like the walking meditation I practiced fifteen years later in Burma. Off-trail was easy during the first several hours, but even with a compass and map, I didn't want to be too far from the track that was trending southeast toward the upper Ba River. Late in the afternoon, having worked my way southward and around what appeared to be an abandoned tribal settlement, I found a dense thicket, into which

I crawled. Hungry, I ate two rice balls, and as darkness crept across the landscape, I pulled the brown netting over myself and my rucksack and went to sleep.

Next morning I thought of crossing the Ba River, then walking east until meeting Provincial Road 2, and finally strolling up to An Khe or maybe even hitching a ride. That was being naïve to the point of stupidity. A feasible river crossing could not be found. So I decided to move back northward until I could ford a tributary stream and then go northeast to intersect Route 19 near An Khe. Before noon I paused, hungry and thirsty, and moved into a thicket for cover. Not far before me a narrower trail crossed the one that I was paralleling. There was some noise, a rustle of foliage, then footsteps. Thirty meters to my right, and coming from the direction of the Ba River, a man appeared, walking briskly northwest. I froze, thoughts of rice ball and nuoc mam completely out of mind. He was dressed like Vietnamese country people, with loose fitting clothes, a floppy hat similar to my own, but sandals rather than boots. He had no visible weapon. A small cloth bag slung casually over his left shoulder appeared to be his only possession. In a few moments, less than required to read this paragraph, with his eyes on the trail he traveled, he passed. The sounds of movement faded and there was silence. I was astonished. My venture had been theory, experiential, not expecting to see another person. Now I was apprehensive that where there was one, there could be others. So I waited about an hour and then resumed my northeast direction.

Returning to Route 19, just west of An Khe, was no difficulty. It was possible to catch a small blue bus back to Qui Nhon. The next day, when recounting my experience for Tuy and Jusiu, they were insistent that I had seen a Viet Cong traveler. Jusiu was especially sure that any Vietnamese alone in that area south of Route 19 was up to no good. Tuy allowed that I could have seen a charcoal worker. Jusiu countered, "No, charcoal workers are always in a team, and they carry a hatchet [riu nho]." I told them that there hadn't been others, or riu nho, but I also had not seen any weapon, only a bag. Jusiu shrugged, "Who knows what was in that bag?"

Once into the woods was not enough. Anyone could have done the same, at least once. I imagined that, when having a chance to tell Noone, Herboldt, and their team about my walk in the forest, the reaction would be to inquire whether I was up to doing it again. So I shuffled my collection of Service Geographique de l'Indochine maps looking for another overnight possibility. I decided to hike between the upper Vinh Thanh Valley and a long, narrow one poking down from Hoai An district. This route would have an advantage by being closer to Qui Nhon and relatively secure, or so an innocent would have thought.

Tuy and Jusiu were much less positive about that area. They raised a reminder that a year earlier communists had briefly seized the outpost at Dinh Quang in Vinh Thanh district. But they did concede that, since the 9th Division began operations, security had somewhat improved. Tuy cautioned me to remember his earlier advice, and Jusiu added, "Don't assume anyone you meet is a woodcutter, and don't expect people to be friendly."

When I spoke with Cao Dan, he said the route that I planned to walk might someday be connected by road, because Provincial Road 3A ran north through the Vinh Thanh Valley, and another section of 3A extended southwestward from Hoai An. The gap that remained, he added, would require serious engineering. I, on my part, did not comprehend the significance of reference to "serious engineering." He looked over my map in detail. "Not believable, not reliable," was his verdict. He said the road into the valley was rough, and that making a ford across the river might not be possible. He expressed doubt we would be able to get as far north on the valley road as indicated by the map. But Cao Dan was agreeable to make the effort, and I will always remember him for willingness to try the difficult.

On the morning of departure, he advised that if we had to stop for anyone, I ought to pretend being a French livestock specialist. I told him that would be difficult because I knew nothing about livestock and spoke poor French. "It's arrogant attitude that counts," he replied. It turned out we were able to make a ford across the river. Cao Dan remembered that years ago a ferry had operated there, but it was gone and the river could only be crossed when the water level was low. He knew ARVN engineers had improved the ford a few months earlier, but he doubted it would endure through the next monsoon season. The only solution, he continued, was a bridge.

There were friendly ARVN soldiers along the way in the lower valley. We slowed, and Cao Dan pressed a few piastres on them, "so happier they will be to greet me on my way out." We continued on through small hamlets, a few homes each. The road was increasingly more test than passage.

We were barely able to get north of Vinh Phuoc when Cao Dan stopped his truck. "This is as far as I can take you." He would work his truck around somehow and stop at each hamlet on the way back, offering to buy pigs for sale in the Qui Nhon market. Cao Dan reminded me to avoid anyone who I saw first and to stay out of hamlets, "because there will be unfriendly people," and he ended with "Good luck![30]

Gazing at the terrain before me, I now saw that the old French map provided only an abstract portrayal of actual topography. Lines ran here and there as though a kind of psychiatric litmus. With my compass and belief that it was better to have a poor map than none at all, I forged forward. There was a trail, apparently well trod, and as on my earlier excursion south of An Khe, I paralleled the track left by others. Here, because the pitch was steep, movement off-trail was much more difficult than expected. I had to move more often on than off, and exposure made me nervous. I pushed myself off-trail as much as possible, but obstacles often forced me back to the path.

In Qui Nhon a couple of days earlier, I had thought traversing hills on my way to the first hamlet in the Hoai An finger valley might require a few hours. In fact, it took all of the first day. I was tired, knocked out on my feet, when I crossed the ridgeline. There were distant dim lights, probably lanterns, in a hamlet. It was time to find a place of concealment, eat rice balls dosed with nuoc mam, cover myself with my mosquito net, and go to sleep.

The next morning I looked carefully at the hamlet to the east. I had a pair of binoculars, almost a child's plaything but effective to my need. I could not discern anything but what I supposed was normal early-morning activity. There were lots of people moving around, children playing, but there didn't appear to be any ARVN. Something about the place induced a bad feeling. I skirted the homes and associated paddy fields, stayed within the cover of trees and shrubs, and moved very carefully.

I covered about fifteen kilometers that day, never comfortable, until I observed a small community with some ARVN strolling around the market. There was an old beat-up flatbed truck serving as the local bus. It looked good to me. The friendly soldiers suggested giving the driver ten piastres for a ride to Bong Son. I offered twenty to make sure the driver was happy. We made a few stops as we traveled the district road. Hoai An town looked interesting, and when we paused in Thanh Tu I bought coconut-flavored candy. Across the river were what seemed limitless coconut groves sheltering An Thuong. I was lucky to have made a long hike without incident and just as fortunately found a pretty clean *phong ngu* in Bong Son. The next day it was easy to bus back home to Qui Nhon.

I needed to catch up with messages from Ev, get together with Howard Walters, meet with Tuy and Jusiu, express gratitude to Cao Dan for his support, and provide my wife with some shared time in Qui Nhon. I also realized that what I gained in confidence and knowledge was meaningless if not applied to field tasking. Ev reminded me to get back to Quang Ngai, resume contact with Vietnamese officials and advisors, and provide him with a sense of how the 25th Division psychological operations plan was being implemented. So obediently, I caught a lift northward on one of the Caribou aircraft stationed in Qui Nhon to support II Corps advisory detachments.[31]

This was only the second occasion to spend several days with Bob Kelly. He was learning about Quang Ngai history and province administration from the province chief, Nguyen Van Tat, and the deputy for administration, Tran Van Phien. Phien was a native of Nghia Hanh district and claimed to have some Cham ancestry in his lineage. Kelly was G-5 advisor to the 25th Division when we first met. Now he was Quang Ngai sector advisor for security. He traveled widely in the province, mostly by road, and was acquainted with a broad cross-section of people in district towns and some hamlets. We went to Mo Duc and Duc Pho districts. In Mo Duc, Kelly spoke with the district chief about making the home hamlet of Pham Van Dong a model of RVN rural development, even if that required extra resources.[32] We had coffee in a small shop on a side street in Duc Pho. The woman who owned the place, and brought coffee to our table, was widow of a senior SVNLF province cadre.

Despite thirteen years' age difference, the more Kelly and I conversed, the more we felt like brothers. We were observing RVN performance in two adjoining provinces, we were more involved with Vietnamese than most Americans, and we were reaching similar conclusions. Bob Kelly was what some would call "an American original." He had joined the army as a teenager during World War II and fought on New Guinea and other islands. He spoke of how thrilled he was to once touch the nose of Dick Bong's P-38 on a remote airstrip. After that war he was stationed in Europe and learned conversational French, which he employed with Vietnamese officials.[33]

After returning to Qui Nhon, Howard Walters and Tuy told me that the 4th Psychological Operations Company was wrapping up an operation in the An Lao Valley, and they invited me to join them for a few days. Tuy's unit was supporting the 1st Battalion of the 47th Regiment to clear and hold the west bank of the Song An Lao. Howard Walters thought applying combined Vietnamese and American resources for psychological (Tuy's notion of political) effect might produce a model for application elsewhere.[34]

The road to An Lao is not obvious. Cross the bridge that spans the An Lao River at Bong Son, then twist the steering wheel sharply to the left and drive west at the base of hills. Soon the road, on the east bank of the river, bends north toward An Lao district headquarters. Every American who loves Viet Nam has a favorite place in their heart. Mine is this valley, especially as I first saw it in early 1963. Where geography allowed, there were small hamlets, rice paddies, and coconut groves. A few bamboo bridges crossed deeper or swifter running channels of the river. Ninth Division engineers had placed a single-file pontoon bridge that facilitated commerce as well as troop movement. In a few places a boat was helpful. There were numerous footpaths on the western side of the valley, but no road. Mountains of steep gradient loomed over all, but especially to the west, as that constituted the beginning of the Central Highlands plateau.[35]

French influence during the colonial period was marginal, and after World War II the Viet Minh, as elsewhere in most of central Viet Nam, governed the valley. After the Geneva Agreement, some of the young men embarked from Qui Nhon to North Viet Nam but promised friends and family members that they would return. Republic of Viet Nam administration of the valley, even after placing a district headquarters at the northern end, was always tenuous. The more inaccessible west bank was again under communist rule from late 1961 through early 1962. Social and market relations between both sides of the valley facilitated political work by SVNLF agents. The west bank, controlled by communists, provided provisioning and recruits further on to base areas Kon Truck and Kon Hannung. In late February 1963, the 1st Battalion, 47th Regiment, was assigned to the valley, and the commander initiated aggressive patrolling combined with Tuy's application of psychological and civic action. The SVNLF territorial unit was displaced westward from Van Trung and Van

Tin hamlets. The withdrawing communists took 149 young people with them. By mid-March those two hamlets were being reorganized as strategic hamlets,[36] but SVNLF guerrillas continued to harass and enter other communities on the west bank.

Airborne loudspeaker and leaflet missions were flown over the west bank and hinterland. The messages described better living conditions in strategic hamlets. Some missions targeted SVNLF personnel who had relatives in the valley. We encouraged return to families, escaping communist control and cruel discipline, and the chance to build a good life in a society where citizens have choices.[37] Within the valley, but on west bank ridgelines, the 4th Psychological Operations Company led by Tuy and Jusiu conducted patrols utilizing night ground speakers directed toward the trails running westward to the base areas. The same soldiers also performed simple civic action, while a cultural team from the 9th Division gave musical and dramatic performances.

At that point in early April 1963, Van Trung and Van Tin hamlets were about 70 percent toward completion as strategic hamlets. An important part of the progress was cooperative effort, including USOM material and emergency food supplement. Based on what I observed, Capt. Nguyen Tuy was the indispensable link for all components of the operation. He spent part of every morning with the 1st Battalion staff at the command post in Hoi Long hamlet on the east side of the river. They reviewed previous activity and planned for the new day. He would typically spend the remainder of that day and night on the west bank. He was constantly moving, encouraging 1st Battalion soldiers and his own men of the 4th Company and making sure that civic action cadre, the medical team, and the cultural troupe were all parts of the overall operation.

Tuy explained that Howard Walters suggested managing as though this would be a model for application elsewhere, and he was trying to apply what he learned at Fort Bragg but transposed to suit Viet Nam. He emphasized helping hamlet residents with any chore or project that could be done simply and immediately. Rather than building a school, he thought, better to repair the old one. Don't build anything unless you are helping people with what they have already begun. "That way, if communists return and tear it down, they are destroying what belongs to the people, not to the government." By personal leadership and personality, Tuy was the essential spark plug. I asked why he didn't push the battalion commander to relocate the command post to the west bank. He responded that the battalion was not his, so he could encourage, set a good example, but not push. "If I push, the other person will push back, and then we are not a team."

The 4th Company conducted patrols cooperatively with the 1st Battalion and at night established loudspeaker positions with defensive ambush points. Broadcasts suggested that persons wanting to return home should escape toward the direction where there were lights in the sky. Coordinating mortars firing flare rounds provided illumination to show the direction for escape home. Those flare-supported loudspeaker missions along ridges west of Tan Son and Tan Xuan hamlets drew results.

A young man, an SVNLF territorial, originally from Tan Xuan, turned himself in to a relative. He had a brother who wanted to come with him, but the brother was caught and killed. Another returnee, impressed as a laborer, had interesting information about Relay Station 06 that supported returnees from the north. These men said that most of the SVNLF leaders were central Vietnamese, but a third youth told us that he met two North Vietnamese with four central Vietnamese who returned from study in the north. They all reported that communist political themes stressed continuation of the fight against colonialism and capitalism. The SVNLF asserted anyone who left the Front would be caught and executed by the Saigon government.

Casual conversation with people in west bank hamlets provided information about communist taxation. Taxes were described as "contributions" and were at a level higher than taxes applied by the government. If anyone complained, the amount would be increased, because complaining proved you opposed the revolution. These poor people, caught in the middle and trying to survive, said that once involved with the SVNLF, even by coercion, it was difficult to break away. Small group indoctrination and the combat cell structure, in which each shared responsibility for the others' behavior, meant that independent action was risky if not impossible.

An older, really old, farmer told us that "liberation people" had held meetings in hamlets during the recent Tet holiday. "The gentlemen told people in the hamlet that they were nationalists fighting American domination." One of the returned young men said they were told Americans were like the French, and the Diem government was a puppet.

One morning I went to the district office and spoke with a young civil officer who was deputy district chief. I showed him my map of the area (another of the 1:100,000 Service Geographique de l'Indochine sheets) and pointed out a wavy brown double line running north into Quang Ngai. It was indicated on the map as *muraille moi*. He responded that it marked the location of remains supposed to have been a wall either built by Cham to hold back tribal incursions or placed by tribes to keep Cham out of their land. He was not sure which was the reasonable explanation, although he thought it more likely that the Cham were responsible. I wanted to go take a look and asked his advice. We studied my map for a few minutes, and then he said that he had seen part of the wall, and it was not interesting. I persevered. More map study. Finally, he agreed to arrange for me to be brought up to the outpost at Hung Nhon on the west bank, and that Dan Ve could assist me in crossing a small stream just north of the post.[38] The wall would then be "not far." He explained that although there was more of the wall farther north on the east bank, security there was poor.

The Dan Ve at the small post seemed friendly and, responsive to the note that I carried from the district officer, ready to escort me onward about a kilometer and over the stream depicted on my map. They halted there and told me they could go no farther, but that the wall was only another twenty minutes at the base of the hill before us. I had come far and was stubborn. Turning back would mean wasted effort, and I would feel diminished. So I walked on. The terrain was mostly open, perhaps once under cultivation but not then.

At the foot of the hill extending to the river on my right, I began to search for a wall, or at least anything that might once have been a wall. The brush there was thick. Suddenly, coming from the west, parallel to the hillside and approaching me, was a man with a rifle slung over his shoulder. I only wanted to find an old wall. He only wanted to be on his way somewhere else. I would have been relieved had he not seen me and simply passed by. But he pulled his rifle forward and raised it while still looking as surprised as I felt myself. I was the quicker for having my carbine chambered and off safety. We were so close that I could not miss. Aiming is as simple as pointing your finger, extension of intention. If something must be done, make sure it is done. I fired several times.

I felt no guilt after, but some deep remorse that two strangers would meet by a hillside and one lose his life. He made a startled defiant move, but it was his country, and I was the intruder.[39] I did not linger in that place. If he had "liberation friends" nearby, they would be mighty angry. I took his rifle, a long and clumsy one, some kind of French manufacture from a time before either of us was born, and quickly retraced my way back to the small stream. The Dan Ve did not wait. They must have heard the shots and decided their duty was back at the outpost. Soon I was there, too. I told them there was a body, a person killed, across the stream by the hill. There were nods and glances from one to another. I offered to leave the old rifle with them, and they could collect the body. They shook their heads negatively, no, better I bring the rifle to district, and they would await instructions.

I told the young civil officer who had reluctantly referred me toward the wall that there was a body in the area where I had been looking. I gave him the rifle. I was not more specific than that, and he asked no questions. One of the district vehicles brought me back to the battalion CP at Hoi Long, and I rejoined Tuy and Walters.

The next day Captain Walters and I went about making farewells, because we would return to Qui Nhon. I saw the district chief off to the side talking quietly with Tuy. They were both looking toward me, not with hostility, but with a kind of curiosity. Tuy never mentioned anything about that conversation, but a few days later in Qui Nhon he told me that he and Jusiu had discussed my walking around and decided I ought to hire a reliable travel companion. They would make introduction to a young Jarai acquaintance of Jusiu.

Howard and I drafted our joint report. We discussed the mix of participating RVN and American civil and military elements. We believed positive results were obtained during the An Lao operation. Although much more was required to maintain progress, we were convinced that a model had been established. We did have some reservations and ideas for improvement, influenced by Nguyen Tuy, who joined us for one long night discussion.[40] We asked Tuy if he would push recommendations in his own report. He replied that would be too soon. He said we should wait about two months and then return to the valley for evaluation. That would be the right time to summarize what was correct and effective and make recommendations for future operations. After listening to Tuy, we agreed it would be premature to push for quantum change. So our joint report focused on the benefit that a well-designed combined operation could deliver to a contested area. Howard summarized, "If we can get all the Vietnamese and American agencies to just work together, that's already a giant step."

I flew to Quang Ngai and shared our draft with Bob Kelly. He was enthusiastic about how the An Lao operation might serve as an example to apply in contested areas like Ba To, Tra Bong, or even toward the Son Tinh foothills. He asked me to get back for discussion with him, other advisors, Province Chief Tat, and 25th Division commander Lu Lan.

We did not think of ourselves as optimists, in late April 1963, but just as surely we were not pessimistic about the potential for the Republic of Viet Nam to organize for effective governance. There were definitely deficiencies in organization and personnel, but we believed those could be remedied. We were sure the fulcrum for change was at hamlet level, because the hamlet was also the basic social community (in central Viet Nam) and the point where resources should be applied for rural development. We thought having the 9th Division and 47th Regiment operational in Binh Dinh and Phu Yen, with the new 25th Division in Quang Ngai, tilted the military balance in favor of the RVN. Despite residual Viet Minh influence in that area, responsible government administration would not be impossible if the correct measures were adopted.

All was about to change.

3
Deterioration

On 8 May 1963 there was an incident in Hue, the former royal capital, that, combined with irresponsible and futile Diem administration response, would have devastating impact on the fate of the First Republic. A scuffle between Buddhist activists and government security forces resulted in several people killed. My first awareness of the seriousness was conveyed by Nguyen Tuy, who told me that he and his company would be staying close to Phu Thanh for the next several days while the 9th Division focused on unit discipline. He added that the 47th Regiment might even withdraw from the west bank of the An Lao Valley. I was momentarily numbed by suggestion there might be a step backward from progress achieved during the preceding month. I asked why a problem in Hue would shake Binh Dinh. We had not previously discussed Viet Nam politics. Now he spoke about historic tension between Buddhist and Catholic adherents, complicated by regionalism and exacerbated by government favoritism for Catholics in assignment and promotion. The two essentials for command or administrative authority, he said, are membership in the Can Lao Party or being Catholic.[1] Both would be best, he said with weary demeanor.

Dave Sheppard, deputy USIS director, called the next day and sought information as soon as possible as to public attitudes in Binh Dinh and elsewhere along the central coast. I took that as a marching order. I had already made the acquaintance of Nguyen Van Phuoc, chairman of the Binh Dinh Buddhist Association; Dr. Nhung, a physician in private practice who often conducted free clinics at the Qui Nhon pagoda; and some young Catholic seminarians who appreciated Free World magazines brought to their center every month. So it would be possible to begin by seeking reaction in the city where I lived and then broadening the base of inquiry when traveling.

Although Phuoc and Nhung met with me separately, their message was similar. First of all, they were well informed (through letters carried by bus) concerning what had happened in Hue.[2] Second, they both expressed hope the government would reach out to Buddhists, especially in Hue, and actively seek reconciliation. "Only the president," said Phuoc, "can do what needs to be done. He should make a grand gesture, go to Hue, apologize, and ask for understanding that all Vietnamese need to work together." Dr. Nhung was pessimistic. He said Buddhist associations in central Viet Nam were not communist, but if the government could not solve this problem, communists could claim religious equality as one of their causes.

I visited a priest at the Qui Nhon cathedral, located across from the market, and then drove the coastal road to the seminary located near the ARVN hospital. Americans were usually well received by Vietnamese Catholics, who assumed most of us were fellow Christians, and this was not the first time I had stopped by for conversation. On this visit I learned that Qui Nhon Catholics were not as well informed as Buddhists, and they did not share Phuoc's insistence that a grand gesture was necessary.

I thought myself tuned in to Viet Nam, especially compared with most Americans, but a few days later, driving north to Quang Ngai, I still had not recognized the seismic nature of what had occurred in Hue. My immediate concern was that ARVN seemed to be retracting. While I passed through Bong Son and Tam Quan, the main streets and shops were unnaturally quiet. You could sense paralysis, and that did not augur well for the effort in An Lao. Arriving in Quang Ngai city, I went to look for Kelly. We called on Province Chief Tat, who, in the manner of the "Chicago School of Politics," told us the government had to be both understanding and firm. We wondered what the relative mix would be.

Bob Kelly organized a government rally in Vinh Tuy, across the Tra Khuc River in western Son Tinh district.[3] Kelly had studied the draft report describing our recovery operation in An Lao, and he wanted this rally to be a trial run for similar efforts in Quang Ngai. I had reservations about what was planned, but my respect and regard for Kelly swept me along. Besides, it was too late to argue for alteration. As it turned out, what took place in one day at Vinh Tuy was symptomatic of RVN failure: short-term effort lacking consistency and durability.

We crossed the Tra Khuc in convoy and almost immediately turned west, passing giant picturesque norias, wheels powered by force of current to lift river water for irrigation. About twelve kilometers on, just past Nui Tron (Tron Mountain, actually a prominent hill about five hundred feet high), we entered Ba Gia,[4] a small market town, and turned north on a smaller road winding between two hills to Vinh Tuy. A Vietnamese-American medical team had arrived even earlier and had already seen more than two hundred persons. Hundreds of rural families were present, and they had to wait until the province chief's party came almost two hours later. An elaborate stage constructed for this event was empty. Music played from loudspeakers, but the crowd was restless. It was hot and there was no water. Finally, the official entourage arrived in a cloud of dust. Province Chief Nguyen Van Tat stepped forward on the stage, took the microphone, and began to speak.

Earlier in the morning Kelly told me the highlight of the rally would be a C-47 flying over the assembled throng following Province Chief Tat's speech. The C-47 would broadcast appeals for Viet Cong to leave the communists and return to the government side. Leaflets (to serve as safe conduct passes) would be dropped so that good people of Vinh Tuy could pass them to relatives and friends.

Well, the aircraft was early on station, or the province chief spoke too long. Before he was finished the C-47 made two low-level passes, observing what was happening on the ground, then circled higher and, using powerful amplified psyops loudspeakers, rudely interrupted Tat by asking, "Ong Tinh, xong chua? Xong chua?" (Mr. Province Chief, finished yet? Finished yet?) Ong Tinh was not finished, and he was not pleased. Absent ground-to-air communication, the C-47 crew formed their own conclusion and made the first leaflet pass. Not all the packages opened, and heavy bundles were slamming into the ground like bombs. Kelly and I took shelter at the off side of an ARVN deuce and a half (standard US Army truck) while I was laughing and he was groaning, head in hands. A leaflet "missile" tore into the canopy over the stage, scattering the official party. Kelly moaned, "I am mortified, I am mortified." I stopped laughing only long enough to say, "Kelly, years from now this will be one of your favorite stories!" He was not persuaded.

At the end of the day, and after the long convoy drive back to Quang Ngai city, we discussed the Vinh Tuy rally. I bluntly told Kelly that it epitomized the worst form of government relations with the rural population: people rounded up like cattle from their hamlets, herded together with no shelter from the sun, no water available, and waiting hours for officials from the province capital. Although there was a 25th Division battalion in the vicinity for security, there hadn't been planning to work soldiers into anything resembling a recovery operation. And, I advised Kelly, that was what was needed in those former Viet Minh areas. Local government had to be constituted in hamlets to represent the people to district and province. "At the end of the day, never mind the loudspeaker and leaflet screwup, we just left. Nothing remained. It's like throwing a giant rock into the ocean. Big splash, and then nothing."[5] Recovering an area is not possible without consistent, persistent, active presence.

The following day, Kelly escorted General Timmes to the province Chieu Hoi center.[6] General Timmes, always interested in a new face and perspective, asked my impression of the reception and reorientation center. The clean, cheerful, physical appearance was satisfactory, and when I spoke with returnees, no one complained. However, I added, while we are trying to bring people back from communist control, the government-Buddhist confrontation will be driving others away. General Timmes frowned, shook hands, and moved off.

The 25th Division advisory team organized a recreational convoy to the beach at My Khe the day before my return to Qui Nhon. Once again we crossed the Tra Khuc, but this time turning east on a dirt provincial road to the coast. My Khe was a semiurbanized fishing community. The broad and sandy beach was accessed by bridge over a narrow estuary. The entire area was bustling with market activity, but there was good humor and social harmony in the noise of buyers and sellers, children calling to each other, and many waving to Americans. Kelly and I relaxed, watching young soldiers at play, and we wondered out loud how many years would pass until My Khe might have a resort motel. On the way back we paused at a bamboo and palm frond shelter to the right of the road and had a bottle of Bia Lon.[7] We were not far from a walled enclosure as extensive as the old citadel in Quang Ngai city. Kelly and I drove into the site and I made inquiry while Kelly patiently waited. Three unofficial Chau Sa caretakers told us that the walls and a nearby gate structure were Cham. I didn't think so. Everything looked to me more like seventeenth- or eighteenth-century

Vietnamese architecture and construction. Then we drove on a few more kilometers to a prominent hillock on which there was a small pagoda. The name of the hill is Thien An, and I thought that could mean "peaceful heaven" or "paradise."[8] Kelly was providing me with an opportunity to converse with resident monks concerning the Hue incident and ongoing Buddhist dissatisfaction. The monks were conversant with Buddhist accounts of the events in Hue and continuing stalemate with the government. Their manner was firm as they told us the government would lose support if the police and army opposed Buddhists. It was warm in the pagoda. The cumulative effect of sun on the beach followed by Bia Lon had me ready to fall asleep right there. We returned to Quang Ngai city, and the next day I made the long drive home to Qui Nhon.

Tuy was organizing the 4th Psychological Operations Company for transfer to Pleiku. The company was a II Corps resource, and headquarters decided it should be colocated with II Corps. At the same time, Howard Walters was preparing for assignment back to CONUS.[9] The combination of these changes had Tuy despondent. I promised to make the road movement with him and pointed out that once he was in the highlands we could discuss the possibility of replicating the 4th by organizing a twin composed mostly of Kontum Bahnar. That raised his spirits, because in early April we had discussed the utility of having a specialized unit to operate north of An Khe and west of the An Lao Valley.

Just a few days before movement to Pleiku with Tuy and his company, Jusiu told me there was a recently captured, "very strong" prisoner in An Khe. He was a Bahnar who had regrouped to the north in 1955 and recently returned to support the SVNLF. The Bahnar were considered by Vietnamese to be the tribe most resistant to being civilized, meaning not susceptible to rule by others. I drove to An Khe to meet the Bahnar captive who impressed a Jarai officer.[10]

The man I found manacled in the district police station was in pain with a roughly dressed leg wound, but his gaze was unafraid. His toleration of circumstance, and his composure, impressed me: "very strong," just as Jusiu had reported. We spoke in Vietnamese, since I didn't know even one word of Bahnar. He smiled as we began to converse and said with some confidence that we could figure out each other's meaning. He began by insisting that he was captured, had not surrendered, and could not have been taken if not wounded.

He claimed to have traversed some part of Laos before crossing back into Viet Nam west of Dak Sut, and when I showed him the old French map that I brought along, he had no difficulty indicating a river trail that ran southeast from the border to cross Route 14.[11] He said he was in Kontum and Binh Dinh for several months before being wounded and captured. He claimed Sedang tribal people welcomed him because they are Bahnar brothers (there may be an ethnic-linguistic relationship), but I noticed he made no equivalent claim for Jarai. He said he traveled easily around Kon Truck and other remote places because it was *que toi*, "my homeland." I suggested it must have been tough going, and he replied, with another smile, that it was not difficult for someone like himself. I asked what his mission was in the South. He responded that he was sent to assess the readiness of the highlands people to support struggle against My-Diem.[12] We had about an hour together before I bid him farewell and good luck. Before I departed, the district police chief told me the prisoner was captured south of Bahnar territory near a stream and trail that approached the Vinh Thanh Valley. He supposed that the captive was on his way to make liaison with the Binh Dinh provincial committee.

As I drove Route 19 back to Qui Nhon, just past Binh Khe district, a thunderstorm threw down such heavy rain that visibility went to zero. I had to pull well off the road, and while waiting reflected on how confident the prisoner was despite his wound and restraints. He had tremendous self-assurance. Although this was the most dramatic example, it was a reminder that all the prisoners and rallied former SVNLF that I had met were impressive.[13] In fact, as a category, they were more imposing than the good people with whom I worked. How could I arrive at this conclusion despite affectionate regard for friends? The only explanation was that the prisoners and ralliers were all connected in some way to the anti-French war for independence. They were patriots. My friends were mostly, not all, but mostly, previously associated with the French losing effort. Before driving forward again, I thought to myself, and even might have said out loud, "This is bad history for us."[14]

I tasted convoy dust from An Khe to Pleiku with Tuy, Jusiu, and the 4th Company, and I also felt the inconvenience of having to travel at the pace of the slowest vehicle. An accident that put one truck overturned off the road halted everyone for a couple of hours. After arrival in Pleiku, Tuy and Jusiu settled the company and then their families. Next day they followed through with their intention to help me hire a Jarai traveling companion.

We went to Plei M—— N——, a Jarai settlement east of Pleiku, where they introduced WR, a young man whose brother was already in the army.[15] WR could speak a little Vietnamese and a few words of French, so we would be able to communicate. I called Ev Bumgardner from the II Corps advisory compound and told him of Tuy's recommendation. His reaction was simple: "Overdue. Hire him on petty cash as part-time driver, even if you are the one driving." So WR returned to Qui Nhon with me and took our small guest bedroom.

On 11 June there was another event in the Buddhist/government chain of cause and effect that increased tension. Dave Sheppard called to tell me that a monk in Saigon had burned himself to death.[16] He asked for reaction from central Viet Nam. My wife and I were startled. We could not imagine the resolve and act of will sufficient for self-immolation. I went around to talk with my usual sources of information on popular opinion. Mr. Phuoc was in tears as he told me that absent change, this sacrifice by Thich Quang Duc would be only the first of many. Dr. Nhung's belief was that Thich Quang Duc shamed the president, and unless President Diem made an appropriate selfless response, the crisis would persist and deepen. Catholic friends told me they were mystified, because their faith would not allow suicide, but self-immolation had happened before in Viet Nam history and had not amounted to much. These two opposite points of view dramatically highlighted a widening gulf between the two religions.

Later in June I spent time in Phu Yen province, including a couple of days in a hamlet near Nui Meo in western Tuy Hoa district. The hamlet, intended to be a combat self-defense hamlet (Ap Chien Dau), had been overrun a few days earlier, and a Bao An (province civil guard) company was attempting to reorganize a defense force. The wooden stake fence had been destroyed, but the greater difficulty was that many young men were missing, presumed to have accompanied the withdrawing guerrillas. The Bao An commander was a mature and dedicated officer but frustrated by the absence of province civil affairs support. Until this visit I was optimistic about Phu Yen, despite what Tuy told me about corruption. No longer.

Returning to Binh Dinh, I met people in Tuy Phuoc and Van Canh districts. Interesting conversations proved country people were becoming almost as well informed about political problems as their urban counterparts. Working closer to Qui Nhon allowed spending more time with my wife, thereby belatedly showing concern for the state of our marriage. Our relationship was deteriorating faster and more completely than was the government's position in central Viet Nam. The fault was my own. She had done more than most would have even attempted. She befriended the province chief's wife and accompanied her on visits around Qui Nhon and even to districts. She organized a special English class that included Jusiu and other soldiers. She endured what most would have called a hardship assignment in a distant province, and she was tolerant of my absences to an extent that surpassed what should be reasonably expected. Days of talking with mutual honesty, absent rancor, yielded the conclusion that I was selfishly more dedicated to Viet Nam, and particularly the notion of myself in Viet Nam, than to consideration for her and effort required to save the marriage. Of course that isn't the whole story; how can a paragraph yield all? But this was the essence. We agreed to separate, and although she returned briefly, that was as much for her own personal farewell to Viet Nam. A divorce was final a few months later.

No matter how relieved one may be to survive a crash landing, literally or figuratively, one needs pause for recovery. Mine for a few days that July was on Phuoc Hai and Phuoc Chau islands. Phuoc Hai is not really an island, but the rocky headland of a peninsula extending south to form one arm of Qui Nhon Bay. I was there with an American NCO who wanted exposure to rural Viet Nam. The boat that carried us was leased by USOM to deliver material to fishing hamlets. Two days on Phuoc Hai, with a sharpened wood palisade around a cluster of homes symbolically indicating a strategic hamlet, was a pleasant change. Except even here there was an unexpected level of hostility against the government. While friendly and good-natured about my awkwardness with their language, these independent fishing families had not a single good word for the republic.[17]

Phuoc Chau, about twenty kilometers south and maybe eight kilometers offshore, was different. People there felt remote from political and military conflict. The island was shaped by two hills with a valley between. People led me to a deep, stone-faced well, still in use, that they said was originally Cham. One family had a collection of pottery, some broken and some intact, collected in nets or along the beach after storms. Friends who knew their interest sometimes gave them something. I did not know anything about Vietnamese kilns in 1963, but, remembering what they showed me, I think they had a mix of thirteenth- and fourteenth-century

Cham pottery and sixteenth- and seventeenth-century Bat Trang ceramics.[18]

Interlude over, I called on Captain Giai, a 9th Division friend, at the Phu Thanh camp. He surprised me by saying there was widespread rumor that the 9th Division would soon transfer to the Mekong Delta. Binh Dinh was the second most populous province in the country and occupied critical geography.[19] Division officers were vague about what reasoning had applied. They thought it could be due to overall government weakness south of Saigon and need for reinforcement to keep control of rice production. I thought to myself that weakening the center to shore up the south was just going to produce problems everywhere, because there would be a vacuum in the center, while 9th Division soldiers relocated to the south would long for home. I could not believe the rumored move would really happen.

I reported to Ev and Dave Sheppard that we were in the eye of a political storm. Passive ARVN posture persisted. VIS focused on explaining government policy to urban constituents in district and provincial towns, where the potential for demonstrations was highest. Driving through Phu Yen, I visited five pagodas in Song Cau, Tuy An, and Tuy Hoa districts. At each stop a photograph of Thich Quang Duc's post-mortem heart was shown to travelers. The photograph "proved" his sacrifice was pure, because the heart was not burned. By the time I returned to Qui Nhon, the same photograph was being distributed in Binh Dinh province, carried from Saigon by Buddhist travelers. Phuoc told me scientific skepticism of the claim for a pure heart was irrelevant, because the political impact of widespread belief was going to be enormous.

President Diem visited Quang Ngai on 1 and 2 August. I was not there, but Kelly sent me a note with photographs.[20] He wrote that the president visited Thach Thang hamlet (about halfway between Route 1 and the sea) in Mo Duc district. "If as much security could be provided in every hamlet as Thach Thang saw today, the war would be over." He also believed that the visit was an example of how beautifully Lu Lan, the 25th Division commander, and Nguyen Van Tat, province chief, could coordinate when the stakes were high for them personally. But in the end, he wrote, like the operation in Vinh Tuy, this might have been just another rock splashing in the ocean.

As the days passed, I learned there really was a plan to relocate the 9th

Division to the Sadec–Vinh Long area in the Mekong Delta. Not a single ARVN officer was enthusiastic about the imminent move. The province chief in Binh Dinh, a former educator, hard-working, who encouraged extension of ARVN and civil administration into contested areas, somewhat reluctantly told me that he didn't see how stretching regiments of the 22nd and 23rd Divisions to the coast would accomplish anything except weaken the highlands while not fully compensating for departure of the 9th. I asked him whether he had represented those concerns to Saigon. His look explained all. One person, even a province chief, could not push back against a palace decision.

I felt adrift and decided to make another long walk. Pulling out maps, and consulting with my landlord/advisor, I asked him to bring WR and me about two-thirds into the Vinh Thanh Valley and drop us off just before Dinh Quang. From there it appeared we could proceed up a trail that ran along a small stream. It was late in the dry season, and travel should be easy. I expected we could be on the plateau and almost intersecting Provincial Route 508 in one day. Cao Dan said that if we got to the road there shouldn't be difficulty catching a ride south to An Khe. We did not mistake his use of *neu*, "if."[21] He was not endorsing this plan. He argued that a big change was under way, and he thought the forest was not so empty as it had been just a few months earlier. He mentioned the Dai Doi Tay Son, an SVNLF provincial company that took its name from the revolutionary Tay Son brothers who overthrew a dynasty. He said a "friend" told him the company would soon expand to battalion, and this meant recruits might be training in the same area where we thought to travel. I was foolishly stubborn. Finally, he agreed to help again. "Let's make this the last time," he cautioned. We bought personal gear for WR at the Qui Nhon market, and I provided him with a large, heavy knife, almost a machete, for which he had immediate affection, but no carbine. I wanted another pair of eyes and ears, not a firefight.

On a beautiful morning in mid-August we set out for the short drive to Vinh Thanh. Cao Dan stayed on the road that ran along the left bank of the river valley and brought us to a turnoff marked on my old map. Now I recalled this was where an outpost had been overrun more than a year earlier. And I remembered that the Bahnar prisoner who impressed so deeply might have been captured somewhere in the area we planned to transit. Strangely, I had not felt as concerned in the northern part of the valley a few months earlier. Now Cao Dan's warning seemed more realistic than when debated in Qui Nhon. But we were not seeking contact, and I figured by moving fast, in and out, others would not even know we were there.

The real problem during the next several hours was that, once again, the Service Geographique de l'Indochine map did not adequately portray the difficulty of passage. The climb from valley to intermediate plateau was more abrupt than I anticipated. In spots there was hardly any path at all. We did move off-track from time to time and then had problems finding the faint trail again. WR was having less difficulty than I, and I knew that in fact he was moving slowly for my benefit. Late in the afternoon I thought we were only about four kilometers from where we wanted to intersect the provincial road. A faint path from the north, not indicated on my map, intersected ours. There was good brush cover right there, and I told WR that we should lay up, eat our rice, and conceal ourselves in brown mosquito netting until the next morning, when we could arrive at the road in less than a couple of hours.

It was just getting dark when we heard voices on the trail descending from the north. Two men appeared, one with a rifle but bearing it casually. They passed our position and headed east along the path we had recently ascended. There was not a glance in our direction. Relief was short, because my companion sprang forth and dispatched the rearmost of the two travelers with the heavy knife I had provided. The other was stumbling backward, trying to bring his rifle to position, when I shot him several times. Once again I felt a sharp twinge for the confrontation and consequence. WR, with a strength I had not thought possible, threw the one I had shot several feet off the trail. He sat the one he had killed upright at the intersection of the trails, and the poor fellow appeared to be gazing back at the direction from where he came. I asked, why? WR responded in French, "C'est la guerre psychologique!"

The one now slumped over and facing away from us had a thick notebook in a shirt pocket and a knapsack that included other papers. I did not ask WR to go where he tossed the other, but we had his rifle, and that was sufficient to feel less than assassin. As a precaution we moved another kilometer or so westward in the dark, to have distance from the place of unintended ambush. I didn't sleep that night, but WR did, and easily. In the morning he was one big, happy smile, and I suddenly understood that whatever Tuy and Jusiu had told him, he believed he did what he was hired to do.

Arriving at the road was easy. Later that morning we caught a ride south to An Khe. We delivered the short rifle, notebook, and knapsack to the district police station where I had spoken with the Bahnar prisoner more than two months earlier.[22] I was able to avoid extensive explanation by simply pointing out on a map where we left two bodies. The ease with which the district police chief was satisfied might have been due to anticipation that he would receive credit. I asked for a ride to the British advisory team, and he surprised me by saying that they were all gone, maybe to Pleiku, maybe even to Saigon. When asked what happened, he replied that there had been a "problem."[23]

I was disappointed, because my juvenile pride had anticipated introducing WR to Noone and Herboldt and reporting that we had been in the forest as they suggested. Instead, we took a bus back to Qui Nhon. I ruminated and slept a little. Arriving at the Qui Nhon bus station, I was concluding that solitary or even accompanied treks ought not become repetitive. Yes, I did it, but continuing self-indulgence could only mean eventually running out of dumb luck. I ought to be working with Vietnamese to identify projects that could support creating a viable independent country.

On 21 August the government raided pagodas throughout the country, especially at Hue and Saigon, in a bold but intemperate stroke to behead the Buddhist movement. Again, Dave Sheppard called for a report on reaction in the coastal provinces. Three days later, after first circulating around Qui Nhon and casually speaking with business people, I went to the main pagoda. Police surrounded the grounds but did not prevent me from entering. Inside the pagoda, Phuoc was meeting with monks and members of the province Buddhist association. They were subdued. Phuoc asked me whether it was true the American Embassy was sheltering Thich Tri Quang. I told him, honestly, that I was not informed. He replied that a relative told him Voice of America broadcast news that the American Embassy had provided refuge for Thich Tri Quang. I repeated that I did not know.

I asked Phuoc what the monks thought would happen next. The several monks spoke among themselves for a few minutes and then replied through Phuoc.[24] The government, by using the army against Buddhists, isolated itself from the great majority of the population. A small number of people are practicing Buddhists. But a far greater number believe they are Buddhists, even though their observance is inconsistent. Phuoc added a thought of his own, "Even many in the army will oppose using the army against the people."

I thanked the monks, Phuoc, and the others, raised myself from an awkward but respectful kneeling position, and prepared to leave. Phuoc followed and asked a favor. He told me a young girl from the Buddhist orphanage in Tuy Hoa was brought to Qui Nhon for a cleft palate operation by the New Zealand surgical team. The girl was ready for return to Phu Yen, but road travel was suspended. I replied that I would take the girl back to Tuy Hoa the next day.

Before returning home, I went to speak with Catholic seminarian friends. You would have anticipated their being supportive of the pagoda raids, but they surprised. Both were disappointed at lack of compromise. One said that in principle he was opposed to any government forcibly entering a church or pagoda. The other commented, "Only communists will benefit." I hastily typed a report, found a C-123 pilot, Capt. Bob Ferry, about to fly to Saigon, and asked him to deliver my envelope straight to Dave Sheppard. He promised, and about four hours later he delivered the report.

The next day, accompanied by Tran Xuan Khoi, another USIS employee recently assigned to Qui Nhon, we delivered the child to the orphanage in Tuy Hoa. At mid-day Khoi and I went to the American sector advisor compound located on the beach east of Tuy Hoa town. After talking for a while, the sector advisor invited us to have the lunch of the day, sandwiches and iced tea, in the team mess. The Americans were surprised to learn we had just driven from Qui Nhon. We informed them the road was open and quiet, with no traffic. A police checkpoint at Song Cau and another in Tuy An had just waved us through.

On our return, those same checkpoints were not manned. There was one at Phu Thanh just after entering Binh Dinh and another right after the turn from Route 1 to Qui Nhon. I had not thought we challenged government authority, but it turned out I was mistaken. Tuyen came by my home office soon after my return. He reported that the province chief was concerned for my safety and had asked the police chief to speak with me that evening about precautions. I asked Tuyen to join us, because he was the senior of two USIS employees in Qui Nhon.

Actually, two province officers called at my home office a little later that evening. One was the province police chief, and the other simply shook hands and introduced himself as Mr. Dung. The police chief opened discussion by saying that the province chief was not happy. He felt some responsibility for my security and would be thought inattentive if anything happened to me. I replied that I always asked advice from friends before travel and that roads were usually safer than rumored. "Officials should get on those roads and see for themselves."

Mr. Dung could not restrain himself: "But you go off roads, into hamlets, into hills. We don't understand. Why are you doing that? What are you doing?"

He had a point. I responded that I was learning about Viet Nam, and it seemed the way to begin was by trying to understand life in hamlets where conflict with the Viet Cong was most cruel.[25]

Mr. Dung was now lead discussant. "You attended a meeting with the Buddhist Struggle Committee yesterday, and today you brought a Buddhist to Tuy Hoa."

I really laughed at that. "I didn't see much in the way of struggle at the pagoda, and by the way, I also met with two friends at the Catholic Seminary. Is that a problem? And the Buddhist who I drove to Tuy Hoa is a nine-year-old girl who hardly spoke a word and didn't seem very dangerous to me."

Mr. Dung was irritated, but the police chief reentered our conversation, summarizing, "Anyway, you might be misunderstood. People will believe you do not support government positions on public order, and then you will be in danger. We ask, for your own safety, that you remain here in Qui Nhon until security is assured."

Obviously a threat had been issued.

The next day I reported the Tuy Hoa travel and subsequent police visit to Ev Bumgardner. He immediately responded, "Well, we'll just have to get you out of there. The pot is boiling, and I don't want you getting burned. Doug Ramsey from the embassy security office has come over to work with us. He has been in Dalat. Now we'll send him to Qui Nhon as your replacement. Spend a couple of days with him and then get yourself down to Dalat. The BPAO [Branch Public Affairs Office] staff there is excellent. They will set you up in the office and show you the residence. But I don't want you getting Dalat comfortable. You will still be my eyes, ears, and hands up in the center. We'll get someone else up there to be the regular BPAO."

Doug Ramsey flew up to Qui Nhon a couple of days later. We had a good discussion about the upper II Corps area. I explained that we were at a hiatus in terms of information, psychological operations, or any other kind of activity. I provided my notes on significant persons in Binh Dinh and adjacent provinces and suggested that, because I was a tainted commodity, Tuyen would be the best person to make introductions. Anyone could see right away that Doug was almost paranormally intelligent, physically active, and a much better speaker of Vietnamese than I. He had taken the full course at the Foreign Service Institute, and I admired his facility with the language. We talked about WR and his strengths as a traveling companion. Doug didn't think he would have the same need, and I knew WR would be out of his element in Dalat and neighboring provinces. Later, I spoke with WR about my move to Dalat, and he affirmed that he preferred to return to Pleiku and work with Tuy and Jusiu. So I gave him three months' pay and a personal bonus, along with a note for Tuy, and brought him to the bus station next morning. In my letter I explained that WR was all Tuy and Jusiu had suggested as a trusted companion, and even more.

Kicked out (no disguising what really happened) of a town and province that I considered home, I made my farewell to Cao Dan and his wife and headed the blue jeep toward Dalat.[26]

4
Demise of the First Republic

There were actually two Republics of Viet Nam. Ngo Dinh Diem and his family established the First Republic in October 1955 with advice and assistance from Americans, none more influential than Col. Edward Lansdale.[1] When President Diem was assassinated in November 1963, the first republic died with him. The Second Republic was not in place until 1967, following adoption of a new constitution and elections for a bicameral assembly, president, and vice president.

The First Republic was slowly, imperceptibly to its supporters, dissolving when John Mecklin called me down from Dalat, and Talbot Huey (BPAO) up from Can Tho to meet with him and Lou Conein at Mecklin's house on Le Qui Don Street.[2] John introduced Lou as an old friend dating from shared time in North Viet Nam almost a decade earlier.[3] Lou was restrained and rather quiet as he inquired about popular opinion in our respective areas. Talbot presented an overview, beginning with the reaction of province officials and then his supposition as to rural attitudes. His conclusion was that there was dissent within the civil/military administration and shunning of government by countryside people. My view was similar to Talbot's except that in central Viet Nam popular feeling already surpassed ignoring the government. People were moving toward opposition, and that included junior officers who felt unjustly stigmatized by the pagoda raids. Echoing Phuoc and others, I said only dramatic change could save the government from disaster, and the longer a change of policy was delayed, the more likely that communists would benefit.

The next day Ev and I had a long discussion about anticipated continuing erosion of the government position in central Viet Nam. It was understandable that for observers in Saigon, with the Ap Bac fiasco a short drive to the southwest, the imperative would seem to be another ARVN division for the Mekong Delta. But stealing that division from the center, a zone where there was already significant transgenerational support for the SVNLF, was going to produce dangerous weakness right in the middle of the country. Ev said that he hoped I was wrong, because the decision to shift the 9th Division was already made, and once the relocation took place, the 9th would not operate in II Corps again.[4] On my part, having no appreciation of the difficulty involved in establishing a binational agreement to increase ARVN by an additional division (as had been done for the 9th and 25th), I simply thought a new division should be raised in the Mekong Delta to meet a Mekong Delta requirement.

Absent his usual suggestion of coffee, Ev got up from behind his desk and paced around, saying that when Howard Walters had stopped by on his way through Saigon, he recounted an incident in An Lao.[5] Ev said the heart of the story was that "you were off on your own, for no good reason, and could have got yourself killed or captured. Instead, you took out a Viet Cong and turned in a weapon. Okay, as far as it goes, but we don't celebrate stupidity. I would recommend sending you home if I didn't need you, but a better you, a smarter you."

He paused while I tried to explain that I had checked with a district officer before going, but Ev interrupted: "You are headstrong and persuasive, and that's a bad combination. Keep it in the past. Some Vietnamese field representatives seem to know what happened. That tells me others might know. So you have a certain reputation. Might work for you up to a point, but beyond, no." He concluded by telling me to hire another traveling "assistant driver" after returning to Dalat.[6] I took Ev's supervisory notice very seriously. His short corrective reinforced the decision that I made on the An Khe bus, to support Vietnamese initiatives rather than seek individual adventure.

I drove back to Dalat on Route 20 from where it branched off Highway 1 several kilometers before Xuan Loc. The road brings a traveler through gently rolling landscape alternately forested or cleared for agriculture. In Dinh Quang there are curious rock formations of great boulders piled on boulders. It is a puzzle whether this is a natural occurrence or an instance of megalithic engineering. I still do not know. More than twenty kilometers farther, one nears foothills, circuits a sizable hill, transits the small Da Hoa Valley, and finally ascends the Blao Plateau. From this point the road continues to Djiring. The headquarters of the 40th Regiment, commanded by Dam Van Quy, was located just outside Djiring, and on this trip I began stopping over to visit him whenever in the area.[7] After that regimental camp the road gradually rises until, about twelve kilometers from Dalat, the ascent becomes steep. Dalat itself, at an elevation just less than five thousand feet, with an attractive small lake, diverse market, pleasant temperature, and relatively wealthy population, was a Viet Nam anomaly. I understood Ev's injunction, "I don't want you getting Dalat comfortable."

I strain the reader's patience by providing an early sixties Viet Nam travelogue. I won't sketch here every district town and hamlet, and you are spared what Dave Sheppard called a minute description of everyone I met on the road or in the field. They were all important to me. The first months in Viet Nam (1962) were a tutorial presided over by Ev Bumgardner. The next several months (most of 1963) were a period of self-study and exploration, allowed, encouraged, and protected by Ev. I was unreservedly loving every aspect of Viet Nam: vibrant colors, especially emerald green rice paddies; smells (including *sau rieng*); excited voices raised in market haggling; waterfalls and rapids in the highlands; sandy beaches along the coast; night in provincial or other large towns with hawkers calling: "Ai muon trung ga, khong," or, "Ai bun bo, bun bo, bun bo." Imagine, if you can, visualize, and feel over time and distance the Viet Nam that was absorbing me.

I took a few days in Dalat to ponder the experience and lessons derived from several months' working outward from Qui Nhon. Binh Dinh and Quang Ngai both have provincial histories that incline the population to insurgency. Quang Ngai traces a revolutionary lineage to Pham Van Dong's birth in Mo Duc and the March 1945 Ba To uprising. Quang Ngai city was an important Viet Minh training site and first headquarters for Inter-Zone V. Binh Dinh tradition was even deeper. This is the home of the Tay Son brothers, who overthrew a declining dynasty in the early nineteenth century. The brothers had a reform agenda before eventually succumbing to the Nguyen dynasty, which acquired power with French support. The Tay Son heritage was claimed by the SVNLF. I was told in Phu Phong that Ho Chi Minh's father was a magistrate in the area before his dismissal and departure for the far south, where he lived as an itinerant medical practitioner. Even today, I call to mind the valleys of Tra Bong,

An Lao, Kim Son, and Vinh Thanh. I close my eyes and see the Tra Khuc, Ca Lui, and Ba Rivers. I remember in An Nhon district, maybe a hundred meters to the west of Route 1, there is a solitary Cham tower. Just past there the highway runs straight north and then makes a sharp right-angle turn westward, all on an embankment. This is a remnant of the defensive wall for Vijaya, the twelfth-century Cham city.

Operationally, I knew now that the forest is like the sea. There are dangers at sea, but prudent attention to planning and method makes risk manageable. The sea and forest can be traversed as well by one traveler as another. There might be greater difficulty in populated areas, depending on local history and sociology. When moving, move quietly and stop often to listen. Don't rush. When in doubt, go to ground. The SVNLF can be displaced by active presence more easily than pushed out by fighting. A good unit is one led by someone who demonstrates care for both soldiers and civil population. Effective recovery of an area (previously ignored or lost to the SVNLF) requires a coordinated operation, presence in hamlets, and persistent, consistent effort. A recovery operation is never "done." Residual Viet Minh influence, transgenerational, a social matrix of support, in the old Inter-Zone V makes that part of Viet Nam the most challenging for any noncommunist government.[8] It is not hard to kill, but one lives with the consequences.

I met the Tuyen Duc province USOM provincial assistant. He was a Churu and spoke Vietnamese as well as his own language. I was impressed with his steady, good-humored self-confidence and area knowledge. I asked whether he could recommend someone for work with USIS as a traveling assistant. He suggested a cousin who lived near Diom southeast of Dalat. So a few days later we traveled from the Da Nhim Dam to the small town of Diom and then to his cousin's nearby home. He introduced me to Touneh Ton. Touneh agreed to the salary offered and was ready to go right away.

Soon it was September, and time to return on the road, by stages, to Binh Dinh and Quang Ngai. A friend in California took my request for special reading material and mailed Mao Zedong's *On Protracted War*, Vo Nguyen Giap's *People's War, People's Army*, and Truong Chinh's *The Resistance Will Win*. I thought it important to read and understand the honorable opposition's scripture. I had copies for Kelly and was bringing them to Quang Ngai.

On this trip Touneh and I went north to Hue and Quang Tri and from

Dong Ha toward Lao Bao on the border with Laos. The mountainous grip enclosing Highway 9 from Cam Lo westward seemed more ominous than the geography of east-west Routes 19 and 21. There you were up through a pass and onto the plateau. On Route 9, mountains seemed to seize the road and not let go. The "highway" itself was not in good condition. I thought to myself that if Giap's army ever moved south to reinforce the SVNLF, it would be hell trying to get them out. For the first time I understood the vulnerability of the Republic of Viet Nam's western border. And, other than to have simply been there, this was the value of having driven Route 9. We were not tempted to linger.

Returning to Quang Tri town, Touneh and I had a light lunch in a small café by the Thach Han River. This town had a traditional appearance and was one of the most attractive province capitals. We found the VIS chief and asked him about governance and public opinion. He told us that if the choice was between communists and the government, most people would choose the government. But the Buddhist protests raised a different question. Could there be a change of government? I had not seen Cham towers in Quang Tri and asked him whether there were any. Not towers, he said, but something interesting in the provincial courtyard. He drove us there to see small pieces of statuary. And he explained that to the west, before the mountains, there were irrigated terraces constructed by the Cham centuries earlier. I thought someday there would be opportunity to see them, but that day never came.

I called Ev from Hue. He let me know I had exceeded my geographic area by being out of II Corps. He was not really angry but said, "I presume we would have heard from you if you made it as far as Hanoi or Vientiane." The city of Hue exhibited greater tension in the streets, market, and shops than did Qui Nhon. I had wanted to visit Linh Mu Pagoda,[9] but it was apparent from a casual drive nearby that there was intense surveillance. An American attempting entrance would only cause difficulty for everyone. I spoke with as many people as possible without obviously taking a survey. It was conversationally clear that President Diem's administration forfeited whatever regard or respect it might have previously held. On a side street along one of the old palace ground walls, Touneh and I found a small restaurant specializing in *banh quay*, a kind of crepe similar to the southern *banh xeo*, but crispier and more delicious.[10]

I did impressionistic pulse taking on the slow return southward to

Quang Ngai. On the second day with Kelly a message from Ev intercepted us. He wanted me back in Dalat right away, certainly no later than mid-October. Touneh and I departed early the next morning. Driving through southern Mo Duc district, we were target for a few rounds fired from long range and striking short on the highway embankment. Touneh was prepared to return fire from his side of the jeep, but nothing could be seen except distant country people in fields. I was reminded of Ev's catechism on the road in Long An: "How many Viet Cong did you see today? How many saw you?" Farther along, a few kilometers south of Duc Pho, workers were clearing wreckage from the railroad where a train had been attacked two days earlier. In Sa Huynh we stopped for tea and coffee and spoke with some 39th Ranger Battalion soldiers, who told us that the area frequently received harassing fire at night. They asserted that Route 1 to Bong Son was no longer secure. Although we found the highway partially cross-trenched close to the provincial border, there was no further difficulty. A couple of days in Binh Dinh, a day in Phu Yen, two more in Khanh Hoa and Ninh Thuan, and then we were back in Dalat before our deadline.

Ev asked me to come down to Saigon right away. When I was at his house for lunch, he revealed that sometime in the next few weeks there could be an attempt to "tip over" the government. He said that what might be tried and what would actually happen "is unpredictable." He wanted to be sure I would be in Dalat, available, and not away on uncoordinated adventure. If I were to receive a message from Ung Van Luong, his assistant, or Col. Le Tan Buu (his Hoa Hao friend), I should act as though it were straight from himself.

I took a couple of free days in Saigon. I had made a friend of Ha Thuc Can, CBS cameraman, months before while in an art gallery deciding whether to purchase a painting. I walked away to think about it, and when I returned the painting was already reserved—for Can. He introduced me to many of his friends, including painters, singers, writers, and collectors of antiquities. From that point on, whenever passing through Saigon, rather than spinning wheels with Americans or wasting time in bars, I sought out interesting Vietnamese. Thanks to their curiosity and friendliness I was considerably introduced to others.[11] During this visit in Saigon it was apparent that many cultured city dwellers, "*attentistes*," anticipated a change of government. But they did not think anything would impact them personally. I did learn that opposition to the Diem administration was not limited to central Viet Nam Buddhists. A university student told me the death of Nguyen Tuong Tam ignited reaction from politically thinking intellectuals. She provided me with her translation of what was alleged to be his suicide note.[12]

For weeks, Ev explained, plans for military seizure of power had been made, rearranged, shuffled, leaked, resealed, disguised from Americans, then shared with Americans until an air of confusion permeated Saigon and the sense of inevitability wavered. Earlier there was a junior officer movement (with Pham Ngoc Thao prominent) and then one based on generals concerned about their own prospects. The two constants were that the US ambassador, recently arrived Henry Cabot Lodge, personally favored change of government, and Lou Conein was the conduit between the embassy and ARVN officers.[13]

On Saturday, 26 October, the government celebrated Republic of Viet Nam's National Day.[14] President Diem invited Ambassador Lodge to accompany him on an inspection visit to Phuoc Long province and then to Dalat for an overnight stay and discussion. I was already back in Dalat when Ev told me over the telephone, rather elliptically, that if there might be a problem for the ambassador staying at the president's guesthouse, then Ambassador Lodge and his wife would shelter with me. I asked how to know whether the guesthouse might be a problem. He replied that someone, known to both of us, would let me know the night before the presidential party arrived at Cam Ly airfield.

The person who rang my doorbell was Le Tan Buu, ARVN, simultaneously Hoa Hao officer who worked in the Directorate General of Information. With no preliminary comment, he stated that it would be appropriate for the ambassador to accept the hospitality of the presidential guesthouse.

The embassy security office telephoned the next morning and said the ambassador would "probably" stay at the presidential guesthouse. But his main point was that Ambassador Lodge knew of a special French restaurant in Dalat, La Savoisien, and he and his wife wanted to take a meal there. The security officer asked for comment. I knew that restaurant.[15] It was about two or three kilometers outside town on a wooded hillside. I told the security officer that, just on the basis of location, and other variables in play, this particular restaurant should be vetoed.

Later in the afternoon I was the sole American waiting on the tarmac at Cam Ly when Ambassador Lodge and his wife arrived on the air attaché C-47. I explained my decision to them (without mentioning that I occasionally ate there), and the ambassador's wife ("call me Emily"[16]) simply replied for both of them, "We can do that another time."

We stood together while the honor guard was drawn to attention and each rifle inspected to make sure there was no ammunition in a weapon's chamber or magazine. In the distance another C-47 appeared, circled, made final approach, and landed. No one disembarked. It was a decoy. Finally, the president's C-47 arrived with appropriate attention from the honor guard. President Diem, in his usual white suit, approached Ambassador Lodge. They exchanged a few words. I stood to the rear and made a respectful nod when the president glanced in my direction. The president and attendants departed in a motorcade for the Dalat presidential compound. Just a few days later Ngo Dinh Diem was dead, with his brother, in Saigon.[17]

Ambassador Lodge and his wife accompanied me for a brief rest stop in my house. He was tired, but the ambassador courteously inquired about my understanding of popular feeling in the provinces where I traveled. I stressed that, generally speaking, there was little affection for the government beyond the community of Catholic believers, still less trust in the government's ability to perform effectively, and no confidence that the government would adopt measures necessary to win respect and trust. Buddhists especially, I went on, believe that moderation of the current policy would be insufficient. Change needs to be bold and dramatic. I offered my opinion that whether the president seized this moment for a new direction would determine survival of the government. This brief meeting was also an opportunity to describe the sociopolitical history of the four coastal provinces from just south of Danang down to and including Tuy Hoa. Communists in this area would be particularly adept at positioning themselves advantageously against an unpopular government or during unsettled conditions that would result from a violent change of government. I was pretty blunt about the transfer of the 9th Division from Binh Dinh to the Mekong Delta being a serious mistake. There was a developing vacuum, and communists were filling it. Ambassador Lodge responded that the decision was made due to criticality of the provinces south of

Saigon. I replied there wouldn't be much left north of Saigon if everything between Pleiku and Qui Nhon were lost.

I could see that I was giving the ambassador more than he wanted, and my opinions were not exactly what he might have expected. The brief conversation at Cam Ly and stopover at my house were noblesse oblige. He was weary, and Mrs. Lodge, a gracious lady, said it was time to proceed to the guesthouse for a real rest before later meeting with President Diem. I sat alone by the little round table before my fireplace after they departed. A violent change of government seemed imminent. Our ambassador was the guest of a president who was about to be deposed. Communists organized and maneuvered in the countryside. I was barely twenty-five, but the sole American on hand to speak with him in Dalat. Everything, I mean everything, seemed very loose to me.[18]

A few days after the 1 November coup and murder of Ngo Dinh Diem and Ngo Dinh Nhu, I drove to Saigon to consult with Ev. He and a number of other Americans were previously so frustrated while dealing with the Diem administration that now they were (I thought) exhilarated by the change and potential for improvement. I was more subdued, but my enormous respect for Ev inclined me to be his listener rather than outspoken skeptic. Ev had documentation proving that our field assistant, Le Quang Tuyen, in Qui Nhon was an informer for the government and that he specifically reported on my activity. I told Ev these were tough times for Vietnamese. Many had relatives with the communists and with the government, friends working with Americans and friends who would not work with Americans, and on top of that we were expecting our employees to report to us about government activity and problems, so it should be expected that they would be asked to report about us to their own government. We might not like it, but reality is basic to playing the game. Tuyen did report but had not exaggerated or misrepresented. I suggested talking with Tuyen, not firing him. I added my belief that Tuyen was one of the smartest people I knew, and I would be glad to work with him again.

I decided to drive out to Hau Nghia, a newly established province, and see what the place looked like. Ev cautioned me to be very careful and avoid side trips off the main road to the new provincial capital, Bao Trai. Provincial Route 8 runs from Cu Chi southwest to Duc Lap and then, with a bend in the road, onward maybe three or four kilometers to the small town of Bao Trai. Not very far away, maybe fifteen kilometers by road, was the Hiep Hoa sugar mill and location of a US Special Forces camp.

I decided to heed Ev's instruction and avoid temptation to head in that direction. It was a wise decision. Two weeks later Hiep Hoa was the first Special Forces camp overrun in Viet Nam. Had anyone driven there in a lone vehicle, there is no guessing what they might have encountered. Bao Trai was the least appealing (I had yet to visit Chuong Thien) province capital I had yet seen. Cheo Reo had a sort of plateau country charm by comparison.[19]

In Bao Trai there was a friendly but harried official who said he was the strategic hamlet coordinator. When I asked about the situation, it seemed, by his reaction, he might shed tears. Strategic hamlets in this part of Long An, he said in frustration, were always imagined rather than actually achieved: "We were just separated from Long An four weeks ago. Now even in hamlets that had fencing, people remove it at night and Viet Cong come and go freely."[20]

I returned to Cu Chi and stopped in that crossroads town for a bowl of noodles. I thought that I might drive farther on Highway 1 and turn onto another provincial road to the Trung Lap Training Center, but others sharing my table, who assumed (as previously in Kien Hoa) that I was a journalist, insisted the only safe road from Cu Chi was Highway 1 back to Saigon. I specifically asked about the road to Trung Lap and was told that only a dummy (*nguoi cam*) would drive there. I decided not to place myself in that category.[21]

In Saigon the next morning Ev asked for my impressions of Hau Nghia. I replied that time there only allowed looking around and speaking with a few people, but I thought the province looked shaky. He suggested that countrywide there might be more relief than fragility because political tension had been relieved: "Hau Nghia will have to catch up." I answered that he seemed to imply other provinces were okay, and I rather doubted that. "My concern would be that the rest of the country might catch up to Hau Nghia."

I was just beginning to formulate my own postcoup estimate of the situation and did, and always would, have such respect for Ev that I was reluctant to be a doubting Thomas. But I went as far as telling him that decapitation of the government, ignoring transfer of authority to the vice president so that a prime minister with new ideas and policies could be appointed, set an unconstitutional precedent. "Anyone with more than two tanks will believe they have license for change of government, now that the first bloody coup is accepted. And, as far as blood is concerned, that stain will be on the generals for years. You told me even paratroopers in 1960 drew a line against killing the president."

Ev loved discussion, give and take, argumentation, and pushing and pulling ideas, and this was no exception. However he was not moved a millimeter by my reservations. He asked me to return to central Viet Nam, get on the road, and give him readings on provinces during the national transition. And he added, "Stay in touch, no disappearing for personal adventure."

Back in Dalat there was a celebratory mood prevailing within official circles. The president had never been popular in this city of relative richness and privilege. All the people with whom I spoke were relieved that the children of Counselor Nhu and his wife were successfully spirited from Dalat rather than abused (or worse) by a mob, but I heard no expression of regret at the death of the two brothers and the republic. An invitation arrived from the military academy commander to attend a "Soiree de Gala Dansante, au profit des combatants tombes au champ d'Honneur le 1er Novembre 1963."[22] I doubted soldiers and officers of the palace guard and Vietnamese Special Forces who died fighting, or were executed for nonacquiescence, were being honored by anyone.

I was still sorting out personal thoughts about the manner in which the government had been tipped over. I was not sorry to see the Diem administration terminate, but the manner by which change of government was effected also meant that we no longer had a Republic of Viet Nam. From that point in November 1963 onward, we would have the Government of Viet Nam (GVN), but absent a constitution. The difference was significant. It was also questionable, but I had not thought to discuss with Ev: Who among those self-interested generals had the smarts and integrity to establish and lead effective, responsive government? I had met only a few of them and would have thought, for example, Do Cao Tri very high on a likeability scale, but I could not imagine him and other generals being qualified to organize a new administration. And I wondered what would happen to good civilian province chiefs such as Bui Thuc Duyen in Binh Dinh. We had been at cross-purposes in August, but that was an intramural issue. He was honest, hardworking, and motivated to serve the people and should have been retained by a new (inevitably) military government at least to represent continuity.[23]

I was eager to get up to Pleiku, find out what Tuy thought about this mess, and learn whether there might be a project to which we could apply combined effort. We had shared an idea about replicating his company, but Bahnar-based and entirely mobile (supplied by air) rather than working from a camp. I thought that while a new government was thrashing around to reglue province and district levels for supporting recovery operations, the new mobile force that we had in mind could disconcert SVNLF units and their movement between Kontum and the Binh Dinh valleys.

Tuy, Jusiu, and I discussed the concept at Tuy's house. They were enthusiastic. We hoped that if we could develop the idea, descriptively persuasive, then we could obtain support for a pilot project, because there was a desperate need for anything that might be operationally valid. We agreed some of the people I had met earlier in Kontum could be helpful. We drove to Kontum the next day and spent a couple of days with the old VIS chief and Bahnar leaders in their communities. I retain memory of fermented beverage drawn from earthen jars, gongs ringing melodically, almost hypnotically, in the background, stomach pain, and headache. Returning to Pleiku, excited, I called down to Saigon from the II Corps advisory compound to keep Ev in the loop.

He didn't want to be in my loop. He had his own that he wanted to wrap around me.

Ev wanted me in Saigon right away for a "most important" new project. I resisted, telling him that I was about to work on something with Tuy, and while he had others in the south (Talbot Huey and Peter Hickman) for his new project, I had commitments. I had a hell of a nerve too. There was silence. Maybe the troposcatter phone system had disconnected. Then Ev asked, with unmistakable irritation, whether there was a problem with clarity on my end. I told him, "No, I can hear perfectly." "So," he said with deliberate firmness, "the problem must be on my line, because I can not have heard you refuse, you would not have even thought about refusing, my telling you to get down to my office ASAP, and I mean tomorrow!"

I went to see Tuy, chastised and chastened, and explained joining him for a return trip to Kontum would be impossible. My good friend was disappointed but understood the predicament. Touneh and I drove like a couple of devils down Route 19 to Qui Nhon, where we left the jeep. Khoi arranged for Touneh's transport to Dalat, and I caught a C-123 to Saigon.[24]

5

Long An Hamlet Survey

I was, some would say, temperamentally adolescent, predisposed to defy authority. So how did Everet Bumgardner bring me to heel? First of all, I owed him loyalty, not because of an organization chart or pecking order of rating officer to rated, but personal loyalty. He taught me, provided latitude, encouraged me by not applying limits to inquiry, and simply required that I continue learning and keep him informed. Second, in difficult situations Ev was totally committed to the mission. He would risk his life, but he was not careless of the lives of others. Ev did not mind disagreement when you could present reasoning different from his own. I liked that.[1]

Ev led in person, not from the rear. "In the field" did not mean an air-conditioned room in a province capital.[2] Unlike many Saigon supervisors, Ev spent several days at a time in the field himself. He relied on Ung Van Luong, his dedicated assistant, to coordinate and maintain all of the office procedures. (After 1975, Luong continued his oversight by working for years to help former USIS personnel come to the United States.) Ev set the example by being attentive to, and supportive of, Vietnamese and American field personnel. When you made a request, you got a response. Delay was not part of his character. He was committed to us, and consequently we were to him. He was a man of his word and expected the same of others. He would help with a problem, and he could keep a secret.[3]

Ev told me, when I presented myself not quite at attention, but contritely, before his desk, that Ambassador Lodge had expressed dismay about the reported collapse of government presence in the Mekong Delta. He was particularly concerned about Long An province, calling it the "gateway to Saigon." He wanted to know what had happened, what was happening, and how rural attitudes were changing. John Mecklin had told the ambassador that USIS could find out what he wanted to know, and then Mecklin turned to Ev for making what was promised come to pass.

Ev explained this would be the US mission's first opportunity to explore what was immediately happening in hamlets, rather than relying on reporting from officials with some vested interest in painting a pretty picture. Ev had already been to Long An, met Province Chief Maj. Le Minh Dao,[4] and discussed a survey of hamlet attitudes with Major Dao and American advisors. The province chief promised to make civic action personnel available, and Ev told him we would provide USIS field representatives as a catalyst. Ev described my experience in II Corps, and Major Dao agreed we could organize and conduct the survey operation as we thought best. "Now you know why I pulled you away from Pleiku. How do you want to organize this project?"

I looked at the map he laid out on a desk. It showed districts in Long An shaded according to population density. My preference would be to begin with hamlets in Thu Thua or Ben Luc districts, because they bordered on Hau Nghia province and were probably most susceptible to SVNLF activity. I thought out loud about organizing three small teams of civic action personnel, six to each team, and include a USIS Vietnamese field employee with each team. So we would need eighteen .38-caliber revolvers and ammunition, one for each of the civic action members, and a submachine gun for each of the USIS employees.[5] I unmistakably insisted that, above all else, I wanted Do Minh Nhat assigned to work with me.

Ev smiled and said he had supposed as much and had already called Nhat to Saigon from Xuan Loc. He expected Nhat to report later in the afternoon, and we could select three more USIS field representatives for the teams. I described a concept of operation to Ev based on my being constantly in the field with the teams, coming back to Saigon about every three days to provide reports. That way information would be fresh by increments rather than stale after all the hamlets were surveyed. Wanting to see my friend Nhat, but tired, I asked Ev to let him know I was glad we would work together again, and we would meet in the morning. Then I went to Mecklin's compound, and, in one of the outbuilding guest rooms (like a small motel room), showered, lay down to consider this new assignment, and so, about three weeks before Christmas 1963, fell asleep.

Early the next morning at a small table in Motel Mecklin I wrote down my basic principles for hamlet survey. I focused for clarity as to what we needed to accomplish, the procedural steps involved, and basic principles of conduct. And I wanted to keep it simple. I drew on what was absorbed from the Bumgardner tutorial, combined with observation and practice in central Viet Nam. I wrote, crossed out, and wrote again. Finally, I thought it was just about right. On the margins I wrote simple equivalent Vietnamese words or phrases that would emphasize the important points. Of course Nhat would be by my side to offer clarification, but I wanted to demonstrate personal commitment.[6]

We met in Ev's office, and three other Vietnamese field representatives joined us. I did not know them as well as I did Do Minh Nhat, but I accepted them wholeheartedly with the understanding that Ev and Nhat would select only men they trusted. We went over the draft principles and had extensive conversation in both languages about how to operate and cooperate. I placed particular emphasis on treating everyone the same, making sure that families accused of supporting the SVNLF were not approached with prejudice.[7] Everyone had rucksacks with personal gear, each of the three men selected by Ev had one of the submachine guns, and in a separate box were .38-caliber revolvers and ammunition.[8] I was sitting, reviewing the concept and operating principles we had just discussed, when John Mecklin came down to wish us luck. He looked concerned. We loaded into USIS vehicles, and then we were off to Tan An, capital of Long An.

Nhat and I checked our three USIS friends into a hotel, then looked for Province Chief Le Minh Dao. He was at his residence. The Tan An subsector intelligence and security officer, Captain Meo, was with him.[9] I explained what kind of reports we expected to provide for the embassy and how we would organize and operate, promising Dao a copy of each report submitted to Saigon. He had no reservation about our plan but suggested beginning in Binh Phuoc district along Route 4 and Provincial Road 22. He said although that area was just outside Tan An, security had recently deteriorated, especially close to the border with Dinh Tuong province. Although we had planned to work first in a different location, Nhat and I on the spot adapted to Dao's preference.

We left with Captain Meo for his office. He would be liaison for the duration of the hamlet survey program. He told us we would have a two o'clock meeting with the assigned civic action personnel. He also advised that, fortunately, so many were available we could make larger teams. "And tomorrow morning," he said, "I will go with you to village offices in Binh Phuoc district, make introductions, and arrange for security with some of my agents and Dan Ve."

In as friendly a manner as possible, but firmly, I told Captain Meo that we did not want larger teams or more teams than the three planned. But we would select volunteers from the larger group assembling in the afternoon. The most important point made was that when we went to the field, we would go directly to hamlets without connecting to village headquarters.[10] I wanted our teams to be different, disconnected from previous hamlet visitations. Captain Meo was surprised, perhaps even somewhat offended, but offered no argument.

In the afternoon we did have an organizational meeting with well more than thirty civic action workers at a government hall in Tan An. Captain Meo introduced us and then considerately (or maybe in some frustration) departed. Nhat called our meeting to order so that we could welcome everyone. I explained the importance of the hamlet survey project and went over the principles of operation. My description and response to a few questions took about an hour. Some expressed surprise that we planned to stay in hamlets overnight and that we would provide our own security. Nhat provided elaboration that was essential to establishing understanding and, I hoped, consensus.

I had thought to move immediately from the organization meeting to the hamlets and was pondering how to reduce our number from the crowd in the hall to the desired level when some of the civic action attendees expressed reservations about beginning that day. According to the lunar almanac (available in every market), this was not an auspicious day for beginning a new venture. There's no point debating the inevitable. We agreed to begin the next morning.[11] I needed to meet with the American advisory team, and Nhat would remain to answer any other questions they might have. Tugging Nhat to the side, I urged him to find a way to pare down to the eighteen that we planned for. I suggested he leave the impression we would begin in Ben Luc, and then at the last minute we could make a change of direction to Binh Phuoc.

Province advisory teams in December 1963 were small and not as unified as they would eventually be organized by MACVCORDS in mid-1967. I met with five or six MAAG officers and Earl Young, the USOM representative. I reviewed what Ev described as lack of reliable information about deteriorating government presence and our planned solution: the detailed survey (physical and attitudinal) of hamlets. They exhibited curiosity and interest, particularly concerning what qualified me for the project. My response was that I had some experience living in the countryside, could speak basic Vietnamese, and feared only failure. The embassy was cited as initiator of the project and principal recipient of reports. I told them that Province Chief Le Minh Dao would get a copy of everything submitted to the embassy. I promised the team a summary report after completing each three-hamlet set, probably about every three days, and the summary would include a copy of each hamlet sketch map.

Ev had previously described Earl Young as earnest, able, and one who would probably ask to be in the hamlets with us. Ev's strongly expressed opinion, and not because of USIS prerogatives, was that I should politely decline. When Earl did ask to accompany, I was respectful of his interest but explained that one American was the limit. My additional, personal (unspoken) reason was that he did not speak Vietnamese. If we had difficulty, especially at night, I didn't want to be responsible for a person who couldn't communicate with anyone but me.

I made a quick return to Saigon and met with Ev for about an hour, describing the day and postponement due to the almanac rule. I told him USOM representative participation was politely declined. Ev agreed, stressing the necessity to keep it simple. "This is something new that we couldn't have been imagined. Don't complicate the essence of what you're supposed to do. This hamlet survey is not a framework for allocating resources and reforming rural development. That might evolve, but right now I just want you to find out what the hell happened in those Long An hamlets." It was dark when I arrived back in Tan An and crashed in a hotel room where Nhat and the other three USIS cadre were already resting.

The next morning, on return to the provincial hall, I was pleasantly surprised to find fewer than half the people who were present the previous afternoon. Curious, I asked Nhat how he managed to reduce the number to what was needed. He told me that after I departed there was a lot of discussion. "Some wanted to know what you meant by immediate punishment if people's belongings were touched or women teased. I told them you're from Quang Ngai, strict, and could even kill someone."

I was amazed. I told my good friend that surely everyone knew I'm not even Vietnamese, and it was too much to threaten anyone. I could only have brought an offender straight to the province chief for punishment. He replied that they only knew I came down from central Viet Nam, and although tall for a Vietnamese, was dark, thin, and spoke with a strange accent. Some guessed I might be part Vietnamese, and Quang Ngai sounded reasonable.[12] "Besides," he continued, smiling, "people who wouldn't steal or bother women had nothing to fear. Now we're at the right number, and rid of troublemakers." I looked around at those who had reported that morning, despite maybe thinking the worst of me, and then went from one to another, shaking the hand of each man and thanking him for coming.

During the remainder of December we would take about three days to survey the ground and popular attitude in each of three adjoining hamlets. By day we worked simultaneously in the three, and then at night we grouped together in one. Depending on the size of each hamlet, we took about three days for a cluster of three, and that would include the time required for a meeting in Tan An to check sketch maps and prepare a summary report on each hamlet. Before we moved to the next set of three, the province civic action personnel were allowed a day for a family visit. At the same time, I would return to Saigon with Nhat and our other three USIS employees. While they had family time, I reviewed sketch maps, reports, and my own observations with Ev. By the next day he would have the reports translated, edited, and ready with maps for submission to the embassy. I carried copies back to Tan An to share with the province chief and advisory team.

The fifteen hamlets in the first phase were only a few kilometers from the province capital, and yet, with only one exception, they lacked government presence. Deterioration meant primary schools were closed and medical stations destroyed or vacant. The SVNLF was a daring presence by day and often right in the hamlets at night. They were not many, but relative to the vacuum in which they operated, even a motivated few could achieve control over the population's behavior.

The one exception was Ap Nguyen Huynh Duc,[13] a hamlet located in Khanh Hau village. Rural sociologist Gerald Hickey studied the community. He found there was a significant degree of social cohesion and community identity because of an active cult committee that cared for the tomb and associated temple of Nguyen Huynh Duc.[14] There was much less SVNLF activity there, and not because of proximity to Highway 4. Adjacent Ap Moi and Ap Thu Tuu were also close to the highway, but with important differences. Ap Moi had the Dinh Tuong boundary hard by its southwest, and the farthest point from the highway for Ap Thu Tuu touched a narrow stream across from Ap An Binh, the most insecure hamlet in the An Vinh Ngai area. Geography counted, but we thought the energetic cult committee in Ap Nguyen Huynh Duc was the decisive factor. In other hamlets government-appointed leaders, schoolteachers, and others had all departed. The cult committee in Ap Nguyen Huynh Duc, continuously in place, provided the community with an ongoing indigenous non-SVNLF presence, and, since it was popular and also nongovernmental, the communists left it alone.

More typically, absence of government activity allowed communist propaganda teams, local guerrillas, and other cadre to enter hamlets and circulate freely among them. In the three hamlets along Provincial Road 22 to Dinh Tuong province, strategic hamlet fencing was removed completely, including the portion right along the road.[15] In these hamlets there were SVNLF propaganda posters right at the entrance and on the walls of abandoned schools. Homes of people who earlier had moved from distant fields were torn down so that those familes would return to their previous location. Just past Vinh Hoa hamlet was a Dan Ve outpost, the last one on Route 22 before crossing the province border. The militia told me they did not dare leave the outpost at night and had requested relocation to Tan An. People told us much deterioration had taken place since the overthrow of the Diem government, but that erosion really began even earlier in the summer. In fact, some families were still not aware the Ngo Dinh Diem government had been replaced.

Almost every family provided information. We explained that we were going to speak with every household, so people understood that by our conversing with every family it would be impossible for the SVNLF to single out those who were most helpful. Our survey team cadre spent significant conversational time with families that were not so cooperative, providing candy for children and cigarettes to older men, so that the SVNLF might even wonder whether their own special friends were receptive to our presence.[16]

There were comments about the government's lack of performance and requests for assistance (Ap Binh Tay wanting a bridge over a small stream), for reopening schools, to all of which we made no promise except to bring them to the attention of the province government. And there were frequent complaints about government misbehavior (theft, abusive language, accosting women) when hamlets were visited for tax collection or inspection. When we asked what might attract people away from the SVNLF, the answer was always some variation on fairness and social justice. People in these Long An hamlets believed those who followed the SVNLF had legitimate grievances.

One night there were a few shots fired into a hamlet where one of our teams had operated during the day. However that team was now joined with the other two, according to our nighttime security plan, in a different hamlet. On another night a few probing shots were fired into the hamlet where we regrouped, but our discipline included not returning fire if an enemy could not be seen. Otherwise innocent families in the supposed direction of incoming fire might be hit by inaccurate response. Predictable guerrilla effort to draw fire, discover our position, and possibly incite civil grievance failed. It was frustrating for the local SVNLF to know we were moving around their backyard, but not know exactly where.

The leader of the guerrilla unit in An Vinh Ngai was a young woman named Kim Loan, whose husband had been arrested and killed by the government. She took up arms in 1961 and acquired a local reputation as a heroine. We were told of her shopping in Tan An and killing a policeman who tried to arrest her. On another occasion she had to flee out the back door of a beauty parlor, and when soldiers searched for her the next day in Vinh An hamlet, she climbed a tree, changed into a bird, and flew away. When I asked the elderly gentleman who gave this account whether people really believed that happened, he smiled and replied he didn't know, "but, she got away, didn't she?"

Kim Loan was originally from Vinh Hoa hamlet, and a sister still lived there. The sister showed me a photograph of Kim Loan and her deceased husband. It was taken in a Tan An studio. They were smiling. I told the sister that I would like to speak with Kim Loan and left a note suggesting we meet in Vinh Hoa on Provincial Road 22. We could both bring a friend as guarantor (*nguoi dam bao*). Two days later there was a verbal reply delivered through her sister. Kim Loan proposed we meet at the far end of the hamlet and bring all our friends. There was obviously lack of trust on both our parts, and we never got together.[17]

Our teams were left alone to carry out the Long An Hamlet Survey. The only surprise visitors were Gen. Richard Stilwell and Col. Wilbur Wilson. They asked to meet at the MAAG house in Tan An. I provided an explanation of what we were doing and how we operated. My appearance was, just out of the hamlets, ragged and unshaven, and my description of movement and conversation in the hamlets seemed at variance with what General Stilwell expected. I could tell that he was uncomfortable having a civilian working with pickup teams of Vietnamese to document poor government performance. I finished. He leaned forward and said, "I don't know, I think we could have pushed the GVN to get in here, find out what we need to know, and share it with us. What do you think, Wilbur?" Colonel Wilson won my friendship forever by replying, "No, I think the kid's right and you're wrong." General Stilwell shrugged, stood, shook my hand, and said, "Well, that's it then."[18]

Once Ev came down from Saigon to join Nhat, the other three USIS cadre, and me for lunch in a restaurant by the river in Tan An. It was a beautiful day. Ev asked whether I wouldn't now agree that delta provinces were the finest part of Viet Nam.[19] He wanted me to consider staying on in Saigon for field assignments in southern provinces. I replied that although I would do my best in any role he assigned, my strong preference would be to return to central Viet Nam. I explained having the desire to work up something with Tuy and Kelly that would build on shared experience.

While we were in Long An, Ev brought Doug Ramsey south for another project. Doug was interviewing high school students about their perception of the conflict and Americans in Viet Nam. Ev said the findings were bleak. It had been anticipated that urban and semiurban students, middle-class, would accept a post-Diem government and an American presence. Doug discovered that expectation was invalid.

On the next coordinating visit to Saigon, and with only three of the originally planned fifteen hamlets remaining to be surveyed, Ev informed me the embassy wanted to continue the project. He promised not to hold me but asked for recommendations. I replied that Do Minh Nhat could run the entire survey operation in the field, and the quality of effort and reporting would be excellent. An American officer could support Nhat by liaison with province officials, the advisory team, and USIS Saigon.[20] So when the final three hamlets were completed, I returned to Dalat and points north. I felt good about our pioneer operation and relieved that there was no loss of life. I never saw a summary report on the first fifteen hamlets. There may be one in retired USIA files. I was told Earl Young wrote a report, but I have not seen it.[21]

When I complete a project, or a period having particular focus, I ask myself what was learned or validated. The ability of small units to operate in the same environment with SVNLF guerrillas was proven in Long An, as it had been on the west bank of the An Lao River several months earlier. Motivation is an important component of success, and people need to believe they are part of something greater than themselves. Personal leadership is basic to obtaining trust of the people for whom you have responsibility. Setting a positive example is necessary for high-quality performance.

The only way for a South Viet Nam government to obtain recognition of independence, and the reluctant, truculent acquiescence of North Viet Nam, was to demonstrate it could govern effectively and defend its territory. Proving effective governance and defense of territory had to begin in the countryside. The way to win in the countryside was to displace the SVNLF in hamlets by inserting our own teams into rural communities so that communist guerrillas would be the outsiders, outlaws, and forced either to fight themselves back in or to return noncombatively to their families.

Now I had new appreciation of the overall difficulty. The Long An project revealed complete collapse of government presence in the hamlets. In the old Inter-Zone V provinces we could attribute absence of rural administration to residual Viet Minh presence consequent to communist governance during the war against France. However, that had not been the situation in Long An. The government began with advantages and squandered opportunity by failing to implement real land reform and ignoring the need for administrative reform at the district and hamlet levels while dissipating energy by conducting a witch hunt for families and individuals who had opposed colonial rule.

I was beginning to feel there were three different American perspectives on the conflict in Viet Nam. Civil and military advisors in the field coped with a reality, mostly problematic, at variance with what had been described to them. Saigon offices urged the field to resolve problems as Saigon defined and understood them, while the embassy and agencies massaged our relationship with the Vietnamese government of the day.

We installed and collaborated with a family dictatorship and later embraced a cabal of generals who were previously French sergeants. Finally, the Washington perspective seemed, even then (to me), clouded with doubt, second guessing, scarcely any knowledge of the Vietnamese we supported, and no understanding at all of the national communist party. Almost every American falsely thought of the communists as an intrusion by North Viet Nam into South Viet Nam. Failure to recognize that the party was national in character and generally central Vietnamese in leadership, with grim commitment to unification, was (looking back) inexcusable. I was thinking, at the beginning of January 1964, that if our policy was to consolidate and preserve an independent South Viet Nam, that mountain was a lot higher and steeper than it had seemed in 1962.

6
Quang Ngai People's Commandos

I first had to return to Pleiku for a meeting with Tuy and Jusiu to follow up on our discussions about replicating the 4th Company. Before getting pulled down to Long An, we were at the point of beginning recruitment for a Bahnar-based unit anticipated to operate entirely mobile between Kontum and western Binh Dinh.

We needed to meet because my perception of the most fundamental problem had altered since we were last together. The An Lao operation and other experience had persuaded us the most important task was to address the vacuum area between the border and the densely populated zone where most people lived. But three weeks in Long An hamlets convinced me we had been wrong. Our priority ought to be creating teams to compete with the SVNLF in and around hamlets.

John Melton arrived in Dalat with his family. He would be the actual BPAO for the city, and that relieved me of administrative responsibility for the post. John made one trip to Lam Dong with me, and from then on he could visit that province from Dalat. John and his family took the large house on Tran Hung Dao Street, and I moved to the adjacent two-room cottage until deciding where to most usefully base myself. Extended time away from Dalat would be personally difficult because of a developing relationship with a young woman, Nguyen thi Kim Vui, and her family.

My jeep was still in Qui Nhon. I flew Air Viet Nam to Nha Trang and then caught the C-123 milk run to Qui Nhon.[1] I spent a few days driving around Tuy Phuoc, An Nhon, Phu Cat, Phu My, and Bong Son to speak with district officials and anyone else I encountered along the way. My impression in early 1964 was that province and district government was a shambles. The Diem administration had placed competent but misdirected personnel in many provinces. The new government of generals assigned less competent people with no comprehensive direction or supervision.

Driving alone to Pleiku, I had the uncomfortable feeling of being observed. A flat tire before Mang Yang Pass caused me to set a personal record for jacking my jeep and changing a tire. Jusiu was in Cheo Reo looking for Nay Luett,[2] so I met with Tuy at his house. I described the Long An Hamlet Survey and gave him a copy of our concept outline. Most important, I spoke with him about how the Long An experience changed my thinking as to what our field operations priority ought to be. What was experienced in Long An, reinforced by observing recent deterioration in Binh Dinh, persuaded me that impeding access of the SVNLF to hamlets should take precedence over all else. Rather than sending a note, I came to Pleiku because he was my advisor, my teacher, as well as my friend, and I owed him a personal explanation. Tuy understood the change of perspective. We had shared the germ of an idea, to promote mobility, rather than camps, in the highlands. The concept was valid, but we would not have a chance to test it.[3]

I was convinced that the sorest need was a competitive presence in the hamlets to force SVNLF guerrillas out. An opportunity for experiment appeared during travel in Quang Ngai a few weeks later. Bob Kelly was now the USOM province representative and shared a house at 179 Phan Boi Chau Street with Bob Day, an IVS volunteer.[4] They made outbuilding rooms available for Touneh Ton and me to use when we were in Quang Ngai. Kelly updated me on what had happened in the province during recent months. There was widespread paralysis accelerated by personnel turnover in all districts and provincial departments. Kelly said the departure of Province Chief Nguyen Van Tat had resulted in a vacuum at the top.

I described the operation of the Long An Hamlet Survey teams and told Kelly I was convinced the immediate need was for an armed, politically motivated force, mobile and unpredictable, in each district to circulate through the hamlets, disrupting the sense of comfort felt by the SVNLF. These new units would complicate recent communist easy access to hamlets. I agreed with Kelly that what was described could be called paramilitary, but I was thinking more parapolitical in that the objective was to develop a politically sensitive force that would root itself into the population.

Kelly said my arrival was timely because a man in Tu Nghia district had recently approached the district police chief and suggested formation of a special mobile unit to cope with the increasingly aggressive SVNLF. The police chief asked Kelly whether USOM assistance could be available. Kelly checked with the deputy province chief for administration, Tran Van Phien (held over by the new military regime), and he approved trying something new. Phien told Kelly to coordinate with the Tu Nghia district chief as well as the police chief, who Kelly thought was most interested in how many piastres would be involved.

With that background I thought our first step should be to speak with the person who initiated this overture. Kelly had his name and location, so the very next day we, with Touneh, mounted our jeep and went to find him. Nguyen Duy Be was at home in a small hamlet a few kilometers south of Quang Ngai city. He was diminutive by physical appearance but had a bright, eager personality and an impressive history.

Like many who lived in Inter-Zone V during the war for independence, Nguyen Duy Be was taken into the Viet Minh. He was trained for leadership in a course conducted at the Quang Ngai training center and then commanded an independent company. He chafed at increased Communist Party control and later deserted in southern Laos, but he was captured and sentenced to hard labor. In 1951 he was released but kept under surveillance until the cease-fire. During the Diem administration he had been a volunteer with Vo Trang Nhan Dan and later with local Dan Ve.[5]

I observed Nguyen Duy Be while we spoke about the need for generating noncommunist political activity in and around hamlets. I began to feel he was a less polished, but as committed, version of my friend Capt. Nguyen Tuy. Sitting in his front yard, Kelly and I listened as Be talked about how a small unit could disrupt communist activities by insinuating itself into hamlets within an operational area. He said every member should be more than a soldier—should be a cadre with exemplary behavior all the time. He believed popular attitudes could be improved by striving to identify with the people rather than forcing people to identify with the government. Helping people with simple tasks in daily life means more than slogans.

We were impressed by his presentation of ideas that emerged from personal experience and that were much in accord with our own views. Be knew Viet Nam was in a difficult period and that the going would get tougher. But he decided not to sit on the sidelines. He wrote in his autobiography that he chose to affiliate with a new special unit because he would rather have an honorable death than a despicable survival. [6]

We returned to Quang Ngai city and spoke with Tran Van Phien about training and operating a new and different kind of unit. We agreed each trainee would be enlisted as Dan Ve, but in a completely mobile unit. Members would have an additional operational allowance, not as compensation for greater risk but so food could be purchased from people in the hamlets. There should be special equipment issue, including (given the developing situation in Quang Ngai) weapons with greater firepower than usually available for Dan Ve. During the short period of intensive training, food and health care would be provided.[7] We talked about a name for the first platoon-sized unit, and Phien suggested Biet Kich Nhan Dan, which I translated for Kelly as "People's Commandos."

I was more than just politely appreciative of the deputy province chief's support and understanding of what would be attempted. If the first unit were successful, expansion would depend on local Vietnamese management for meaningful continuation. Back at Kelly's house we agreed that at the beginning USOM funds would cover training costs (food) and the operational allowance. We knew if a request were put to MAAG for three or four dozen weapons, we would be told issue was impossible for unauthorized programs: "Cease and desist!" Kelly planned to rely on Joe Vaccaro and his contacts for arming the first unit.[8] I told Kelly that we needed to keep Ev informed.

Ev was not personally familiar with the An Lao operation of a year earlier, so I described what we intended as an extension of what was recently practiced in Long An. He understood how Nhat and I shaped and ran the hamlet survey teams, and he endorsed that demonstration of small-unit ability to work in contested rural areas. So Ev had context for agreeing to our proposal, and he was ready to support us.[9] He suggested rather than our going to Saigon, he could fly to Nha Trang, where we would meet him. Kelly was itching to make the drive down the coast anyway, and this was a convenient opportunity for riding shotgun. We fixed a meeting in Nha Trang for three days later and prepared to depart for Qui Nhon.

During the drive, I realized we would have to ask for two or three more field representatives for motivational instruction. I knew we could count on Tran Xuan Khoi from Binh Dinh and Nguyen Ho from Quang

Ngai, but I wanted to ask Ev for Le Quang Tuyen. Despite his having reported our (my) activity to Binh Dinh province police in 1963, Tuyen, I knew, was one of the most intelligent young men in USIS. Additionally, Ev would also expect something on paper describing how we planned to train the first Biet Kich Nhan Dan unit and what we proposed for operational procedure. So that night in Qui Nhon, in the office of my old house, I drafted a training outline and operations guide.[10]

Kelly and I had already tossed around ideas, debated them, sometimes with Tran Van Phien and Bob Day participating, and thereby shaped ideas about how a new and different kind of unit should train and operate. We were influenced by our own experience during the previous two years, some understanding of Mao Zedong's practice, and secondhand understanding of Viet Minh training.[11] Our goal was to equal the SVNLF in motivation and unit loyalty. The new force we had in mind would operate by constantly moving in and around insecure hamlets in a district. We described to ourselves (as practice for description to Ev, instructors, and eventually trainees) a well-armed platoon that would operate from inside hamlets outward, rather than from outside hamlets inward. We envisioned them as being alert at night, shifting location, always prepared. During the day they should rest, take turns for sleep, but always be conversationally friendly with everyone in the hamlet. They would be motivated to help hamlet residents with simple tasks by bare hand, sharing labor, for immediate impact, with nothing promised for later. We believed that a unit like this could win respect, trust, and eventually (from some in the hamlet) cooperation in the form of actionable information. We were sure mobile presence of this kind, in an area that previously offered easy access, would be so disruptive that the SVNLF would have to respond. Well armed, established among the people, prepared to resist, our unit would be capable of protecting itself and an attacked hamlet. SVNLF guerrillas would be gradually displaced to a less densely populated area where the regular army could challenge them.

What else would make this unit superior to others? We expected that question from Ev. Our answer was that the most important difference would be that they were local people armed, trained, and empowered to defend their own hamlets in active rather than passive (outpost) mode. Special training, with encouragement and support by Deputy Province Chief for Administration Tran Van Phien, would provide enhanced unit motivation. Why wouldn't we advise these volunteers to enlist in existing government forces? We saw the general failure of army organization and affiliated district and province militia in Quang Ngai. Local initiative should not be stifled by embrace of existing organizations already defeated in spirit.

We drove south through Phu Yen province, stopping briefly in Song Cau and Tuy Hoa. The VIS chief, whom I had met and spoken with a few times in the past, was extremely pessimistic, claiming that since withdrawal of the 9th Division, security in Phu Yen had spiraled downward. He told us that making the drive to Cung Son, a trip I had taken a year earlier with Bob Burns and his assistant, Lam Tuan Lam, would now be impossible. We were sure to be killed or captured, was the way he put the odds. Kelly was ready to take that challenge, but I convinced him we had been provided good-faith counsel, and besides, we had an appointment the next day in Nha Trang.

Ev looked over our draft outline and listened carefully to our description of how the new unit would operate. He agreed, and advised us to move quickly. Otherwise, he said, organizational and jurisdictional rivalries would coalesce on one point of agreement: an unauthorized parapolitical venture should be quashed, along with the persons involved. He urged Kelly to be careful about sharing information. Ev promised three USIS Vietnamese field representatives to work with us during training. These would be Le Quang Tuyen (whom I requested), Uyen, and Xang. Khoi from Binh Dinh and Nguyen Ho from Quang Ngai would also assist. We had a lead (through Vaccaro) on weapons for the unit, but we told Ev we needed pistols or revolvers for the instructors. He replied that .45-caliber pistols would be available. Ev committed to assuring cover by describing our venture as psychological warfare training, in the event that anyone asked.

Before parting, Ev, rather sternly, warned us, "Look, don't think I just gave license to start cranking out commandos like sausages. Do the first one, test it, let's see the results, and then consider a second, a third, and how to proceed from there, step by step with me informed."[12] We saw the logic of caution. I would return to Saigon and follow through with the Vaccaro connection for submachine guns. Ev explained he also wanted me to speak with the USIS cadre who would be assigned to the Quang Ngai project. Kelly would take Air Viet Nam back to Quang Ngai and make sure arrangements stayed on track. Ev suggested that if other units were organized in the future, Kelly could contact Ralph Johnson in Danang for assistance in covering training expenses and weapons. "But, let's wait and see some results first."

I saw Ev and Kelly off at the airfield and drove to Dalat with Touneh, who had accompanied Kelly and me on the drive from Quang Ngai to Nha Trang. A couple of rounds were fired at us when we transited the desolate area just before beginning the abrupt climb to Da Nhim. A neat hole with a concentric web pattern in the windshield was evidence that now no road was safe. We thought two rounds were notification of trespass. I was glad Touneh was by my side. And from that day on I always drove with a companion rather than alone.

A couple of days later, in Saigon, our contact agreed to arrange delivery of crates containing M3 submachine guns ("grease guns") to Quang Ngai airfield on a date in mid-April.[13] There was time for me to see Vietnamese friends in the city. They clearly lacked enthusiasm for the second military government.[14] Saigon friends could not understand why I stayed away from Saigon. They questioned me at length about my travel in the countryside and what I experienced, but they had no desire to see for themselves. I explained it was impossible to understand Viet Nam without examining the basic level where most people lived, and the hamlet was that base. Among these well-educated, mostly young Saigonese there were significant differences of opinion, but they all agreed I was *ky qua*, "strange," "eccentric."[15]

Ev asked me to take a look at Long An. I visited Captain Meo in his office and inquired whether any improvements, positive results, were obtained following the December hamlet surveys. His answer was that, of course, the district and province levels were now well informed about popular feeling, and they responded to hamlet concerns. Since I already knew from the second-phase report that the principal consequence was officials criticizing people who spoke candidly, my initial impression of Captain Meo was confirmed. He was a smart, tough operator who was more concerned with the well-being of the influential than of poor farmers.

Touneh and I drove down Provincial Road 22 through the An Vinh Ngai area to the lonely outpost at Vinh Hoa hamlet. We found it destroyed. A few rangers were holding the position until a decision came down to abandon or rebuild. They told us the outpost was overrun about three weeks earlier. They did not know what had happened to the Dan Ve. They added that they did not enter the nearby hamlet, and no one came to talk with them.

On the way back to Tan An, we pulled into Vinh An hamlet, where in December our survey team befriended three elders, brothers, who might have been in their sixties. One of them was the storyteller who had described Kim Loan's escaping arrest by changing to a bird and flying away. The brothers were excited to see me again, an entertaining diversion for them. We all had small glasses of *ba xi de*.[16] They assumed Touneh was another American. We assured them he was a citizen of Viet Nam, but from a tribe living near Dalat. They asked a lot of questions about Dalat, his education, how long he had worked with me, and his marriage, children, and monthly salary. They were impressed, amazed, really, by his speaking fluent Vietnamese. Right there, with that one family, Touneh fractured a Vietnamese cultural prejudice. The brothers told us that after the hamlet survey team had left, maybe three weeks later—less than a month, anyway—district and village officials had paid a visit with soldiers escorting. Some families were accused of supporting the communists by criticizing the government. Of course, one said, we were all going to be in trouble anyway because everyone knows liberation gentlemen (*may ong giai phong*) do visit from time to time. "And some of them, especially Chi (Sister) Kim Loan, would like to meet you, too."[17]

I met Le Quang Tuyen and Uyen in Ev's office. We discussed their travel to Quang Ngai in early April. I explained that the work would be instructing in a special training course, with concentration on motivation. Our training program would be different from instruction previously experienced. We planned to organize the training in hamlets, on the move, with discussion and questions enlivening each session. They expressed some concern. If we trained while operational, unit members and instructors would tire. There would be difficulty scheduling sleep and arranging for local food purchase. Soldiers were used to training in a camp or center. I insisted that, although of course there would be difficulties, since our opponents could solve them, then we could too. Promising that I would be right there with them, sharing the same conditions, they agreed to try. Tuyen and I sought opportunity to speak privately. I told him it was understood his first loyalty was to country, and that was the context for his reporting my activity to the security service in Qui Nhon a year earlier. It was past.

Ev had a long talk with me about the early 1964 changing situation. He was not feeling positive about the shift from Military Government 1 (Minh-Don-Kim) to Military Government 2 (Khanh), and he expressed late regret for the absence of constitutional process the previous November. "It is as you said: now anyone with more than one tank will think they can grab the brass ring." I asked him, since we had liaison with the coup plotters last fall, couldn't we have helped Minh and his group form an effective government by the end of the year? Ev shook his head: "I don't know Rufus Phillips very well, but he might have had a chance. Didn't happen. The ambassador had pretty tight control over who talked to the generals, and then Phillips left in December. We never had a handle on what you called a shaky situation. The new government should have shown initiative in December, but now if anyone is positioned to exploit new opportunities, it's the Front."

This was the first time I saw a disheartened Ev Bumgardner. I asked about his impression of Nguyen Khanh. He replied, "I understand he has been a capable combat officer. His intent may be honorable. But I don't know anything that argues for him being more capable than others to form an effective government."

Touneh and I drove back to Dalat by a different route. We took Highway 1 past Xuan Loc through mixed plantation and forest to arrive at Phan Thiet on the coast. We stayed a night in that town of nuoc mam fame, then drove north to Phan Rang. This area was the last stand for sixteenth-century Champa; there were still some Cham living there, but their presence was a faint residue of past glory. We stayed another night in Phan Rang. Talking with VIS and American advisors gave me the impression that deterioration there was not as severe as in Binh Dinh, Quang Ngai, and Long An. My supposition was that even the SVNLF had to prioritize. They would apply greater effort in more important provinces, especially where they may already have local advantage.

Briefly in Dalat, we sorted out what would be needed for an extended stay in Quang Ngai. Driving would require about three days, the first day to Nha Trang. We always stayed at the Giang Hotel. It was clean, each room had its own cold-water shower, and the price, for being half a block from the beach, was reasonable. I sought out a friend, Charles Fisher, who frequently road-traveled in II Corps. He was a technician with the American company that did maintenance on the troposcatter communications system.[18] I asked him how Route 1 looked to him in the previous couple of weeks. He said there was no problem as far as Tuy Hoa, but in Tuy An district he had heard sporadic gunfire in the distance. Even though the road was open, and he didn't see anything specific, he had an insecure feeling about that place.

The next day nothing unusual transpired while we drove through Ninh Hoa and on up to Tuy Hoa. We paused there and spoke with the deputy province chief, who candidly told us that he thought government rural presence had peaked in June 1963, even with Buddhist unrest, because strategic hamlets were carefully planned and gradually implemented in Phu Yen. Success, compared to Binh Dinh, he said, was partly because Phu Yen was more manageable by total number of hamlets. He thought Binh Dinh might have twice as many, maybe even three times. When I asked about Major Dong, the former province chief accused of corruption, the deputy replied that Dong had squeezed money but had achieved good results despite not being perfect.[19] When asked what accounted for the change since last summer, he replied that the Buddhist/government crisis, followed by withdrawal of the 9th Division and then the November coup, all combined for paralysis.

In Qui Nhon I went around to visit the same Buddhist and Catholic friends who were candid discussants the previous summer. I was relieved to hear that there was no expression of recrimination. However, Nguyen Van Phuoc, Cao Dan, Hong Nam (an observant pharmacist), and my seminarian acquaintances all described the situation as "unsettled and dangerous." No one had suggestions for stability. A common refrain was lament for departure of the 9th Division.[20]

Immediately on arrival in Quang Ngai, sitting down with Kelly, I learned he had already spoken with Ralph Johnson's assistant, Guy Boileau, and obtained agreement for long-term support for our project. That made me uneasy, because we had not even fielded the first commando unit. Moreover, Ralph soon arrived and told us there was a snag to Boileau's commitment for delivery of weapons, because approval of the corps commander was necessary before introducing them into a province. Ralph said he would straighten the problem out, but this marked the beginning of some friction between Ralph and Bob Kelly. My good friend thought

Ralph an Abercrombie & Fitch dilettante compared to real field operators. Ralph felt previous experience in China and Laos qualified him to provide guidance. Kelly wasn't having any of that. Finally, we all agreed that waiting until a month or so after the first unit was operating before tweaking the concept Kelly and I had developed made more sense than arguing. But from then on it seemed as though I presided over group therapy whenever we were all together, and I wasn't the best person for that.[21]

Additional volunteers for Nguyen Duy Be's unit in training raised the total to thirty-nine. We began special training in mid-April 1964 by asking each participant to write a short autobiography, paying special attention to three questions: Why do you fight communists? What is the best way to defeat communists? Why did you volunteer for this special unit? The intent was to have trainees thinking about political purpose and their individual role right from the first day.[22] Another benefit was that instructors could study the biographical material to understand the volunteers' background.

During two weeks of guided instruction my impression was one of rising combat spirit and identification with the mass of people living in Tu Nghia hamlets. I was wary of overestimating the effect because, first of all, Nguyen Duy Be's leadership was crucial and unique, and second, every special unit based on volunteers begins with predisposition for good morale. During training the unit was called forth to engage a communist element that had entered a nearby hamlet. Two guerrillas were killed and one captured.

I departed for Quang Tin and other provinces farther north. USIS had responsibility for advising every province to establish a psychological operations center to coordinate VIS and ARVN information programs. My personal quest was to meet Nguyen Chanh Thi, who had returned to Viet Nam and active duty from exile in Cambodia a few months earlier. Knowing he was a leader in the 1960 paratrooper coup attempt, I wanted to learn what he thought about developments since President Diem's death. Before leaving I reminded Kelly (as Ev had cautioned us) to just monitor the Tu Nghia unit for a few weeks before making additional commitments. "And no arguments with Ralph!"

Touneh and I stopped in Tam Ky, capital of Quang Tin province.[23] We stayed the night in a small *phong ngu* just behind the town's bus station. The next morning we met VIS staff at their office. I was surprised to learn they had already worked with province headquarters, an ARVN Regiment (6th of the 2nd Division), and sector advisors to establish a psyop center. Later, when speaking with American advisors, they expressed enthusiasm for the concept. The Americans were insistent that direct information work should focus on hamlets in the lowland districts. The interior districts of Hau Duc, Tien Phuoc, and Hiep Duc were too insecure from late 1963 onward.

North of Tam Ky, on the left as one drives toward Danang, are Cham towers that might be of the eleventh or twelfth century. Touneh and I stopped to stretch our legs and take a look. Walking toward the site, we found an animal sculpture in a field. It was almost entirely covered by dirt. We approached two farmers working nearby. Although they were friendly, it was obvious they didn't want extended conversation. Usual curiosity was lacking. They advised us not to stay.

At Dien Ban, just over the Thu Bon River, we drove east toward the coast and river town of Hoi An. Now capital of Quang Nam province, centuries earlier this was a significant trading center.[24] The VIS office there was focused on information activity in town rather than throughout the province. There wasn't any planning for a psychological operations center. An American advisor described security as good along Highway 1 but a "light dimming" in the western hills.

I was politely provided a short meeting with the 2nd Division commander, Ngo Dzu. He was rotund, jovial by initial appearance, but after speaking awhile it seemed he was a little depressed. When I asked about security in Quang Tin, he spoke about communist pressure, erosion, deterioration, and government presence "melting." I asked him about 2nd Division deployment, and he responded that the division would hold its positions. He was responsive to queries but emitted, by his speech, the vague impression that the division lacked aggressive leadership. When I inquired about his family, I was surprised to learn he was from Qui Nhon. We talked about Binh Dinh, and he spoke of the people from his home province as being very tough, but it was as though they were somehow different from him. When I politely excused myself, he asked where I would go. Replying that I would see Nguyen Chanh Thi in Hue, Ngo Dzu rather apprehensively said, "Thi is very fierce."[25]

I found Nguyen Chanh Thi at 1st Division headquarters, and on first glance he certainly did have a sort of "lean and mean" appearance. But that was relieved by a frequent infectious smile. Trying, as always, to speak Vietnamese, I seemed to amuse him. He wondered at my strange accent. I told him that, aside from the expected American accent, my first teacher for one month in Washington was from Sadec, and then I lived in Binh Dinh and probably picked up something there. He laughed at the explanation and suggested that, since he had a strong Hue accent, we should just use a mix of whatever would work.[26]

Thi explained that he was born in a district southeast of Hue and during World War II had joined the constabulary for a salary to support his mother and brothers. He thought the experience would also prepare a young man for whatever would come after the war. He was serving in Binh Dinh while the French administration collapsed when Japan seized complete control. He began to make his way back to Hue when he was arrested by the Viet Minh and placed in prison at Ba To. Thi described terrible conditions during detention, with many dying due to lack of food or illness. He escaped after two years. Returning to Hue, Thi learned that his mother had been killed more than a year earlier during a Viet Minh campaign to collect jewelry to support the struggle for independence. For that, he told me, he could never forgive the communists.

We spoke about changes since November. Thi began by saying he was glad to be able to return, but deeply regretted the death, the killing, of Ngo Dinh Diem. He insisted that when leading paratroopers against the Palace in 1960, the purpose was reform, and he would never have killed President Diem. Thi recalled that in 1955 he commanded the 5th Airborne Battalion in support of Ngo Dinh Diem against the Binh Xuyen. Generals who killed the president, he said, should not have so generously and proudly rewarded themselves. Thi shook his head while saying that they became drunk (*say qua*) with new power. Meanwhile, they lacked a plan for what needed to be done. Communists were more active, and they did have a plan. So, he concluded, he supported General Khanh for a new beginning, a new administration. "But we need a real government, not a soldier government; officers should get back to war and out of politics." For someone who advocated removing the military from politics, he was very politically aware himself. I regretted not having more opportunity for conversation but had already presumed on his friendly nature, so I expressed a hope we would meet again.

Then it was back to Quang Ngai, and Kelly suggested return to the

Thien An Buddhist temple on the small mount north of the Tra Khuc, where there are beautiful views of the surrounding countryside, hamlets, and paddies. The monks remembered us from our 1963 visit and were not offended by a few questions. They told us "liberation forces" (*quan giai phong*) were stronger than before, and we should be careful. The warning was kindly, but I thought their use of the term *quan giai phong* was unusual for implying a kind of legitimacy.

We spent a day with Nguyen Duy Be's commando unit operating mobile within and among Tu Nghia district hamlets. They were in An My Trai on the south bank of the Tra Khuc. We were unannounced, so Kelly and I felt good, even validated, witnessing unit members working with hamlet residents. Some of the commandos were helping farmers with irrigation, two-man teams rhythmically swinging a woven bucket to lift water to a higher level. To everyone's amusement, I tried. The exercise was more difficult than it appeared to a casual onlooker. I knew from past awkwardness that I couldn't dance, and now I learned I couldn't gracefully irrigate. Be told us they had engaged in some firefights, but so far the communists seemed confused by suddenly finding government activity where it hadn't been. He also told us Quang Ngai security would worsen while the 25th Division prepared for departure.

During May 1964 I did not spend much time in Quang Ngai. ARVN was thrashing around in western Quang Ngai, the Do Xa area, looking for what was supposed to be a communist regional headquarters. I thought that was a waste of time and operations energy. Bob Kelly knew more about the province than any other American. He was resourceful and courageous and loved to work with Vietnamese at all levels. His contribution as organizer, expediter, and discussant with province and district officials, while initiating the Quang Ngai commando program, was indispensable. It was thanks to Kelly that two doctors, Frileck and Venema, volunteered to provide medical screening and treatment for unit volunteers.[27] Kelly had everything in hand, and I understood the smartest move would be to keep my own hands off for a few weeks.

I went into the highlands and sought out Tuy to describe what was being done in Quang Ngai. He rather grimly said that it was a late effort. He was most concerned about the almost open border with Laos and Cambodia. The number of Special Forces camps had increased, but he felt the direction from any camp in which patrols would move, and how far, was predictable. He recommended going to Cheo Reo to meet Nay Luett for discussion of the highlands problem. When we met in Cheo Reo, Jusiu was with him. They described a need for a federation of highland tribes that could popularize limited highland autonomy. Both thought this would energize tribal resistance to communists. He and Jusiu believed that, without introduction of a new dynamic, tribal societies would continue apathetic. I mentioned Tuy's critique of camp strategy. They responded that a camp approach was inescapable, because it was already widespread and accepted by both Vietnamese and American governments. But both believed it could be possible to utilize the camps as political points of attraction, if their thinking for limited autonomy was accepted. "Camps that are not so useful militarily can be important politically," was Jusiu's formulation.[28] Nay Luett suggested that I travel to Banmethuot to meet Y' B'ham Enoul, deputy province chief for Darlac. He described Y' B'ham as acknowledged leader of the Rhade, a Christian (he said that Y' B'ham was Rhade for Abraham), and accepted by other tribes as a spokesman.

I could not go to Banmethuot for the kind of discussion that we were having. My opinion was that no Vietnamese government would entertain proposals for any degree of autonomy; it sounded too much like splitting the country as French colonials had done. If there was any hope at all, and a very slim one, they needed to find Vietnamese who could represent their point of view. The problem was that any Vietnamese who might do so would be suspected of seeking commercial advantage. I thought it more realistic to find ways to compete with ethnic Vietnamese in the highlands. Ask missionaries for fewer Bibles and more help organizing agricultural cooperatives to claim vast areas before others did. Get young men into NCO schools so that they could win acceptance as a useful militant segment of society, like Sikhs in India.

I stayed with them for another couple of days. We went into the woods and had some ambush adventure together. Attachment to their cause was tempting, but I thought it would be a diversion from the principal problem: winning the conflict in ethnic Vietnamese hamlets. This was my last opportunity to be with Jusiu. Nay Luett brought me to his home, or, as he put it, "one of my homes, I have many." He presented me with a long, almost sword-length, bayonet that was stamped 1917. We seemed to have made a connection, but I realized much later, when talking with Gordon Huddleston (who was one of Nay Luett's Hoa Cam instructors), that everyone who spoke with Nay Luett felt connected.[29]

I drove again, with Touneh, to Saigon to provide Ev with an evaluation of what was happening in central Viet Nam. I was not so prescient as to predict the tribal uprising, primarily Rhade, which erupted a few months later. We did talk about my conversations in Cheo Reo, but he grimly remarked that the tribal future was bleak no matter whether North or South won. Ev asked me to check in with the Embassy Special Assistant Office (a term much used in the American mission to refer to the CIA attachment), express appreciation for support, and provide a general description of the Quang Ngai training program. The officer I spoke with told me that what we were trying in Quang Ngai sounded a lot like what his office was already supporting in other provinces. He made arrangements for me to visit the Cat Lo camp near Vung Tau, where training was in progress for those other programs.

I was glad to have an opportunity to observe and exchange ideas with people experienced in small-unit motivational, psychological, and intelligence training. Maj. Le Xuan Mai was the overall camp director, and Capt. Nguyen Xuan Phac was his assistant. Mai was quiet but very much in charge. Phac spoke almost colloquial English; *reckon* (as in, "I reckon that . . .") punctuated the conversation.[30] They told me that none of the Americans connected to Cat Lo spoke or read Vietnamese, so I understood Phac's role was just as important as Mai's. They talked about training content and method. What they described seemed reasonable, and I benefited from the discussion. But we had one fundamental difference. Kelly and I consciously turned away from a "training camp" or "training center" approach to organizing units. We wanted training done operationally right in the hamlets. We recognized that was more difficult, but we believed it was the most dynamic and effective way. As Mai and Phac talked about content and instructional process, I supposed there was inevitable training center rote teaching. I asked about small-group discussion, was told there was some, but had a feeling not much took place.

Change was taking place in USIS. John Mecklin, ill, had already departed and was replaced by Barry Zorthian. Sanford Marlowe replaced Dave Sheppard as deputy director. Most unfortunate, from my perspective, was that Ev Bumgardner was bureaucratically eclipsed by the placement of another officer, Lewis Pate, director of the Field Services Center, between Ev and Director Zorthian. Ev was now senior field representative to someone who (in the Viet Nam context) would not have qualified to be his assistant.

Ev counseled me to be extremely careful around orthodox senior officers. He advised that although he personally had not hit it off with Zorthian, he did think the new director was shrewd and would understand that what we were doing in the field reflected positively on USIS. Ev was planning for home leave and not sure what circumstances would apply to his return. He urged me to prepare a report right away on training and operation of the first Quang Ngai commando unit, and to be generous in crediting the role of other agencies.[31] "Exaggerate if necessary, but recognize all parties. That's the way to retain cooperation and support." Ev suggested talking with a solid journalist if it appeared the program might be shut down as unauthorized "pirate activity."

"Finally," he added, "at some point what you and Kelly are doing might be impossible to ignore or suppress, and then someone will take it over. If we knew how to operate in Viet Nam, an expanded program would just be turned over to you guys while others support, so that you would organize in a nonbureaucratic way, maybe different from province to province, maybe not even applied in every province. But the big boys on the country team are not going to acknowledge that an army major on loan to USOM and a kid in USIS came up with a solution better than what they had on the table. If this happens, grit your teeth and cooperate. Help the big boys, because something is better than nothing." This was typical Ev, drawing a lesson from any situation.

Now in mid-June Touneh and I returned to Quang Ngai. We spent two days and nights with Be and his Tu Nghia district People's Commando unit in the field. This was an opportunity for evaluating and thinking about what might be done next. In addition to one engagement, surprising an SVNLF unit moving between two hamlets, I observed good (wonderful, I thought) behavior on the part of the commandos. Conduct was friendly and respectful of personal property. There were instances of spontaneous simple civic action, encouraged and sometimes led by Be and his deputy. They did quickly what could be done simply with little effort, a real contrast with usual soldier behavior.

I shared Ev's cautionary counsel with Kelly. He showed me a captured

communist document complaining about the effectiveness of the Tu Nghia commando unit and advising avoidance if possible. Kelly told me that
in the most recent month reported, the commando unit had killed more
guerrillas than the entire 25th Division. Specific numbers aside, what was
the difference? The division, operating by regiment and battalion, conducted large-formation operations almost guaranteed to result in little
or no contact.[32] The locally operating Tu Nghia People's Commando was
motivated to make contact in and around hamlets on terrain they knew at
least as well as their SVNLF opponents did.

While Kelly and I talked about our feel for effectiveness of the first Biet
Kich Nhan Dan platoon, I described my orientation visit to the Cat Lo
training camp near Vung Tau, and my conviction that we were on the better track by pushing enhanced training in the field, in the hamlets where
a unit would operate. In fact, I said, we can do even better if we decide to
organize additional units. I think during our first training cycle there was
more distance between instructors and trainees than desirable, and we
need to assure even more small-group discussion for commitment.

Kelly told me the Nghia Hanh district chief had already requested a
specially trained and equipped commando unit. Deputy Province Chief
Phien concurred, and Ralph Johnson and Guy Boileau agreed to provide
financial and material support. I responded that first I needed to get up to
I Corps and look at what was being done with psychological warfare centers in a couple of provinces, but I would send a message from Hue with
suggested dates. And I told Kelly that we would make improvements for
both training content and methodology.

While in Hue there was time to consider all the factors, other than
field training, that together were the foundation for success. Participants
were all volunteers. They were native to the district where we trained and
operated. Many had prior military experience and exposure to political
argumentation. Now I decided we should better align our instructors and
training with those characteristics of the volunteer commando units. If we
were to expand the project, we would need additional cadre instructors,
and we should begin by developing that capability in the province. I decided in the next cycle we would bring back instructors who had worked
with the first platoon but add four additional USIS cadre who were central Vietnamese. I would place one of them, Phan Manh Luong, in overall
charge of the second training cycle.[33]

I sent Kelly a message suggesting 2 July as the starting date and asked him to speak with Tran Van Phien, asking for good candidates from the provincial government to attend and participate with a view to eventually becoming instructors. If the People's Commando program should expand in Quang Ngai, local leadership should prepare to take control as soon as possible. Phien would need a minimum of five instructors, so more candidates ought to be provided, because some would be dropped or drop out. I also acknowledged that an important difference between the SVNLF and the GVN (one disadvantageous for ourselves) was lack of emotionally persuasive political content. Before we started with a unit for Nghia Hanh, I wanted to discuss that problem with Kelly and Phien.[34]

When I brought the new team, headed by Phan Manh Luong, to Quang Ngai and mixed them with instructors who had worked in Tu Nghia, I almost immediately understood that I would need to work group therapy on the Vietnamese side even more than with fellow Americans. I should have, but had not, foreseen the consequence of altering leadership and mixing cadre from the Center with others from the North.

Kelly and I spoke about his discussions with Tran Van Phien, who was, even before we trained a unit in Nghia Hanh, now proposing we organize and train a People's Commando platoon in each of the lowland districts. So we went to province headquarters to seek a meeting with him. Phien greeted us for a few minutes but said that he was so busy he would prefer we meet in the evening at Kelly's house. At first Kelly, though he was smiling, was not happy because he felt Phien was letting us know the project was less important than other business. On the way back to his house I advised Kelly my feeling was completely opposite. Phien was signaling that our district commando training and operations were too important to treat as a routine office matter.

Meeting with Phien that evening was basic for acknowledging that, as the program expanded, we would work with volunteers from existing Dan Ve units. We were not going to do basic training, although I did intend to conduct reorientation as to effective ambushing and movement. Volunteers in each district would be young men who wanted to be more active and were willing to dare. I described my intention to increase small-group discussion and include some political perspective by acknowledging corruption and poor government performance, but to define the local environment as their own arena for becoming the voice of the people.

Eventually they could control government through elections rather than be controlled. And, based on a thirty-nine- or forty-man unit, I wanted one of them to be elected political officer in each unit. That person's responsibility would be to check everyone's behavior and assure commandos' personal concerns were not overlooked. Phien's careful response was, "I agree in general, and will not disagree in particular."

In later separate discussion, Ralph was nervous. He thought a copy of the POI (program of instruction), a course outline, was necessary for his Saigon office. Kelly and I believed we needed to be daring, not faint-hearted, so we should ignore what we supposed were Saigon's concerns, because so far Saigon had only delivered failure. I promised to give Ralph a copy of our POI, but later, because it was still evolving.[35] He told us that, in addition to the Quang Ngai observer-candidates, he would bring some from Quang Tin and Quang Nam preliminary to introducing the People's Commando program in those provinces. He wondered how those people would react if they found Quang Ngai training included criticism of the government and promoting elections. I replied that they would think we were not fools. I believe Ralph understood I was not crazy, but my approach might have seemed reckless, and he was uncomfortable.

We began training in Nghia Hanh on 2 July 1964 while Kelly was preparing to depart for home leave. He had lived in Quang Ngai two years, had traveled the whole province, slept in hamlets, and was acquainted with a very broad swath of Vietnamese. I did not know another sector advisor or USOM representative as much into a province of assignment as was Kelly. It is testament to the USOM Rural Affairs Office that Kelly was first taken on detail from the army, and now USOM planned to bring him back as a regular employee. During Kelly's projected absence, USOM posted another army officer, Ron Theiss, on detail to Quang Ngai. Ron was smart and wanted to learn a new game. He came into the field with us in Nghia Hanh and later accompanied me on a two-day drive to Nha Trang. But it wasn't possible for anyone to take on in a matter of a few weeks the persona that Kelly developed over two years.[36] So now I would be dealing with, other than field training and operations, two significant problems.

The first problem was of my own making. I had overestimated my ability to unite previous instructors and the new group led by Luong. I thought at a minimum we could have combined effort that would be effective, if not completely harmonious. Tuyen, Uyen, and Xang were not comfortable with the new formula that called for an instructional cadre with each squad to guide discussion to understanding of local and national difficulties. In this approach there was recognition of corruption and other government deficiencies, but instructional cadre emphasized potential for improvement and local self-government that communists would never allow. The goal continued to be a totally mobile platoon having loyalty to the hamlets in its home district and to themselves. I insisted that, even more than with the first (Tu Nghia) platoon, instructors move with the unit and eat and sleep (when possible) with the unit. Living conditions during the second training cycle, and from now on, were much more arduous than during the first training experience (and that was no picnic) in Tu Nghia. Phan Manh Luong was, like myself, not long on patience. The central Vietnamese that he led were congruent with his embrace of the alterations I introduced. The others were not.

The second problem was circumstantial but no less significant. Ralph would not go toe to toe with Kelly over jurisdictional responsibility and control. That was partly because Kelly and I were not sure whether we would stop with one unit in Tu Nghia or expand. As long as Kelly was on the scene, his knowledge of districts, and relationship with Tran Van Phien (fortuitously, the next-door neighbor), made his role absolutely indispensable. Now, with Kelly's departure, Ralph had rationale for bringing one of his own people to Quang Ngai rather than working through Ron Theiss. Actually, Ralph was bringing two representatives to Quang Ngai, and they were both Australians: Capt. Ian Teague and noncommissioned officer Ron Clark.[37]

I had serious discussion with Ralph about this fait accompli. I understood his reasoning, thanks to Ev, better than he thought. But I supposed Ralph might have asked for my thinking about what sort of person could best fit the program. My view was that he had now introduced not just new persons, but a major change. Whereas Kelly could speak French and some Vietnamese and had a special relationship with Deputy Province Chief Phien, and I spoke Vietnamese in the field with units in training or operating, the two Australians did not have non-English language capability, so that introduced the complication of an interpreter. I told Ralph that my long-term vision would be having Phien in charge of the program with support from a couple of Americans, one from his office to relate to Phien and another who would visit teams in the field. Ralph replied that he had made the decision with his own office in Saigon, because as supporting agency, his office had to be the coordinator. Since, from my perspective, this was an uncoordinated decision, I could see that coordinator was intended to be controller.

While we were still training in Nghia Hanh, Ralph made another visit from Danang. He advised there was Saigon static, primarily from MACV, with respect to the Quang Ngai People's Commando program. The sensitivity seemed part disbelief that nonmilitary people were training and operating armed formations and part concern about impact on the manpower pool. He asked if I had thoughts for rebuttal. I told him that in essence we were improving people already organized as Nghia Quan but inadequately motivated and ineffectively operated. CIA should suggest to MACV that improved district forces by any name would be better than perpetuating failure. I told him that I had another idea, too, but would have to think on it awhile.

A year and a half earlier, in 1963, when I was first in Quang Ngai to work on a draft psychological operations annex for the 25th Division, I had asked about Vo Trang Nhan Dan (Force Populaire) because of its possible support value to an overall division and province plan.[38] Kelly, Walters, and I learned from Quang Ngai discussants that that program, initiated by Ngo Dinh Can, was most effective closer to Hue and, perhaps because of the Hoa Cam training center, had some presence in Quang Nam. We were told that in Quang Ngai the organization really only existed as a courtesy to Ngo Dinh Can. Whatever there was (and I think not much) in Quang Ngai by way of structure, training, and methodology evaporated in November 1963. Kelly and I never gave a thought to Force Populaire, and (as noted in chapter 6, note 33) much fewer than a quarter of the people we trained had that background. Nguyen Duy Be had some Force Populaire experience, but his Viet Minh orientation was more of an influence for him in that he often used that as a reference when speaking with Kelly and me. Our model was derived from what we understood of the Viet Minh/SVNLF synthesized with ideas of what needed to take place in Quang Ngai hamlets.

So when historian Tom Scoville speculated, "Scotton may have gotten that idea from Diem's brother in I Corps who had something called the force populaire, and I think the antecedents to this go even further back,"[39] he was completely wrong. How did that error get loose and running in the first place, and how did it gain some currency? I think there are three reasons:

1. I was never concerned with reports and justifications for Saigon, and Ralph needed to produce an explanation of the resources applied to the Quang Ngai project. Describing what Kelly and I were doing as a sort of Force Populaire revival was useful.

2. There probably would have been acute indigestion in Saigon if the program were initially described as a variant on a Viet Minh model.

3. Citing a fictive Force Populaire root might have made it less obvious that we were working inside the overall manpower pool.

Meanwhile, in mid-1964, I was blithely telling Phien and other officials that "of course, we are working with volunteers from existing Dan Ve units."

7
Expansion and Control Issues

During the first four days of Nghia Hanh training there was increasing tension between the two groups of instructor cadres. On 6 July, Tuyen, Uyen, and Xang asked to be removed from the project for return to Saigon. They explained that they did not understand the changes to training procedure and were uncomfortable being entirely in the field, sharing living conditions and food with the trainees. They also grumbled, less specifically, about the dangerous environment where we were training. I think I could have persuaded them to stay, but on reflection I decided to cut that Gordian knot rather than keep an unsatisfactory situation festering. I sent them to Saigon and recommended against any disciplinary measure.[1]

These three instructors also submitted their own memorandum explaining that the reason they did not agree with conducting small-group discussion was because trainees do not like to express ideas. They criticized some of the vocabulary that Luong and I introduced. Especially unsettling for them was my insistence that they live with commando trainees, "because the daily living standard of ourselves and the SDC in the countryside is quite different." Another problem was perception of danger. The area where we trained during the first few days was in and around a hamlet about two kilometers from the district headquarters. Armed SVN-LF agents frequently penetrated another hamlet just about half a kilometer distant. Nervous about their personal safety, Tuyen, Uyen, and Xang tried to persuade Luong to pull everyone back to a relatively secure area in the district town and reduce the hours required for daily instruction and patrolling. I believed that yielding to their request would be a giant step rearward from what we wanted to demonstrate to commandos and instructor candidates from Quang Ngai and other provinces. So I was relieved when they departed.[2]

My intention had been to immediately expand the number of USIS field cadre with experience, field-proven, for intensive small-unit training programs. By overlooking what I should have recognized as cultural (regional) and ego sensitivities, I inadvertently risked negative impact on the Quang Ngai program. I was grateful when Phan Manh Luong and other USIS field cadre conducted such productive training that their performance more than compensated for my mistake.

I knew province staff observers, attending as candidate instructors, would report the dissension they witnessed. When the Nghia Hanh course was almost complete, and I was convinced we had attained a higher standard, I called on Tran Van Phien to describe and apologize for my mistake. He eased my distress by asking, "When six Vietnamese are arguing, how many people are really involved?" I'm sure I looked confused, and I could only reply, "De hieu, sau nguoi" (Obviously, six people). "No, seven," he said, "and the seventh is the one who listens and then makes a decision. You were the one this time. Too quick and some would feel they were not allowed to speak, and so the argument continues. I know what happened, and I think you decided at the right time." I still knew I had made a mistake at the beginning, but Phien made me feel better about the resolution.

Although we introduced improvements into our two-week training, the objective really remained the same: Motivate people to defend locally by operating from within hamlets out, rather than from outside hamlets. The operating intention was to have a mobile unit, rather than an outpost, defend an area. The unit should be politically charged, in that its foundation would be positive relations with fellow citizens in their own neighborhood. This meant that successful ambushes and patrols would be the outcome of political presence. Acting politically put them much more in direct competition with the SVNLF, for whom everything was political. Before making a trip northward, I called on Phien again. We agreed to organize and train a unit for Mo Duc in August.

When I sent my report to USIS on 6 July, describing I Corps and Quang Ngai activity, my intention was to visit provinces farther north and push for effective psychological operations centers. But the four-day instructor snarl persuaded me to stay in Quang Ngai through the two-week Nghia Hanh course. Finally Touneh and I could get back on the road. It was not possible to obtain commitment for a coordinating center in Quang Tri and Thua Thien. On the USIS side, we lacked a regional BPAO in Hue because the incumbent departed prior to arrival of the next officer. So the cultural officer who worked with the Vietnamese American Association (VAA) was supporting English teaching and libraries in Hue and Danang, with only minimal time available to look after other USIS interests.[3]

The situation in mid-1964 with respect to USIS Vietnamese field representation was dire. The only functioning psyop center in I Corps was located in Quang Tin. So I placed one employee, Dung, in that province to support VIS, ARVN, and American advisors. As I had brought Luong into the commando field-training project, only Nghi and Duc remained to work in Quang Tri, Thua Thien, and Quang Nam. I eased the situation somewhat by persuading Nguyen Chin to take up duty in Quang Nam.

Other than a paucity of resources, the other factor inhibiting local interest in psyop centers was that the SVNLF was increasingly assertive. I thought increased communist propaganda activity in hamlets amounted to a clinical indicator of a weak, sick GVN. The response to SVNLF political action should have been countervailing political action, but instead the reaction was typically military, sometimes blind firing into the hamlet where communists were reported to have been. SVNLF selection of targets was more deliberate. Hai Lang district headquarters (Quang Tri) was overrun in early July. Touneh and I took fire in the same area from a hamlet well back from Highway 1. The railroad was torn up for a considerable distance after having been previously repaired following a similar incident.[4] Nam Dong, a Special Forces camp, was almost overrun by hundreds of SVNLF on 6 July, and, although the camp valiantly held, the attack showed a rising SVNLF tide. GVN preoccupation with declining security was not conducive to obtaining support for psychological operations, even though the need was now more acute than before.

I was concerned about the nature of the transition under way from Kelly, as principal coordinator for special units in Quang Ngai, to the two Australians representing Ralph. The important point was not organizational jurisdiction. I just was not sure the two Australians, solid in the field and fun to be with in town, fully understood and wholeheartedly accepted that these new units were primarily political in nature. By their presence in hamlets, engaging with the population and confronting the SVNLF as a by-product, these units were exemplars and effective agents in political warfare. Everything that the SVNLF, directed by the communist party, attempted had a political purpose. We likewise needed to remind ourselves that our prime function ought to be political presence in hamlets. Opportunities for inflicting casualties would be derived from challenging the enemy where it counted most.

I took a couple of days in Hue to produce a short summary outline on the nature of politically effective forces applicable in Viet Nam. First, I set down some of my thoughts on a yellow lined pad, then later I laboriously two-finger typed out selected passages. I cribbed, without mercy, from Mao's *Strategic Problems of China's Revolutionary War*, substituting Viet Nam for mention of China. I mixed my simple ideas with what I plagiarized to prepare a paper to pass to Ian Teague while traveling south through Quang Ngai.[5]

Ian, Ron Theiss, and I discussed the fundamentals in this paper. I felt we were knitting together, but at the same time I knew that Ian, especially, would take his cue from Ralph's office. Tran Van Phien and I met at his house. We confirmed that I would return, with instructors, later in August. Ron Theiss decided to accompany me on the drive south to Nha Trang. The first day, with an evening in Qui Nhon, was uneventful. On the second day, south of Song Cau on a hillside, we met Charlie Fisher driving north to Qui Nhon with a young lady. He flagged us down and shouted a warning, "Be careful, or be fast, but keep your eyes open. About ten klicks south, VC all over the highway." He grinned, maybe because he was going the other way, and drove off.

Ron and I briefly consulted, looking into each other's eyes for sign of hesitation. I repeated one of my gut beliefs, "Roads are only insecure because people fear them!" We made sure rounds were chambered in our weapons, nodded to each other, and remounted our jeep. Ron had a grease gun, and I advised, "If anyone tries to stop us, or fires, make a lot of noise with that thing." I would be braced on the steering wheel, intent on getting us through and well beyond a bad situation.

We got to the approximate area where Charlie had reported "swarming," and there they were, a few black-clad, excited men firing shots in the air and waving their arms while frightened-looking people fled up the road toward us. I accelerated, everyone scattered, and we plunged through the gap at better than 100 kilometers an hour. The disturbers of the peace pointed weapons but were astonished and ineffectual. Not a shot was fired by anyone as we sped around a fortuitous curve and away. Only then did Ron laugh with relief. "That's one hell of a thrill," he said, "but one I'd rather not repeat."

Eventually in Dalat again, I found a message from USIS asking me to look for Malcolm Browne, an American journalist staying in Dalat for a few days while working on a book. The information section thought we ought to offer facilitative assistance. I found him in a small hotel. We talked for an hour or so. He was married to a woman from Kien Hoa, he thought the world of John Vann, and he believed South Viet Nam was not placing the right officers, such as Tran Ngoc Chau, in senior command. Bearing in mind Ev's suggestion that, if the Quang Ngai project appeared endangered, I might consider speaking with a reporter; and Ralph having told me that negative opinions were expressed in Saigon, I wondered whether Malcolm could usefully make our case. When he asked who my supervisor was, and I replied, "Ev Bumgardner" (although technically that was no longer the case), Malcolm said with enthusiasm, "Lucky! We all like Ev. You couldn't be with a better man." So it did seem Malcolm was the right person.

My instinct was to not tell Ev that I was going to unwrap the Quang Ngai commando program. By my playing a lone hand, Ev would be as surprised as other Saigon officers. Ev would be "covered," as he had covered for me in the past.

So the next day, after Malcolm described the scope of his book, Viet Nam as representative of a new kind of war, I told him there might be another interesting angle for him. I explained that in Quang Ngai province USIS had trained two special commando units, one for each of two districts, and that they were platoon-sized and well armed. I described their tactic of working from within the hamlet outward rather than the reverse and told him that they were causing communist elements to be cautious and had captured more weapons than the nearest ARVN division. I described a couple of difficulties they were encountering in the field but summed up by letting him know our effort was so successful that the province wanted us to train in four more districts, beginning with a third unit in August. There was, though, some risk that the program might be canceled. "Why the hell would that happen?" he wanted to know. I explained there could be a couple of reasons: one, irritation with civilians organizing, training, and fielding special teams in cooperation with province, and another, concern we were raiding a manpower pool expected to support ARVN, Bao An, Dan Ve, and National Police.[6]

Malcolm considered what I told him, then replied that for him the crux was not impact on manpower tables, but whether a new approach improved field performance. He said that if I didn't object, he would do an immediate article for AP, and although that might make a problem for me, it would also make terminating a successful program more difficult. Later in the evening I called USIS to report that I met with Malcolm Browne to offer assistance and we discussed some USIS programs.

Malcolm did file an AP story that was picked up by other publications in the United States and placed in translation with some Vietnamese newspapers. Ev called and told me, "Well done, but hunker down, Saigon warriors are having ulcer attacks." Lewis Pate, director of the USIS Field Services Center, reprimanded me. Even nine months later when he wrote the annual evaluation of my performance, he noted: "Adverse publicity concerning the nature of his work caused some consternation among his superiors."[7]

I think two factors operated in favor of the program: proven success and the institutional interest of Ralph Johnson's office. But Malcolm Browne's article also made it difficult for anyone to oppose continuation and expansion. When Ralph and I spoke a few weeks later in Quang Ngai, he recalled our earlier conversation: "When you told me you might have another idea, I never thought you meant going public. I wouldn't have gotten away with that." I didn't tell Ralph that I hadn't exactly gotten clean away myself.

More than a year later, in late 1965, when we were working with a different kind of special teams in Binh Dinh province, Ev asked me, "Do you know why you weren't burned over the Malcolm Browne story?" And he answered his own question, "Because senior officers had the bright idea of sending you to talk with Browne in the first place." My only personal regret was that there were some, in Ralph's office, who concluded I had engaged in self-promotion, when what I really did was promote the Quang Ngai project at a time when I thought there was risk of its elimination.

Now, with general agreement, albeit reluctant on the part of some, for expansion of the proven Quang Ngai format (training and field procedure), the next sensitive question was, under whose aegis would we proceed? Already scalded on the issue of manpower pool, I decided to be passive on the question of organizational primacy and control. I was mindful of Ev's premonition that "big boys" would arm wrestle over who ought to have ownership of a new successful program. So when Ralph, in conversation with Ian and me one night in Quang Ngai, asked what steps I thought ought to be taken for expansion to other provinces, I stuck to immediate business. We needed to maintain excellence of training and performance of commando units in Quang Ngai. "Let's do that, keep cooperating, get Kelly back from leave, and then reach agreement on what constitutes success and how we might expand."

We did organize and train a Mo Duc district commando unit in early August. Phan Manh Luong and the other USIS cadre worked Quang Ngai candidate instructors into each session so that they were more active participants. I visited the two existing units on field operations. There was an intense engagement one evening after people in a hamlet pointed out where communists usually approached from the foothills. Our ambush was successful, resulting in three guerrillas killed and two (wounded) captured. Most important, I had dramatic evidence of hamlet families and the People's Commandos knitting together. When I met with Phien, we were optimistic about local initiatives stabilizing the countryside and then eventually energizing it politically. I was, however, still concerned about the imminent departure of the 25th Division. Although the division seemed flummoxed by its difficulty in coping with small, irregular guerrilla elements, when the SVNLF pulled together larger formations to confront hamlet-based commandos, then regiments and battalions of the 25th would be in their element. Unfortunately, Col. Lu Lan was feeling pressure to complete division relocation to the Saigon area. The only alteration to the plan was leaving the 51st Regiment in Quang Ngai and forming a replacement regiment in the south.[8]

USIS sent a message through the sector advisor telling me to be in Pleiku on the morning of 16 August 1964 because Ambassador Taylor would be arriving for a briefing and discussion of the II Corps situation. On the tarmac at Pleiku I had the opportunity to speak for a few minutes with II Corps commander Do Cao Tri. When asked if he was at the airfield to greet Ambassador Taylor (and I assumed he was), Tri surprised me by replying, "No, just departing for an important meeting in Vung Tau with other generals." Then Ambassador Taylor's aircraft arrived, and so Do Cao Tri welcomed the ambassador after all, but then he quickly moved away to his own C-47. Ambassador Taylor was perplexed. He asked where Do Cao Tri was going, not understanding why the corps commander would not attend him. I informed Ambassador Taylor that Do Cao Tri was on his way to a meeting with senior generals in Vung Tau.[9]

During a discussion with American advisors at II Corps headquarters, Ambassador Taylor appeared irritable. At one point he asked why South Viet Nam soldiers were not fighting harder to save their country. The question indicated such a vacuum of knowledge, my own condition two years before, that it was hard to formulate a response. I answered that the basic reason was lack of motivation. Ambassador Taylor replied he would have thought fighting to save their families was sufficient motivation. Then I told him if that were the case, everyone would be even more risk averse, because family interest would dictate doing whatever would be necessary (or from our perspective, as little as possible) just to survive. General Taylor, a lean, austere figure, was not comfortable with that thought. I was never in another meeting with him, but on the basis of that short encounter I thought he was remote from Viet Nam reality.

I was definitely disconnected in a different way. I knew a lot about hamlets, field operations, and GVN difficulties but was specifically ignorant of DESOTO patrols, Oplan 34A, and rising tension in the Tonkin Gulf. I was astonished when informed of air strikes against North Viet Nam. When I learned of the Tonkin Gulf Resolution, I was doubtful, and I mean full of doubt, that my own government knew what it was doing.

Returning to Quang Ngai was a great relief. I decided to drive to Thuan Hoa, where the 25th Division was originally organized and trained. This was only about eleven or twelve kilometers west from the province capital. What interested me was that, on my old French map of the area,[10] another four kilometers west of Thuan Hoa at the base of Nui Ho Dinh, there was the brown wavy line (first noticed on my An Lao map) with the same *muraille moi* notation. Irresistible. Some RF soldiers were disassembling the old training center. Poles, boards, doors, and window frames that could be used elsewhere were being loaded on a few trucks. A friendly ranger NCO was the general supervisor. This time I would not go off alone on a vague archeological exercise. Pointing out the area on my map, I asked the sergeant if he was familiar with it. He replied that yes, he was, and then he asked whether I would like to go take a look. This was beyond what I could have reasonably expected but exactly what I had hoped for. I asked whether the location, just at the foot of a sizable hill, was safe. He replied, yes, by day.

So with a couple of RF soldiers in the rear of the jeep, westward we drove, slowly, because as we got closer to the hill our road was increasingly narrow and rutted. The base of the hill, even though this was still the central coastal dry season, was covered with pretty thick growth. I could, with help from the friendly RF soldiers, poke around a little. There were rocks scattered here and there. I could see they might once have been in some better order, perhaps foundation for what could have been greater. We were about to leave when three genuine woodcutters appeared, returning from the hills and bent under the loads they carried by shoulder straps. I offered water from my canteen and, tempted, they paused. With help from the sergeant (since a countryside Quang Ngai accent is truly extraordinary), I asked whether they knew anything about a wall nearby the hill. Right away they knew exactly what I asked about. They spoke among themselves, and then the one I took to be eldest told the sergeant and me that there were still places where sections could be seen, but this close to hamlets, people had been taking rock and stone since their grandfather's time to use as post foundations when building homes. And that is as close as I came to rediscovering the mysterious wall that showed on my maps.[11]

Ian Teague and I continued cooperation for training and fielding units. For me personally, there wasn't any issue about who was directing, who was in charge, or whether there was subordinate order. Ian and Ron offered me a place to stay whenever I was in Quang Ngai city. I concentrated on quality of training, and when in the field with an operational unit, I considered that simply as follow-up to training previously provided. I still thought of Tran Van Phien as the primary officer because, without his concurrence and support, there would be no expansion. I assumed that after-action or monthly reporting would be Ian's responsibility. I understood Ralph's point about his office needing to monitor because of applied resources, and that would also be necessary in the next phase, when units were prepared for Son Tinh, Duc Pho, and Binh Son districts. I had already expressed concern about change in emphasis, accidental or intentional, but did not want to pound the same nail over and over again. I thought that, overall, every person involved, from beginning until now, especially instructors, Phien, and the volunteers themselves, accepted the validity of emphasis on local training for local volunteers to defend their own area by acting as a permanent political presence.

I did have two big-picture concerns by late August 1964. I thought we should resist the temptation to centralize our Quang Ngai formula and make it a prescription for every province. Second, ARVN was not weaving regiments into a coordinated web with RF and PF. Withdrawal of the 9th Division a year earlier, and now most of the 25th, left no margin for error or absence of reality-based planning. I thought back to I Corps travel, how intimidating it was to gaze westward from jungle-covered hills and abrupt mountains toward the almost completely open border from Lao Bao all the way south to Loc Ninh.[12]

I was in Qui Nhon when the National Salvation Movement (Hoi Dong Nhan Dan Cuu Quoc) took control of the streets. The roughest element was reinforcements arriving from the fishing hamlets on Phuoc Hai Peninsula, which I had visited more than a year earlier. I learned from a few of them that, earlier in the summer, their homes were bombed and strafed. Now communist cadre encouraged them to come to the province capital to protest and demand reparations. They didn't know anything about the national political situation.

But on the part of Qui Nhon community leaders this was definitely manifestation of widespread negative reaction to Nguyen Khanh having grabbed complete power. A tempering influence on the dangerous situation was well-organized Buddhist and student teams leading chants, counseling nonviolence, and distributing drinking water to the hundreds of demonstrators. My old friend Nguyen Van Phuoc assigned four students to accompany me and provided a yellow armband that he insisted I wear. Former landlord/trek facilitator Cao Dan walked along with me. With their assistance I could circulate freely, even go in and out of the province headquarters, which was defended by RF but surrounded by demonstrators. I negotiated agreement that demonstrators would not force entry to the compound if their representatives could present a petition of grievances. The deputy province chief agreed to receive them and their petition. Separately, working with Phuoc and Cao Dan, we calmed a situation at the province radio station. Telephones worked, and I could keep USIS informed of the situation.[13]

While training a commando unit in the next Quang Ngai district, I had the opportunity for long talks with Phien about national political and security developments. He now believed communists had the political and military initiative. The government lacked a clear, convincing political message. He doubted a Nguyen Khanh administration would be popular, but if it could be fair and administratively responsive, if really open elections were held, then there was still a chance. "Elections, choice," he said, "are the one thing that the communists will not give people." I asked what would happen if communists won election in a hamlet or even a province. Phien replied, "Let them, let them have responsibility, let the people see that the government will accept fair and open election results, and then people might demand that communists do the same."[14] The next day we went to see the original Tu Nghia district commando platoon. We spoke with unit leader Nguyen Duy Be and the district police chief. Phien had already told me he was planning on bringing Be into province headquarters to be responsible for coordinating all the Biet Kich Nhan Dan. Be had visible mixed emotions about the change. He hated to leave men he had led day and night in the field. The district police chief tugged me off to the side and asked whether there would be advancement or other reward for him. I replied that I had no idea about that. All was up to province.

During August and September 1964 the incidence of being fired upon while driving roads once considered safe could not be shrugged off as a minor risk. There seemed to have been what one with nautical inclination would have called a sea change. Blue paint on a vehicle provided no magic. Dr. Stan Frileck, who previously made the Quang Ngai–Saigon–Quang Ngai round trip with me, suggested that Medico was interested in buying my jeep for use in Saigon. I had flown up from Qui Nhon, and now Capt. Van Ivy brought me back on one of the UH-1 helicopters that replaced the old underpowered H-21 flying bananas.[15] A final three-day drive to Saigon from Qui Nhon reinforced memory of people and places along the roads of central Viet Nam. Medico paid a fair price for my jeep, but I was sorry to leave it behind.

The government, such as it was, seemed adrift with no functional motor or anchor. In mid-September there was a half-hearted coup attempt. The instigator was Lam Van Phat, of perpetual conspiratorial nature, who had recently been dismissed as minister of the interior. Somehow he persuaded a few other more respectable officers (also dissatisfied with Khanh and their own career prospects) to participate. Surprisingly, Hoang Van Duc, IV Corps commander (who did not have a reputation as a political dabbler) involved himself with Phat. There were so many people who had, at a minimum, some knowledge of the affair and did not disapprove, that when the attempt collapsed, there were extensive dismissals and reassignments. I don't think there could have been a better indicator of the shakiness of any government with Nguyen Khanh fingerprints on it. This period marked the beginning of the rise of Nguyen Van Thieu.[16]

It was fortuitous that I was in Saigon in late summer 1964 just when country team intramural wrestling for control of an expanded Quang Ngai–style program was in its final minutes. The three contenders were MACV, USOM, and CIA. Having lost a half-hearted play to have the district/hamlet commando concept removed from the board, MACV basically stepped aside.

USOM had three advantages. Within the foreign affairs establishment, USOM held principal responsibility for rural development. Therefore, USOM had the capacity to sustain a program with funding to support instructors, training costs, and field supplements for operational units. The project was initiated in a province where a dynamic provincial representative (Bob Kelly) was the facilitator and coordinator on the American side. He was involved from the beginning in thrashing out concepts and demonstrated talent for working effectively with Vietnamese at all levels. Moreover, George Tanham and his deputy, Col. Samuel Wilson, managed the USOM rural affairs effort.[17] However significant those plus factors, a major drag on USOM potential was the persona and policy of the new USOM director for Viet Nam, James Killen. Ev described him to me as officious and ineffective without the grace or wit to get out of the way. Rather than engage more effectively with Vietnamese, his policy choice was disengagement.

Sam Wilson had me over to his apartment in downtown Saigon for a couple of long sessions to describe Quang Ngai hamlet-based local commando units while he took notes. Ev advised me to avoid getting irritated by Sam's initial sweet-talk approach. "It's only habitual case officer technique," he told me. "Just give him what he wants. Sam's smart. He's going to figure out you don't need complimentary lubrication."

I described operational principles, field training content, and the need to be an element for fostering local Vietnamese political leadership. Just because we established a forty-man unit appropriate for Quang Ngai did not mean that the same TO&E should pertain in Ninh Thuan or Long Xuyen. We talked about how the spirit and conduct of facilitating American officers ought to be as "irregular" and committed as that of Vietnamese volunteers. And, I told him, I did not have an immutable preference as to which agency of the US mission should take the leading role, but the agency head should be totally engaged, otherwise any push to shove would lack staying power. What struck me, even as we spoke, was that we were talking about responsibility for a major, potentially determinative program, and USOM Director Killen was not exhibiting personal interest or even curiosity.

Peer de Silva's approach was very different. He invited me to his office for two long talks. He flew to Quang Ngai to speak with people working with the first units. He demonstrated the command interest that is necessary whenever a new operation is launched. Sharing my wristband description of field training content and operating principles was easy. But beyond that, I believed the reason for relative success in Quang Ngai was because we worked from analysis of a local problem to a field solution without the imposition of a template from above. I was hoping to persuade him of six points that seemed fundamental to me:

1. I held a jaundiced view of centralized training and believed field training was essential.

2. Although there would be an occasional lapse to hunter instinct, I did not see these teams tracking Viet Cong beyond hamlets into the bush, because that would pull them away from the people. I explained what I meant by rooting ourselves into hamlets (just as our opponents sought to do) and then working from the inside out rather than from the outside in.

3. There was nothing sacred about the size of units or the weaponry defined for them in Quang Ngai. They could be very different for another province.

4. Everything we did would have political impact, and the intent of these units should always be political, with weapons in support, taking care that we did not drift to the reverse.

5. These units could stimulate local political development. We should welcome that.

6. Any American (or Australian) assigned to the program should be imbued with an irregular spirit, abjure creature comfort, and risk going native.

I was a "loose constructionist" and had the advantage of no one (other than Ev) telling me what to do, but I also believed people function most effectively when some sense of organization allows each to know what others are doing and how one's own part fits the whole. I was surprised to see little coordination at the highest level in Saigon. In provinces everyone saw other advisors day by day, and information was exchanged and promises of support were given on an informal basis. That was not typical of Saigon bureaucratic behavior. Moreover, there wasn't good linkage between Saigon and the field when it came to what I called recovery operations.[18] In the spring of 1964, for example, there had been some frail effort to rescue the strategic hamlet program by a more cautious approach, renaming the concept Ap Tan Sinh (New Life Hamlets), but provincial officials and advisory teams received little guidance and less support.[19]

Ralph flew down from Danang and brought Ian Teague with him. They found where I was staying with a friend and invited me to join them for lunch at Ralph's house. I liked both of them. I did agree with Kelly that Ralph was something of a dandy, but we all have profiles that may bother others, and within the limits set by his organization, he was supportive with finances and weapons. And, strangely, I felt real sympathy for him. I was sure he went out on a limb by extending assistance to a project that he may have reported as initiated by himself.[20] Now he was in a bind for not being able to fully describe all the elements of the program. I had twice delayed, in effect denied, providing him with a program of instruction. My reasoning was that the POI was really flexible and modified slightly with each session. And of course placing it in channels prematurely would have risked some bureaucratic Saigon warrior getting involved. But now we had coalesced the fundamental points, order of emphasis, and practice of eliciting trainee participation in small-group discussion. It was time to give Ralph what he needed. I spent most of that day writing an outline, dictating some elaboration, and responding to their questions.[21] I was certain CIA would be designated the lead agency for expanding the program. I was convinced that was the proper decision, and I wanted optimum prospects for success.

Before leaving them, I quickly reviewed some of the issues raised in discussion with Peer de Silva. I still thought it was possible project expansion could be in the dynamic manner that I believed essential. Ralph brought me into his real world by considerately, almost gently, speaking to a couple of the points that I advocated.

"We might try a province-by-province approach with field training," he said, "but we will eventually move to training at a central location, maybe pretty soon, because time is short, we don't have enough field instructors, and we do have training capacity in Vung Tau. So that also means there will be a standard template. And Frank," I remember that he paused and spoke quietly, "not many of us are going to be anywhere near going native. There are prohibitions that apply. Maybe there's you, Kelly, and a few others, but not enough. I think we'll ask for Kelly on loan, but not you." Ralph placed a friendly arm on my shoulder as he brought me to the door and said, "We don't like divided loyalty, and I don't believe it, but there are some who think you're uncontrollable."[22]

Before departing Saigon for return to central Viet Nam, I went to III Corps headquarters, intending to introduce myself to the corps commander, Gen. Tran Ngoc Tam. He was absent, however, preparing for assignment as military governor of Saigon, part of the fallout from the failed Phat/Duc plot. I introduced myself to a major on the staff by explaining that I had just spent most of the past few months in Quang Ngai, knew Col. Lu Lan slightly, and wondered what the 25th Division would have for area of operations. The officer's friendly reception reconfirmed my previous experience and continuing appreciation for Vietnamese hospitality and courtesy. He explained that, while the 5th Division would focus on the area northeast of Saigon, in particular threats from Zone D, the arriving 25th would focus on Hau Nghia and Tay Ninh. Recalling my brief exposure to that area, I thought it a tall order.

I returned to central Viet Nam by the familiar Flight 719 milk run along the coast to Qui Nhon. This was mid-October 1964, and, unknown to me, the 95th PAVN Regiment was moving southward from North Viet Nam.

Once more in Quang Ngai, I talked with Tran Van Phien about the need to maintain a Quang Ngai identity even as American presence increased (little did I know). I visited a special unit in training, looked at two units in the field, and with Nguyen Duy Be spent two nights with his old platoon in the Tu Binh area. I knew this was a sentimental farewell. Ian Teague was as friendly as before, but we both understood that I was now essentially divorced from the program that had been part of me.

8
Upgrading District Forces

I closed out of Dalat in late October 1964 and relocated to the south. Kim Vui also moved, retaining her family villa in Dalat but renting a small house in Saigon in order to resume her singing career. Bob Kelly was back in Viet Nam, employed by USOM and on loan to CIA while the original Quang Ngai program was modified and extended to other provinces in central Viet Nam. Renamed (by Americans) People's Action Teams, the PATs (as CIA termed them) were expected to provide sturdy resistance in the populated countryside while the government reorganized for better overall performance. MACV asked USIS to loan me for organizing and training one special platoon in each of the districts in the national pacification area around Saigon.[1] We began with the six Gia Dinh districts that were contiguous with or very close by the capital. My friends Phan Manh Luong and Tran Xuan Khoi remained in central Viet Nam to assist Kelly, but Do Minh Nhat and I reunited with some of the USIS cadre who had worked in Long An almost a year earlier. Even while beginning to work with platoons in Gia Dinh, we sought to recruit additional persons who could train to qualify as instructors. We identified some through recommendation from existing instructors. Ev Bumgardner introduced good prospects. We found a few in the Chieu Hoi program.[2]

Beginning with districts in Gia Dinh was by request of Gen. Pham Van Dong, whom I had briefly met more than a year earlier. He was now commander of the Capital Military District comprising Saigon and Gia Dinh.[3]

I explained our methodology, both instructional and operational, to him and his American advisor, Colonel Sapp. I particularly noted the point that because each unit would be mobile, weaponry must be upgraded to individual automatic weapons and one heavy automatic rifle per squad. They agreed and urged beginning as soon as possible.

I checked in with the USIS office, still in the downtown Saigon location, to provide Director Barry Zorthian and Lew Pate (Field Services) with an explanation of how we would be responsive to the MACV request. Director Zorthian said my assignment was at the direct request of General Westmoreland, "and so I will have personal interest in what you do." He went on say that after the first unit was in field training for a few days, he wanted to see for himself what was taking place. Lew Pate spoke with me privately, and his attitude was significantly different. He said my reporting was "sketchy" and not always "full disclosure." He frowned while calling me a maverick, lacking respect for senior officers, and seeming to enjoy "ruffling feathers." I told him we had better go back and speak with Barry so that a more compatible person could be identified to work with MACV. Lew stopped short, grimaced, and suggested, "You just watch your step."

When I mentioned Lew's view to Ev Bumgardner, he smiled and said the problem stemmed from Westmoreland's direct request to Zorthian. The matter was so far above him that Lew felt insecure about a situation he didn't comprehend. "Just remember that Zorthian is the one who needs to understand what you're doing. He wants success for USIS, and he will support you."

Ev advised me to meet as many Vietnamese generals as possible. "They are going to be in charge for a long while, nobody else in USIS will know them as well, and that will armor plate you bureaucratically." He elaborated by saying that I should forget about Nguyen Khanh, "because Americans are all over him, like flies, and his sun is setting."[4] Ev suggested I go down to IV Corps to meet Gen. Nguyen Van Thieu. When I told him that Vietnamese friends thought Thieu was a lightweight, Ev laughed: "Maybe he is, but that might allow for floating to the top. None of the others feel threatened by him, and when they do, it just might be too late."

Tan Binh was the first district scheduled for special unit training. It included an area of urban neighborhoods to the southeast of Tan Son Nhut airport, a semi-industrial zone (mostly textiles) to the west, and then from Ba Queo on through Vinh Loc, a rural stretch of hamlets up to marshes on the border with Hau Nghia. Despite proximity to the national capital, SVNLF activity in and around those hamlets had recently increased. I went to the district headquarters with Do Minh Nhat, and we met Maj. Lam Quang Thoi, recently appointed district chief. Major Thoi, on first acquaintance, had a languid countenance. He seemed skeptical concerning a young American instructing one of his local-force units, but he became more comfortable as we conversed. He agreed to provide a Browning automatic rifle (BAR) for each of the assigned squads.[5]

We trained and maneuvered within the four hamlets of the Vinh Loc area. An airborne company occupied a mud-walled outpost about a hundred meters from the Vinh Loc elementary school. They ran patrols westward to the marshy province border. We ambushed to the north toward the Hoc Mon district boundary. Our training, featuring small-group (almost cell) discussion guided by instructors, led participants to conclusions established in the program of instruction. Practical exercises, working with hamlet residents and establishing night ambushes, seemed as effective here as in Quang Ngai. Once again, we were proselytizing for defending the population by being in the hamlet and working (ambushing) out, not outside the hamlets disconnected from the people in isolated outposts. Do Minh Nhat capably coordinated and supervised instruction. Major Thoi made a few visits, at first to determine whether our training was as advertised and then later, including a couple of nights, because he became a believer.

I had already met Col. Lam Son in Nha Trang several months before when he temporarily commanded Viet Nam Special Forces. Now, in mid-November, he was deputy to General Dong for the Capital Military District (CMD).[6] I learned very quickly that Col. Lam Son was someone you could not drink under the table. He held strong views about other ARVN officers and was candid when expressing opinion. He agreed with the need to upgrade district forces, keeping them attached to a locality but mobile rather than stuck in outposts. He did express, not as an excuse but from his perspective, the thought that mobility was hampered by inadequate *phuong tien*, "means." We went around and around in cognac-lubricated discussion. I reiterated that the necessary mobility, within an area of several hamlets, required strong legs, not helicopters and vehicles. I think finally, after excessive (at least for me) cognac, we were in agreement that expectations should be no less than what SVNLF local forces demonstrated. Lam Son promised to attend a training completion ceremony for each unit in the CMD.

I decided to meet with the ARVN Political Warfare Department to assure no misperception that our training trespassed on their charter. Gen. Mai Huu Xuan had just taken command as chief of political warfare in October. He had a speckled past (Col. Lam Son was not an admirer) as a French colonial policeman with the Sûreté during the early 1950s; then he had entered ARVN as a colonel in 1954 and headed the Military Security Service. He agreed to a meeting so I could explain what we were doing to energize Nghia Quan as a well-armed, mobile, political presence within hamlets. I was surprised when two officers from Taiwan (Republic of China) also attended. They were in Saigon to provide suggestions based on their political warfare experience. I need not have wondered whether Mai Huu Xuan would be curious about local forces competing politically with the SVNLF. It was almost immediately apparent that his sole interest was in being the watchdog for securing ARVN loyalty to the government.[7] But at least, if asked by others at USIS, I could claim to have touched base with ARVN POLWAR and so to have assured absence of project conflict.

Barry Zorthian reminded me that he wanted to see the first unit in training. We drove along Highway 1 as though going to Hoc Mon, but after passing the western perimeter of Tan Son Nhut about six or seven kilometers, we turned left at Ba Diem. From there we drove through densely populated Tan Thoi Nhut and then several more kilometers across open land and paddy fields to Vinh Loc.[8] We carried small battery-powered, transistorized HT-1 walkie-talkies (provided by the USOM Public Safety Division) for squad and instructional cadre communication. I used one to make sure I linked with Nhat when bringing Barry into a hamlet where instruction was under way. Barry Zorthian was a World War II Marine Corps officer, and he was quick to understand our intent and methods. He was a committed supporter from that day forward.[9]

We were ready to graduate the Tan Binh unit. We provided a unit flag with the name of the district and Quyet Tam Bao Ve Nhan Dan (Sworn to Protect the People) prominently embroidered. Following Major Thoi's inspecting graduates, Col. Lam Son presented the flag. Nhat, Major Thoi, and the colonel had previously consulted among themselves and made a decision that surprised me. They wanted to issue new uniforms in camouflage pattern. They believed this would reinforce the special spirit we wanted to encourage. My concern was that we should be wary of a drift toward military appearance. I always liked discussion and working to consensus, but on the question of camouflage issue, I was outvoted, so I yielded.

Ev reminded me of his suggestion that I find a way to meet Nguyen Van Thieu, then commanding IV Corps. When I mentioned to Pham Van Dong that the training "he was pioneering" would be suitable in the Mekong Delta, and that I could explain "his program" to IV Corps, he was so responsive that he sent a message to Can Tho. So I did talk with Thieu and described the program for improving Nghia Quan performance by making their presence in hamlets politically relevant. I explained current instruction in Gia Dinh and suggested it could be available for expansion to the Mekong Delta provinces sometime in the spring. Thieu was an attentive listener who revealed little of his personal opinion.[10] He said he would give careful attention to what we discussed.

A central point for coordination was needed to check implementation and quality control when the MACV program would expand beyond Gia Dinh. I could make arrangements with CMD for units organized and trained in districts bordering Saigon, but more general liaison for broader issues should be with Headquarters, Regional Forces (RF) and Popular Forces (PF), commanded by Gen. Tran Ngoc Tam, previously III Corps commander. I met General Tam and Colonel Collins, his senior advisor, at their headquarters. Four American captains were also waiting there for the first meeting. They were assigned to observe and learn special unit training and operations for wider application with PF and CIDG.[11] Capts. Jim MacGill and Giac Modica were detailed from MACV, and Capts. Jim Drinkwater and Phil Werbiski were attached by the 5th Special Forces Group. I was especially glad to reconnect with Phil.

In early December 1964 we prepared for the next training cycle, with those four captains participating. We would be in Hoc Mon district. The district chief, Maj. Nguyen Van Vy, was an amiable, slightly pudgy, mustached Vietnamese edition of Casablancan Claude Raines. When we briefed Major Vy on the mobile platoon and field training concept, we told him that, in accordance with General Dong and RF/PF headquarters agreement, each squad would be issued a BAR, and we would be responsible for other equipment enhancement. On the day before training was to begin, Major Vy told Phil Werbiski and me that he would not issue three

BARs for a platoon that ordinarily would have one. We replied that when we returned the next day, if three BARs were not on hand we would cancel the training. We found the platoon leader and gave him the same message.

When we returned the next morning, the platoon had three BARs, but Major Vy was furious, not at all amiable, because the unit had gone to the district armory and forced staff to provide them the automatic rifles. Major Vy was trying to determine an appropriate punishment short of execution. I could see that he would have loved to include us in whatever might be applied. Phil bought a bottle of cognac in a shop right there in Hoc Mon and, during a long discussion, we persuaded Major Vy that the unit's initiative should be rewarded by assignment to the toughest part of the district.[12] In the days that followed, Major Vy frequently observed field training and even spent a night with us in a hamlet. The four American captains, who had previous tours and could speak some Vietnamese, were excited because what we were doing answered some questions they had previously asked themselves: How is it SVNLF units have superior motivation? How can we improve the behavior and political effect of our own people? Is this war winnable?

Peer de Silva visited this unit in training, and we had another good discussion. He felt that his office needed to move quickly to train and field units in a number of provinces, and if that meant compromising the tailored approach I advocated, then urgent need would have to take precedence. I suggested, aware that he meant central training in Vung Tau, allowing each province to make some modification after their units returned home. He was noncommittal, but the visit was an opportunity for us to express appreciation for the material support and encouragement his office had provided during the previous several months and continued while the MACV program started up.[13]

When I was in Gia Dinh, Bob Kelly was in Binh Dinh province working with Maj. Nguyen Be, deputy province chief. Kelly sent a message through Ev to let me know he was coming to Saigon with Major Be and needed to meet. When we three got together at the apartment USOM reserved for him in Saigon, Kelly and Be shared important information. First, GVN presence in the Quang Ngai and Binh Dinh countryside had collapsed. Even some district towns were not safe, and some districts would be abandoned. An Lao was one of them. When the last post in a district was withdrawn, the administrative area would be abolished so that the communists could not claim they had "liberated" a district. Second, he confirmed that the original Quang Ngai program based on local field training was now reconfigured and dependent on training in Vung Tau. Overall, he said, even at Vung Tau there were not enough qualified instructors. So teams returned from Vung Tau little better than before they went. And that, he said, brought him to the reason he wanted me to speak with Be.[14]

When teams returned to Binh Dinh from Vung Tau training, Be had their uniforms dyed the same deep purple color as that of clothing worn by farmers in much of central Viet Nam. Then he added provincial personnel to each People's Action Team (PAT) and reorganized it as a fifty-nine-person unit to work in areas he was trying to secure. Finally, he provided refresher training for reorientation. The mission of the Nguyen Be redesign was clearly recovery and stability (pacification) operations. He believed in the necessity and validity of his approach, and Kelly agreed.

There was an American coordinator, Major M, for the People's Action Teams program. According to Kelly, the major was a Special Forces officer on loan, spoke no Vietnamese, had little familiarity with the province, and spent most of his time in an air-conditioned embassy house secured by Nung guards. Major M had an interpreter who convinced him that Be was a clandestine communist. M was inclined to believe the accusation because he and Be were in dispute over how to organize and run PATs in Binh Dinh. Kelly thought there might be an attempt to remove Be and replace him with someone more pliable.

I explained that involving me would be a mistake, because it would be perceived as trying to assert influence in a program from which I had already been removed. I suggested Kelly get to Pleiku and, using persuasive language with Gen. Nguyen Huu Co, describe what Be was doing as the only positive feature of an otherwise grim situation. I told Be that, in my opinion, local modification is necessary to keep the program relevant. I scribbled a note in Vietnamese for the province chief, Lieutenant Colonel Tuong, expressing my hope to return to central Viet Nam but explaining that I was stuck on assignment in the south. I wrote that I had just met Major Be, learned about his shaping teams to be effective in Binh Dinh, was impressed, and hoped to get back to help.[15]

Kelly, Be, and I went to a Hue-style restaurant picked, of course, by Be. This initiated our practice of searching out central Vietnamese restaurants whenever we got together. During the shared meal and discussion, we arrived at mutual conviction. If the southern half of Viet Nam wanted to establish a noncommunist independent political identity, it would have to be based on self-governance in the hamlets. Kelly and I had found a brother.[16]

In January 1965, having integrated four American captains and expanded the number of qualified instructors,[17] we were able to organize, train, and field special platoons in Nha Be and Binh Chanh districts. During training in Nha Be we had a good night contact not far from the border with Can Giuoc district, the easternmost district of Long An province. The following day, General Westmoreland helicoptered in with General Dong and Colonel Sapp for a look at how we trained and operated. I asked Do Minh Nhat to provide the visitors with an explanation of our procedures. I could make occasional elaboration, but Nhat was in his element in a way that would not have been the case in an air-conditioned briefing room.[18] Our presentation took place in a hamlet during group discussion. General Westmoreland asked Nhat whether adding a dependent housing component to the program would raise morale and attract volunteers. Nhat responded that dependent housing would reduce unit effectiveness, because if families were collected in one place, the natural tendency would be to focus on protecting that location. Leaving families scattered in their own homes was inducement for mobility to protect an area rather than one position.

A few days earlier, district advisor Capt. Jim Ray had been killed across the Saigon River in the Rung Sat.[19] General Westmoreland knew Jim Ray, just announced as a White House fellow for his next assignment, and he felt a personal sense of loss. He asked whether having supporting fire, artillery, immediately available might have made a difference. I doubted artillery would have been helpful, because Captain Ray was killed in the initial contact, and then the few guerrillas withdrew. By the time rounds could be on target, there would have been no target. General Westmoreland suggested that preparatory fire could have helped. I responded that in that case the difference would have been casualties for fishermen and woodcutters and no contact with Viet Cong. I had the feeling General Westmoreland was trying to conceptualize firepower for tactical advantage. Opportunity for further discussion then and thereafter was limited.

We continued to expand our pool of USIS field instructor/operator cadre. One new participant was Tran Huu Tri, a courageous and perceptive former member of the 40th Regiment who had completed his ARVN term of enlistment. David Engel and I met him at Djiring in 1963, and he contacted David after returning to Saigon in 1964.[20] I went to find him at his father's house, described what we were trying with local militias, and offered him an opportunity for adventure and brotherhood. Who would hesitate? Tri was resourceful, smart, with self-taught, almost colloquial English language ability and sincerity that won friends. He was good at incorporating former SVNLF into our own USIS cadre program.[21] His accent was southern, but like Do Minh Nhat, who spoke northern, he transcended regionalism and befriended all cadre and trainees. In this respect they were alike; not surprisingly, everyone eventually accepted them as coleaders.

We finished training a special unit in the Cho Dem area of Binh Chanh. This district was another that one might think fairly safe because of its proximity to the Phu Lam checkpoint and metropolitan Saigon-Cholon. But SVNLF political activity was everywhere, and guerrillas made incursions from an extensive pineapple and sugar cane area to the west. In February a sharp engagement resulted in the death of the Binh Chanh platoon leader and a need to reconstitute the unit. We were already planning for training in Go Vap and Thu Duc, but fortunately we had sufficient instructors/operators to meet the unanticipated need.

Meanwhile, as Kelly indicated, expanding People's Action Teams encountered difficulties in late 1964 and early 1965. One of the most significant was a shortage of good instructors experienced in other than hectoring lecturing. Some of the cadre in our expanded MACV-USIS program were approached by persons in the PAT program and enticed by higher salary and other considerations.[22] An officer from Peer de Silva's section came to meet me in Thu Duc. He explained that they did not want to poach, but really had a desperate need. Fortunately, we were developing such an extensive organization that there was no temptation to react negatively.

Nhat and I met with our cadre in the locations where they were deployed. We explained that all of us were working for the same objective, a South that could compete with the North. The effort could be applied in different, complementary ways. I told them that I understood the need to support family, so if they could have a better salary than what USIS offered, then go and transfer. We would still be friends.[23] Several decided to take employment with the PAT program. Those who decided to remain with the MACV-USIS project were the cadre with whom we had the tightest bond.

I reflected on how uninformed we Americans were about rural actualities and attitudes. I felt area recovery operations (pacification) would be ineffective without knowing about recent events and citizen reaction in hamlets. Colonel Collins brought me to dinner with General Westmoreland (at his Tran Quy Cap residence) one evening, and that provided an opportunity to make the point. General Westmoreland nodded. Before I left, Colonel Collins told me to prepare a concept paper. That was easy, simply the Long An Hamlet Survey recooked.

Nguyen Khanh dismissed the Tran Van Huong civilian government in late January 1965. Disarray was still the salient GVN administrative characteristic. Dissolving an ineffectual government was still within his power, but beyond that Khanh himself was stymied. Even if he brought forward a plan for national revival, no one would discuss it with him. He was a spent force. On 20 February there was another failed coup (with Pham Ngoc Thao a key instigator), but other generals decided they already had had enough of Raymond. The Armed Forces Council, with Nguyen Van Thieu prominent, voted "no confidence" and compelled Khanh to depart Viet Nam.[24]

South Viet Nam was still far from establishing a constitutional government. What followed was a military directorate. There were shifts of command and replacements in provinces and districts. Pham Van Dong was relieved of the CMD command in April and replaced by Col. Lam Son, one of the most likable and honest officers I knew, but the economic and political convolutions of labyrinth Saigon were beyond him. Lam Son was later reassigned to III Corps as deputy commander.

On the American side, I was so distant from the 1965 level of important decision making (that is, the country team, expanded and glorified by the new title Mission Council) that those persons may as well have been on the moon. I knew a few of the personalities, and, based on experience concerning the issue of support to hamlet and district irregulars, my sense was that there seemed to be more competition than cooperation among them. I thought the Mission Council was more focused on explaining itself to Washington than taking a clear-headed look at what needed to be done in the provinces, districts, and hamlets. I spoke with Sam Wilson one day and suggested reviving Joint Province Committees, but this time including representatives of all the agencies. I thought if we could achieve team spirit in the provinces, that was better than nothing.

There was frequent discussion within Special Forces about the ultimate purpose of our presence in Viet Nam. Was it to contain China? Vietnamese history suggested the way to contain China would be to step aside and allow Viet Nam to unify and be the cork in the bottle. Lt. Col. Charles Spragins, 5th Special Forces Group deputy commander, gave me his 1964 Army War College paper arguing the case that military government could establish preconditions for democracy. He called it PREDEM. Phil Werbiski and I considered his point of view but were not persuaded. We believed that, absent an Ataturk, military administration was not a probable route to representative government, and in fact allowed the SVNLF to claim plausibly that only they represented change.[25]

Capt. Jim Drinkwater brought an instructional team to Cu Chi district in Hau Nhgia. That area was so infested with SVNLF guerrillas and political operators that the team was barely one step ahead of "Charlie." Jim received a Bronze Star for his leadership during one engagement. Giac Modica had another team in Thu Thua district of Long An, where they found the GVN was barely hanging on to a few hamlets around the district town. Phil Werbiski and Jim McGill took a third team to Sa Dec to begin working with Nghia Quan, deeper in the Delta. I recall getting my hands on an AK-47 for the first time that spring. We were impressed. I moved among all the teams, looking for problems and providing encouragement. Gen. William Peers, SACSA (special assistant for counterinsurgency and special activities to the chairman of the Joint Chiefs of Staff), arrived in Saigon for discussion with Barry Zorthian. They reached agreement on terms for reconfiguring USIS as a countrywide joint office (JUSPAO) with assigned military personnel.[26]

Barry suggested General Peers look at the USIS-MACV special training for district mobile platoons. I brought him to Hoc Mon to meet the district chief and platoon that had demonstrated initiative by forcing issue of the required BARs. I described the training and operational intent to have armed representatives, more "tuned" than the usual soldiers, motivated to act sympathetically, that is, politically, with the rural population. General Peers understood immediately, thought the approach absolutely essential, but commented, "It's awfully late to finally begin in the right direction."[27]

Project expansion requiring occasional liaison in Saigon made it possible for some side inquiry into other aspects of Viet Nam. Buddhist friends brought me to meet monks in the United Buddhist organization. I was not yet Buddhist, but I thought that with enduring roots in Vietnamese society, especially in the provinces, Buddhist associations could take part in noncommunist political development.[28] There were internal divisions (more apparent in 1966), but when I spoke with Thich Thien Minh and Thich Huynh Quang, assisted by a layperson, I was impressed by their commitment to constitutional government and direct elections. Some Americans thought Buddhist leadership naïve, narrow-minded, and ill-informed, but that was not my view. The real difficulty was absence of communication with the military government. It seemed, given the tortured history of Vietnamese politics, that was due to military leadership's wish to avoid giving offense to Catholics.

I called on Dr. Phan Quang Dan, recently elected to the Gia Dinh province council. He was a popular opposition political figure during the Diem presidency, had some involvement in the 1960 paratrooper coup attempt, was jailed on Con Son (the island political prison), and still possessed (I thought then) tremendous leadership potential. We had an interesting discussion about fault lines within Vietnamese society. I suggested if the military were not reaching out to civilians, then civilians like himself could reach out to the military, starting by visiting some military commands, schools, and units (RF and PF) in Gia Dinh. "Oh, no," he replied, "the generals wouldn't like that at all."[29]

I had another brief meeting with Nguyen Van Thieu. He had just been promoted to lieutenant general and was about to be (but not yet) named chairman of the National Directory. Referencing our short discussion in Can Tho a few months earlier, and reporting that Nghia Quan enhancement was indeed now introduced in Mekong Delta provinces, I brought up an essential point that I hoped he might convey to other generals: "Opportunity to be in hamlets for days at a time, to converse with people most at risk, convinces me that whatever might happen on battlefields, competition in hamlets where most people live is the most important factor. If you can win the people's understanding you will have a real South Viet

Nam identity, and the quickest way is through elections at all levels." My time with General Thieu was but a few moments. I was not representing an office of the US mission or even an official position, just expressing personal opinion. Compared with a few months earlier, he seemed more opaque, more guarded, perhaps even suspicious. I may not have adequately conveyed what I felt most deeply. Even if he understood, Thieu was now playing for all the marbles with others even less likely to be receptive to the case for immediate 1965 elections.[30]

What was I doing, poking around like that? I was still trying to learn as much as possible while looking for anyone who believed the essential task was to find a common way, a common cause, for most Vietnamese to pull together. If that meant I wanted to learn everything, of course it was impossible, but by making the effort I would be more knowledgeable than through stove-piped inquiry.

I was sensitive to the need for high-quality Americans to work with Vietnamese in programs having potential for local political development. The first captains assigned with me had previous one-year tours and language competency. Most recently assigned officers were not at the same level. There just were not enough to go around. Capt. Jean Sauvageot made me realize the gap between desirability and reality. Jean had been in a district in Dinh Tuong province, and like me he loved being in hamlets, learned Vietnamese to a level that surpassed mine, and was ranger-qualified. He was providentially assigned to lead and support small teams entering hamlets to acquire information and report problems, in accordance with the concept proposed to MACV through USIS. We spent some time in the field, and I remember thinking, "If we had a hundred like Jean, we could energize Nghia Quan in every district to leverage political dynamic at the basic (hamlet) level." My next, regrettably realistic, corrective thought was, "Wait a minute, we won't even have a dozen guys like this."[31]

The army, although recognizing the special abilities of people like Charlie Beckwith and Dickie Meadows, still had a tendency to assign anyone of a certain grade to any slot at that grade. When we had a number of captains deployed with instructional cadre training teams, I wanted a major assigned to coordinate. The right person could have done that and been an expediter and inspiring leader. I asked for Jack Gibney, who was previously effective in Phu Yen province and later on the Hop Tac staff. I received a reply from MACV informing me that Major Gibney was already in an important assignment: planning. "Major J" was assigned instead, and that unfortunate officer failed to grasp the essence of what we were attempting and in other important aspects did not obtain the respect of the more experienced captains.

John Paul Vann was back in Viet Nam in late March 1965, and USAID hired him to work in rural affairs. John took assignment to Hau Nghia, and a tougher location (although by this time there were other places just as tough) could not be found. Other than an assertive, dynamic personality, he also had the advantage of having Doug Ramsey as assistant province representative. The two of them together were like seeing a sawed-off Batman and tall, lanky Robin. Like Bob Kelly three years earlier in Quang Ngai, they were all over Hau Nghia and cultivated a good personal working relationship with the province chief. They shared most of their meals with Colonel Hanh and his family.

I was assigned a small town house in Tan Binh district adjacent to one provided for Doug Ramsey. Our houses were informal meeting and transient sleeping facilities for us and for others passing through Saigon. John, Doug, Ev, Phil Werbiski, and I were the core of frequent discussions. Vietnamese friends often joined. We exchanged information, debated, and arrived at some conclusions about what ought to be done in a combined or joint way with Viet Nam in order to avoid failure. We had deep reservations about the wisdom, or lack thereof, in committing draftee-based regular force divisions and brigades (and Marine regiments), but we argued ourselves into supposing that perhaps time would be bought during which change could be implemented. I thought we needed joint command for influencing ARVN promotions and assignments, and the others agreed. They were less sure about the "encadrement" concept Phil and I promoted, whereby all US units would have ARVN attached, and GVN units, especially RF and PF, would have Americans.

All of us were contributors to a paper, "Harnessing the Revolution in South Viet Nam." Although Americans, our opinions were significantly shaped by exposure to Tran Ngoc Chau (for John and Ev) and Nguyen Tuy, Tran Van Phien, Do Minh Nhat, and Phan Manh Luong in my own case. The first very rough draft was patched together in June 1965. It included some revolutionary suggestions: immediate elections and a strengthened court system to deal with corruption, joint command, and encadrement. Then John and Ev urged setting aside joint command and encadrement to a later date. They felt we risked choking the horse by pushing for too much, and General Westmoreland (while balking at those two recommendations) would oppose changing the advisory approach. Ev said the US Embassy would have a collective stroke over recommendations that trespassed on their political preserve. So we made substantial changes, but the second edition retained the quotation from Dang Van Sung and stressed that we were burdened by perpetuation of reactionary governance with, in fact, some of the same Vietnamese lackeys holding positions similar to those held under the French.[32]

The second draft proposed a three-year pilot project in three provinces, wherein the broad spectrum of government authority would be vested in the province. All forms of US assistance would be coordinated within the province, and there would be one US manager responsible for leading the team in that province. I prepared a summary paper describing motivational training, and John and Ev agreed that the proposal for three test provinces should include that kind of training for all civil service and military personnel in each selected province. All who participated in discussions reviewed the second edition, and we agreed John should be listed as the author and circulate our think piece among people he knew in Washington.[33]

I had one more chance to push for encadrement, to try and obtain something positive from the introduction of US forces. I had a long discussion with Gen. Tran Ngoc Tam.[34] I knew he was appreciative of the positive results attained by Nghia Quan platoons that had received enhancement equipment and training. I urged him to propose, and then insist, that several hundred American soldiers, organized in five-man teams, be specifically assigned to districts for the sole purpose of rotating among PF platoons to improve performance and liaison with other forces. I suggested that although the teams would be assigned to districts, his command should be the point of coordination. We who already had experience with the concept would help him develop an introductory course for new participants, including quick-start language learning of the four hundred most essential phrases and vocabulary. I was sure that early beginning for this program would minimize misunderstanding, demonstrate American sincerity, strengthen PF resolve, and be the foundation for developing a body of American military officers with sensitivity for the Vietnamese.

General Tam understood the proposal and potential advantage for himself, but he did not commit. He was as resistant to the notion that Viet Nam should place conditions on US assistance as Americans were to the idea that quid pro quo be required in return for help. So in mid-1965 both sides settled for the lowest common denominator.[35]

Reflection, 1965

We were not aware the 95th and 32nd PAVN Regiments were already in II Corps and about to be joined by the 101st and 18th Regiments. I don't think anyone on our side understood the nature of the quantum change that was occurring. Yes, we were introducing US ground forces, but I heard only discussion about taking on main-force SVNLF and stopping infiltration by NVA fillers. I do not recall anyone anticipating our US brigades against their PAVN regiments in the way that erupted several months later. Why was that? I think we assumed communist strategy was limited to rural-based revolutionary war and would not change.[1]

We knew, by our group discussion preceding John Vann's circulating the "Harnessing the Revolution" paper, that MACV rejected a Washington suggestion for some form of encadrement. But I continued to hope the subject would be reviewed as the need became more obvious. I also knew MACV rejected combined command, citing Nguyen Cao Ky's and Nguyen Van Thieu's objections. I believed the initial GVN hierarchy denial was a given, because, absent our influence, inept and corrupt military officers and civil officials could continue in office without American comment. But I thought eventual recognition of desperate circumstances would allow for reconsideration, and even something less, like a joint coordinating staff, would be better than nothing.

The SVNLF expanded its reach in populated areas, and this allowed for increased recruitment and training. The results were not only additional or expanded units, but also creation of specialized attack sapper (*dac cong*) elements for attacking discrete targets. The fall 1964 mortar attack on Bien Hoa Air Base that destroyed and damaged B-57s, the 6 February 1965 attack on the Pleiku army aviation airfield, and the 10 February bombing of the American enlisted hotel in Qui Nhon demonstrated ability to maneuver in and around GVN urban centers and specifically target and execute missions. I had thought expanding the number and variety of SVNLF units would result in logistical difficulty. Although I knew that food was requisitioned (as a form of tax) or "volunteered" in the countryside, my understanding of how the SVNLF purchased pharmaceuticals and textiles in towns for delivery to base areas was minimal. I did not imagine the volume of supply from the north, either by trail or by Cambodian port, nor the creativity, discipline, and energy that would be applied over time to sustain the effort.

I think even if I had been supernaturally advised of what was coming, I would still have argued that the center of gravity for us should be developing attachment and loyalty to a separate southern identity,[2] and that would have to be based on stimulating political development right away. I wanted one war, not two wars (ARVN and other) or three wars (US, ARVN, and other), but the only player who seemed to understand the one-war concept, with everything having political impact and purpose, was the Viet Nam Communist Party.

Could strategic hamlets have worked? I kept thinking about that during the spring of 1965, because my own approach, influenced and reinforced by Nguyen Tuy, Tran Van Phien, and what I heard of Tran Ngoc Chau's program in Kien Hoa, was to work insistently at the hamlet level. Getting into hamlets and then "working from the inside back out, forcing the SVNLF to have to work from the outside back in," was absolutely basic. This was not inconsistent with strategic hamlets. However, strategic hamlets were imposed from the outside and hurriedly executed.[3] And that earlier effort lacked political content and featured underarmed, or even unarmed, hamlet defenders. Rather than just abolishing village elections, President Diem could have converted the village level to support and coordination (rather than supervision) on behalf of the province while carrying out hamlet elections as part of his hamlet development and security concept.

When the inadequate GVN hamlet approach was halfheartedly revived in 1964 as Ap Tan Sinh, there was no consistent and persistent follow-up from the national government through the provinces. As the war increased in scale during the spring of 1965, the GVN and American reaction was to think in terms of battalion engagements, districts lost or held, and territory/population control percentages. So distracted, our side lost sight of the most critical long-term factor, the people and their attitude.

Whenever I thought about the advantages of holding elections, I remembered again the murderous overthrow of President Diem. I understood his regime's deficiencies, but the murder was a massive impediment to establishing legitimate constitutional government. Reactive execution of Major Nhung three months later only added bloodstain to ARVN generals' uniforms. The only way to achieve a clean slate was through elections.

I had already been in Viet Nam three years and was missing, in some vague way, family and former friends. As others had done, I departed for leave. I had not imagined that, almost as soon as I was home, I would begin to count the days until my return to Viet Nam. Others surprise us, and sometimes we surprise ourselves.

9
Long Way Home to Central Viet Nam

Bob Kelly was also taking home leave, and we planned to travel together. Our commercial flight made an unscheduled stop in Phnom Penh, then we bumped through cloudy skies most of the way to Hong Kong and an overnight in Kowloon. When we arrived in San Francisco, there was an airline strike of some sort, no flights available. We rented a car and headed cross-country to Kelly's home in Allegan, Michigan. One would drive while the other slept. Somewhere around the continental divide, on my shift, I had to stop because antlered creatures were bounding across the highway. Later, when Kelly woke and I told him, he said that I must have imagined them.

I barely remember meeting Kelly's wife and son. I just crashed on the bed they showed me. They were awfully gracious for having a bedraggled stranger on their hands. Kelly had mentioned me in letters, but reading about someone is not the same as knowing the person. I woke to voices raised in disputation. While I slept, Kelly had informed his wife that he would return to Viet Nam. My appearance in the kitchen was cause for armistice. I hardly knew what to say but did acknowledge Kelly's important work and express appreciation for his kindness and friendship. His wife was not mollified. I was grateful for coffee and a doughnut. Amazingly, Kelly's wife invited me to stay, but I explained having a schedule to meet in Washington. Kelly followed me out to the rental car in his driveway, imploring me to stay just a few more hours. I shook my head, "Kelly, this situation is one where I'm no help."

Other than coffee, gas, and toilet stops, I drove straight through to Washington. As I entered the city, it was less than seventy-two hours since we had left the San Francisco airport.

I was not in sync with early summer 1965 Washington. The USIA East Asia Office was interested in my sense of what was happening in Viet Nam, but when I raised the need for political development from the ground up, eyes glazed. The area director told me that the embassy in Saigon and the Department of State were prioritizing stability at the top. He looked at me strangely, as though thinking it peculiar I would not know that.

The deputy area director brought me to the Department of State for a meeting of the Interagency Viet Nam Coordinating Committee, chaired by Leonard Unger. I briefly described rural Viet Nam characteristics and development of specially trained and motivated small units working at the hamlet level. During the discussion that followed, I mentioned that the PAT program was becoming more military, while the MACV-supported Nghia Quan (PF) were more politically aware than before. Both Langley (CIA) and DOD representatives were irritated. They told the committee they wanted to be on record as disagreeing with my view.

I had blundered, and bluntly, into a thicket of jurisdictional sensitivity. The military representative was insistent that the district platoons, recently enhanced, were now just better trained and equipped soldiers. He was surprised when told that each platoon I worked with would elect a political officer. The agency representative was angry because I asserted that the originally parapolitical units were now more military in character than a year earlier, due to the changing environment and background of newly assigned province coordinators. My opinions were not conducive to interagency harmony, and it was obvious Leonard Unger was not comfortable. I told the group that I had an "experience basis" for evaluating the situation, and no one else in the room could say that. I was not asked to return.

I drove to Fort Bragg to spend a few days with friends. I felt more engaged in conversational give-and-take about Viet Nam than in Washington. I could have stayed longer, but that would not have met the intent of "home" leave. So I returned, not quite the happy native, to Massachusetts. My brother David had just completed his first year in medical school. I saw extended family members and demonstrated more regard for them than I had when I was an inconsiderate adolescent. I spent a few days on Cape Cod. One could not imagine a finer spot in early summer, unless you were still yearning for the An Lao Valley, symbolic of places where best friends remained behind.

Heartache for Viet Nam induced restless anticipation for departure. I did not meet anyone outside of Fort Bragg and Washington who cared about Southeast Asia, even though our country was making a historic commitment of a draftee-based army.[1] I called Kelly, but his wife hung up the phone. I thought it better not to try again; I would either see him back in Viet Nam or not. But I would not complicate his life by telephoning through his family. I was supposed to stay on leave until late August but doubted I could make it.

I telephoned a friend in Washington and conspired to have a telegram sent to my home leave address requiring my return to Viet Nam as soon as possible. For my mother's sake I pretended to be disappointed. A few days dragged until return to Washington for ticketing. When Vietnamese and American friends met me at Tan Son Nhut, I had a singing heart. Born again!

Ambassador Taylor had departed, and now we had an Ambassador Lodge reprise. I was not, from the bleachers, enthusiastic. Taylor, even with his distinguished record of service to our nation, had not at all understood Viet Nam. I had no reason to think the second coming of Lodge would be different. I was inclined to hope that General Westmoreland, younger, with a fresh eye, could comprehend the essential and provide the political as well as battlefield strategy lacking up to now.[2]

Gen. Ed Lansdale, infected (as were many) by what Jean Lartéguy (Osty) called *le mal jaune*, was also again in Saigon. John Vann knew one of the members of the team arriving with Lansdale, and he brought Dan Ellsberg around to meet us. We were impressed by his quick intellect and desire to get into the field, understand problems, and be an asset to the Lansdale team. We also met General Lansdale a couple of times and agreed among ourselves that he was a wily but personable "uncle" sort of figure. His only rival for the title of "easiest person to sit down and talk with" would have been Col. Sam Wilson, professionally trained to gain one's confidence and a master by natural talent.

But John, Ev, Kelly, Phil, and I could not understand the vagueness of Lansdale's 1965 mission. It was one thing for us to have lack of role definition, because we could exploit that elasticity in the field. But we thought a senior officer needed a license with weight. Lansdale was going to be bumping elbows with others who asserted primacy in their respective fields. If Lodge really supported Lansdale, he would have made him something such as Deputy Ambassador for X. Then, as among canines, there would have been acceptance of Lansdale's place in the pack. But instead, all the Mission Council dogs saw him as a rival.

We thought the Lansdale team composition was also a problem. He brought along too many players attached to his past. This provided personal comfort, but not much in the way of contemporary knowledge and skill. These were interesting people—Napoleon Valariano and Charles Bohannon, for example—but they were not clued in to 1965 Viet Nam. Lou Conein, for whom we had great personal regard, absolutely scared some members of the American Saigon community. Lansdale might have been able to make common cause with Barry Zorthian, but by bringing Hank Miller as his own information/psychological operations specialist, he caused Zorthian to join the opposition. His mission would have been better served if he had brought Ellsberg and just a couple of old friends with him and then built a new team from persons already in Viet Nam.[3] Eventually, as original members departed, that did happen over the next couple of years, but it was too late. General Lansdale had our respect because on the broad issues his views were almost congruent with our own. But he did not make a significant difference. And it could have been otherwise.

A message consequent to my opinions expressed in Washington preceded my return to Viet Nam.[4] I was accused of having made comments injurious to CIA programs in Viet Nam. Some of the office staff, reacting to the Washington message, seemed cool and unfriendly. One let me know that I was cut off from the warehouse. Another commented that, after all the support provided, I had stabbed them in the back. Peer de Silva, with whom I might have mended that bridge, had been wounded in the spring 1965 car bomb attack against the embassy. There wasn't any basis for personal relationship with the new station chief.

I was not comfortable with this new situation, but I had been the one in hamlets for days at a time, none of them, so I was the one who had a field-tested basis for evaluation and comment. Of course I simply could have nodded my way through Washington and Saigon, keeping my mouth shut, but at cost to my personal sense of integrity. Admittedly, that was also just not my nature.[5] I regretted the outcome, but if expression of different opinion is not acceptable, then why the hell do we have interagency committees?

Capt. Phil Werbiski, a brother, was back with the 5th Special Forces Group. Ev suggested, and Barry Zorthian agreed, that I spend time with Phil establishing a motivational training program that could be applied in CIDG companies. We prepared a joint JUSPAO/5th Special Forces Group project outline, complete with financial breakout.[6] Some of the original USIS instructional cadre chose to remain with the expanding MACV program; others, including Do Minh Nhat, Tran Huu Tri, Bui Dang Su, and Dang Van Sau, associated with the 5th Group when I did. As 5th Group commander Colonel McKean and deputy group commander Spragins had met me before, their taking me on loan from USIS was an easy step.

Colonel McKean said he wanted us to concentrate on CIDG improvement, particularly camp relations with surrounding populations, while encouraging selected young officers and NCOs to understand the political dimension of the war. He suggested informally considering me a major so that Vietnamese and Americans would understand the relationship with Phil and other captains while also facilitating reporting directly to himself.[7]

During August we conducted special training in Chau Doc province by settling in with an instructional team at the An Phu Special Forces camp. This part of Chau Doc pokes into Cambodia along the two great branches of the Mekong. Kandal and Prey Veng provinces are on the Cambodian side of the border. The Vietnamese side, by recent history and family practice, was predominantly Hoa Hao. The area Hoa Hao commander was Maj. Le Van Phoi. We lived in the perimeter huts with locally recruited Hoa Hao CIDG when in camp. Most of the time we would take a company several kilometers farther upriver, close by the border, and train while operating. As in the past, this procedure strained instructors and soldiers but produced the quickest results.[8]

Beyond An Thanh, where the river is the border, we noticed modest water traffic by day and then an increase at night. Phil and I, with youthful exuberance, drew up a plan to check night river movement.[9] We went to the B Team for discussion with Major Arnn prior to meeting with Major Re, the province chief. I can only describe the province chief as shocked that we had so quickly moved from observation to supposition to plan.

He told us he would speak carefully but honestly on a delicate subject. The night river traffic consisted, in part, of commercial traders who paid fees. Major Re, with embarrassment, allowed that the IV Corps commander required monthly remittance to supplement his income, and he was sure that other province chiefs cooperated too. Major Re looked pained. He said under those circumstances he could not approve interruption, even by checking, as we proposed.[10]

We left and returned to the B Team house. Major Arnn told Phil and me that he would submit a report summarizing what we had learned. Several days later he confirmed he had made the report to the C Team in Can Tho but had no response. Meanwhile, I decided to drive downriver to Can Tho and try to meet the IV Corps fee collector. My route was to Long Xuyen, then through Thot Not, mostly along the Mekong, and thereafter away from the river on Interprovincial Route 27 to Can Tho. I went to IV Corps headquarters and had no difficulty arranging to see Gen. Dang Van Quang.

We were not alone. A lieutenant sat on the side and took an occasional note. I told General Quang that I appreciated the opportunity to discuss training for improving Nghia Quan platoons and CIDG companies. I described some of what was taking place in various provinces and explained that since I had previously spoken with General Thieu when he was IV Corps commander, I felt following up with his replacement could be useful. General Quang, maybe ten or twelve years older than I, had a confident but chubby posture. Since I mentioned General Thieu, he let me know they were longtime friends. Classmates at the (French-period) Hue Officers School, "we are always in communication." Because Thieu was now chairman of the military directory, in effect chief of state, Quang was letting me know that he had a Big Brother.

We concluded our discussion after I suggested that improving attitudes toward the government could influence the war positively for the GVN if the right steps were taken. I advocated public punishment for corruption as a way to win trust from the people. We parted with his appearing puzzled by my visit. I returned to Chau Doc with little satisfaction. We never had another conversation. When I described the meeting to Major Arnn, he said, "You do like going out on a limb, don't you?"[11]

We continued, even as we worked in and out of camps, to seek persons we could qualify for special assignments. Some we found within CIDG companies and others by simply being alert to possibilities. In the same way, we also acquired Americans who were attracted to our unorthodox operations profile. Most Americans would be inside the camp inner perimeter in a "team house" or bunker, whereas we would be outside the camp, or if at camp, then on the outer perimeter with CIDG. When a curious young officer or NCO asked us questions, we could lure him our way. Gordon Huddleston, mustang lieutenant, was one. Sgt. Lonnie Johnson was another. We continued to troll Chieu Hoi centers for prospects. A good man who had been 9th Zone deputy party secretary (name withheld) decided to join us, and he became one of our finest cadre instructors. Dang Van Sau, formerly a regrouped SVNLF company commander and concurrent battalion medical officer, one night after a border ambush extracted a bullet by lamplight from one of our CIDG. I never doubted the commitment and loyalty of our cadre, and I felt privileged to be among them.

In Chau Doc we were remote from battlefield change. Beginning in late spring 1965 and continuing through the summer, while SVNLF units had increased in number and size, PAVN regiments were arriving in the Central Highlands. US Army and Marines forces were committed to Viet Nam. The nature of the war changed. Previously, communists described the conflict as "special war," one that was fought with advisors and by proxy. Now they were applying the term *limited war*.[12]

Decisions made in Washington during winter 1964–65 had resulted in the deployment of American maneuver units to this California-sized country. Facing defeat in the advisory and special war, recognizing irrefutable evidence of a tectonic shift in favor of the SVNLF, Washington panicked and made a strategic decision absent understanding of Vietnamese history and the Communist Party's commitment to unification above all else. The Communist Party, with enlarged SVNLF and some PAVN regiments in the South, was not intimidated. Success in battle at Song Be, Ba Gia, and Dong Xoai and general GVN collapse in Quang Ngai and Binh Dinh whetted communist appetite for early, conclusive victory.[13] GVN prospects were grim. But the Communist Party, conditioned by its experience in defeating French colonialism, underestimated the shattering impact of US ground forces and supporting air and artillery fire that was about to alter battlefield conditions.

Purely coincidentally, I was recalled from Chau Doc to Saigon. The circumstances of US involvement in Viet Nam, and the direction that I took with encouragement and guidance from Ev Bumgardner, meant being only nominally a Foreign Service officer. USIA paid and supported me, but I took assignments that stretched, and then snapped, any definition of an information officer. Barry Zorthian was a realist and quick learner. He understood what I was doing and could use that to benefit USIS competitive standing in the Mission Council.[14] When I arrived in Saigon, Ev collared me at Tan Son Nhut, and we drove straight to lunch with Lt. Col. John Bennett, who would replace Lieutenant Colonel Spragins as deputy commander 5th Special Forces Group. Bennett opened by telling us that there was a sense, even in Special Forces, that Phil Werbiski and I might have gone "off the reservation." He wouldn't even ask whether we had crossed into Cambodia, because, "I don't want to know. But it's the right time for you and Phil to shift your attention to central Viet Nam. We're sending Phil and Gordon to work with camps up there, and maybe you and Ev will be in the same neighborhood. Come back and see me before you leave Saigon."[15]

Ev brought me to his place for cleanup. He explained that, with the organization of JUSPAO, Barry was provided a general officer to serve as his overall deputy for expanded field operations. Brig. Gen. John Freund had moved into JUSPAO in July from a previous assignment in II Corps.[16] Ev explained that we had a meeting in the afternoon with Barry and General Freund, and we would be given a new assignment in central Viet Nam. "I'm not going to tell you anything more because I don't want you getting negative before the meeting even starts. Just hold your temper, listen, and we'll talk about it later. But remember, at least this will be a chance for us to work together."

We met with Barry and General Freund in Barry's PAO office. Barry obviously knew beforehand what General Freund would say. Since Ev had hinted broadly that he was informed as well, I was the sole ignoramus. General Freund began by mentioning the GVN spring and summer 1965 collapse in Binh Dinh. He said that as a countermove, the United States had secured Qui Nhon and environs with US Marines, because the harbor and junction of Routes 1 and 19 would be essential to recovering lost territory. A brigade of the 101st Airborne Division was operating along Route 19 in support of the 1st Cavalry Division (Airmobile) now deploying into An Khe. A Republic of Korea division was setting up base camp in the Van Canh Valley with the mission of securing southern Binh Dinh. Although I was not quite staggered, it was still hard for me to picture what he described.

General Freund assumed that as SVNLF units in Binh Dinh province shifted northwest in response to pursuit by allied forces, a vacuum would develop in the densely populated coastal districts, and communist political cadre would exploit negative aspects of foreign soldiers on Vietnamese soil. He said that he wanted Ev and me to bring an instructional team to Binh Dinh for the purpose of assisting the Ministry of Information and Binh Dinh province to organize an armed propaganda presence to compete politically with communists in recently recovered areas, beginning with the district closest to Qui Nhon.

For just three or four seconds I was speechless. Did he realize what he had just said? We were going to organize to compete politically, but without content, against a national communist party, and we were going to begin in one district of maybe the toughest province in the country. General Freund smiled, expectant. Barry and Ev were looking at me too. I could see from his expression that Ev was not enthusiastic, but he was not argumentative either. Well, I made up for that by strenuously resisting. General Freund was adamant. Barry obviously supported the general. At least, I told myself, Ev was part of the package. I yielded.

Ev told us he had to get back to his own office to get organized for travel. General Freund asked me to join him so that we could "get to know each other." Once we were alone in his room, he motioned for me to have a seat, and he took one opposite. He leaned back in an informal manner and said, "Look, we don't know each other, but a few people here tell me that you and Ev are the best field operators around, but others say you're a couple of wild Indians. JUSPAO has a lot of sorting out to do in the next few months, and I don't want you getting caught in a meat grinder. You two are not popular with senior officers, and right now the only thing I can do is put you in the field under my auspices. Barry agrees. I defined a task that only you and Ev can handle. Get up there, give it your best effort, run around with your Special Forces friends, and do whatever else makes sense, but don't fight me on this."

It is remarkable how context and private discussion illuminate.

I went back to the 5th Group TOC and waited with Phil Werbiski until there was an opportunity for us to speak with Lieutenant Colonel Bennett.

I described the meeting with General Freund and explained my reservations. Bennett said I was foolishly checking a gift horse in the mouth instead of being relieved someone had just given me a ticket back to the field.[17] From his point of view, he thought that while Phil looked to apply motivational training in central Viet Nam camps, and I assisted on the side, we could also think about how Special Forces could be most effective in the new environment. "No wild ideas. In fact nothing on paper, just see me in Nha Trang or here in the TOC."

A few mornings later, Ev and I loaded a jeep, several cadre, personal gear and equipment, and ourselves into a C-7 Caribou for the long flight to Qui Nhon. The day before departure, we visited the Ministry of Information. We were told every hamlet had an information employee, almost always a resident of the hamlet, who received a modest salary from the ministry through the province VIS. Some of the hamlet representatives might have withdrawn to refugee camps because of decreased security. There were no central records in the ministry, but there should be a registry at province. As we were leaving the ministry, an elderly gentleman who had silently attended our meeting waved us into his office. He confided that hamlet information representatives were never supported in a meaningful way by ministry or province. He said the program was ineffective, and many of the names might exist only on paper. Walking to our jeep, Ev remarked that sometimes you get good news and sometimes not so good. I replied, "Well, anything we can do up there is going to be an improvement."

I had been away from central Viet Nam for about a year. As our aircraft began descent from the south toward Qui Nhon airfield, I was astonished to see more than twenty ships standing offshore. Helicopters, many with sling loads, were shuttling back and forth from supply ships to the interior. I thought this looked like reenactment of the Normandy landings. For the first time I had visual understanding of US multidivision deployment. I was suddenly struck by the thought that we would win by pouring in enormous resources, hundreds of thousands of troops, but we would win the wrong way, not by applying proper strategy and tactics but by smothering Viet Nam with material and scorching the countryside. When I told Ev what I was feeling, he replied, "Let's see. This definitely changes the war, no doubt; but winning the war, maybe not."

We consulted with Province Chief Le Trung Tuong, known from

Quang Ngai, and good friend Maj. Nguyen Be, the deputy province chief for security. They were an effective combination. Colonel Tuong had supported Nguyen Be several months earlier when there was conflict with the CIA province representative who objected to alteration of the PAT format.[18] Ev and I asked for their suggestions and support for our mission to organize armed propaganda teams. We told them we would come back after speaking with the province VIS. We also asked permission to spend a few days with two or three of the rural development teams that Be organized.

We went to the same VIS office on Vo Tanh Street that Dr. Bunce had visited two and a half years earlier. The VIS chief was not the same. We presented a copy of the letter from the ministry authorizing us to organize and train hamlet representatives to work in teams. After a lot of symbolic hand-wringing and expression of difficulty due to inadequate funding, our hosts produced a "partial list" of hamlet representatives in Tuy Phuoc and An Nhon districts.

I spent most of the next morning going around Qui Nhon visiting friends. Cao Dan was despondent because ambushes and fighting adjacent to highways made travel and livestock transport impossible. He was surviving by purchasing locally, not far from Qui Nhon, and then selling in the city market. Nguyen Van Phuoc, Buddhist lay leader, told me with some embarrassment that he was considering opening a massage parlor. He said he was ashamed, but since Americans occupied Qui Nhon and consumer prices increased, he had to do whatever was necessary to support the Buddhist Association and his family. I also spoke with three schoolteachers, Catholic seminarians, the director of the Chinese language school, and the BGI bottling plant manager. Only the bottling plant manager was enthusiastic about US troop presence.

Nguyen Be told his staff to locate as many of the Tuy Phuoc hamlet information representatives as possible. While the search was on, Ev and I took three of our cadre instructors on a familiarization swing through southern Binh Dinh. Jack Gibney had escaped Hop Tac purgatory to assignment with the Air Cav and was on the G-3 staff. We stayed in An Khe for the night and were astonished to see soldiers working under lights to clear the new base area as far as Hon Con.[19] The next morning at the Air Cav fueling point, by the airstrip next to an abandoned French plantation house, we swapped a bottle of Hiep Hoa rum for a tank of gas.

On the way back to the coast we paused in two hamlets of Binh Khe district. We talked with people returning home after a few months in refugee camps. Communist slogans were on many of the houses. People generally gave wanting to flee air and artillery strikes as the main reason for abandoning their homes. One woman told us that she could live with communists but feared she would not survive the war. Complaints about the brutality of Korean soldiers were common.[20] We drove into Tuy Phuoc district and east of Nui Ky Son, finding many destroyed or abandoned houses in that area. Later, the district chief told us damage was even more extensive north of the river at Go Boi and throughout An Nhon district.

We learned the 1st Brigade, 101st Airborne, operating in southern Binh Dinh while the 1st Air Cavalry and Koreans established themselves, was planning an operation into the Vinh Thanh Valley. The purpose was to clear the valley so that enemy forces could not operate from there against Route 19.[21] I went to brigade to offer a description of the valley as I understood it. There was no interest in what I might have had to say. Everyone was busy with maps, communications traffic, and conversing with each other. Finally, a major asked what I wanted. I responded that I had been into the Vinh Thanh Valley a couple of times in 1963 and would be glad to share my impression. He just looked at me and then said, "It probably has changed a great deal since then. You must have been with Vietnamese. Now you'll see how an American unit operates." In the next two days the 101st bumped into some serious opposition, lost helicopters, and suffered killed and wounded before getting support from the Air Cav.[22]

Major Be's people did locate most of the strayed hamlet information representatives. Our plan was to incorporate five or six of them from as many contiguous hamlets and train them to operate in that cluster of small communities as an armed propaganda squad. Phil Werbiski and Gordon Huddleston promised we could draw equipment from Nha Trang (5th Group headquarters) in return for a promise that we would be responsive to some of their needs. We expected that once an armed propaganda team was operating, VIS would continue paying salaries and provide printed material for distribution. We began to train in hamlets around Tuy Phuoc district, employing our experienced USIS cadre to demonstrate technique and lead trainees through group discussion to understanding and commitment. As with other projects during the previous two years, we brought them into the areas where they would operate and shared conditions and some risk with them.

Since there were no problems, I asked Ev for approval to slip north to I Corps for a few days. I wanted to see Kelly, and maybe Nguyen Chanh Thi, and have a look at US Marines. Ev was agreeable but cautioned me to avoid controversy, keep a low profile, and return in a week or less. If asked, he would inform the curious that I was examining potential application of General Freund's armed propaganda concept in other provinces.

10
Binh Dinh Conflict

B ob Kelly was in Quang Nam province. The fall 1965 environment did not allow road travel, so I caught a C-130 up to Danang and then hitched a ride south to Hoi An. Kelly was enthusiastic about Marine Corps small unit operations, and particularly the initiation of combined action platoons that encadred Marine squads with Nghia Quan platoons in hamlets. He explained the combined action approach was started near Phu Bai in August and in the beginning was based on the company level. But the acronym CAC (combined action company) is pronounced like a Vietnamese slang expression for penis, so it was changed to CAP (combined action platoon), which more accurately reflected the level of encadrement anyway. Kelly knew that I would be eager to see one.

We visited two combined action platoons. My impression was unreservedly positive. That is not to say that I thought there couldn't be problems with combined platoons eventually scattered in hundreds of hamlets. Of course there might be some difficulty in assuring that the platoons were mobile and not holed up in outposts, but the potential benefit to rural defenders, and to Americans learning how to operate in the populated countryside, was unlimited. I told Kelly this seemed similar to what we tried to launch in Quang Ngai, only in combined action platoons a partnership with Americans would be constant rather than occasional.

After Kelly returned to Hoi An, I called on Nguyen Chanh Thi, who had taken command of I Corps in late 1964. He was surprised but pulled me into his office. Right away he wanted to know where I had been for the past year. I briefly described work with MACV and Special Forces and asked him about developments in I Corps. He reviewed the general deterioration preceding arrival of US Marines but said securing support from the region's population was still what would determine losing or winning. He told me that earlier in Saigon, in June, when Nguyen Van Thieu was made chairman of the Directorate (de facto chief of state) and Nguyen Cao Ky took the office of chairman of the Executive Committee (de facto prime minister), he could have received support from other generals for one of those positions. He decided not to make the reach because he was not comfortable removing himself from I Corps, and he believed the country should have a civil constitutional government.[1]

He acknowledged the necessity for US direct involvement (that is, Marines), but he worried about the communists calling Americans new colonialists, new imperialists. I responded that, especially in the countryside, popular attitudes would be shaped by what the people witnessed. In that connection I described the combined action platoons I had just observed. If this program were adopted everywhere, benefits would be: (1) Nghia Quan (PF) units would immediately have improved support, (2) People in hamlets would see Vietnamese and Americans cooperating for local security, (3) air and artillery strikes would probably be applied with greater care, and (4) US Marines would begin to accumulate a body of Americans who knew how to work cooperatively with Vietnamese. I suggested he consider making combined action platoons his policy for I Corps. Thi asked why I couldn't find a way to stay, and I explained being on assignment in Binh Dinh, with just a few days to come and see friends.

On the C-123 ride south along the coastline, weather was poor with low, scudding clouds. We were under the ceiling so as to pop in and out of Quang Ngai and then low-level our way to Qui Nhon. From minimum altitude I could see even more of the widespread destruction that we were told occurred from spring 1965 onward.

Ev and I spent days and nights with the instructor cadre and the armed information teams in training, occasionally returning to Qui Nhon for discussion with Nguyen Be and Le Trung Tuong. Despite some of the appearance of an American garrison town, Qui Nhon still retained traces of earlier innocent charm. I showed Ev the two Cham towers on the northern side of the peninsula shoulder and introduced him to friends within the city, the Hue restaurant near the bus station, the delights of the Phi Diep ice cream parlor, and the genius mechanic who could revive any crippled vehicle.

We took opportunity to accompany friendly forces on operations into

Phu Cat and An Nhon districts. On foot, in and out of shattered hamlets, it was apparent that what we were told about devastation was not exaggerated. The situation in Binh Dinh had been so precarious during the spring and summer of 1965 that Special Forces camps at Plei Ta Nangle and Kannack were untenable.[2] Some additional Special Forces reinforcements were brought into the province from Okinawa to bolster local forces until regular US units arrived. These teams advised and operated in Bong Son, Hoai An, Binh Khe, and Tuy Phuoc but were withdrawn or relocated as first US Marines, then the 1st Brigade of the 101st, the Korean Division, and the 1st Air Cav deployed.[3] We spoke with many of the district advisors, a mix of those who had survived the spring-summer collapse and some who were recent arrivals. Their consensus was that application of firepower on Viet Cong in the populated areas doubled or even tripled after the arrival of American and Korean forces. Some hamlet residents who lived by night in crude bunkers told us that most residents fled because of frequent artillery fire.[4] We went with Major Be north to the Bong Son and Tam Quan area, where we observed that air support to ARVN and US ground units was tearing up the northern side of the province to an even greater extent than that which we had observed in the south. My recollection of havoc in the area west of Route 1 from Gia Huu northward up the coastal valley toward the Quang Ngai border is still vivid.

Nguyen Be was not discouraged. He did not excuse the erroneous, inadvertent pouring of artillery and air strikes on Binh Dinh's rural population, but he did understand that a partial vacuum developed in much of the countryside as SVNLF battalions reeled back into interior valleys and mountains from the coastal plain. He intended to fill that vacuum with the fifty-nine-member rural development teams he was organizing. He asked Ev and me to encourage some of the VIS hamlet cadre we trained to volunteer for work with his teams. "Every willing hand is needed," was his approach in late 1965.

An American unit invited Ev and me to their Thanksgiving dinner. We were tempted, but our theology was to share good times with our cadre, so we politely declined and decided to organize a holiday meal with our own team. Several cadre had come to Binh Dinh with us, and others we had recruited locally. Rice and local vegetables would provide the bulk of the meal, but we decided to include roast chicken as a special treat. I planned to divide our total number into small groups, place each with a Vietnamese household, and ask the lady of the house to prepare the meal in return for generous compensation. I wanted the chicken to be a surprise, and so, confident of my language ability, I made the arrangements myself. I emphasized that I wanted the chickens cleaned and then roasted whole, not chopped up in small pieces as was usually done to facilitate eating with chopsticks. Considering the number of people we had, and calculating four people to each of five eating units, I bargained for five chickens.

On that pilgrim day, with Ev and me in different households of a small hamlet, I was disappointed when our meal was delivered with communal bowls of rice and vegetables, accompanied by a plate of chopped-up chicken. I thought just one of the ladies had not understood. Toward the end of the meal I circulated among the other houses and was dismayed to find that each chef had finely chopped the roasted chickens. I apologized to Ev, explaining that I had thought my language ability better than it proved to have been. Ev laughed, enjoying the situation at my expense. "Oh, no," he said, "The ladies understood all right; but how many chickens did you pay for?" I had to admit that I paid for five, but there was no telling how many we were served.

A few days later, Ev returned to Saigon, called back by General Freund to represent USIS in discussion of a new national pacification program. Roast chicken aside, we had shared a good couple of months together.[5]

Up until the fall of 1965, although PAVN presence in central Viet Nam was acknowledged and prisoners confirmed PAVN unit designations, battles were still between SVNLF forces and ARVN, now supplemented by US regiments and divisions. The mid-August fighting on the Van Tuong Peninsula in Quang Ngai was between the US Marines and the 1st Regiment of the SVNLF. It was the first large-scale battle involving Americans as principal combatants, but the first major engagement with PAVN regiments took place in the highlands from mid-October through much of November.

Communist intent was to attack (and overrun) the Special Forces camp at Plei Me, ambush any relief force arriving from Pleiku, and secure domination of the western approaches to Pleiku.[6] Le Trung Tuong assured me that regiments of the PAVN 325th Division were also in the highlands. He said the PAVN 101st Division was somewhere north of Kontum, and he believed the 95th was north of Route 19. Although what he told me lacked precision, no one was denying that PAVN was significantly in the war. He also claimed there was a new PAVN 3rd Division, including two PAVN regiments along with one that he thought was SVNLF formed by recruitment in Binh Dinh. And it was not as though PAVN entry was the only problem. The ARVN 7th Regiment (of the 5th Division in III Corps) was defeated at the Michelin plantation, and the victor was a homegrown SVNLF formation beginning to expand to division size.[7]

This was no change of degree; the war was fundamentally altered by arrival of PAVN and US field units. I thought back to the assumption Nguyen Tuy, Jusiu, and I made in early 1963, that small mobile (not camp-dependent) Bahnar-based units could make movement difficult for the SVNLF between Kontum and the An Lao Valley in Binh Dinh. More than two and a half years later our central Viet Nam environment had so changed that what seemed possible then might as well have been in a previous century.

Phil Werbiski was working from 5th Group headquarters in Nha Trang. He brought Special Forces cadre instructors into camps in southern II Corps, while Gordon Huddleston continued to do the same in III Corps and IV Corps. We visited camps that Colonel Bennett asked us to examine with respect to CIDG morale. Few camps had the demographic base of young men necessary to organize and sustain four or five companies.[8] This meant that, unlike at the beginning of the CIDG program, personnel were often recruited (even impressed) from other areas. The more intimidating the operational area, and the greater the number of nonlocal CIDG, the worse we would find morale to be.[9] Phil, Hud, and I arranged to meet as often as possible. One of them would deliver the payroll for Special Forces instructional cadre working in Binh Dinh. I met them in Qui Nhon, where we would spend time with Nguyen Be and then proceed to a unit in the field and overnight with them.

USIS, reconfigured as JUSPAO in 1965, had an American field representative working on civil information and psychological warfare in each province. The Binh Dinh province representative was Major Gomez. Messages for me were sent through him, and they would accumulate until he could pass them along. That was how I learned one morning that Carl Gebuhr would arrive in the afternoon. He was the recently arrived chief of the JUSPAO Field Development Division.[10] Gordon had been planning to return to Nha Trang and then onward to IV Corps, but he told me that he would, if I didn't mind, stick around to "watch the Newcomer Show."

So we met Carl at the Qui Nhon airfield. It was my practice to be respectful on first acquaintance, and I gave him credit for flying up for an overnight visit. I introduced Gordon as the visiting Special Forces officer who brought administrative support for personnel who were participating in the JUSPAO hamlet information program that supported recovery operations in Binh Dinh, arguably the most important province in Viet Nam. Before learning of our visitor's arrival, we had already planned lunch with Colonel Tuong (province chief) and Maj. Nguyen Be (deputy province chief and sparkplug for civil operations), so of course we invited Carl to join us.[11]

Colonel Tuong, while we ate in a small local restaurant on Vo Thanh Street, described the spring/summer 1965 collapse, the arrival of US forces, and the difficulty of establishing security. When he expressed appreciation for Americans who were risking their lives to help his country, Gebuhr demurred by saying, "I'm not here to risk my life." Le Trung Tuong, surprised, not sure what was intended, decided he needed to return to province headquarters. Gordon was frowning but held his temper. Nguyen Be smiled, but after Tuong left he said, "Of course no one wants to lose life, but sometimes we find something worth the risk."

We accompanied Be to visit a Korean artillery unit while he discussed clearance procedures, and then Gordon and I brought Carl to join an instructional team that was training a new mobile information team in a hamlet not far, maybe just a kilometer, from the Tuy Phuoc district headquarters. I introduced all of our people, pointing out which were USIS employees and giving them an opportunity to say something about their work. Later, as instructors and trainees prepared for night ambushes around the hamlet, Carl shared a spartan rural meal with us. We talked about the project in Binh Dinh, evolution of hamlet-based programs, the USIS role, and the significance of Nguyen Be and his rural development teams. Our visitor was direct in stating his belief that we were off on a non-USIS tangent that he could not support. When he asked, after dark, when we might find a hotel, we took pleasure in telling him that he was in the hotel. It was a long, uncomfortable night for him.

I understood, from what he told us, that USIS would not long have a future in small-unit counterinsurgency training, and as I reflected on the new situation applying in Viet Nam, I realized that the change would not be solely due to Gebuhr's negativity. The war itself was in metamorphosis, with PAVN application directed by the Communist Party on the opposing side, but on our side a feeling that the United States now had the kind of war (big-unit, big ordnance–expending) that it knew how to win. I asked Gordon to speak with Phil Werbiski and Colonel Bennett about taking the USIS cadre who worked with me onto the Special Forces payroll. Gordon promised that he would get back with a response.

Phil Werbiski sent a message suggesting we meet in Saigon in mid-January 1966 to arrange voluntary transfer of USIS field cadre to Special Forces. He had approval from Colonel Bennett, who was also anticipating our promised oral report and discussion on Special Forces in the new Viet Nam environment. Before leaving Binh Dinh, I spent more time with Nguyen Be and promised to return as soon as possible.

Colonel Bennett told us our observations would be shared with Colonel McKean, who was then focused on strengthening existing camps to avoid any being overrun and abandoned. That provided us with the perfect opening—while recognizing that the camp approach was inherited and that camp defenders put up valiant resistance—to question the fundamental camp concept in the new operational environment. I began by summarizing in a couple of sentences the history of the first camps, stemming from the Buon Enao project in 1961, when the camp was a training center convenience, to camps becoming the focus, with a need to relocate populations to support the camps. Phil chimed in with a litany of the steps whereby SF camps became havens rather than patrol bases. First of all, he said, our people are not in the trenches and bunkers with the CIDG; they are in an interior fortified minicompound. Then one of the rotational teams will jerry-rig some kind of shower facility, the next team will scrounge a hot water heater, another will get fans for the team house, and little by little the human urge for creature comfort begins to separate us from those we should be with all the time. Huddleston's analogy was to the four Fs taught at Fort Benning: it is basic to find, fix, fight, and finish the enemy. By anchoring ourselves to camps, we had solved the first two of the four steps for our opponents. We were found and we were fixed. Communist forces could easily go around our camps according to the radii of our patrol patterns. Our conclusion, based on the January 1966 environment, was that Special Forces camps were judas goats occasionally attracting a major attack that enabled MACV to apply maximum firepower and follow up with conventional forces. This is strategy of sorts, but not one that adequately engages Special Forces capabilities.

Judging from the look of disappointment on his face, Colonel Bennett had not anticipated blanket disavowal of the camps. He asked whether, without (sarcastically) dumping the whole program, there might be some way to make better what (sarcastically) we are stuck with. I had a couple of suggestions. One stemmed from Jusiu's comment in 1964 about camps having potential political significance. I suggested closing vulnerable camps but retaining some in tribal areas as political centers of gravity, emphasizing civil affairs, education, and medicine. In those camps, located within traditional tribal areas, the camp commanders should be tribal leaders. Then personnel from closed camps could operate on a mobile basis in and out of the trail systems used by communist units. Lots of air supply and maximum mobility would be required. We were advocating a sort of SOG/Delta, but oriented toward populations within the country. Colonel Bennett shook his head: "We're not exactly looking for Band-Aids, but you guys are proposing radical surgery."

John Vann had earlier moved from Hau Nghia province to be III Corps USAID representative and had just recently left Bien Hoa to be USAID representative to the Rural Development Ministry. Ev Bumgardner, after leaving Binh Dinh, was spending a lot of time there too. They were both committed to helping Tran Ngoc Chau take hold of a national program for countryside recovery. Until his arrival in Saigon as national director of the Pacification Cadre Program, Chau was on his second assignment as Kien Hoa province chief.[12] Mark Huss, then with USAID, invited me to lunch with Chau. Three years earlier I was so unformed and uninformed that it was no surprise Chau did not remember our previous brief meeting in Ben Tre. Chau briefly reviewed the essence of his approach: involving local people to solve local problems (including lack of security) by organizing teams to identify grievances and take steps for reform. His teams targeted individual communists, but only as a last resort. I thought the description of what he had tested in Kien Hoa, and wanted to apply nationally, was complementary to what Nguyen Be was trying in Binh Dinh. The approach they took made more sense than any of the ineffective post–strategic hamlet paper exercises. I expressed my appreciation to Chau for meeting him again, but told him I expected to return to central Viet Nam as soon as possible. I stressed that he couldn't have more understanding and supportive friends than John Vann and Ev Bumgardner.

After lunch I went to the Ministry of Rural Development and found

John and Ev in the office building behind the main ministry.[13] They were excited about prospects for this new government effort focused on programs in the countryside. They described the new minister, Gen. Nguyen Duc Thang, as the perfect "ministerial umbrella" for Chau, an understanding general officer with support from Prime Minister Nguyen Cao Ky. He would assure that Chau's initiatives were acceptable to senior echelons of the government. I was, maybe habitually, somewhat skeptical. I knew Thang was considered one of the completely honest, financially clean, incorruptible generals, but I doubted he understood hamlet reality.[14] I reminded Ev about Nguyen Be's experience with the national PAT program, wherein he was expected to be the grateful beneficiary and administrator of a CIA operation. When Be took steps to nationalize and provincialize (in Binh Dinh) the program for local relevance, he encountered resistance, with only Kelly as interlocutor and supporter. I supposed that Chau, to whom both Ev and John felt strong attachment, was at risk for being thought by powerful others as simply administrator of a CIA/ministry program that needed no adjustment.

On the next day, Saturday, 15 January 1966, Phil Werbiski, Huddleston, and I completed the paperwork required to place all USIS special cadre, including friends from the Long An hamlet survey, Quang Ngai commando program, and more recent activities with the 5th Special Forces Group. This measure provided them with organizational and payroll protection while assuring, Phil and Hud promised, that they would continue to be available to work with Ev and me as needed. Late in the day Phil went to the main PX to purchase a tape deck system, while I went in search of Vietnamese friends. We didn't meet until the following afternoon, when Phil brought his new purchases to Doug Ramsey's place so that Doug could give him a quick introduction to system connection and operation and recommend additional items for enhanced performance. In the evening we met with the Vietnamese cadre, and all, including Doug, went to dinner at a restaurant between Saigon and Cholon. The next day, Monday, 17 January, Phil and Hud left early in the morning for Nha Trang, where they planned to meet with the Project Delta (Detachment B-52) commander, Charlie Beckwith. Doug returned to Hau Nghia province, where he was USAID representative in replacement of Vann. I stayed in Saigon to touch base in JUSPAO and spend another night with Kim Vui. I expected to return to Qui Nhon on the following day.[15]

When John found me Tuesday morning and reported that Doug had been captured the previous afternoon, he could only be described as profoundly shaken and really pissed that I was unreachable until the next morning. Vann was intensely loyal to people who worked with him, and that applied in double portion to Ramsey, with whom he had shared field duty in Hau Nghia and who had replaced him in that province. Furthermore, when you were John's friend, you were expected to be available on short notice. By the time he caught me, John was hopping with unexpended energy.

We immediately went to Bao Trai and consulted with the province chief. His assessment was not encouraging, but Vann, to his credit, was irrepressible. He activated messages to contacts in rural areas, people who knew him, describing Doug's work to provide assistance in hamlets and asking for help in obtaining his release. We returned briefly to Saigon. John worked USAID and embassy channels for approval and support for an unorthodox attempt to recover Doug. He got authorization for a trade, in effect ransom, that would include medical supplies for distressed civilians. Sam Wilson and George Jacobson arranged availability of an Air America helicopter on standby in case a pickup could be arranged. While John was pushing to get what he believed would be necessary, I spoke with General Freund and got his concurrence for working with Vann. Then I went out to Tan Son Nhut and, very Vann-like, leaned on a friend to take me on a short hop for an aerial view of the Trung Lap area where Doug had been captured. I was not optimistic. Just beyond Trung Lap isolated hamlets were replaced by plantation and jungle that swept, like a green sea, all the way past the Michelin plantation onward to the Cambodian border. I sensed that Doug was probably long gone, but, knowing the extensive kin relationships and Vietnamese skill in coping with ambiguous situations, I did think there was some chance to make a trade.

Most of the Special Forces cadre who spent the weekend in Saigon had already dispersed to assignments. All of the remainder volunteered to accompany John and me into Hau Nghia. On Wednesday the 19th I selected two, Nguyen Thanh and Do Dinh Duyet, to accompany John and me while we explored possibilities in Hau Nghia. Don Besom, a USIS Foreign Service officer with JUSPAO field operations responsibility for Hau Nghia, also wanted to come with us. We welcomed his company as an additional shooter in case of need.[16] We all stayed, crowded, in the small Bao Trai

USOM house. During the next three days we were in and out of several hamlets. Our two Vietnamese cadre friends could be off in one direction, while John, Don, and I went to Hiep Hoa and the surrounding area. We drove in John's personal vehicle, a small white, obviously civilian sedan, on provincial and interhamlet dirt roads. Gold star SVNLF flags were planted on both sides of Highway 1. Over the provincial route to Hiep Hoa there was an elaborate bamboo arch, almost an "arc de triomph," surmounted by three flags and a large poster of Ho Chi Minh. In hamlets just outside Bao Trai we saw young men, by dress and demeanor obvious SVNLF boys on leave, who frowned or glared. We ran into an attempted ambush, John, Don, and I, on the provincial road by So Do hamlet, probably only three kilometers from Bao Trai. The grenade I threw over the sedan roof, and the cloud of dust as John accelerated, provided conditions for escape. On the final day of our effort, John, Thanh, Duyet, and I reached a small hamlet north of Phuoc Hiep, in the direction where Doug had probably been led. John and I took tea with hamlet leaders and their holiday guests and weathered SVNLF cadre who seemed surprised but Tet-tolerant of our presence. I made the case for Doug's release, and in response a note was passed to me that confirmed his capture and detention until (as I interpreted the text) hostilities were over.

We had gone as deeply into the Hau Nghia countryside as feasible. We believed, based on what we were told, that Doug was alive, but he was no longer in the area.[17] The extent of SVNLF public presence in the area was impressive, more extensive and visible than I had expected. We were witnessing political action energized from within hamlets and districts by communist cadre rather than typical and anemic GVN directives from the ministries and province downward. We saw on Hau Nghia roads and in hamlets, late in January 1966, striking evidence of SVNLF presence and acceptance and GVN irrelevance.

Returning to Saigon, John and I parted. He appeared burdened by heavy regret that Doug might have been captured because he, John, had not stayed longer in Hau Nghia. I told him that, although we all cared for each other, encouraged each other, and helped when we could, bad luck or adverse circumstances could take any of us down. I believed this, and I think that he did, too, but even the obvious did not comfort him. I sought out his good friend Jake Jacobson and suggested he keep an eye on John, lest he have an Air America helicopter drop him off north of the Michelin for making a solo effort to bring Doug back. I was serious. That's how Vann seemed to me.

I went to JUSPAO to report lack of success and to let General Freund know that I was returning to Binh Dinh, where he could continue to contact me through Major Gomez. General Freund was not in the office, but his deputy, Bob Delaney, absolutely accosted me in the central reception area, almost screaming, "You've been on thin ice!" At first I wasn't sure of his meaning. Nobody needed to tell me how thin the ice was in Hau Nghia, but his attitude was accusative of operating illegitimately. So I calmly, for me, replied that my time in Hau Nghia had been cleared with General Freund. That further provoked him: "The general isn't running JUSPAO, not yet anyway." We were just short of coming to blows, which would have been a pleasure for me but a one-way ticket home rather than enduring satisfaction. I only said, "Well if you are ever captured, you should hope someone will care enough to look for you." It was several months before we spoke again.

Aware of Vann's emotional state, it didn't occur to me that I was having my own peculiar response. I went from the JUSPAO office to the home of Kim Vui, the woman whom I loved. She was holding court with musicians and artists. I took her by the hand and led her into the kitchen. I told her that we wouldn't be seeing each other again, that I could not divide myself between the provinces and Dalat/Saigon. Our lives were on roads too far apart. She wept and I left. I went to the 8th Aerial Port at Tan Son Nhut and caught a C-130 that was going up to Nha Trang.

What the hell had I just done? For the past two years she had been kind, loving, not insistent, and she came twice to provinces so we could have time together. She knew most of my friends, and I knew many of hers. She had brought me into her family. I learned something about Viet Nam from her. Now I had hurt her deeply. At the time I did not understand that my uncompromising quixotic impulse, extreme rededication to the field, was reaction not just to a friend's capture but also to the contrast between people suffering in the war and my own relatively comfortable life. Months later, when I thought about the timing, I realized how irrational we might be, even while counseling others to stay steady. We all make mistakes in our professional and personal lives, and this is one I will regret to my last breath.

I found Huddleston. He wanted to hear about how John and I ran around Hau Nghia chasing information about Doug. After describing how disturbed John was feeling, I admitted maybe having a reaction myself. All I wanted to do now was auger in where the war was fought. The best place for me was back in Binh Dinh, supporting Nguyen Be's effort in hamlets, but if there were opportunities to hitch on to US or Korean operations, I would do that, too. Hud told me some locally trained instructor cadre were assisting Be in reorienting teams returned from Vung Tau training, and several others were available to work with Special Forces. He said he would come up to Binh Dinh once in a while.[18]

So at the end of January I was profoundly disturbed but at home again, back in Binh Dinh, but a Binh Dinh that was being punished. Friendly forces were beginning to get a grip on the Vinh Thanh Valley, but the toughest spots would be the three districts of An Lao (An Lao Valley), Hoai An (Kim Son Valley), and Hoai Nhon (Bong Son–Tam Quan Plain).[19] Late on 27 January three Delta (Detachment B-52) teams were inserted into the An Lao Valley to assess and provide intelligence for a 1st Air Cav brigade that intended to operate there. Right from the start the Delta teams were struggling to survive. The situation swiftly changed from insertion for reconnaissance to need for extraction. Coordinating support from the cavalry was difficult. The Special Forces team at Bong Son got a helicopter to mount an ad hoc effort that rescued some, but it resulted in a life-threatening wound to B-52 Detachment commander Charles Beckwith. Delta was shaken, with dead, wounded, missing in action, and the detachment commander now lodged in the intensive care unit at the 85th MASH at Qui Nhon.[20]

This was the beginning of an extended operation initially (and accurately) named Masher but later renamed White Wing to reflect pacification correctness. By either name the conduct of operations extended through 6 March. Air support consisted of more than one thousand strikes and more than a thousand tons of bombs. Napalm was widely employed. I never got figures on artillery, but I suppose research could provide figures for cannon fire. Almost three hundred Americans were killed and more than nine hundred wounded. The 1st Air Cav reported about thirteen hundred PAVN and SVNLF killed, and the Koreans and ARVN claimed to have killed several hundred more. I could not obtain figures for civilians killed or wounded and homes destroyed, but thousands fled the fighting to take shelter in refugee camps. Although there were MACV rules of engagement, my impression was that once a US unit established contact, those rules went out the window. When GVN clearance was sought, approval would invariably follow. The GVN tendency, knowing arrival of US forces had saved their bacon, was to avoid questioning American operational conduct.[21]

At the beginning of February 1966 a conference of subsector advisors was called in Qui Nhon. Americans in districts were sympathetic to (and dependent on) RF and PF. Their comments were revealing. Training needed to be strengthened. The leadership factor was most important, even though family benefits and pay procedure was sloppy. The predisposition of RF and PF soldiers to go absent without leave (AWOL) was a persistent problem. Forcing PF to serve as RF yielded poor results. I looked at RF training in the Phu Cat Training Center. AWOL was common, especially for trainees from Binh Dinh. At the end of January, from a total of 811 RF in the camp, 165 were AWOL on 27 January. Of those AWOL, 150 were from Binh Dinh. Capt. Harry Johnson was the Binh Dinh sector RF/PF advisor. He said the problem in the training camp was that instructors themselves did not stay overnight. The commander was not effective, and there was no discipline, no gate, no pass system.[22]

My attention shifted to observing Korean and American operations in mid- to late February. When not with cadre instructors or Nguyen Be's hamlet development teams, I looked for friendly units in contact.[23] Hud was up to check on me so often that he seemed to be always just coming or just leaving. Ev, informed by him, came to Binh Dinh for a couple of days and asked me to rein back and focus more on the psychological aspect of "pacification." When Hud was next with me while accompanying an operation in Phu My (where we saw incredible bravery by PAVN soldiers), he said, "I know why you're doing this; it's because you don't have to." That strangely made sense.

Billy McKeithe was assigned to us from Delta after the disaster in An Lao Valley. We were together for a few weeks, working out of the Vinh Thanh Special Forces camp. Most of the CIDG were brought into the valley from two refugee camps. Their lives were dismal. Our instructional cadre sought to motivate them for defense of the valley that was their original home. We taught that whatever else happened anywhere in Viet Nam, they could take responsibility for defending their own land. We took questions about corruption, and our cadre replied that the problem resulted from appointing officials who were not accountable to local people. "Win the war in Vinh Thanh and then you can keep the corruptors out of the valley, too."

I began to refocus on the political aspect of war in the countryside. As I did so, the frenzy that had affected me since Doug's capture slowly subsided. As I stabilized, Billy McKeithe was also emotionally processing his recent An Lao experience. Talking with Billy helped place my own experience of a captured friend, and failure to recover him, in comparative perspective. Billy and his team were running for their lives, almost from the moment of insertion, and three of the six members were quickly killed. Billy's steadiness helped balance me. Our cadre took to him like a brother returned to family. He and Tran Huu Tri were soon close friends. In mid-March we prepared to depart Vinh Thanh to increase support to Nguyen Be's work in the expanding "pacification" area. When we lifted from beyond the camp perimeter, our helicopter crashed, rolled over, and finished upside down. I remember a quick thought as we rolled: "Twenty-seven years old, and gone." But I was wrong. I wasn't finished. We pulled survivors back to the trench we had vacated. Billy had a broken collarbone but was in good spirits. Much later we were lifted out to Qui Nhon.[24]

After sorting out who required hospitalization or other medical treatment, and allowing all others twenty-four hours' leave, I went to see Major Gomez to check on messages. I was told to call Saigon right away. Of course Ev was the person I wanted to speak with. After I brought him up to date on completion of the mission in Vinh Thanh and the crash, I described an opportunity to work with Nguyen Be pushing fifty-nine-man rural construction teams onto the Bong Son Plain for salving damage caused by the Masher/White Wing operation. Ev replied that we could talk about that possibility later, but he had an immediate task as higher priority. He said CBS was sending a team to look at pacification in Binh Dinh province. Ev explained there were really only a couple of places where pacification worked at local direction; one had been Kien Hoa (but Tran Ngoc Chau had already been brought to Saigon in December and was having "conceptual" difficulty with CIA), and the other was Binh Dinh and Major Be. He said the consensus of Tom Donahue, Lansdale, Vann, and himself was to recommend Binh Dinh.[25] Charles Collingwood would be the face and voice for a special one-hour production, and he was accompanying the team. "Take them right into the hamlets, protect them, assure their security, but unobtrusively." I let Ev know that I understood it would be a setback if Charles Collingwood got whacked in the middle of a hamlet undergoing pacification.

Just as I knew Saigon had little knowledge or understanding of what happened even twenty kilometers from the capital, I was likewise insulated in Binh Dinh. Ev surprised me by mentioning, almost casually, that Nguyen Chanh Thi had been removed a few days earlier from I Corps command. Sympathetic antigovernment demonstrations erupted in Hue and Danang in spring 1966. Ev told me Thi was allowed to return to Danang for stabilizing the situation. "But you stay away. Collingwood and the CBS team arrive tomorrow, and that is your immediate responsibility."

I went to see Nguyen Be to discuss the CBS project: where to bring them, how to arrange security, and the important role that he would have to play. We decided to place the CBS team to the north side of Ky Son Ridge about twelve kilometers (as the whirlybird flies) from Qui Nhon and five kilometers from Tuy Phuoc district. The CBS team could observe rural recovery ongoing in Xuan My and My Trung. An enhanced Nghia Quan platoon would cover the area to the west. One RF company would cover from Loc Le through Tuan Le, and Be planned to place a fifty-nine-person rural construction team in Tu Thuy close to the road that led to Go Boi. We believed that placement and frequent checks would keep the area peaceful as long as needed. Be felt that our arrangements were not absolutely necessary, but advisable insurance.

I asked him what he knew of the political problem involving Thi, Buddhists, the Saigon government, and Americans. He had a pretty clear picture of what had occurred. Friends sent him letters from Hue, Danang, and Saigon. He summarized by offering his opinion that Thi had offended Ky, Thieu, and other influential generals with frequent accusations of systemic corruption. Thi advocated appointing civilians to provincial leadership, and that threatened breaking the chain of corruption that corps and division commanders exercised through influence over appointments. Be felt that, although Buddhists were disappointed by Thi's not having offered them stronger support in the past year, they still thought of him as the least objectionable general and the only one who understood their commitment to national and local elections.[26]

Be agreed with the need for exterminating corruption, because he understood the phenomenon was an advertisement for the SVNLF cause, and in particular because it was recently prevalent in Binh Dinh. There was a new province chief in Binh Dinh. Le Trung Tuong had been reassigned to Pleiku on the II Corps staff. The announced reason for this transfer was that with so much action in Binh Dinh, the II Corps commander, Gen. Vinh Loc, wanted someone at his corps headquarters who was familiar with the ground situation. However, we soon learned that the new province chief, Lt. Col. Tran Dinh Vong, had no qualifications other than being a Vinh Loc family relative.[27] There was always money to be made from corrupt inefficiencies and lack of inspection that characterized GVN civil and military administration. But in Binh Dinh there were a couple of dramatically new and lucrative opportunities. Not all, but a significantly high percentage, of the logistics for the 1st Cav and the Korean Division arrived through the Qui Nhon port. The Han Jin (Korean) truck company had a contract for transportation, and manifests ceased at the dock. The second opportunity, and one that most outraged Nguyen Be, was construction in 1966 of a new airbase in Phu Cat, with funding to reimburse families who would be displaced. It would appear, by the number of names listed, that the affected hamlets were the most densely populated in all Viet Nam.

We met the arriving CBS team at the airfield. Charles Collingwood was friendly and began conversing with Nguyen Be about Binh Dinh province history and pacification problems. Bernie Birnbaum (almost immediately nicknamed "Burning Napalm" by Tran Huu Tri) was the program producer, P. B. Hoan was the sound technician, and my friend Ha Thuc Can was cameraman.[28] Pretty soon I was showing them a map on which the program area was circled, and then I learned we had one conceptual disagreement. I liked Maj. Nguyen Be as the story focus, because his maverick style and stand against corruption made him vulnerable to attack by GVN snakes. Positive portrayal on American network television might provide some protection. My reservation had to do with the working title for the program: "The Other War."

I expressed my opinion that the notion of positing "the war" (presumably the big battlefield war) and then "the other war" was a mistake, because it implied that one was prime and the other secondary. The Communist Party, I said, understood there was just one war, but multidimensional and multifaceted. At different times and in different places one aspect might be emphasized more than another, but the guiding principle is that everything is intended to have political impact. Collingwood was a patient listener, but he finally replied that conveying understanding of the over-all unity of war in Viet Nam would need yet another separate program. Their charge right now was to come back with a TV special that addressed "pacification." Well, it was their initiative, their money, and Be needed the favorable exposure, so when the program aired later that spring, it was "The Other War."

I returned to Saigon for a few days in late March and discussed Binh Dinh circumstances with friends in the embassy and elsewhere in the US mission. John Vann described the difficulty that he and Tran Ngoc Chau were experiencing with CIA's relationship to the rural development program. General Thang was expecting Chau to administer a program already acceptable to Prime Minister (de facto) Nguyen Cao Ky and the American Embassy. Chau thought he was brought up from Kien Hoa to replicate what was already proven in that province. There were two prin-cipal points of contention. The first was, according to John, that the CIA wanted the teams to be basically the former PAT format (evolved from the 1964 Quang Ngai commandos), with enhancement of six to ten men for pacification work, for a total strength of about fifty. Chau wanted each team to have the strength of eighty, with much more emphasis placed on hamlet political, economic, and social development.[29] John said there might be embassy compromise at fifty-nine. I smiled and told John he should let Chau know the compromise was based on what Nguyen Be applied in Binh Dinh after his own dispute with CIA.

The second point of contention was less specific but as important to Chau. He found the Cat Lo training center (Vung Tau) was both less and more than what it was represented to be. It was less Vietnamese in ap-pearance than it should have been, and Americans were less informed about instructional content than they should have been. The camp was more than it appeared in that some Dai Viet tint was applied to instruc-tion without the knowledge of the CIA advisors, who spoke no Vietnam-ese. When Chau moved down to Vung Tau to exert personal control, "the turkey stuffing hit the fan," as John put it. There was a "vest pocket revolt," he said, that only Chau's leadership skill and Sauvageot's timely reporting managed to resolve. John thought Chau had worn himself out contending with both Americans and General Thang.[30]

Chau's predicament, as described by John, caused me to think about my own situation. I was a USIS officer in JUSPAO, but atypical of USIA. The three who best understood what I could do were Ev Bumgardner, General Freund, and Barry Zorthian. But Ev was returning to Washington for a domestic assignment, General Freund expected to receive a brigade command, and Barry had so many responsibilities that we had limited contact. I was anathema to both USIA officers above me on the organization chart, who hated my taking direction from General Freund rather than them.[31] General Freund suggested considering a direct commission into the army. He discussed the possibility with General Westmoreland and brought some forms for me to fill out. I went before a panel of officers who examined my experience and qualifications, and I was cleared for commissioning as a lieutenant. All I needed to do was sign the papers.

Lieutenant Colonel Bennett and Capt. Gordon Huddleston (recently promoted) intervened.[32] Expecting that friends in Special Forces would applaud my decision to enter the army, I went to the TOC on Pasteur Street to look for, above all, Phil Werbiski, but he was at the C-5 camp, Ho Ngoc Tao, in Thu Duc district.[33] Deputy Group Commander John Bennett was in his office, and I shared my news with him. He was startled but recovered quickly and got my promise to have dinner with him and Huddleston that evening. We went to a European-style restaurant in Khanh Hoi, just over the Trinh Minh Bridge.[34] Colonel Bennett made three points in counseling me to stay "semicivilian." First of all, I had been providing direction for captains and counseling field-grade officers. Accepting commission as a lieutenant didn't recognize my field accomplishment at a higher grade. Second, Special Forces was not a career branch, so I could be tossed around as the army saw fit and might wind up "riding in a tin can on the desert at Fort Hood." And finally, although aggravated by two civilian officers above me on the JUSPAO organizational table, I shouldn't assume that the same situation doesn't occur in uniformed service. "You might just exchange one for another." Huddleston added, "As long as you're with JUSPAO, we feel we can reach out and get your help more responsively than if you're a lieutenant somewhere."

Without citing the career coaching provided by Colonel Bennett, the next day I informed General Freund that I had reconsidered alternatives and decided to stay with the civilian Foreign Service. He told me General Westmoreland would be disappointed and that the recommended grade for entry might be reevaluated to captain. I replied that his interest was appreciated, and grade had been a consideration, but not the only one. He shook my hand then and concluded, "Well, you could have had a place in the army, unorthodox, but solid."[35]

I returned home to Binh Dinh and reengaged with Nguyen Be. We spent a couple of days around Ba Canh hamlet in the Dap Da (Stone Dam) area. This hamlet is located within the site of the former Cham principality of Vijaya. Of course the Cham were long gone, but I purchased a bronze spear point from a farmer. Major Be was having serious difficulty. His outspoken criticism of fraud in connection with the relocation fund for the Phu Cat Air Base, and his accusations of misappropriation and dishonest accounting and of corruption in the Qui Nhon port facility, all placed him in opposition to the 22nd Division commander, Nguyen Thanh Sang. One morning Major Be found me in Binh Khe district. He had been informed that an assassination team, with the acquiescence of Lieutenant Colonel Vong, was looking for him. We talked about what to do. I suggested he leave his jeep at the district headquarters. If this was a false alarm we could return for it the next day. Meanwhile, we should go to Qui Nhon in my jeep; he could make inquiry and then determine a course of action.

We went to the JUSPAO office and used the telephone to contact friends in province police and at the 22nd Division liaison office. Unhappily, he received confirmation his life was at risk, not from communists but from corrupt forces within his own government. We talked about options and agreed he had best get to Pleiku and bring his own account of what was happening direct to Gen. Vinh Loc, the II Corps commander. Of course we both recognized that Vinh Loc was complicit in the chain of corruption, but face to face with Be it was most likely that Vinh Loc would provide protection rather than appear to be part of an assassination scheme. I described the situation to Maj. Charles Francis, commander of the army aviation side of the Qui Nhon airfield. He agreed to provide a special flight to Pleiku. I brought Be to the airfield, concealed under a poncho liner in the back of my jeep, and we went straight to the airplane where Major Francis was waiting.

The next day I went to Pleiku and obtained an appointment with Gen. Vinh Loc.[36] His disdain for plateau hill tribes and dalliance with a Saigon singer were well known. He understood that I was not the usual uninformed American. Being brief and direct without being accusatory, I told him any investigation would show a level of corruption in Binh Dinh that betrayed the national interest by allowing communists to claim comparative virtue. Involvement of the 22nd Division commander and province chief would probably be proven. The corps commander could demonstrate his own honesty by protecting Major Be and assigning a new 22nd Division commander. My concern, I assured him, was for his own good reputation. That was duplicitous, perhaps, but for a good cause, and I left the corps headquarters without seeking Major Be so that if my visit were mentioned to him, he would be genuinely surprised.[37]

I returned to Binh Dinh and from Qui Nhon flew north to I Corps and surreptitiously spoke with Nguyen Chanh Thi. The atmosphere in Danang and Hue was tense. Although (de facto) Prime Minister Ky and Chief of State Thieu had on 14 April pledged to hold elections for a constituent assembly, Buddhist leadership and citizens in general were mistrustful. Thi thought that if honest elections were held, a new government might restore him to command, possibly even as minister of defense. He believed the most urgent need was to purge corrupt military officers from national service. Corruption could not be tolerated, because an officer was supposedly a capable combat officer. He said that in fact he could name many corrupt officers, but not a single one who was both corrupt and an effective commander.[38] He summarized the overall situation as stabilizing based on the expectation elections would be held.

Thinking that May 1966 would be a period characterized by the government's accommodation of elections, I returned to Binh Dinh and hamlets in An Nhon and Phu Cat that were still being worked by province teams Nguyen Be had fielded. I called down to Saigon, informing John Vann that Nguyen Be was in Pleiku, temporarily assigned as deputy province chief (for security) for Pleiku province, and told John that Be could be available to work in rural development if Tran Ngoc Chau approved. John said he would follow through on the suggestion.[39]

A few days later, back in Binh Khe district, I was surprised to learn that Prime Minister Ky had ordered troops to I Corps to suppress the movement that forced government acceptance of elections.[40] I surmised Ambassador Lodge might have encouraged Ky, because the principal consideration for the American Embassy always seemed to be "stability." The operation brought central Viet Nam close to civil war. Although the situation was most acute in I Corps, Qui Nhon and Binh Dinh in general, despite overwhelming presence of US and Korean forces, were also tense.

The Saigon government gradually gained full control of Danang, Hue, and Quang Tri, but there was smoldering resentment and definite estrangement from national governance.

I began to feel that one American's complete attachment to the field was not going to make much difference. I reconsidered the hasty, cruel, personal choice I had earlier forced upon Kim Vui. Ev sent me a message via Huddleston advising me that she was in Dalat, and I decided to seek her and ask forgiveness. Remembering cold showers at her villa, I scrounged, trading a few captured weapons and an SVNLF flag for a hot water heater at the army airfield in Qui Nhon. Huddleston helped me arrange a Caribou flight, as a navigation exercise, that would bring me to Nha Trang and then Dalat. If Kim Vui were responsive, then the same aircraft would fly us further to Saigon to meet with Ev and see a lawyer about necessary procedures for marriage. Hud flew with me and remained with the aircraft parked at Cam Ly while I delivered the heater as a preliminary to personal discussion. It was painfully clear that I was too late. I returned to Cam Ly, angry with myself. Hud wisely refrained from expressing consolation. Then followed a long flight back to Qui Nhon.

Into early June I continued alternately spending time with civil teams in hamlets and hitching on to operations conducted by ARVN, Korean, or US Forces. I just didn't care much whether I lived or died. The 1st Cav believed it was defeating the 3rd Gold Star (Su Doan Sao Vang) Division. And actually that was true, but repetitively, over and over. The 3rd, composed of the 2nd (possibly SVNLF) Regiment, 18th PAVN Regiment, and 22nd Regiment, established a recycling schedule wherein at any one time the regiment just smashed by Americans was withdrawing westward for reconstitution, the regiment previously battered was completing reorganization, and the third regiment would be moving forward to replace the one withdrawing. The process was not as smooth as the 3rd would have liked, but there was a formula, and year after year the 3rd was a predictable presence in northern Binh Dinh.[41]

I noticed that the typical American attitude toward the Vietnamese was callous disregard. Americans of all grades often joked about Vietnamese technology being defined by picking up one thing with two sticks or carrying two things with one stick. Xenophobic pride in American capability and culture obstructed consideration for Vietnamese. Even senior officers frequently made sarcastic comments about the odor of nuoc mam.[42] A derogatory definition of the South Viet Nam flag is too malicious to re-peat. Vietnamese, for their part (and perhaps in reaction), sometimes re-ferred to specific Americans (even when they knew that I overheard and understood) as *no* (thing or animal) or *thang* (child or inferior). We were allies who understood very little of each other.

11
Roles and Missions

I was feeling increasingly worn out, worn down, but attributed that fatigue to life on the run, perhaps complicated by my recent personal tailspin. Then one morning, while pissing in some bushes, I noticed my urine stream was coffee-colored. Whoa! I sought out a medic and asked him whether there was any explanation. He checked my eyes and replied, "Yeah, your liver is dissolving, and we're going to get you out of here." So, first by helicopter, then by C-130, I finally washed up in the US military hospital on Tran Hung Dao Street in Saigon and was placed in a ward where all the patients had hepatitis. An orderly sent a Thai nurse to clean me up and explain the rules. "No getting out of bed except to use the toilet. Eat everything provided. Ring a bell whenever you want ice cream." One of the other patients was almost pumpkin-colored. A patient died the second night I was there. I had been ignorant of the danger in hepatitis. I was lucky. On just the sixth day my blood cleared, so I was released the next day.

The embassy provided temporary housing in Saigon, which I shared with a USAID officer. I was weak—terribly and uncharacteristically weary. It required conscious, directed effort just to get up from a chair. Friends came to visit and distract me from the depression of being housebound. I learned from them that Nguyen Chanh Thi had returned to Saigon from Danang and Hue but was under close surveillance.[1] The only good news was that Thieu and Ky reiterated on 20 June that there would be elections in September 1966 for a constituent assembly. People expressed some skepticism as to how open and fair those elections would be.[2]

I wasn't fit for the field, the field environment as I understood it. Huddleston came by, amused at my predicament, and we discussed allocating several of the experienced Special Forces instructional cadre to work with Nguyen Be at the Vung Tau training complex. Phil Werbiski also wanted some of them to be assigned to work with him at the C-5 Ho Ngoc Tao camp. So I was comforted by the illusion that, despite illness, I was still somewhat relevant.

Barry sent a note asking me to see him. He revealed that George (Jake) Jacobson was going to do a review of roles and missions in Viet Nam, and Jake had asked that I be assigned to work with him. For the past several months I had, in fact, been observing and evaluating the roles of elements operating in Binh Dinh, so I believed myself ready to contribute.[3]

I energized sufficiently to go see Jake in his office. Up until now we had not worked together. I had a better feel for Sam Wilson, and of course John, but Sam, John, and Jake were often in league with each other, so we were comfortable for having that context. Jake allowed that he knew I was recuperating from hepatitis knockdown but said the first few days would be organizational anyway. He asked whether I knew of PROVN, a study prepared in DOD, and he seemed surprised that I did. I explained that "Harnessing the Revolution" had circulated in Washington a year earlier (and I knew from Vann that Jake had brought copies to friends in DOD when on leave in July 1965) and was reviewed by the PROVN group, and John had shared their reaction with me. "I might have known," was his response.[4]

Jake indicated a telephone directory–sized chunk of paper on his desk and said, "There it is. Want to take a look?" It looked too heavy for someone like me who needed maximum effort just to get up from a chair. I asked whether he had read the whole thing. Jake had looked at what he believed were the most important sections. He added that PROVN began by looking at the environment in which pacification had to be applied and concluded that the US needed to improve management structure for all forms of support provided to the GVN. The focus of PROVN, Jake told me, was that US and ARVN efforts should be in securing the population rather than lunging out in search of main force SVNLF (and PAVN) units.[5]

There had been a general feeling, accelerated by President Johnson's comments at the Honolulu Conference in February 1966, that more had to be done—economic, social, and political—in rural Viet Nam.[6] But there was no agreement in Washington or Saigon as to what was involved and what measures needed to be adopted. Jake said that earlier in the spring, while I was in Binh Dinh, Deputy Ambassador William J. Porter was tasked by Ambassador Lodge to be coordinator for pacification, but it was a grandiose title for amorphous authority. Lodge, Jake said, wouldn't really delegate more than fictive responsibility. Col. Sam Wilson (of the Jacobson, Vann, Wilson triumvirate) was placed in a new position, mission coordinator.

Jake described his charge, a US mission roles and missions study, as something different. It would not be a response to or elaboration of PROVN, but a completely fresh examination in a timely manner. I suggested that, in order to preclude our study from being seen as a reaction, he not show PROVN to any of the persons selected as team members.[7] Moreover, I went on, I knew the DOD group felt "Harnessing the Revolution" erred in suggesting three provinces for trial rather than applying a solution for the whole country. And I felt the most obvious PROVN weakness was that it had taken a full year for study before its conclusions were presented. It lacked timeliness. So I suggested that Jake make sure his license was catholic, with nothing immune from examination; have recommendations for applicability countrywide; and deliver the product within a six-week window. Jake in turn advised me that, on advice of John, he would expect me to advocate realistic assessment and vigorous debate but commit to bringing sensitive issues to him for private discussion.

We were assigned a conference room in the USAID II building. USAID also provided an administrative secretary, Esther Arguinez, to assist Jake in keeping the project organized and sensitive material, including notes, under control.[8] We took, at Jake's direction, three approaches to the task before us. Although each member selected for the study group had experience in Viet Nam, we made in-depth field trips by small teams of two or three persons. We were not a traveling circus. Second, we devised and sent to province advisory teams a detailed questionnaire. And third, we debated, exchanged observations, and argued among ourselves to conclusions on a broad range of the elements engaged in pacification.

My own travel was first to Binh Thuan with Steve Ledogar, a State Department officer on detail to AID. We confirmed that the actual situation in that province, a low priority for both SVNLF and the GVN, was not as positive as official reporting indicated. This wasn't surprising to me, and Steve's experience also convinced him that, given human reluctance to appear negative on paper, a person would be more inclined to candor when you shared a night on his ground.[9] The second province, visited with Lt. Col. Bill Young of MACV, was Quang Ngai. We were with Nguyen Duy Be for a day, seeing one of the original Quang Ngai units in Nghia Hanh district, and then we drove to the Son My area in Son Tinh district, where families were returning to hamlets recovering from the 1965 through spring 1966 fighting.[10] Dan Ellsberg (still with Lansdale's liaison team at that point) and I made a short visit to Hau Nghia, a province that seemed untouched by GVN attention and was still SVNLF-ascendant. Finally, Pat Patty from the embassy, Bill Stubbs (USIS officer on detail to the embassy), and I went to Long An province. We took special interest in the dysfunctional relationship of numerous US and GVN intelligence organizations. I brought Pat and Bill to Vinh An hamlet, where they spoke with residents to obtain a firsthand understanding of what had occurred, and was still ongoing, in Long An. Other team members in varied combinations visited so many provinces that Jake had to reel us back for discussion of the replies to our province questionnaire.

The responses varied depending on circumstances of the province itself and the composition of the American advisory team. Careful examination and analysis helped us identify broad areas of field agreement that supplemented our own individual experience, our recent field trips together, and the beginning of debate in our conference room.

We were all pledged to objectivity and independence of thought, but it would be unrealistic not to acknowledge institutional or personal predilection. Each of us had been in Viet Nam for one to four years. Jake himself totaled twelve years in-country. Three of us spoke fair Vietnamese. Dan Ellsberg's thinking was, like John Vann's, considerably influenced by conversation with Tran Ngoc Chau. Lt. Col. Bill Young, a straight arrow all the way, would have been conflicted if inquiry were broadened (not to be the case) to include the impact, positive and negative, of US and Korean military operations on pacification. Steve Ledogar and Bill Stubbs, I thought, had less predisposition than any of the rest of us. Pat Patty would have been in a bind if the study group returned recommendations that were contrary to station policy. Jake's intent, as chief of the interagency group, and responsible to the ambassador, was to deliver a report with recommendations that could induce change absent any hand-grenade effect.[11]

More than anyone else, except perhaps Jake, I had my own agenda for weaving into study group deliberations: First, I wanted inclusion of national elections at all levels of governance as the indispensible engine for noncommunist political development. Second, I wanted a group recommendation of joint or at least combined command to get a handle on RVNAF personnel decisions so that the best would be assigned and promoted rather than the family- and crony-connected.[12] And third, I still wanted what I called "encadrement"—inclusion of Vietnamese with US units and Americans with Vietnamese units. Despite knowing that some Mission Council members were ambivalent about elections, and despite MACV's having vetoed combined command and encadrement more than a year earlier, I thought the roles and missions review opened a door for reconsideration.

I struck out right away on my first preference. I had committed to Jake for bringing sensitive issues front and center to him for personal discussion. Jake explained it was tricky enough dealing with information flow for the ambassador without exciting him about elections beyond those already promised for an assembly in September. On my personal second and third wants, Jake encouraged me to make my case with the group, but be advised I would be "paddling upstream against COMUSMACV current."

How did my effort fare? Not well with respect to joint or at least combined command. The group, following vigorous debate, concluded that high-level joint, or even combined, command would not be acceptable to Vietnamese for reasons of national pride and not acceptable for the American (MACV) side because of distaste for involvement in messy Vietnamese intrigue. I was bitterly disappointed, because I felt reform had to begin at the top, better and honest officers would accept binational responsibility, and to hell with those who wanted to perpetuate what was failing.

My third want, encadrement, obtained limited acceptance. One of the study recommendations was for combined operations, and Marine Corps "combined action companies" (before the nomenclature change to "combined action platoons") were specifically cited for emulation. That was a good beginning, but it was not possible to decide on wording requiring immediate CAP expansion for all PF platoons in every province. And although I recall mention of benefits accruing from Vietnamese soldiers with an American unit, we didn't get that option moved forward as an action recommendation.

So as far as my personal agenda went, my batting average was maybe .167. Swinging for the fence promoted intense group discussion but didn't get me on base. On other points, my input was conducive to group consensus on the need for change. Although we were constrained to use the term *revolutionary development* (because it reflected Ambassador Lodge's preference), that was not a term employed by Vietnamese and did not convey what might have been possible. The final report cited the difference between Vietnamese and American terminology. I wrote a three-page paper, at Dan Ellsberg's request, on the difference between revolution and reform, and in our group discussion I argued that reform needed to proceed vigorously, even harshly, if necessary, from the top down, with conspicuous punishment of parties who would not reform. This case for a corrective was included in the section discussing problem areas, and we painted a bleak picture of GVN prospects absent change: "There is a deadly correlation between corruption at high levels in an administrative system and the spread throughout the system of *incompetence*, as higher-ups encourage and promote corrupt subordinates, and protect them from the consequences of poor performance of duty or direct disobedience of orders. Such a system demoralizes and 'selects out' the able and the dedicated who do not play the game, and thwarts any attempts at reform initiated at intermediate levels. There is no escape from the requirement that reform, unlike revolution, must start at the top."[13]

I was disappointed we could not reference the devastating impact of US firepower on the countryside. It was recommended that the issue of the negative influence of air and artillery strikes on rural attitudes, and their adverse effect on "pacification," should be the subject of a separate study. We all understood this was a weak response to daily tragedy, but Jake ruled on this one. We had just had an argumentative meeting with DEPCOMUSMACV General Heinges in which he told us what ought not be within our purview. Jake felt we were going to have enough contentious recommendations without pushing an issue that could be separated out for later consideration.

We had a session with Col. Ted Serong,[14] who was fostering Police Field Forces. He wanted Police Field Forces to have a separate command organization, but we were going in a different direction. Our group concluded that RF and PF should be redesigned, trained, and fielded as province and district constabulary, with Police Field Forces integrated. We specifically mentioned that a constabulary police approach could provide advantage after a ceasefire. We also advised placing the new province and district constabulary within the Ministry of Rural Affairs rather than the Ministry of Defense. I thought Serong was correct about a need for rural police, but two years after helping initiate commando units in Quang Ngai, I also believed we should not continue proliferating special-purpose units.

And in that connection, we found that melding some of what Tran Ngoc Chau had done in Kien Hoa (counterterror teams) with what Kelly and I conceived in Quang Ngai (People's Commando teams), had also resulted in metamorphosis. Embryonic formations became People's Action Teams (PAT), Provincial Support Units (PSU), Armed Political Action (APA), and, eventually, Provincial Reconnaisance Units (PRU). For these other than RD Cadre groups, some commonality, without stifling local initiative, was required. And a GVN sponsor, a ministry or special branch, was desirable so this activity would not be unilaterally American.

Closely related to our recommendations for special-purpose units was conviction that we had to dramatically improve intelligence coordination. Although many of our advisable steps were politely ignored by agencies that would have been inconvenienced, this one was so obviously a need, and so suited to the direction that CIA needed to take, that it provided a small push toward district and province coordination that eventually led to beginning intelligence coordination and exploitation (ICEX) in June 1967, with province intelligence and operations centers (PIOCs) and district intelligence and operations coordinating centers (DIOCCs).

The advisability of each province chief's having operational control (OPCON) of all units within their province was basic to each study group member's individual experience and reinforced by our visits to provinces and the questionnaire responses. Revitalizing each Province Committee for Rural Development and reinstating the province committee sign-off for expenditures would also strengthen the province chief against importuning division and corps elements that sought diversion of resources. Unfortunately, those steps, which we all agreed were essential, were not meaningfully implemented.

The Roles and Missions Study provided a revealing portrayal of what was happening in Viet Nam in the summer of 1966. Some good recommendations were placed before the US mission for action. Were there any points with which I had personal disagreement on which I was outvoted? I remember three.

There was a recommendation for housing for RF/PF (eventually constabulary) dependents. I was sure that, while well-intentioned, that would simply result in those local forces exerting principal effort to protect their dependent area. Or, if tin roofing, concrete and rebar, and timber were provided for individual houses, then that would single out those families for reprisal or envy. "Just pay them much better," was my alternative.

CIDG camps, the report concluded, should only be located in remote areas where there was no base for recruitment. That recommendation was designed to preserve populated areas for RF and PF operations and recruiting. But I thought it would result in more A Shau Valley situations, in which the tribal presence was too resistant or slim to provide adequate numbers of CIDG, so dragnetted urban delinquents would be flown into distant camps with tragic consequences. If there was no recruitment potential, then there should be no camp (leaving aside the whole issue of camps themselves as Phil Werbiski, Huddleston, and I had discussed with Colonel Bennett).

The Roles and Missions Study Group endorsed "hamlet festivals" and "county fairs." A US, sometimes a US and ARVN, unit would surround a hamlet and cordon it from the outside, presumably trapping SVNLF agents or members inside. Hamlet residents would be removed from the hamlet for checking of ID cards and questioning by GVN officials. Vietnamese police and intelligence specialists would enter the hamlet and look for concealed SVNLF documents, persons, or weapons. I had seen several such events, and at about half of them an American military band from the parent unit played upbeat, happy tunes in the background. The rural families were penned and unhappy, but an illusion of meaningful counterinsurgent activity was established. I found the practice nauseating, and I couldn't understand why only one other (Bill Stubbs) agreed with me.

The recommendation to disband ranger units was one with which I reluctantly concurred. Some Vietnamese friends were rangers—good men like Tran Van Hai, just named commander of rangers, and Son Thuong, commander of the 39th Battalion (brutal but effective)—but I recognized a problem of overall unfavorable conduct. I thought the basic problem was the rangers' excessive dispersal and inadequate support, which led to a mentality that allowed them to treat civilians and prisoners meanly because "we are treated meanly." If the best ranger battalions were retained, but reorganized in a Ranger Division, like the Airborne Division and Marine Division, then flexible ranger task forces could be organized to deal with specific situations. The remainder of the ranger battalions could be assigned to stiffen CIDG camps with improved logistics or disbanded. I recognized this would require a major RVNAF reorganization. The worst case would be perpetuation of numerous uncoordinated, poorly supported, overcommitted bastard battalions, and that is what happened.

If one could have taken the best parts of the summer 1965 "Harnessing the Revolution," winter 1965/66 PROVN, and summer 1966 Roles and Missions Study for application with strong leadership, then we could have had more effective support to rural development and perhaps even political development one year before MACVCORDS was organized. But the determined leadership that the time and circumstances required was lacking. Instead, we suffered from fog and polite obstruction, polite in the sense that there was not so much argument as there was simple lack of cooperation. The Roles and Missions Study was predictive, in that there was a suggestion for a new DEPCOMUSMACV for advisory effort and revolutionary development.[15] Although this alarmed some civilian members of the mission, it did foretell a step taken (with modification) a year later.

At the end of August, Jake told me, when I made a respectful farewell, that MACV had just issued its own roles and missions statement in a message to the Joint Chiefs and CINCPAC. It was called something like "Concept for Operations in South Viet Nam." Jake described it as more a response to PROVN and rationalization of current practice than a fresh look at our challenge. I was due in Washington for China language and area study. Jake told me I could probably see a copy in Washington, but I replied that I doubted it would have much applicability for either China or Taiwan. "Oh, but you'll be coming back here, you'll see." We both laughed.

USIA had an experimental program for Chinese language and area studies, and Talbot Huey (my colleague from 1962 to 1963) and I would be the lab rats.[16] Rather than the usual enrollment at the Foreign Service Institute, we would enter the George Washington University language program and take a graduate-level course on contemporary China. Four years of Viet Nam intensity placed me out of kilter on the urban GWU campus. I found, unlike a year earlier, lots of discussion about the war, but not much interest in Viet Nam, country and people. Students would patiently listen to a description of Viet Nam's historical background and the complexity of an internal war. But when I stated my belief that there was nothing wrong (morally) with attempting to assist South Viet Nam to establish an independent identity, listeners would quickly bring the matter back to themselves: How will the war impact me?

So recent was my arrival in Washington that, imbued with fervor for hamlets and fresh from immersion in roles and missions, I felt a fiduciary responsibility to bring the inside story to friends' attention. "Harnessing the Revolution" was essentially an insurgent essay and had not received the higher-level consideration that it deserved. PROVN was shrugged off too easily by MACV. It should have been unacceptable for the Roles and Missions Study to be ignored. Robert Komer had been special assistant to the president for Viet Nam "pacification" since late March. Ambassador Bill Leonhart was his deputy, but the two most important members of his small staff were Dick Holbrooke and Lt. Col. Bob Montague.[17] I had known them both since 1963. I did not have a copy of the study with me but have always had a fine memory, so I shared my fresh recollection with people working in Washington. Hunger for new, relevant information presented the opportunity to build on what was in the formal report. There were always questions, and responding allowed me to advocate the broadest possible elections,[18] consideration of combined (if not joint) command, and encadrement. Jake guessed I was not confining myself to classrooms, as he wrote: "I am told that Ambassador Leonhart took a copy back to Mr. Komer's office. Either this is true or they got one from another source or you have been filling them in rather fully because cables have been shooting out this way."[19]

Gen. Nguyen Chanh Thi was living in a small apartment on Connecticut Avenue. Sam Wilson had seen to bringing Thi's three children to America.[20] They were in a Virginia boarding school, and we drove to visit them. On another occasion I brought Thi to visit West Point. In every conversation my friend was optimistic about his chances for returning home. He believed, despite his own prickly persona and poor relations with many general officers, there would be eventual recognition of the need for proven combat commanders. Without telling him and damping his spirit, I was less optimistic.

A good friend, Floyd Brown, made space in his apartment on Pennsylvania Avenue near Washington Circle. I could walk to classes at George Washington. Friends from Viet Nam, now posted to Washington, Fort Bragg, Fort Benning, or even farther, reached out for reconnection. Often they would reminisce about their assignment in Southeast Asia and express interest in returning.[21] Sometimes they referred others to me for discussion about Viet Nam. Helping people who wanted assignment to Viet Nam was easy for me to do by simply raising those interests with friends who could turn personnel wheels.

I was not comfortable at George Washington University. The language class was about twice the size of what was standard at FSI. I already knew some Chinese, understood the tonal aspect, and could pick up vocabulary quickly, because there were Chinese loan words, particularly economic, military, and political, introduced into Vietnamese during China's roughly one-thousand-year rule. The language teacher at GWU was teaching according to the Chao phonetic system rather than the Yale script or even Hanyu Pinyin. Since the Chao system gave tones by varying the spelling of syllables, whereas the Yale and Pinyin systems applied diacritics as necessary (like alphabetized Vietnamese), I felt the Chao phonetics were esoteric and a diversion from really learning Chinese.[22] Our teacher was equally disturbed when she checked my notebook and found that I was using Vietnamese to phonetically write Chinese.

Dennis Doolin, a visiting professor from Stanford, taught the graduate course on contemporary China.[23] Talbot and I thought the course text was so theoretical as to be divorced from the real China. We felt unrest in China, already obvious by the autumn of 1966, could be tracked back to 1964, when Beijing University was suspected of being insufficiently "red."[24] We pointed out that the textbook strikingly omitted description and analysis of the PLA (People's Liberation Army), even though the PLA would probably have to be used to hold the country together. Doolin actually agreed with us and said that we would cover the PLA during class discussion. When that happened, it was pretty much a conversation among the three of us, because the other graduate students were not experienced or well informed.

So in the fall of 1966 I was in Washington, out of Viet Nam, but with Viet Nam still in me. One day, while I was briefly visiting Dick Holbrooke in the Executive Office Building, he revealed that all the American civil agencies in Viet Nam were about to combine field elements.[25] He said the new organization would provide focus and improved coordination and facilitate implementing some of the Roles and Missions Study's recommendations. A couple of days later I had a brief discussion with Bob Komer, and in his usual assertive fashion he stated that I was wasting time in Washington when there was important work to be done in Saigon. He told me to think it over and, if willing to return, just send a personal note to Deputy Ambassador Porter, and the ball would start rolling from there. I had a premonition that if Komer took even casual interest in my return to Viet Nam, he would not be far behind.

When checking with the USIA personnel office concerning possible assignments after the two-year China study program, I was told candidly that a future assignment might be something like assistant cultural or information officer in Singapore, Hong Kong, or Taiwan. "After all," one personnel officer said, "we really didn't know what to do with you when you came back here in September."

So at the beginning of December I wrote a note to Porter. I remember saying (I did not keep a copy of the letter) that I could return if he thought it useful. The reassignment gears meshed swiftly. Dan Ellsberg heard I was returning and wrote a letter kindly suggesting we share the house assigned to him. My orders placed me with the Evaluations Branch of the still-forming Office of Civil Operations. I took a few days to see friends and family in Massachusetts. Dwight Owen, a college student, visited in my mother's house and asked about taking a summer job with USAID in Viet Nam. I encouraged him to seize that opportunity for field experience before continuing studies. Right after New Year 1967 I launched back over the Pacific. Jake was right, I was going back, and even more quickly than he could have guessed.[26]

12
Office of Civil Operations/MACVCORDS

One of the first persons I went to see after processing was, of course, Jake. He had license for a good-humored jab at my early return. Jake was the new mission coordinator, replacing Sam Wilson, who had transferred to Long An province to test, in person, the concept of a single-manager advisory team. Jake brought me up to date on the view, or at least his view, from Saigon. He said the mission approved 80 percent of the Roles and Missions Study's recommendations, but most were not really implemented. Jake told me the impetus for pulling all the civilian agencies together stemmed from the October Manila Conference, but he thought there must have been prior intent. He looked expectantly at me, as if I must have known something, having just arrived from Washington.

But I had no idea what Washington might be planning. And that was the total truth. I had not even been a fly on the wall during my four Washington months. However, I did share my impression that Robert Komer was not a patient man. He would expect results, not complicated explanations, and if the new OCO did not fire off to a fast start, then OCO as OCO would not survive. But, I added, better to have civilians in Viet Nam try to organize themselves before someone else did it for them.

Jake frowned. Usually outwardly ebullient, he didn't appear sure that a fast start for OCO was likely. I asked what he thought were obstacles to a unified civilian effort, and he simply replied, "Take a look, go see John, see Kelly, talk to your friends, and then let me know what you think."

The Office of Civil Operations was provided its own premises, the former USAID II building. Even physical proximity of civil elements working on provincial recovery was a giant step forward. There would be more informal discussion and exchange of ideas than previously. I was assigned to work for Paul Hare, a State Department officer on detail to OCO. He was chief of the Field Evaluations Branch and wanted to organize the office to produce reports that would be accurate and immediately relevant. He explained that the staff, just assembling, would travel extensively and submit reports for the highest levels of the US mission. Paul asked me to settle in quickly and get back to him with ideas on how best to proceed.

One difficulty was that other Americans coming on board as field evaluators lacked the kind of field experience that Jean Sauvageot and I had accumulated by going from hamlet to hamlet with small teams of Vietnamese. This meant that, even if their ability to speak Vietnamese was as good as ours, they didn't yet have the deftness for eliciting information from Mr. and Mrs. Rice Farmer. Fortuitously, my need to address an entirely different problem provided a way to strengthen the newly organizing evaluations branch immediately. Gordon Huddleston, still with 5th Special Forces Group, knew I was back, and he was looking for some help.

With Phil Werbiski and me both away from Viet Nam, Hud had in late 1966 inherited responsibility for the field cadre who worked with 5th Special Forces Group, and he still had concern for those who went to the Vung Tau training complex to work with Nguyen Be. Some of them had begun with USIS in the Long An Hamlet Survey and later worked with the Quang Ngai program, then in districts around Saigon with MACV and up in Binh Dinh and elsewhere with Special Forces. Despite casualties, we maintained the strength of this talented group at more than seventy, counting both Special Forces and Vung Tau components. When this sort of work under JUSPAO auspices was about to be concluded in the spring of 1966, we arranged for armed political instructional work, with associated personnel, to be acquired by Special Forces.[1] That step was taken with approval of Deputy Group Commander Bennett and Group Commander McKean.

In late June 1966, Huddleston explained to me, Colonel McKean completed his one-year tour and was replaced by Col. Francis J. "Splash" Kelly, previously 1st Group commander on Okinawa. When someone arrives in replacement of another, it is tempting to wire a few things differently just so all concerned will be aware there is a new person in charge. Something of that sort was operative in the 5th Group in the summer of 1966.

According to Hud, Colonel Kelly was eager to make a positive impression with General Westmoreland, so he wanted to shift the 5th Group entirely away from community development and into a combat role. Camps would continue to be fortified, and, beginning in II Corps, Mike Forces would be used as a "mobile guerrilla force" directed against communist sanctuary areas.[2]

I told Hud that we shouldn't be critical of the mobile guerrilla concept, because it sounded similar to what we had suggested to Colonel Bennett almost a year earlier, and maybe Colonel Bennett had a transition discussion with Col. Kelly. I suggested, "The whole camp issue is something best left alone." I also, for the first time, told Hud that when I had met Colonel Kelly the previous summer in Nha Trang (with Jake), my impression was that he was most concerned with the appearance of his office.[3] Despite that encounter, it did seem to me that Colonel Kelly was smartly making Special Forces more mobile as a strike force. Our difference would have been that his moving away from appreciation of political effect was not as sensible.

So then Hud got to the heart of his tracking me down. He presented a loose-leaf folder and opened it to the first item, a message from the commanding officer, 5th Special Forces Group, to all four corps special forces teams conveying his decision that, effective 15 January 1967, motivation indoctrination training would be discontinued, and training personnel would not be paid after that date. Colonel Kelly had first requested termination the previous July, after Colonel McKean departed, but MACV had refused because special cadre training was judged by MACV to be important support to "revolutionary development" and of value in disseminating information about the September election for a constituent assembly. The request was repeated on 24 October and approved by MACV on 12 December 1966.[4]

The solution to both our problems lay in determining how to transfer the best of our special cadre into the OCO Evaluations Branch and allocate others either to work with Nguyen Be or possibly to support John Vann in III Corps, where he was already OCO regional director. I knew John would be receptive because, during our attempt to retrieve Doug Ramsey, he had witnessed how our cadre could enter contested areas and acquire information. Nguyen Be was always in need of good instructional personnel. I only needed to convince Paul Hare that this was a tremendous opportunity to enhance Evaluation Branch potential. I told Hud not to worry, just temporarily move the cadre to Vung Tau, with Nguyen Be's approval, until arrangements could be made with Vann and others.

Paul immediately grasped the dynamic in joining American evaluators with experienced Vietnamese field operators who had demonstrated problem-solving skills. He told me to implement their hiring and entry into OCO as soon as possible. With Paul's support the necessary paperwork was processed in a few days. The only snag was that some of our people were former SVNLF, and I had to explain why we were hiring "ex-Viet Cong." Fortunately, I knew each man's history and could provide personal attestation of their loyalty, at risk to life, already demonstrated in the field. During the next few weeks Paul allowed me to informally orient and train less experienced American officers in the way to cooperate with Vietnamese cadre. My procedure was to bring Americans into the field with two or three Vietnamese cadre. We would go to the countryside, examine a situation, and then on departure sit down with the local American advisory element to describe our findings.[5] Complete reports for higher authority would be prepared after return to Saigon.

Dan Ellsberg and I traveled to northern Binh Dinh, southern Quang Ngai, and Quang Nam. Dan was working more for Deputy Ambassador Porter than for General Lansdale, producing memoranda on the state of security and rural recovery operations. Dan was my "landlord" in that he provided a place to hang my hat when in Saigon. He did not speak Vietnamese, but he is one of the most intelligent and perceptive (two characteristics not always found together) people I know, both in Viet Nam and subsequently.[6] We talked with members of a US Marine battalion (my memory is 3rd Battalion of the 7th Regiment) in Duc Pho district, the southernmost Marine contingent in I Corps. When we inquired about their mission, one Marine replied, with a smile: "Blocking force to keep the Army out of I Corps." Actually, the Air Cav, frustrated by the success of their perennial opponent, the 3rd "Gold Star" Division, in slipping battered regiments (especially the 2nd SVNLF) north for recovery, had already run some operations into Quang Ngai. The Marines, as fine a force as ever deployed by the United States of America, were somewhat overextended in having to cover the DMZ, the western approaches (Route 9 at the Laos border and the A Shau Valley), the densely populated coastal plain, and the western mountains and interior valleys of Quang Nam, Quang Tin, and Quang Ngai.[7]

On seeing abuse of detainees, I intervened. People who may or may not have been communists or combatants were being roughly treated. We flew some of them to Quang Ngai city, where they would be interrogated. I was uncomfortable about the lack of a systematic approach for screening captives. It was insufficiently understood that people living in a hamlet simply cooperated with whichever side held governing authority (power) on a given day. Understanding the rural environment, especially in central Viet Nam, and awareness of the sociopolitical history of those provinces would argue that accommodation to the SVNLF did not mean enthusiastic support for the SVNLF. I asked an ARVN interpreter, who I stopped from abusing an elderly man, why he cruelly treated another Vietnamese. He responded that the man was "same same Viet Cong . . . he lives with the Viet Cong."

In Quang Nam we met two embassy officers, not Vietnamese speakers, who described a new approach for sharing intelligence and compiling dossiers that would yield so much information the SVNLF would be "flushed away." Ellsberg wanted more details: who would act on the dossiers, detention procedures, administrative processes, assigning priorities. The two lost patience and repeated, "Flushing them away, flushing them away!" Dan said that he got the hydraulic analogy, but just who installed and maintained the plumbing? I was interested in their insistence that something systematic was being attempted with information collected about persons filling SVNLF positions. I remembered our "roles and missions" experience, when we would find several GVN and US intelligence organizations in a province with little, if any, sharing. What these two described as a district intelligence center in Dien Ban district seemed like a positive step toward targeting specific communist agents rather than the general population within which the agents sheltered and operated.[8] If the concept worked, then the GVN could discriminately seek out communists rather than indiscriminately target an entire area of hamlets.

I took time to learn about OCO structure and operations. John Vann was one of the regional directors, for III Corps, and it was easy to get to Bien Hoa and have long catch-up conversations. Ev was in Washington helping to set up a Viet Nam Training Center to provide courses in

Vietnamese and country and program orientation. Sam Wilson was in Long An province testing the single-manager approach to organization on the American side. John, like Jake, assumed that I knew more about future plans for OCO than was the case. I told him the same thing already expressed to Jake: time is short, and OCO will have to prove itself in a matter of several weeks or dissolve. But, I advised, even just getting civilian agencies to work together is important, because if MACV takes on rural development responsibilities, having civilian functions incorporated as a block will be better than by separate sections.

I went to Kien Giang with Tran Huu Tri for a quick look at rural development. Exposure to the Mekong Delta was important, because I knew much less about that part of the country than I did about central Viet Nam. The RD Cadre team we observed was applying itself to the tasks learned at the Vung Tau training center. Province advisors were optimistic in describing progress except for difficulty along the borders of districts adjoining Chuong Thien and An Xuyen (Camau) provinces. There was more concern expressed about the Cambodian border as sanctuary for supply and basing of SVNLF units than I had heard in the late summer of 1965.

Back in Saigon, I finally made time to take a look at Nguyen Chanh Thi's old bungalow at 9 Gia Long Street. Before I left Washington he had asked me to check on the condition of the house and make myself known to the old gentleman, "Bac" Sau, who was taking care of the place in his absence. He described Uncle Sau as a fine old fellow, a refugee from North Viet Nam to Phnom Penh after 1955, who had owned a small restaurant in that city and had befriended Thi and some other officers (including Marine Corps officer Pham Van Lieu) when they were exiled there in 1960.[9] In 1964, Bac Sau left Cambodia and traveled to My Tho, where he stayed with Pham Van Lieu, then chief of staff for the 7th Division, and Sau finally moved to Saigon several months later. Bac Sau told Thi that he also wanted to serve the country. "But he is too old," Thi told me, "so I just let him take care of my small house while I was in I Corps. He's still there because the government has not seized my home."

So that is how I met one of the cleverest intelligence operatives of the war. Whenever I spent several days in Saigon, we would meet and share a meal. He was well informed concerning developments within South Viet Nam and was conversant with the archeology, history, and arts of Viet

Nam. He always criticized communists while affirming that many who followed the party were patriots.

I thought by mid-February 1967, a month after my return, that I had a sense of OCO and its capabilities. I was sufficiently sure of my appraisal to share it with Bob Montague. OCO was slow to organize, especially at the province level. Two of the appointed regional directors (Vann in III Corps and Vince Heymann in IV Corps) had a sense of purpose, but leadership on the civilian side in I Corps was ineffectual. A regional director had just been appointed for II Corps. Agency heads were dragging their feet when it served their individual interest, and they were getting away with it. Deputy Ambassador Porter, a good man, was aware of the need for more active performance but distracted by traditional embassy DCM responsibilities. Assignment of Wade Lathram, formerly deputy USAID director, to be in charge of OCO was a mistake. Lathram knew very little about Viet Nam. He had proven ability as an administrator of established programs but not the leadership required for organizing something completely new.[10]

My assessment was so bleak that I would not commit it to paper, but I did share my conclusions with Jake (who had asked me to get back to him with my thoughts) and John Vann. I asked them both why they were not candidates to head OCO. Jake said that he would not have been in the running, even if he wanted to, because it was a given that with so many USAID resources involved, a USAID officer would have priority. He went further and said that another possibility might have been Sam Wilson, but Sam wouldn't touch it because he had other interests. I asked about John, and Jake replied, "Hell, JUSPAO might have concurred, but everyone else in the mission would have revolted."

I visited John in Bien Hoa, and he expressed agreement with Jake's estimation of his own chances for having been placed in charge of OCO: "Maybe suggesting Lansdale could have been more irritating, but it would have been close." Vann went on to add that if OCO was about to crash, it's best not to be the pilot facing a board of inquiry. I told him that I guessed the next step would be to fold OCO into MACV, one would hope with an understanding general officer in charge.[11] We talked about potential implications and advisable measures. Vann could take steps to strengthen province chiefs by simply ignoring ARVN divisions in the process of directing OCO support to rural development. On the American side, he could make sure that he would write the province senior advisor personnel evaluations, even for military officers, rather than having them prepared by the ARVN division advisor. I told him that I had rated some army officers in 1965, and he definitely had the throw weight to do the same.

There were some energetic players for OCO, including Paul Hare, Frank Wisner (effective liaison between Deputy Ambassador Porter and OCO Director Wade Lathram), and some junior officers, and from Washington on TDY (energetically), Bob Montague and Dick Holbrooke, who on Komer's behalf tried bring OCO to takeoff speed. But there was too much dead weight, too much drag, and insufficient power to generate lift. I did not know what the next step would be, but I was positive there would be change. And I was convinced that the Evaluation Branch, led by Paul Hare, should be retained in any new structure. My hope was that the Evaluation Branch, with the experienced Vietnamese component included, would add value by providing an unvarnished reality check for the highest levels, shine light on counterproductive GVN and US behavior, and recognize GVN and US personnel whose performance was effective and honest.

Huddleston was diagnosed with tuberculosis and evacuated to Japan. I had letters from him, almost immediately, seeking assistance for return to Viet Nam as soon as he could get medical clearance. Paul Hare went TDY to Kien Hoa province to cover an advisory vacancy, so when I found training center problems in Vung Tau, I addressed my report through Frank Wisner for Ambassador Porter. Before going to see Major Be at the end of February 1967, I had thought problems of American insensitivity (stupidity) had been resolved the previous spring. I was surprised to learn that a neocolonial pattern of behavior persisted on the part of some Americans. The result was festering discontent detrimental to training rural development teams. Nguyen Be had already informed General Nguyen Duc Thang of the situation.[12] Ambasssador Porter took measures to alleviate the situation.

When Bob Montague abruptly departed Saigon in late February, he wasn't even sure himself what Komer had in mind. On 15 March 1967 the picture became clearer when President Johnson announced that Ellsworth Bunker would replace Ambassador Lodge and Bob Komer would head up "pacification" operations.[13] A conference was held in Guam 20–21 March. Bob Montague attended, flying with Bunker to prep him on Viet Nam background. Bob was positively impressed by Bunker and described him as more energetic than Lodge.[14] President Johnson took the Guam occasion as opportunity to stress the importance of elections, and that resonated with Ky and Thieu, because the Constituent Assembly, elected the precious September, had just (on 18 March) adopted a new constitution that called for electing a bicameral legislature, a president, and a vice president in early September 1967.[15]

Bob Komer, with Lieutenant Colonel Montague, came to Saigon to work out the details of a new organization. Paul Hare was still in Kien Hoa, and Komer and Montague absorbed me into their operation. Paul gracefully accommodated to the situation, simply noting, "At the time of my return, Mr. Scotton was working directly for the Deputy to COMUSMACV for CORDS, Ambassador Komer, though we continued to work together on a close daily basis." While undertaking special assignments for Ambassador Komer, I continued to assist Paul with respect to field evaluations and incorporating Vietnamese cadre formerly with Special Forces.[16]

OCO was in transition to (not yet announced) MACVCORDS, and I had frequent discussions with Komer and Montague. I believed as a new organization was shaped within MACV (but distinctively), it would be absolutely necessary to acquire the most knowledgeable civilian personnel rather than strive for numbers. Komer felt the priority should be to fill slots as soon as possible, because we lacked sufficient field-experienced individuals. The immediate consequence was that CORDS absorbed many USAID people, such as Clayton McManaway, who were brilliant administrative "systems specialists" but with no field experience, who knew little about Viet Nam, and who could not speak the language.[17] It was also difficult for officers newly assigned from outside the USAID charmed circle to be recognized for their ability and ideas. Ev persuaded a senior USIA officer, Jim Tull, to take posting to OCO, but Jim was looked upon as an outsider despite my effort to make introductions. I advised him to seek a province assignment and get out of Saigon.

One of the OCO/USAID administrators asked me to examine the single-manager test that Sam Wilson was conducting in Long An. Since the conversations leading to our 1965 "Harnessing the Revolution" paper, I had been always supportive of the single-manager concept but recognized potential flaws: It could stifle initiative if an anal-retentive personality was in charge, and the GVN might misconstrue the US model as an incentive to strengthen division and corps over province chiefs. Looking at the test in

Long An was an opportunity to call attention to single-manager complications just when we Americans were about to make it a principal part of our advisory program. I went to Long An in late March and spent a few days talking with Long An province officials, ARVN 25th Division officers, and four of the district chiefs.

On the GVN side, management of the war had always been understood to be about territorial security. Through 1963 the Long An province chief (with Bao An and Dan Ve) had been the single manager. That was compromised in 1964 when ARVN regiments began extended operations in Long An, and those regiments began taking operational control of RF and PF in their area of responsibility. By the end of 1966, command of forces in Long An had been divided between a regiment of the ARVN 25th Division in northwestern Long An (with OPCON of RF and PF), province (sector command) in the central portion of the province (with control of RF and PF), and another regiment of the 25th in southeastern Long An (with RF and PF OPCON). On 1 March 1967 the GVN made a significant structural change. The III Corps commander, Le Nguyen Khang, and the 25th Division commander, Phan Trong Chinh, assigned a 25th Division officer, Colonel Luyen, to be the newly created brigade commander of both regiments in Long An.[18] He simultaneously took responsibility for all civil functions within the province, and now (like the regiments) the province chief was subordinate to ARVN brigade, division, and corps. The United States' appointment of a single manager provided an apparently convenient pretext for something similar on the GVN side, but brigade commander Colonel Luyen told me difficulty between the 25th Division commander and the province chief was the actual reason.[19] In any case, I found significant ill feeling between brigade and province.

So, on the GVN side, there was much more concern for their own structure rather than interest in American organization. They were impressed with Sam Wilson as a person, not by his position description. That was consistent with what I had observed elsewhere. The most important consideration for Vietnamese was who the advisor was, his background, his friends, his degree of commitment. The reason that Sam Wilson was persuasive in Long An was because he was Sam Wilson, not because he sat on top of a pyramid. Whether to take his experience in Long An as a template for expanding single management to every province raised the issue of making the right personnel assignments. We were having difficulty staffing regions and Saigon headquarters to satisfaction. Could we give assignment of high-quality single-manager province advisors the priority required? Finally, explication of the Long An situation allowed me to raise the question of whether a US single manager should also have complete advisory responsibility for ARVN and US units in a given province.[20]

Coincident with examining GVN response to the single-manager concept in Long An, I also had opportunity to observe the RD Cadre situation. I visited a couple of teams with the Vietnamese province RD Cadre coordinator. He told me SVNLF guerrilla units were dispersed, but that our own effort also lacked focus. "Look at An Vinh Ngai just outside of town. We can't seem to hold that area, and yet we go to Rach Kien and Long Huu." He had eight teams in the field, with one at Vung Tau for training. Over one hundred cadre had resigned because of poor security and low salary. He requested that the team in training be used to fill gaps within the eight field teams. His own morale was not high. "The RD team knows what happens when they leave. Everything goes back to what it was when they came."[21]

I asked about elections at the local level. He replied that they were not significant. "The same people are being elected, or people the government wants. It is a ruse to deliver the vote in the Presidential election for a certain person. People feel they must vote to obtain the voting card and protect themselves against trouble by the government. Why do you fool yourself to think anything different? The important elections will be for President and a new Assembly."[22]

While my two priorities were being responsive to Komer and Montague and providing encouragement for the Evaluation Branch, occasionally other officers in OCO (supposing I had more access than was true) would pass me their drafts for review and comment. So despite myself, despite personal field history, I was circumstantially beginning to orbit around Saigon concerns. One day, absorbed by a pissant problem, I went to see Frank Wisner at his OCO desk. Frank was conversing with an advisor from Kien Phong province, and he introduced us by commenting that the advisor was reporting a problem with police manning canal checkpoints and extorting money from merchants and other travelers. Stupidly focused on what concerned me at the moment, I made a flippant and irrelevant response. Of course the advisor was angry, Frank was embarrassed, and I realized that I had become a self-absorbed Saigon shithead. Later in the day I apologized to Frank, and two days later I took an Air America helicopter to Cao Lanh. I found the advisor who I had treated disrespectfully. He was not happy to see me. After I apologized, we talked about some ways the problem of local corruption might be addressed. When I left he was still not entirely satisfied, and he had cause.

Late in March 1967, then, I wondered whether to continue in what was shaping up to be a troubleshooting staff position revolving around Saigon issues. I felt suffocated. The USAID Training Center, John O'Donnell presiding, had me back to Honolulu at the end of the month to talk about changes in revolutionary development. Travel, which provided opportunity for attention to personal life and implications for my work, brought me to an important decision. I would either obtain a field position or depart.

Friends knew I was on the cusp of a decision. There were some options. RAND expressed an interest in my exploring employment with them. Ev called to let me know that he could arrange a place at the Viet Nam Training Center in Washington, and USIA confirmed that assignment to the FSI China language program would be possible. Dick Holbrooke kindly wrote a letter offering his personal view that even if I had accomplished nothing "beyond the signing on of the survey cadre that were about to be dissolved by Special Forces, that in itself was worth the whole business from our viewpoint."[23] Dick and others were careful not to advise any particular option, but their concern and thoughtful expressions of understanding were helpful while I was sorting out my thinking.

Sam Wilson initiated and was presiding over an interesting experiment in recovery operations. His concept was to use US and ARVN forces to saturate and comb through an area of Long An province, then activate the Chieu Hoi program to convert all the area young men, in place, to enlistment in local Nghia Quan while restoring local government authority. The test area was Long Huu in Can Duoc district.[24] Sam was reporting the operation and continued stability of the area as a successful model for implementation elsewhere. Deputy Ambassador Porter was very interested. He asked me to make an assessment. I read the MACV operation summary that described combining elements of the US 9th Division with the ARVN 46th Regiment (of the 25th Division) to take Long Huu. The SVNLF appeared to have been surprised, and there was no armed resistance. According to Sam's subsequent reports, all young men were now members of local Nghia Quan, government services were being extended through the hamlets, and local government was restored. Long Huu was a beacon for hope in Long An province.

I hadn't seen Sam in a long while because, when I went to Long An to consider the single-manager concept a few weeks earlier, my focus had been on how the GVN reacted, so I spoke only with Vietnamese. Now, along with two American evaluators (John Lybrand, former Special Forces, and Jerry Dodson, recruited from Binh Dinh) and two Vietnamese evaluators (Tran Huu Tri and Dang Van Sau), I took an Air America helicopter to Long Huu. We landed on the northern side of the island at Ap Cho (Market Hamlet), the center of GVN and US advisory activity. We met with Maj. Tran Truong Nghia, Can Duoc district chief, whom we had known two years earlier when training and operating an enhanced Nghia Quan (commando) unit in Binh Chanh district. Major Nghia assumed that I had arrived to organize a similar unit for Long Huu, but Tri explained that we were only there for a couple of days to evaluate what was working in Long Huu that might be applied elsewhere. Major Nghia told us Colonel Wilson was at "the American residence," and I asked him to inform Colonel Wilson that we were in Long Huu and would call on him later in the day.

Our plan was for Sau to spend as much time as possible with the former SVNLF who had rallied under the Chieu Hoi program and were now enlisted as Nghia Quan. If Sam Wilson's concept was working, these people were at the heart of his success. Tri, Jerry, John, and I set off to walk the island. We wanted visual appreciation of the hamlets and terrain and opportunity to speak with people who lived away from Ap Cho. It was only about three kilometers to Ap Tay on the south. The road had a familiar cross-stitch pattern of trenches that allowed people on foot or by bicycle to weave passage but obstructed government vehicles. We found families all had bunkers dug beneath their homes, not as fighting positions but for protection from government artillery. We spoke with several families, mostly Cao Dai, and they expressed lack of trust in the government and belief the communists would return. Even now, they said, we should take care, because some "liberation gentlemen" remained well hidden on the island.[25]

From Ap Tay we walked along paddy dikes about two kilometers to Ap Trung, located along the road between Ap Cho and the old fort. There we found soldiers of the ARVN 46th Regiment holding a prisoner taken early that morning. He was not mistreated, just being held until a squad came from Ap Cho to take him there for interrogation. He told us he had crossed over to Long Huu the night before. When we asked whether any others came with him, he replied, "Many! And after them, many more." I could not imagine a more courageous person in the same situation. The ARVN soldiers themselves were surprised that we approached from the south, since they said that part of the island was not secure. We headed back toward Ap Cho, rejoined Sau, and listened to what he had discovered. Then Jerry, John, and I went to find Sam Wilson.

Sam was at the "residence," a large building that was the coordinating point for Americans coming and going on Long Huu. When we arrived, Sam was strumming a guitar and singing with a small group. He had received our message from Major Nghia but wanted to know why we hadn't come to see him before going elsewhere. I explained that, according to standard practice, evaluators would look at an area or situation first, and later, when possible, provide feedback before departure.[26] So time would be saved because there is one protocol meeting rather than two. "Besides," I said, "you're so persuasive you could get a dead horse up and running; we needed to look at Long Huu for ourselves before you convinced us that we should just talk with you and then go home." I was insistent on this point because, if we could establish the right SOP despite Sam's aggravation, the Evaluations Branch would have a legitimate precedent for routine practice everywhere.

"So," Sam asked, not in good humor, "do you have feedback?"

With regard for his feelings, because he had so much invested in the appearance of success, we told him that much of the island was insecure. An ARVN company at the old fort, and another at Ap Cho, anchored government presence, with some patrolling along the connecting road, but there was nothing in the southern part of the island except a lot of unhappy people in hamlets who resented return of the unpopular village government that was previously run out by the communists. Those people in the old village government, I asserted, are the very people who provide the communists with a rationale for revolution. They are the wealthy landlords, Diem government appointees, tax collectors, and local bullies. Sam was taken aback. "It can't be that bad!" he said.

It's even worse, I replied, because the assigned RF company and returned police have mistreated local people, and the so-called Chieu Hoi ralliers (*quy chanh*) are really a mixed group of true ralliers and captives. Out of that group there are few true volunteers for the local Nghia Quan. Some were forced to pretend they joined in order to fill ranks for the ceremony that was held to celebrate restoration of Long Huu to the GVN, and a district officer (Lieutenant Rac) collected money (illegally) from each person for an ID card. Although complaints to Major Nghia resulted in return of the money and departure of Lieutenant Rac, ill feeling still prevails. Those more than one hundred who were supposed to receive Chieu Hoi certificates allowing them to return home are still waiting, treated as detainees. The certificates are with the village chief, who, returned to power, fears those men who previously opposed him.

I do not think Sam was sorry to see us go. We incorporated our basic observations into one report and attributed them to Sau, because I wanted to make the point that having a few former SVNLF as field evaluators provided us with special insight into contested environments. A few days later I told Jake that although Sam could sell anything to anyone, in Long Huu reality trumped personality.[27]

Leadership changes in the US mission during the spring of 1967 eased the transition from OCO to MACVCORDS.[28] In early May, when Bob Komer was appointed a deputy for MACV and the decision to make OCO a robust part of MACV was announced, new ambassador Bunker was about to arrive, with Eugene Locke as deputy ambassador. Departure of Ambassador Lodge and Deputy Ambassador Porter allowed Komer a clear field upon which to exercise his forceful personality. Locke knew nothing about Viet Nam but a great deal about LBJ and his preferences, so his role would be to maintain order among other mission agencies so that Komer would be insulated from intramural squabble. Wade Lathram was named assistant chief of staff for MACVCORDS, and his retention was a point of contention. If his leadership of OCO was not sufficient, why retain him? John, Jake, and I talked about this one night. I thought it unimportant, because Komer and Montague would provide the energized leadership. John thought die-hard OCO loyalists would organize around Lathram and retard CORDS development. I told John that I thought "die-hard OCO loyalist" was a farcical term, and Jake assured us both that from his perspective (as mission coordinator) this was simply an instance of organizational politics intended to placate USAID. Komer, newly minted

DEPCOMUSMACV for CORDS, was provided with a military deputy, Maj. Gen. George Forsythe. General Forsythe was influential in explaining army concepts and procedures to Komer and explaining Komer and CORDS to some of the military commanders.

One day Komer called me in to talk about Viet Cong infrastructure (VCI), saying that he wanted counter-VCI action to be a principal part of the total pacification effort. During the Roles and Missions Study we had found that proliferation of intelligence agencies, with little exchange of information, meant that coordinated, specifically targeted operations were a mirage. So on principle I was in favor of comprehensive overhaul, based in part on what was initiated in Quang Nam province. But two considerations needed to be acknowledged and built into any national program. First, we needed to define what we meant by infrastructure. I had my own ideas about that, but most important was to have a definition specifically agreed to by Vietnamese and Americans. I told Komer at the moment it was one of those terms casually tossed into conversation, but when you asked for an exact definition, the response was usually an embarrassed stammer. Second, due to more than a thousand years of Chinese occupation, more than a hundred years of French intervention, and strong clan and provincial loyalty, Vietnamese are prone to conspiratorial political activity in which revenge is a means or even a goal in itself. The potential for abuse in a system that depends on "sources" identifying others as communists or communist supporters is enormous—and impossible for non-language-qualified Americans to check. In order for a new program to avoid repetition of the Diem-period denunciation campaigns, something like provincial council review of cases and a public defender ought to be part of any new plan. Komer nodded. He told me CIA would provide a draft paper on organizing to attack communist infrastructure. We didn't discuss the subject again.[29]

Two years earlier the desirability of joint command was denied, but the question of how to work "levers" for obtaining Vietnamese government commitment and performance at all levels persisted. Lt. Col. Volney Warner had previously been assigned to Komer's office in Washington. He drafted a paper on leverage, the techniques that could be used in the advisory role to persuade a counterpart to take action. Komer asked me to review it and provide additional comments. I thought it was a refreshing and candid look at a perennial problem. Lt. Col. Jack Gibney joined us temporarily to discuss and then help me draft another paper on the same subject. We spoke with a wide range of Vietnamese and Americans on both sides of the advisory relationship. We prepared a rough draft and carried it to Hue for Bob Kelly to review. Then I rewrote our draft for typing and submission. We concluded, and placed our bleak assessment right in the first paragraph: ". . . that United States influence over virtually all aspects of the GVN's conduct of the war is minimal—much less than that required for realizing the goals of both the GVN and the United States, much less than that warranted by the nature and scope of the United States contribution, and even much less than that which is tolerable within the limits imposed by Vietnamese nationalist sensitivity."[30]

We specifically identified the heart of the leverage problem as being the will to use available levers and then stand up to countervailing resistance. Much of our paper was in agreement with Warner's draft and represented amplification of his message. A strong and necessary consideration, we felt, should be approval at each level by an American representative before US resources were released.[31] We also defined removal of ineffective officials as the ultimate test of any leverage system. We identified certain levers that, given "will" equal to "intent," could most effectively be activated. While we advocated taking the long view, and understood the hope that increasing numbers of Vietnamese officials would be motivated to perform with distinction and honor, we recognized that many others would not, and the leverage that ought to be applied against that category is the power to remove: "Anything else is begging the issue." It was a stark presentation, neoimperialist in appearance, but many Vietnamese friends (including Tran Ngoc Chau, Nguyen Be, and Do Minh Nhat) assured us, "Look, just by being here you are interfering; the important question is for whose benefit is the interference? Why do you provide your lifeblood and resources while accepting corruption and inept performance?" So we thought it best to write severely, because the institutional tendency, sensitive to counterpart relations and "rapport," was always to water down proposals for strong action.

In later discussion with Komer and Montague, it was apparent that Komer seized on the final paragraph. He wanted to place priority on the issue of corruption. Komer asked our opinion about developing a system of filed information on officers believed by US officers to be corrupt and undermining of government rural administration. My response was that information provided by advisors should be specific rather than general accusation, and material should be held in his office with limited access. Subsequently, "corruption files" were initiated, and later, under Bill Colby, they were maintained first by Ev Bumgardner and then me.

Dan Ellsberg was working on a "think piece" paper about the presidential elections scheduled for September. His working title was something like, "The Coming Election, the Ky [Nguyen Cao Ky] Candidacy, and the US Stakes." Dan worked at home while recuperating from illness. Since I had a room in the same house, we often exchanged ideas. My considerations were two: it was a step forward to have any elections at all, but it was regrettable that the real election (for most Vietnamese) would be made by the military leaders when they selected one of two claimants as the military candidate.

Tran Ngoc Chau was a significant contributor to Dan's thinking about the election process, and Chau was planning to run for election to the Lower House as a deputy from Kien Hoa. One day, returning from the temporary CORDS office, I saw Colonel Chau's eldest daughter leaving her school. Knowing that Chau had already returned home, and since I had been to his house before, I offered her a ride. Wow! When we got to the driveway gate, Chau practically exploded from the house, highly offended that his daughter would be descending from an American vehicle. As soon as he saw that it was me, he calmed and said, "Oh, it's only you." Two years later my next appearance at his home would be even more dramatic.

USIA was seeking my response as to whether I would return to Washington to resume Chinese language and area training. Bob Montague knew I felt stifled by the headquarters environment but advised that Komer's preference was to continue me in a troubleshooting role working out of Saigon. They invited me to dinner for resolution of the matter. I was determined to settle for nothing other than being a province senior advisor. Moreover, assignment to Quang Ngai, Binh Dinh, or an equally tough province was my goal. I supposed soliciting assistance from John Vann or Bob Matteson would enhance my prospects.[32] But sense of self, of what I was able to accomplish in the field, my pride, deflected me from asking others to intervene. I thought I should make my case and stand or fall on my own.

I fell. Komer did listen patiently. Then he told me that I was too young, "just twenty-eight and lower in grade than what was expected for a province senior advisor." I was not cowed. I replied that age and grade aside, he could not find a more capable and Viet Nam–experienced candidate for any of those two province assignments. Komer acknowledged that I had a point or two, but he had to consider the combined civil and military personnel structure when he made assignments. He asked whether I might consider a different province and mentioned one. I replied that I didn't just want to be a province senior advisor; I wanted to be one in a province that was a tough environment and where significant contribution would be expected. He expressed regret that I could not compromise, and I expressed appreciation for dinner and consideration of my request.

The next day Bob Montague told me that he tried to change Komer's mind, but his boss was "as inflexible as you. He thinks if you get into one of those high-priority provinces you will start to work your own agenda for encadrement, some kind of province joint command, and out-of-sync leverage. He told me that one John Vann is enough."[33]

Bob asked whether I had any thoughts to share before departure. Thinking back over the past couple of years, and recent discussions in Binh Dinh and Quang Ngai about order of battle (OB), I told Bob that I thought the American mission had an unrealistic image of diminishing communist strength. And that lack of realism was the basis for the notion that we could "attrit" communist forces to the point where they would wither away or become so incapable that we would win. Bob asked me to explain.

"In Binh Dinh and Quang Ngai you will be given a list of PAVN and main force SVNLF units that are in the sector, never mind that a couple of those units will be on both provinces' OB sheets, because they drift back and forth along the province border. But there isn't any appreciation, certainly not with good numbers, of local force guerrillas, and the supporting SVNLF elements like 'liberation youth' or groups that provide services like food, prepositioning supplies, and cleaning [recovering weapons, wounded, and bodies] the battlefield."

Bob saw my point and elaborated by saying, "Yes, and those people become fillers to the units that we do list."

"Even worse is that we do kill, wound, and capture significant numbers of those uncounted enemy elements, and then even though they were not part of our base calculation, they are subtracted from, let's say, the six hundred thought to be the total for the 2nd SVNLF Regiment. So we imagine that our impact is greater than it is."

I suggested to Bob that ICEX as it fully formed could provide better identification and numbers for the non-main force units, especially local forces, and I also suggested that, since this is a political war, responsibility for evaluating and calculating effectiveness of other than main force units should be with the civilian side of the mission, not MACV.

Bob asked whether I might be available for TDY sometime in the future. I replied that I really needed to get serious about Chinese language study, but after several months of calligraphy I might appreciate a break.

Reflection, 1967

It was hard to leave Viet Nam. I thought, just before departure, that I could love someone. John Vann said he expected me to be in and out of love but never married. But I had some honorable intent. She was the daughter of a prominent Saigon commercial/political figure. Her father checked with Lansdale as to my character and thereafter was agreeable to our continuing a relationship.[1] One would not say this was an instance of opposites attracting, but I was different from other young men she knew. I may have been seeking to bring part of Viet Nam away with me. Our plan was for her to come to Washington in the fall so we could decide whether our feelings were as constant far from Viet Nam.

Before Chinese classes at the Foreign Service Institute would begin, there was time for travel to New England to see family members and have a few days on Cape Cod. Inevitably, I thought a lot about Viet Nam, friends there, the direction of American operations and policy, and whether we would make it to the mountaintop or lose our way in impassable terrain.

I believed we Americans were still not thinking clearly about Viet Nam and the magnitude of the task we had assumed in 1965 when our government decided to commit a citizen army (by selective service) to war to preserve a foreign government of questionable competence and legitimacy.[2] We still knew practically nothing of our opponents, and we usually perverted what we did know.[3] We thought that by vocabulary we could actually delegitimize the opposition. The US mission in Saigon directed that PAVN (People's Army Viet Nam) be referred to as NVA (North Vietnam Army), and MACV decreed that US units might encounter "meeting engagements" but never be ambushed. We facilely accepted and used the French colonial term *pacification* and, when the need for something different was obvious, were told to adopt the term *revolutionary development*.[4] The Vietnamese themselves never used that descriptor, so our well-intentioned but clumsy terminology just contributed to linguistic confusion. My own preference, often suggested but never accepted, was *recovery*, as in "recovery operations" or "Ministry of Rural Recovery," because in most situations we were recovering an area from previous SVNLF occupation or ascendancy and because there was usually "intensive-care" clinical need to provide hamlets with recovery assistance.[5] The notion of "the Other War" (denial of Clausewitz) inadvertently caused a fractured approach to the phenomenon of revolutionary war in Viet Nam. There was one war. The war was multisided and multidimensional, but it was one war. Why did we persist with vocabulary that was not conducive to clear thinking? The answer is simple: reluctance to challenge hierarchy. When the president, ambassador, or COMUSMACV bless terminology, it is as if a voice speaks from a flaming bush. Disagree and get burned.

Americans are, or at least in the middle of the twentieth century were, very good barnyard carpenters and handy mechanics. We liked to tinker, to invent, to make improvements. And so we considered insurgency susceptible to mechanical solution. It could be resolved, suppressed, "countered" if the proper procedure would be applied, the components assembled in correct order, irritants lubricated. While thinking about our allies it was usually with frustration at their inability or unwillingness to embrace and implement our tutorial. When Tran Ngoc Chau or Nguyen Be initiated local programs independently, the Amereican response was initial excitement and support, followed by insistence that the local Vietnamese initiative be altered to suit an American-designed model. Friction was the inevitable result.

As we were oblivious to the political core of the war, our purely military intervention was also off-target. Communist equipment, especially for III Corps and IV Corps, might come from Cambodia, but personnel (and logistical support for I Corps and II Corps) would always come down the trail (now road) system through Laos. And that Laos corridor was what Clauswitz would have recognized as our opponent's most vital and vulnerable point. We could never apply sufficient sealant to Viet Nam's western border, so our best option was for US units to cut North Viet Nam's reinforcement/supply route through Laos. In mid-1967 we had the punch to do it. Casualties would have been high, but no higher than what were suffered as we fought "whack-a-mole" style on South Viet Nam soil. We would have been internationally accused of and cursed for widening the war, but our position could have allowed replacement by UN peacekeepers, if any dared. We ascribed great significance to preserving a distinct South Viet Nam, but we were unwilling to do what could have most hurt the communist commitment to unification by any means.[6]

Central Viet Nam protest movements had pressured the GVN to provide elections, first for a constituent assembly in September 1966 and
now for a bicameral legislature, president, and vice president in early
September 1967. But it was doubtful that real choice would be allowed.[7]
I had good friends, including brave and committed ARVN officers and
noncommissioned officers, but there were too many incapable and out-
right corrupt personalities in command positions, and that, combined
with a pervasive attitude that "the Americans will win the war for us,"
made energizing ARVN at large (distinct from a few elite units) problematic. Civil ministries were moribund. Ap Tan Sinh, modification of
strategic hamlets, morphed into Ap Doi Moi, with equal ineffectiveness. In all my hamlet days and nights (admittedly mostly in contested
areas), I encountered no civil ministry personnel, only RD Cadre teams
and military units. So when RD Cadre teams moved from one hamlet to
another, there was a vacuum in their wake.

Our presence in Viet Nam, more than two years after committing Regular Army and Marines operational units, seemed too heavy in Central
and South Viet Nam. Since we were unwilling to deny enemy movement
through Laos, the weight of our operations fell most heavily on the very
people who we claimed to be protecting. Whether wise or foolish, there
we were, and we should have made our presence count for more than
just local frustration of the force we defined as enemy. We had military
intervention but not positive political intervention. Instead, political aspects of the one war (as our opponents saw it) were always subordinate
to military considerations. The more I thought about where we were in
the briar patch, the bleaker prospects seemed for our American venture
in Viet Nam. What did that mean? It meant we were stalemated. The twin
arms of the Viet Nam Communist Party, PAVN and SVNLF, would trade
their lives for attrition of the US will to persist. I concluded, with some
difficulty, because of personal commitment, that our US goal should be
honorable (or least painful) disengagement.

Was our cause, assisting noncommunists to develop and defend a
separate political identity based on south and central Viet Nam provinces, realizable? Yes, but not as the GVN was constituted in 1967. We had
not, with few exceptions, been as enthusiastic about elections as we
should have been. Given choice between unpredictability (as a feature
of the election process and result) and stability, we opted for "stable"

leadership, no matter how corrupt or incapable. The SVNLF had developed tremendous political and military momentum during 1962–65. It would have taken, for any chance of success, introduction of a magnetic political process to change the game from the one that they were winning. Simply placing US forces in the field as a counterweight did not work. And we had placed our maneuver forces in the forests, hamlets, and paddies more than two years before pulling together an "other war" component for engaging the civil population.[8] MACVCORDS was late.

But I had residual hope, slight hope (wistful wishful thinking), that if we rectified terminology, realized the inadequacy of positing the GVN to its own citizens as "less oppressive" than the communists (therefore worthy of respect), and then adopted combined command and encadrement as elements of urgently needed change, several years of more reasoned application might (*might*, not *would*) obtain an independent South Viet Nam. We could only break the summer 1967 stalemate by completely damming the Laos corridor and acting much more politically. But our opponents could break the stalemate by raising the level of American casualties to a point that would be unacceptable to American voters while at the same time demonstrating to Vietnamese that the SVNLF and PAVN were not going away. While at an awards ceremony at the White House in late August 1967, before resuming Chinese studies, I had opportunity to speak at length with Harry McPherson and others. I expressed those views at lunch. Later, in a discussion with Hans Heymann and Dick Moorstein, I unequivocally told them that, despite CORDS, our approach to the conflict was divided between "chasing the NVA" and pacification.[9] A vacuum had developed between the populated areas and frontier battles, and the communists would exploit that opportunity for maneuver.

The young Vietnamese woman did come to visit my family and me in Massachusetts. We spent a few days together in Washington, then concluded, each according to our own reasoning, that the feelings that had sprung from a few days in Saigon were fading. I bent myself, literally, to the task of becoming an adequate speaker and reader of Chinese. During the next couple of years there were occasionally other women, but none could compare with Kim Vui, and Viet Nam was always on my mind.

13

Away but Still Connected

ow it seemed my view of Viet Nam in late 1967 was from too far away, looking through the wrong end of a telescope. Friends sent letters describing changing circumstances and sharing their opinions. Since they told me what each thought most important, this chapter includes excerpts from those letters and notes.[1] I indicate if the original is not in English. The order is chronological, but arranged as one set pre-Tet 1968 and a second set post-Tet. I also provide italicized remarks for context before resuming the narrative with an account of travel on orders to Viet Nam in December 1968 and again, sub rosa, in July 1969.

> 8 September 1967
>
> The election is over. No comment for the presidential, but there are matters of doubtful honesty for the senate. Unfortunately our ticket is the principal victim of the dirty rigging. Claims and protestations are going on. But the result is uncertain because it seems that the reason of the robbery is a policy from an unknown superior.
>
> *Tran Van Lam*[2]
>
> 26 September
>
> I am happy to say RD goes well in Binh Dinh principally because of the FW security. . . . The CORDS crowd is the best I've seen . . . and by the end of the year most of the Senior District

Reps will be civilians—Hawaii Vietnamese trained who <u>care</u> about what they are doing.

Frank Wisner

14 October

Not too much has changed since you left. . . . Neither the war nor the pacification program are making any real progress. . . . I Corps has negative progress, II Corps minimal progress along the coast, III Corps a standstill, and in IV the infrastructure keeps getting stronger. . . . The VC have slowly been taking over hamlets in Sadec. (Ex. 89 hamlets secure, 86 next month, 81 next month >79 >now 73.)

Jerry Dodson[3]

27 October

I don't know if I will be able to come and visit you or not. There is only one way I can explain to you without telling you a lie. I extended 6 months in Viet Nam. I don't know what made me do it. But I did.

Don Pilkington
USMC[4]

9 November

Since your departure I haven't had your letter, but have news of you from your friends in Saigon. . . . Write. . . . When you were in VN we were like family. I hope that you will do all you can for our dear friend and work with him for our countries. [Translation]

Sau
9 Gia Long[5]

10 November

We had some difficulties in August when I was away, with two of the military (now gone) who tried to take over. It took three or four weeks to untangle and caused misunderstanding in Saigon. . . . I have been spending one night, sometimes two, in a hamlet overnight with the RD team, village or hamlet chief, RF or PF leader, and someone from Province. We cross-question each other for four or five hours and it has given me a much better feel for the situation.

Bob Matteson
Deputy for CORDS
To CG IFFORCEV[6]

13 November

Although the recent elections represent the most significant progress on the Vietnamese side, the major difficulty in this country continues to be our inability to stimulate and cause to evolve a government that can win the respect of a majority of its people.

John P. Vann

25 November

I am due for duty in Danang on the 10th of Dec. . . . Everything is now organized. It has been a good year. Not very revolutionary, but certainly better than any other year with its annual pacification plan. If those bastards at home don't sell us out, we may win this thing yet.

Kelly

10 December

The cloud hanging over everything is corruption—particularly in Saigon. The T-K government is not popular. . . . We lost our first Province Senior Advisor—Tuyen Duc—where Frank Wisner will be in January. . . . The VC have been coming out of the woodwork strong. They show no signs of surrendering, collapsing, or fading away.

Bob Matteson

John Vann was in the United States on leave and came to Washington for briefings and informal discussion. One night he stayed in my small Arlington apartment on North Vermont Street. Coincidentally, my brother David and a medical school classmate were also there. They listened to John describe a disappointing meeting with Governor Romney and a frustrating encounter with NSC Advisor Rostow; then John quickly sketched the problematic situation that prevailed in Viet Nam at the end of 1967. It was classic dynamic John Vann. My brother still remembers the man who spoke with him and his classmate as though they counted for as much or more than Rostow.

12 December

Back to R&E Division, we are all right, John and I work very closely. He has helped us everything he can while Paul and you aren't with us this time. I feel something wrong (US side) since Paul left VN for his long vacation. We do need Paul a lot.

Do Minh Nhat[7]

12 December

It is becoming more difficult for me to remain flexible as the organization is becoming more bureaucratic day by day. I have talked to Komer and should Paul not return to his former position we will have a change. The reasons for our problems are not all in the leadership. We do not have the maturity on the civilian side we once had, and the military runs from worthless to outstanding.

John Lybrand[8]

Christmas Card 1967

My main mission in life is to help Major Be for I can think of no better way to help both our countries than to help Be—he really is a great man I believe. . . . I guess you realize that Be has so won the American Community that where before some had many baseless reservations about him, now he is sort of an "institution" if you know what I mean.

Major Jean Sauvageot
National Training Center

Christmas Card 1967

1968 ought to be the year for peace, that peace among all of us more and more longed for, as fine as the Spring (festival) 1968. [Translation]

Sau[9]

27 December

Chau Doc is still the same. The GVN continues to regard all of Hoa Hao country as did the French—as a féodalité. They still permit the Hoa Hao to decide who will be appointed to key jobs. The result is that most important positions are filled on the basis of Hoa Hao loyalty rather than on the basis of demonstrated competence. We are still saddled with a bunch of "assimilated officers" from the old Hoa Hao Army—men who may have been good fighters in the past, but who are totally unfitted for administrative and staff jobs. . . . Progress is being made here, but precious little of it in the pacification program. We are clobbering the enemy on the field of battle, but we ain't so far winning many hearts and minds.

Jim Tull
Province Senior Adv.
Chau Doc

4 January 1968

I have just finished the special assignment in Q. Ngai and Q. Tin. Very interesting and exceedingly difficult to maintain complete objectivity. I know that some people won't like my findings. In fact one highly placed CORDS official asked me, "How are you going to white-wash this one, Kelly?" I explained that the price of my self-respect came a damned site [*sic*] higher than the report.

Kelly

12 January 1968

This morning I talked the province Chief into making your old buddy, Maj. Phoi, head of the Provincial RD Council. I know Phoi will hate me for it, but I just <u>had</u> to get somebody I could work with in that key position. Phoi, I'm sure, would rather fight. But, in his present position he can't even do that [because] . . . there are so many jurisdictional disputes that he has, in effect, no command.

Jim Tull

23 January 1968

I just got back from Hue last week. Tri, an officer from Evaluations, and I tramped around first semester RD hamlets in Thua Thien for about two weeks. . . . Only broad conclusion after looking at Ap Doi Moi is that where there is good gov't and good local officials, the RD program works—where there aren't, it doesn't. . . . I'm very disturbed about the future of the Evaluations Branch. Ever since Paul left in November we have become increasingly irrelevant. . . . We can't get any of our reports out of the office (the military keep delaying them and sending them back) and we aren't listened to like we were pre-November.

Jerry Dodson

28 January 1968

Tet is breaking out all over—and so are the VC. Binh Dinh—particularly An Nhon and Tuy Phuoc—have been set back and, to a lesser extent, Phu Yen around Tuy Hoa. Even Tuyen Duc is not safe anymore. I am told the security is worse than anytime in the last three years. . . . Pleiku is—at the moment—having the greatest difficulty. Hopefully the end of Tet will see the VC activity taper off.

Bob Matteson

Bob Matteson was describing preliminary movement of SVNLF cadre and units positioning for the 1968 Spring Offensive that, after debate within the Communist Party, was intended to break the stalemate that existed in mid-1967. There was some expectation that a major communist effort was about to be mounted (increased truck traffic on the trail system, AK-47 and B-40 equipment upgrades for SVNLF units, our cadre reporting to John Vann that "ant hills were erupting," and Vann making input to Fred Weyand), so the communists did not achieve complete surprise. But the scope and scale of attack were inconceivable by the GVN or American allies. Prepositioning of communist units and supplies was a logistics and command feat of excellence unsurpassed in the history of warfare. It is striking that although the general population did not rise up in support of the communists, neither did they betray communist preparations for the offensive. Except in III Corps, where Vann and Weyand had well-founded apprehension, the communist summer/fall frontier strategy (Loc Ninh, Song Be, Dak To, Khe Sanh) provided an opening for attack into towns and areas thought to have been pacified. The offensive began in the morning of 30 January 1968 with attacks in I Corps and II Corps and was general throughout the country on 31 January. The impact on American public opinion, and President Johnson's reevaluation of the war and his personal plans, was enormous.

15 February 1968

There's not a lot of damage to the city [Quang Tri] physically speaking, but in terms of personnel and psychology, there's serious damage. The vast majority of civil servants were caught in Hue over TET and the VC/NVA killed three hundred of them. . . . The

VC hold most of the Trieu Phong RD area. If we try to retake it, there's going to be a lot of refugees, civilian casualties and homes destroyed.

The Cong still hold half of the city [Hue] as of today. There is extensive damage, and . . . there is fighting on the outskirts. I haven't found out what's been happening in the RD areas. . . . Bob Kelly has gone back to Hue as acting PSA.

We've suffered a loss, but the VC did not gain their objective of a popular uprising. Anti-VC sentiment is running high, but the gov't does not seem to be capitalizing on it.

Jerry Dodson

20 February 1968

Morale has declined in the Evaluation Branch, it's hard to get our reports up through channels and we're detailed to a lot of diversionary crap.

The larger situation in Vietnam is bad. The ball game is over and we might as well throw in the towel. I was in Kontum and Ban Me Thuat [*sic*] a couple of days ago. Kontum is 20% destroyed and BMT 55% after our air strikes and artillery were called in to drive out the VC. Destruction is extensive in I Corps and the Delta. For those of us who love Vietnam, withdrawal is the only solution.

Jerry Dodson

23 February 1968

South of the river every house is shot up. Burned cars, tanks and trees litter the streets. Rocket and 8" holes are all over the place. . . . All of the houses and shops around the big market and up the canal, where the sampans were always parked, are all destroyed. Napalm, CS, 8" and 500 pounders are used every day.

Charlie came in town at about 0430 30 Jan. Unopposed! NVA were escorted in by the local VC. Locals wore white armbands, main force wore red and NVA wore yellow. . . .

Those bastards in Saigon have no idea of the magnitude of the problem. The dumb shits are asking, "What is the status of your 68 plan?"

What makes me so mad is those fuckin generals of ours who say, "we knew it was coming," as though they let it happen. And now with a stunning defeat on their hands are claiming body count victory.

Kelly
Hue

26 February 1968

All the troops we've fought have been well equipped, even to the extent of such niceties as gas masks, rocket launchers, and recoilless rifles (not to mention plenty of guts). . . . I can sum it up best by saying that in my three previous years here I never bothered to draw a flak jacket from the supply room, now I never go without it. . . .

We encountered a sizable enemy force (estimated to be the Quang Tri—Thua Thien—Hue Front Hqs and its supporting units) in a hamlet called La Chu, just southwest of Hue. I understand it was the model RD spot, the showcase for all VIPs, in this part of the country. Now a prudent bird will carry his own provisions when flying overhead. Fortunately, the people bugged out as soon as the NVA moved in (so a POW said), and I say "fortunately" advisedly, because as far as I can tell our course of action would not have been different in either case. Whether we know NVA/VC are in a hamlet or only suspect that they're there makes no real difference to the commanders I have observed in the past two weeks; more often than not (in fact, almost invariably) they will prep the area before moving in, and the civilians are expected to look after themselves. . . . Kick me in the ass if I ever pretend that the rules of engagement really inhibit my operations when in fact I'm virtually indiscriminate in applying firepower.

CORDS is out at the new MACV Hqs. . . . I only talked to Montague for a little while, but here's a few things I remember. Komer (says Montague) sees eye to eye with Westy on current strategy and does not feel (a la Matteson) that too many Dak Tos are coming at the expense of RD security. . . . Chau[10] is a nice guy but is something less than clear in his own mind about what needs to be done in VN and how to go about it. . . . Leverage can only be applied at the highest level—i.e. by Komer, Westy, Bunker, et al. Considerable friction exists between Komer's office . . . and Wade Lathram and Co. Jerry Dodson . . . confirmed the estrangement between CORDS proper and Montague. . . . Lathram has apparently given instructions for his people not to have any direct contact with Komer's office.

(Name withheld at his request)
Multiple tours with the 1st Air Cavalry

7 March

Tuy Phuoc is really in bad shape. All the pacified area next to the bay is heavily damaged and the district is so insecure that you can only drive on the road to Go Boi and Highway 1—no RD cadre are in the hamlets and nobody forages into the countryside. An Nhon is also bad—heavily damaged and highly insecure. Phu Cat is not damaged, but it is insecure. The city of An Khe is secure, but hamlets off the beaten path are penetrated by the Cong. The northern districts are as always—full of NVA and VC.

Jerry Dodson

11 March

[The enemy] since December has pushed us out of 45 hamlets—8 of them 1966, 67, 68 RD hamlets (people and all), knocked out 6 PF outposts, bridges, roads etc. He is taking considerable losses . . . but appears happy to do so in order to erode GVN confidence + discourage Americans. He has not surprisingly been completely successful. GVN reaction has on the whole been good—much better cooperation + energy between the administration + civilian leaders than I've ever seen . . . but . . . the security forces and cadre scattered + the roads [are] an off + on again thing.

Frank Wisner
Dalat

23 March

I've seen enough to convince me that you were right last November when you said we had to negotiate an American withdrawal. Things are that bad in Viet Nam. You may remember that at that time I disagreed with you still thinking there was some possibility of pulling this thing out of the fire. Last November there was a possibility of doing that, but that possibility no longer exists. . . . I hope we handle the diplomatic aspects of withdrawal better than we have handled the war. This involves making the proper assurances to our allies, and explaining that Vietnam is a special case and the US is not withdrawing from Asia. It involves making provision for those people who have fought with us to leave Vietnam. . . . It involves an orderly withdrawal and a transition period before communist rule. . . . Moreover, I don't feel that Komer, the J-2, J-3, are really happy with me due to my negative reporting.[11]

Jerry Dodson

29 March

Friend Thi has an odd sense of timing. I was carrying out quite a campaign for his return, in my quiet way (including talks with Thieu and Ky), when Thi sounded off about what a bunch of bums they all are. Or, at least, so it was reported in Saigon. I've picked myself up from the floor by now and will go back to work patiently on the problem. Give him my affectionate regards, and some adhesive tape for his mouth.

Ed Lansdale[12]

31 March

[On speaking with a group of Vietnamese about the post-Tet situation, their views were]:

1. The VC won a great victory—even if they didn't achieve all of their goals.

2. The Thieu government is universally disliked because it tolerates corruption, is not democratic, is a military dictatorship, was elected by fraud, and is a US puppet.

3. Ho Chi Minh is the true nationalist hero and well known to most Vietnamese.

4. Most people would choose peace under the VC to war under the GVN aided by the US.

Bob Matteson

2 April

[Translation] The war is increasingly fierce. One never knows how the thinking of the American people will emerge.

LTC Nguyen Tho Lap
Fort Leavenworth[13]

2 April

First, Westy gets kicked upstairs. Then, yesterday LBJ announces the war's de-escalation and his own political defenestration—all in one swell foop! Like most province capitals, we were hit pretty hard beginning at 0300 31 January. The VC attacked with an estimated 2 battalions, and took over the center of town. . . . Our military losses were light, but many civilians were killed or wounded, and 1100 houses were destroyed (mostly by our own gun ships). . . .

Tremendous (GVN) performance in Chau Doc is largely because of Hoa Hao leadership, organization and internal discipline. . . . It was the most heartening thing I have ever witnessed in Viet

Nam . . . proved to us again that we (the US) cannot win this war. But it also proved that the <u>GVN</u> can win it—with our help.

Jim Tull

14 April

Over the past five to six months we have been slipping. Nothing spectacular mind you, just slipping. Otherwise known as regression. The RD teams are doing poorly, have bad morale and high desertions. I would like to see them all drafted and work simply with the PF, local officials, and CG cadre. Perhaps we could retain a small number to form into elite teams, like the PATs of old. But god, we have gotten complicated, and perverse as a result. . . . The problem, as I see it, is that any time things get tough for the opposition he can simply introduce some more troops and upset the applecart. That's what happened last August when they infiltrated one NVA Bn into the province.

Paul Hare

25 April

I hope the day is close when we will meet in Viet Nam. Certainly when you come you will see the sadness in Viet Nam, destruction in Hue because of bombing, and outside Saigon, people suffer. We will have a lot to discuss when we meet. I always remember you.

Sau

21 May

I took over this battalion in March when my predecessor got killed. It's the same outfit I was exec of in the spring of 66. In all honesty, I'll admit that after 2 1/2 months of my leadership, the battalion has virtually the same strengths and weaknesses as all other US battalions over here. In other words, the problem areas are pretty much what I'd expected—extremely weak NCOs. No use of camouflage and concealment, extravagant use of equipment, excessive

reliance on firepower at the expense of maneuver at company/
platoon levels, virtually no night offensive action—but effecting
beneficial change in these areas has been much tougher than I'd
expected. I sense some improvement but that may be wishful
thinking. I just came back from the A Shau; spent about a month
out there. A pretty successful operation, but like <u>everything</u> else,
the effects will wear off quickly.

(Name withheld at his request)
Multiple tours with the 1st Air Cavalry

27 May

I've been assigned to 199th Inf. Brigade, Gen. Freund's Brigade. . . . So far, my unit is located near II Field Force HQ, on Bien
Hoa highway. . . . Everyone in my family is in good health but nervous, due to tense situation in Saigon causing [*sic*] by VC attacks.

Sgt. Tran Huu Tri[14]

*Although Viet Nam was always in my heart, I concentrated on devel-
oping FSI-level proficiency in Chinese. Letters from Viet Nam decreased as
some friends completed assignment and departed, while at the same time I
was landing in Taiwan the summer of 1968. The FSI field school was located
in Tai Chung, where the United States had a colocated operating base with
the ROC Air Force on the Ching Chuan Kang (CCK) airfield. Two USAF
C-130 squadrons flew missions all over Asia. Catching a ride to locations in
Southeast Asia was like catching a bus in an American city: know the stops
and be friendly with the drivers. Gordon Huddleston, successfully treated
for tuberculosis, attained (through my intercession with Bob Montague and
John Vann) return to Viet Nam; Phil Werbiski would go from Fort Benning
to Laos; and I expected to see them both in coming months. Wade Lathram
departed Viet Nam in the spring and was replaced by Bill Colby. The most
important consequence for me was Ev Bumgardner's reassignment to Viet
Nam, specifically to work in Colby's office. I knew that I could rely on him to
keep me informed.*

19 September 1968

Thieu is turning Vietnam into a DIEM-LAND. Once again we go forward on all programs and security, but backwards on political and social justice. ARVN is still the most hated enemy to 35% of the people we just surveyed. Really a damning report. 8% of the people think ARVN can replace the US. Most people feel safer because they think the VC are weaker not the GVN stronger. It really does not matter for it will give the US a chance to get out while it <u>looks good</u> before Panic "does the GVN in."

RF/PF is the answer to populated areas—But MACV continues to give ARVN 1st priority for manpower. If there is <u>any</u> god, they will lose.

Ev Bumgardner
MACV JOIR

•••

The language school in Tai Chung was productive in direct proportion to the effort made. Our student body, of about thirty, included representatives of civilian agencies and military branches. Classes were one on one, changing instructors every hour. Each instructor could either teach general content or lead the students into specialized topics and vocabulary. Although Vietnamese and Chinese had very different linguistic origins, the result of Viet Nam having used Han characters for several hundred years produced cognates, and that helped me. Still, pressure to intellectually perform was constant. I had a set of 1:50,000 maps for Taiwan, and occasionally, most often with other students, on my own a couple of times, I would take three-day hikes into the mountains. Stretching my sinews along trails relieved mental tension.

Significant personnel changes were made to MACVCORDS in November 1968. Bob Komer departed and was replaced by Bill Colby, who had already been AC/S CORDS (in replacement of Lathram) since late spring 1968. George "Jake" Jacobson, would be named to follow Colby as new assistant chief of staff. Ev and Bob Montague stayed with Colby for several months. John Vann moved to Can Tho to be the CORDS deputy for that region.

In mid-December 1968 I received a message from Bob Montague asking me to go TDY in Viet Nam. He wrote that Colby, on his and Ev's recommendation, had something he wanted me to consider. A few days later the language school executive officer told me the DCM's office called from Taipei and wanted me to report to the DCM. I supposed that this was preliminary to flying down to Saigon, so I packed the rucksack that I kept for hiking in the Taiwan mountains and drove north.[15]

I was consequently irritated when DCM Oscar Armstrong informed me that he would not approve travel to Viet Nam on TDY. He said the request was incomplete and irregular: "We don't ask for officers from Viet Nam on TDY. Why should they ask for someone from Taiwan?" He seemed not only peevish, but also suspicious. I thanked him for his interest but said I needed to report his reaction to Saigon so it would be understood that I was not the one being unresponsive. Before he could recover control of the conversation, I went to another office and called MACV to inform Bob Montague of the obstruction. Bob was furious. He told me to stay away from the embassy for a couple of hours while he made sure the DCM received an attitude correction.[16]

When I returned in the afternoon, the DCM's secretary told me travel orders were being prepared and should be ready in an hour or so. A more courteous Oscar Armstrong invited me into his office. While waiting for the orders, we had coffee and chatted about the language school, intricacies of written Chinese, and life in the Foreign Service. When I had the orders in hand and was about to leave, he asked, "By the way, what will you be doing in Viet Nam?" Actually I had no idea, since Montague and Colby would tell me after arrival, but I took some pleasure in (ambiguously) replying, "I can't share information that's need to know and time sensitive." His facial expression was a mix of aggravation and confusion.

My arrival just before Christmas meant that many Americans, including Ev, were absent on holiday leave. Bob told me to take a few days looking at security and rural development in the countryside, then to come back to MACV headquarters to share impressions with him and Colby preliminary to discussion. Jake provided a room in his house adjacent to the embassy, and I took a couple of days to find Vietnamese friends in Saigon and catch up with their opinions. When I entered the Continental Hotel to meet with Ha Thuc Can and others, I unexpectedly found Senator Tran Van Lam, his wife, and another distinguished couple being accosted by three drunken American soldiers. I persuaded the soldiers to move further down Tu Do Street. Tran Van Lam asked me, "How can this happen, how can this happen?" I replied that this is what happens when a country cannot defend itself.[17]

I flew north and found Buddhist Movement friends in Hue and Danang circumspect in expressing opinions. They understood, as they had not in earlier years, that they and their aspirations were stuck between two giant millstones. I caught a ride with a convoy to Quang Ngai. Tran Van Phien, talking in his home, offered his opinion that the war had entered a new phase. He referred back to the "special war," as we experienced it in 1964, when US advisors worked with GVN forces to try and contain the SVNLF. Then, he said, we transitioned quickly from a limited-maneuver war between a larger and more capable SVNLF/PAVN force and ARVN units assisted by the United States to a general war with US units fighting in the Center and South while bombing the North. The new phase would be a test of comparative endurance. The communists could not beat the Americans, and the Americans should realize that the communists would not surrender or just go away. One would have to outlast the other, and this would mean years of effort. He believed the determining factor would still be political. Could a Saigon government acquire legitimacy? Seeking legitimacy, he said, entails risk, because it would require working with persons who previously opposed the government.

I flew to Qui Nhon and spoke with people who knew me as a sort of neighbor in 1963 and 1964. Onetime landlord Cao Dan was again able to conduct some business in livestock. Travel south to Phu Yen was safe, but he would not risk road travel to Pleiku. Buddhists in the main Qui Nhon Pagoda described the Tet Offensive (eleven months earlier) as a shock for the government, but one for the communists as well, since they were unable to hold territory. I spoke with American advisors the next day. Their feeling was that improved security increased support for the government. We had quite a debate, because I felt that pushing the communists back would naturally mean less overt support for them, but regard for the government had to be acquired over time. They cited restoration of the railroad from Phu Cat south to Cam Ranh as a dramatic indicator of improved security. But when I said, "In that case I'll take the train to Nha Trang rather than fly," their reaction was, "It's safe for Vietnamese, but not Americans."

I stayed New Year's Eve with Tran Xuan Khoi and his family, and on

1 January I took the train from Qui Nhon to Nha Trang. The journey required two days, because the roadbed would not allow a speed of more than thirty or forty kilometers an hour. The cars were all freight, so passengers—a mix of soldiers and civilians—sat or sprawled on the floor. The best spots were adjacent to open doors, because one could catch a breeze and gaze at the countryside. At each of many stops people got on or off. Everyone was surprised to find an American as a fellow passenger. Even the RF soldiers assigned to ride the train on security detail found it strange to have me with them. Lively conversation always began by exploring details of personal life, then it proceeded to the historical and political. The first day was uneventful, with only three or four rounds fired at the train just south of Song Cau. I thought the intent was simply to advertise SVNLF presence, "We're still here!" We took our overnight in Tuy Hoa, and the next day, with an extended stop near the large airbase at Tuy Hoa South, headed to Nha Trang.

The only problem on this portion of the trip was that a young girl, fourteen, she told me, happened to climb into our car. One of the RF soldiers grabbed her and began pulling her toward one end of the car. When she protested, I intervened. We had ourselves a tense situation. I was armed, and there was gang reluctance to provoke gunfire that could result in death or injury for some of them. We trundled along in an atmosphere of mutual mistrust. The girl told me she was on the way to see her brother, a ranger wounded somewhere in Phu Yen, now in the ARVN hospital at Nha Trang. I approached the deprived, disgruntled RF soldiers and explained that the girl was going to visit her wounded brother. I asked them to help me make sure she would find him.[18] The remainder of the passage was more agreeable for all of us. When we arrived at the Nha Trang railyard, one of the RF soldiers stepped forward as guide to the hospital. Exiting onto the street, we were pulled up short by an American MP jeep, whose occupants were curious about me, in the company of two Vietnamese, dressed field casually and carrying an exotic Swedish K weapon. Fortunately, I had a note from Lieutenant Colonel Montague, on MACV letterhead, identifying me as person on a special mission and requesting assistance as necessary. Allowed to proceed, we found the hospital and connected brother and sister. The RF soldier and I went for coffee, omelet, and bread near the Nha Trang market, and I thanked him for his help. I never saw any of them again. I hope they all found their way out on the other side of the war.

A couple of days later I was sitting in Ambassador Colby's office. We had met once previously, but this was our first opportunity for real discussion. He inquired about my impression of the situation in central Viet Nam. Keying my comments to views expressed by friends in Quang Ngai and Binh Dinh, I suggested (per Tran Van Phien) that we were now in a new phase of the war that would be based on relative endurance. I mentioned my travel on the railroad and said that although I would not make much effort to open the line all the way, where it did operate trains were a positive symbol for the government, because their restoration reminded people of better years when the railroad was part of their daily auditory and visual experience.

He said citizen attitudes were exactly why he asked Colonel Montague to bring me in for consultation. He wanted some way to be informed about popular attitudes with respect to a variety of matters, including political issues broadly defined. I suggested that the potential was already present in CORDS: those experienced cadre who were once with USIS and Special Forces, then OCO in the Evaluations Branch, and now in MACV. Working with Americans who were experienced in cooperative endeavor, those people could organize a system for making rural inquiry on a regular basis. Over time one could discern trends. The only anticipated caution would be (sharing my perception of President Thieu as suspicious of others' motives) that the effort to appreciate public attitude should be described as a form of pacification studies, with specific topics ranging from social and economic to very broadly political. Some province chiefs would be more understanding, or tolerant, than others.[19]

Ambassador Colby asked whether I would be willing to return on assignment after completing language training.[20] I responded that I would consider the option, if there were one, very seriously, but I was not a very good organization man. I candidly mentioned fundamental disagreement with the way we operated in Viet Nam. He replied that the command predisposition was for progress reports, and he wanted someone who would bring problems to his attention. He had in mind requesting me as replacement for Ev, because he didn't think Ev could stay in Viet Nam for much more than another year. I immediately replied that his two indispensable assistants had to be Montague and Bumgardner, and bringing me as replacement for Ev would not provide equivalent value. "Well," he smiled, "we will see."

Several weeks later, using the C-130 "bus service" operating throughout Southeast Asia, I flew from Taiwan to Thailand and reconnected with Phil Werbiski, now in Laos as a major and liberated from what he called Fort Benning purgatory. Phil was with Project 404 working from the Defense Attaché Office in Vientiane, making frequent trips in and out of Lima sites to assist Lao defense forces. He described the need to train competent combat air controllers. I wondered how he would react to the possibility I might return to Viet Nam, but I suppose a subliminal motive was to let him know I was halfway to marriage. I had been spending some Taiwan time with a young woman of the Tayal tribe. She was pregnant and, like too many males in similar circumstances, I was not as responsive as I should have been. I told Phil my reservation was that if we married and I returned to Viet Nam, I might not survive.

"Survive," he exclaimed. "Who's going to survive? What's survival got to do with anything? We've known each other for seven years. Now I'm in Laos, and you're going back to Viet Nam. Hell, a year from now we'll probably both be in Cambodia! You already mucked up your life three years ago. Forget about survival, we're not going to survive, just do what you should, and that's all!" I returned to Taiwan. Sa Yun and I endured an "unofficial" tribal marriage ceremony in her village, while I acquired the extended family data necessary to submit an application for authorization to marry a noncitizen. Three months later Phil was killed in a crash north of Long Chieng.[21] My son was born on 17 September, and his middle name is Philip.

A few messages about me were exchanged between Saigon and Washington during the spring and early summer. Ev, John, Jake, Bob, and, with their encouragement, Bill Colby wanted to bring me back to Viet Nam. USIA balked (by USIA telegram 6632), and Ev sent me a copy with a scribbled note telling me, "They say you don't finish till March 70."[22] Colby responded to USIA with a letter repeating his request to have me join him. He provided reasoning and a commitment to provide opportunity to use Chinese as well as Vietnamese.[23] USIA declined. Instead, I was scheduled for transfer to Kuching (in Sarawak State of Malaysia on Borneo) in late 1969.[24] That seemed to settle my 1970–71 place of assignment, and as I worked through the processing required for government approval of marriage, it was understood I would go to Kuching in the fall, return to Taiwan for marriage when approved, and finally bring my wife and son back to Borneo with me.

But first there was another trip to Viet Nam. At the end of June, John sent a secure message asking me to see him in Viet Nam, right away and low-profile, on a matter of great importance to him, Ev, Jean Sauvageot, and other friends. I couldn't even guess what he was talking about. I knew, more than most, about his complex personal life, but I couldn't figure how that would be relevant to Ev and Jean. I did understand needing to arrive in Viet Nam unannounced and undocumented. Darryl Johnson, a State Department officer studying Chinese in Tai Chung and a former Peace Corps volunteer in Thailand, had already suggested making a trip to Southeast Asia as an "area studies" component of our program. I made arrangements with the CCK C-130 group, promising to bring back an AK-47 for the commander, and we were off—first to Thailand. I was glad to have that diversion, because it not only made whatever Vann had in mind appear incidental, but at last there was opportunity to catch up with Dick Noone, who in 1963 had challenged me to "enter the jungle." We met at the SEATO headquarters on Sri Ayuthaya Road. Dick welcomed my visit, and we conversed for a couple of hours. He described recently searching for missing Jim Thompson, saying that the jungle would always have secrets to keep.[25]

Darryl and I also traveled north together and, thanks to his Thai language ability, had interesting conversations in Chiang Mai, Lamphun, and Pasang. On 4 July we took picnic lunch with the advisory team in Phitsanuloke and then a flight (barnstorming-style) to Udorn for a look at Issan, Thailand.[26]

When we arrived at Tan Son Nhut on 6 July, it was so late we had to sleep on base. I phoned John, let him know that I was in-country, and said I needed a description of his problem. He told me a full account would be provided when I got down to Can Tho, but, if at all possible, I should make arrangements to get someone escorted safely out of Viet Nam to Phnom Penh. I was confused and couldn't imagine what personal relationship required extracting someone. I decided to make contingent arrangements but not to implement them if the problem was one involving a woman.

Whatever was bothering John, right up to the point of finding out, I had to make this visit appear exactly like any other foray into the country I loved. Sometimes with Darryl accompanying me, and sometimes alone while he met colleagues in the embassy, I went to see special units previously trained in Vinh Loc and Hoc Mon, called on Tran Van Hai (National

Police director),[27] had lunch with a couple of knowledgeable journalists, shared a supper with Bac Sau, and on the margins arranged for a helicopter on stand-by, an escort, and connection to a Cambodian friend in Phnom Penh. Implementation would be contingent on learning the identity of the mystery person.

On Wednesday, 9 July, Darryl and I drove through Long An, visiting one of the hamlets surveyed in December 1963, speaking with some people, then to My Tho for a short talk with Le Minh Dao and over to Chau Thanh district for pickup by Vann's LOH. I was surprised to find that Huddleston was crewing (not piloting) the LOH, so we reconnected. The next day we spent time with Sgt. Lonnie Johnson; Air America pilot Len Wiehrdt, who often flew us in and out of locations in 1965 and 1966; and some new IV Corps PAAS cadre being trained by Gordon.[28] Hud told me that he had it "straight from Colonel Vann" that Colby and Ev were bringing me back to replace Ev. My response was that it would not be easy.

When John and I finally had an opportunity to talk, he opened by revealing what he called a "shameful US 9th Division rampage" through upper Mekong Delta provinces. Claimed success for sniper kills, John said, did not distinguish between enemy and civilians killed at long range, and night heliborne killer teams simply fired at any movement after supposed curfew. John told me the "Bloody 9th" claimed a kill ratio of one American to forty-six enemy combatants, but only one weapon captured per twenty-four enemy claimed killed. Emphasis on sniper action produced many of the suspect kills, because if American soldiers found it difficult to identify true Viet Cong face to face, how were they capable of differentiation at a distance? The two provinces where the 9th most often operated (Kien Hoa and Dinh Tuong) averaged five hundred civilian casualties admitted to friendly facilities every month in each province. The remaining twelve provinces of IV Corps together had an average total of only four hundred.[29] That was depressing, but unless Vann expected me to kidnap General Ewell (9th Division commander), this was not the urgent matter that spurred him to insist on arrangements to help someone out of Viet Nam.

It was Tran Ngoc Chau. John and I had a long talk covering some of his relationship with Chau back to 1962. I was familiar with some of the personal history. John and Ev told me in 1966 about Chau's older brother, Hien (a Communist Party member and PAVN officer) making contact, Chau's response, Vann's peripheral (and fruitless) involvement, and awareness within the US mission of that contact.[30]

John reported that Hien (as the law of averages would have it, no matter how clever an agent) had recently been captured. President Thieu, despite previous friendship, looked upon Chau as a threat to his administration because Chau had recently advocated that the legislative branch initiate a peace dialogue with the SVNLF.[31] Chau, Vann said, was at risk for arrest and trial or possibly even assassination. John told me that he, Ev, and Jean Sauvageot were instructed to cut contact with Chau and his family. Now I understood. I had a fig leaf of apparent innocence, because no one anticipated I might appear from Taiwan and visit Chau. I told John that, if Chau agreed, he could be pulled out in a day. John described an alternative he had in mind involving a helicopter, a life raft, and paddling to a Cambodian beach. I told him that sounded too desperate, because even if Chau was a good swimmer, who knows whether the beach would be friendly?

Back in Saigon again, on Friday evening, 10 July 1969, Darryl and I went to Chau's house on Ngo Tung Chau Street in Gia Dinh. Having Darryl with me provided the appearance, I hoped, of a casual social call.[32] The discussion between Chau and me was intense and emotional. Chau expressed his feeling that he was being sold out by Americans whom he had trusted. I responded that although not speaking for all his friends, my simply being there with an offer for an exit was proof some friends cared and would risk much for him. He grumbled that if he was not being sold down the river, maybe we were just standing on the side watching him drift away. I insisted that wasn't fair. He played a high-stakes game, the highest, and was paying a price. The only matter we could discuss was whether he accepted the offer for safe departure.

After about two hours Chau concluded that his sense of honor would not allow him to run, sneaking, from his own country. "If I were to leave, to run, that would allow the president and others to claim it proved I am a communist and a coward. I will stay."[33]

I bade him a respectful farewell, not imagining it would be almost forty years before we would meet again. Assisting him would not have been just another adventure, not an excuse to prove I still had "the touch." I trusted John, Ev, and Jean on the specifics, and I was ready to act on the basis of that trust. I would have helped Chau for the same reason I had assisted

Nguyen Be three years earlier. These good men represented hope for a nondictatorial future.

I cancelled the special arrangements, and Darryl and I took a flight to Cam Ranh, then a C-130 for the return to Tai Chung. Back in the language school, I prepared a short, three-page memorandum on our travel in Thailand and Viet Nam, referring only in one oblique sentence to an evening visit with Tran Ngoc Chau.[34] That was the form of CYA that Ev taught: "If you go to the edge and beyond, provide yourself with cover by mention of the event as an inconsequentiality."

Capt. Howard Walters and Le Quang Tuyen in Van Canh district, Binh Dinh province, October 1962. (Photo VIS Binh Dinh province)

A briefing in Qui Nhon, January 1963. Left to right: Dr. Ken Bunce, David Sheppard, Le Quang Tuyen, Binh Dinh Province Vietnamese Information Service (VIS) Chief Mr. Tram, Frank Scotton, and Ev Bumgardner. (Photo VIS Binh Dinh province)

Author with Dan Ve (Self Defense Corps) troops in An Lao Valley, April 1963.

At an overrun outpost temporarily held by rangers at Vinh Hoa hamlet, Long An province, March 1964.

Do Minh Nhat briefs General Westmoreland, January 1965. Left to right: Colonel Sapp, Do Minh Nhat, General Westmoreland, Frank Scotton, and Capt. Jim Ray.

Author talking with the Hoc Mon district Special Platoon commander, March 1965.

Author in Thu Thua district, Long An province, while with the district mobile platoon, May 1965.

Capt. Phil Werbiski (left), Frank Scotton, and Capt. Art Bair (commander, Detachment A-424), An Phu district, Chau Doc province.

Bob Kelly after visiting a combined action platoon in Quang Nam province, October 1965.

Author with Maj. Nguyen Be, northern Tuy Phuoc, October 1965.

Author with cadre in Qui Nhon before leaving for Special Forces camp in the Vinh Thanh Valley, February 1966. Tran Huu Tri is at top center. Three others are former SVNLF combatants.

Maj. Nguyen Be (standing, left) and a CIDG unit in training, Vinh Thanh Valley, March 1966.

Author with team leader Phai while securing the area in Tuy Phuoc district for a CBS television program team, March 1966.

Author with Tran Huu Tri at Tien Giang market, Binh Dinh province, April 1966.

Jerry Dodson (left), Frank Scotton, and John Lybrand at Long Huu Island, Long
An province, April 1967.

Author with Lt. Col. Le Minh Dao, then Dinh Tuong province chief, July 1969.

Daryll Johnson (left), Frank Scotton, and John Vann in Sadec, July 1969.

Isolated ARVN Fire Support Base 5, southwest of Dak To, June 1971.

Author with an ARVN 1st Division soldier near Hue, June 1972.

Note: Unless otherwise indicated, all images courtesy of the author.

14
Borneo and Return to Viet Nam

China area and language study completed, and following the birth of my son (David Philip) while still waiting for final approval of "official" marriage to Sa Yun, I left them in the mountains with Sa Yun's extended family and in early November 1969 flew to Kuala Lumpur. This was my first experience with a "regular" USIS. The ambassador was Jack Lydman. He had a theatrical background and World War II experience that he shared with Public Affairs Officer Earl Wilson and me during lunch. He inquired about my Viet Nam experience and suggested it might be useful in East Malaysia, where there was a simmering ethnic Chinese–based insurgency. Earl Wilson was an experienced USIS officer who understood the need for focus in outreach programs. In those precomputer days he introduced a contact records system based on manual key-sort manipulation.

I was USIS representative, and vice-consul, for East Malaysia and Brunei. That territory was the northern third of Borneo, with the southern two-thirds being Indonesian Kalimantan. Brunei is independent (still), and East Malaysia is divided into the states of Sabah (formerly North Borneo) and Sarawak. The consulate was located in Kuching. I succeeded Bob Peterson, who returned to Washington for Japanese language training. There was a consul and an assigned communicator for secure messages. As soon as I arrived, the consul departed with his wife and children for a long-anticipated family vacation. He was not gone long before I had to cope with applicants for visas to the United States. I had no preparation for the visa interview procedure. If the applicant seemed like a good person and had a reason for travel to the United States, I approved a visa. When the consul returned from holiday he was astonished at the number.[1]

I began travel into the interior. There really was a low-grade simmering insurgency. You could see antigovernment communist slogans in some communities, Chinese characters painted on walkways from riverbanks to town markets.[2] Hundreds of captured insurgents were held in a detention center outside Kuching. I spent part of a day interviewing some of them. The vehemence of their commitment to the Chinese Communist Party and Cultural Revolution values surprised me. Vietnamese communists never, in my experience, made reference to China, but these ethnic Chinese insurgents in Sarawak did so as a matter of course. The heat of the insurgency was felt mostly in riverside, pepper-farming Chinese communities, but not in the Iban, Melanau, and Malay populations.

Capt. Walter Wong of the Sarawak Rangers invited me to accompany him up the Rajang River past Kanowit, Song, and Kapit and then even farther, either on the main Rajang or its tributary, the Baleh.[3] Travel was first by motorized fast boat, then eventually by paddled dugout. We moved and spoke with people along the river by day and then slept in longhouses at night. Each visit occasioned a celebration with chants, gongs ringing in hypnotic rhythm, and abundant intoxicating *tuak*. We were often with Malaysian district officers. At night I was struck by hearing nostalgic references to former British colonial officers or school headmasters who were "tough, but honest," or "demanding, but caring." In comparison, I never heard positive reminiscences expressed by Vietnamese for French colonials.

Temenggong Jugah was chief minister for Sarawak and Walter Wong's uncle. We were together on two trips deep into the interior. He was received with reverence in each longhouse community. Sarawak politics were basically tribal in nature. Each of the principal ethnic groups had parties that ostensibly represented their interests. The more I spoke with some of the leaders, and observed their behavior, the more I understood that party and communal leaders used influence for their own benefit. The federal government was adept at playing personalities against each other to benefit Malay and Kuala Lumpur interests. Jugah is probably the best example of that Sarawak phenomenon. He was an upper Rajang River Iban heroic figure during World War II, when he led resistance in the area against Japanese occupation. Illiterate, he had his name tattooed on his forearm so he could copy the letters when signing papers.[4] He was an important player in the 1963 maneuvering that brought Sarawak into the Federation of Malaysia and prospered by receiving financial opportunity favors from the Malay-based federal government. A pattern was established whereby Iban politicians would promise Iban longhouse communities improved services, get elected because they were Iban, and then pursue their own personal aims rather than overall Iban needs.[5]

Ling Bing Siew led in fact, though not by name, a party representing Chinese commercial interests. His base was in Sibu, and we met on two occasions. More interesting was the Sarawak United People's Party, led by Stephen Yong. Very different were the Melanau, early inhabitants of the northern Borneo coast and among the first Bornean converts to Islam. Religious affinity and lifestyle provided linkage with Malay interests, so this community played a sort of balancing role in Sarawak. I made sure USIS resources, including the prestigious "leader grants," were broadly applied rather than directed toward one ethnic or political identity.[6]

I returned to Taiwan when my marriage to Sa Yun was approved, and our legally recognized ceremony in Taipei was witnessed by vice consul and friend Bob Perito. Then, with Sa Yun traveling on a Taiwan passport, we moved with our son to Kuching.

I was committed to doing my best in Malaysia. There were some amusing interludes in the spring of 1970. Vice President Agnew made an official visit, and I was pulled up to Kuala Lumpur for work on protocol and security. I was at the golf course when one of his errant drives struck a Kuala Lumpur journalist, who was too close to the line of fire. When US Marine helicopters flew down from Viet Nam (to transport the vice president's group between a rubber plantation and the parliament building), some journalists questioned the significance of conical hat silhouettes painted on the nose of one. More pleasant was escort duty for Boston Celtics coach Red Auerbach and John Havlicek.

So far as I knew, my assignment to Kuching would continue for the expected two- or three-year duration. I received a lukewarm officer evaluation report prepared by the information officer, who also functioned as deputy to the country USIS director. I thought that officer's attitude was skewed by envy for my easy access to Earl Wilson and Ambassador Lydman, but decades later I discovered there was an additional factor. Every rating, in those days, had a Part II attached to the basic evaluation report but not shown to the rated officer. In my case the information officer provided insulting commentary concerning my wife and son. Had I read what was written while we were face-to-face, my reaction would have been explosive. To his credit, reviewing officer Earl Wilson wrote that the rating officer's speculation "should be discounted."[7]

Jodie Lewinsohn replaced Earl Wilson, and she wanted to close out the USIS branch office in Kuching and redesignate the position for country field operations and base it in Kuala Lumpur, but with program and travel responsibility throughout Malaysia. I was responsive because I believed something like the Bumgardner field operations model could be applied. My only reservation was preference for slow implementation that could provide time for USIS Kuching personnel to find other employment.

On an extensive trip to Sabah, I flew to Tawau on the eastern coast, met with district officials, and was schooled on some of the legal and extralegal aspects of Borneo timber enterprises. After arriving in Sandakan on the northeastern coast and inquiring about the possibility of overland travel to the west coast, friendly officials provided information about an Australian company, Snowy River (I think), that was contracted for preliminary work on the route. I took a bus to the advance road engineering station at Telupid. The team kindly put me up in camp for a night. The survey engineer pointed out a track that he said traversed jungle to a small town called (by my memory) Paganatan. From that point it would be possible to get transport to Ranau and then Kota Kinabalu, the state capital. The next day they delivered me across a small stream by boat, and I set off along a path. The trail became less distinct, then faint, and finally disappeared. But I had a compass, map, and the sense of invulnerability that had previously accompanied me in Viet Nam. Still, I eventually found myself forcing, breast stroking, my way through thick tropical growth, and fatigue and frustration forced frequent rest stops. It was several hours before I emerged in the town that was my destination. The people there were surprised to have a lone traveler appear from the southeast, but they hospitably provided tea, rice with some chicken, and a place for rest. The next day a district vehicle from Ranau, on routine travel to outlying towns, offered a lift to Kota Kinabalu.

I just wanted a clean room in a modest hotel and good food in a local restaurant, but an invitation arrived for the evening meal with Tun Mustafa, the chief minister (actual ruler) of Sabah. The bearer told me that Ranau district had informed the chief minister of my travel, and he was curious. Friends in Sarawak had described Tun Mustafa as a dictatorial character with less interest in accommodation and compromise than their own politicians. His forceful personality was obvious, as was a belief that Sabah, positioned between aggressive Indonesia and an ungovernable Philippines, remote from Kuala Lumpur, needed a firm hand (his) at the wheel.

After returning to Kuching, I learned Sa Yun had experienced adventure of a different sort. In my absence two thieves attempted entry to our home at 10 Jalan Pisang, but she had asked two Iban girls (who worked for us) to stay with her while I was away. The three women armed themselves with kitchen knives and choppers, turned on all the lights, and made as much noise as possible. Discouraged, the troublemakers ran away. Here was an early instance of successful people's self-defense.

I had been back in Kuching but a few days when Jodie called with her decision to close Kuching as soon as possible. Two days later, the embassy in Kuala Lumpur received a telegram immediately reassigning me to Viet Nam. Part of the package included expeditious naturalization for Sa Yun and "family separation" separate-maintenance government housing in Taiwan for Sa Yun and David Philip. We flew to Los Angeles and stayed with Dan Ellsberg for a couple of days. He brought me over to see his office at RAND, and one evening my cousin Bob Warren joined us from the Marine Base at Camp Pendelton. Dan did surprise me by showing us some sections of the Pentagon Papers in his house, but I supposed he had administrative approval, since he was one of the principal writers. We talked about Tran Ngoc Chau, his arrest, and the inaccuracy of charging him with working for the Viet Nam Communist Party. Dan said that each Washington administration had determined that anything was justifiable in order to avoid losing the war, and he now believed anything was justifiable in order to end it.

We proceeded to Washington DC for Sa Yun's naturalization. Coincidentally, Jean Sauvageot and his wife, Huong, were there for the same purpose, and we applied for our wives' passports on the same day. Jack Gibney arranged for us to borrow another officer's (Art Cates's) car so that we could drive to Fort Bragg, where my brother David and his family were stationed. In less than two weeks we flew back to Taiwan. I placed Sa Yun and our son in Taipei (USAID-managed) government housing and returned home to Viet Nam.

Three years earlier, I had declined a staff position and would not have accepted any assignment other than province senior advisor in a tough environment. Now in early 1970 I was returning to a country that I loved as my own to serve on someone's staff. The difference wasn't because I was three years older and married. The determinative factor was that the US presence and organization in Viet Nam was three years older. In the summer of 1967, as CORDS organized, the new structure was still in a flexible birthing phase. It would have been possible to innovate in one of the provinces where I had field experience. Now, in 1970, although not entirely ossified, the position description for province senior advisors was one part of a large machine wherein expectations were predefined and limits accepted.

Staff executive assistant to Ambassador Colby, Ev had assured me, was not like being personal assistant to a celebrity personality.[8] He described Colby as always accessible, always curious, and with more awareness of the reality of Viet Nam than any other senior officer. I already had a strong positive feeling from my short discussion with Ambassador Colby in January 1969, when he told me that he wanted someone bringing problem reports rather than progress reports.

My affinity for Viet Nam, the part of me that was Vietnamized before Vietnamization, friends there, continuing conflict, a sense of unfinished business—all acted like a magnet to draw me back. Suppose you were deep into a grand historical novel, but then, after having placed it aside, the book were to go missing. Someone else could describe how the story ended, but you would be dissatisfied. The Vietnamese-American experience and the American civil rights movement were the two great "historic dramas" of my generation. I was immersed in one and would see it through.

Despite five years in Viet Nam, 1962–67, all the letters from friends in 1967 and 1968, and two purposeful trips there in 1969, I needed reexposure to the rural environment, reconnection with Vietnamese and American friends, and an understanding of CORDS as it operated in 1970.

Reacquiring field sensitivity was my first priority, and that was eased by Ambassador Colby's absence for travel to Washington. Tony Allitto had just joined the office as reports officer replacing Dennis Harter. Tony came up from Soc Trang, where he had been a district advisor. I was eager to get back to central Viet Nam and capture a feel for 1970 reality. Tony wanted to come along and look at a part of the country that would be new for him. We concentrated on meeting people in Hue and seeing old friends in Quang Ngai and Binh Dinh. Most surprising were the two nights we spent with Maj. Nguyen Tuy and his wife.[9] Now Binh Dinh sector commander, Tuy was not the young, energetic officer who had set an example for me in 1963. He seemed worn down, and I wondered whether my appearance was the same for him. Late on the first night, a small guerrilla unit attacked a bridge just outside Qui Nhon. The radio linked to sector crackled. There was a lot of talk but no action. Finally, Tuy, Tony, Tuy's wife (!), and I suited up, armed ourselves, and drove to the bridge. We were the reaction force. *Khong kha nang* (not capable, i.e., unprofessional) was Mrs. Nguyen Tuy's verdict.

My overall impression was that there was apparent stability in central Viet Nam. I call it "apparent" stability because quiescence was obtained by the massive infusion of US forces in 1965–69 and consequent widespread destruction of rural communities, and now those American landscape-altering forces would redeploy home.

John Vann was still in IV Corps. I visited him and Wilbur Wilson (his deputy) for a couple of days. Vann was his usual irrepressible self, convinced that the accelerated pacification program (initiated in late 1968) was the foundation for assuring eventual success. "Now there is a basis for outlasting the North," was the way he put it. We had different viewpoints, because I was not persuaded the current flow of "pacification" would not be followed by another ebb, perhaps precipitated by communist response to the departure of US units. Do Cao Tri was in disfavor and generally out of the country from late 1964 (including brief assignment as ambassador to Korea) until 1968, but in August of that year he was made III Corps commander. It was said, with equal accuracy, I thought, that Tri was one of the most ambitious and business-oriented generals and at the same time one of the most capable. When I saw him in Bien Hoa, having first met him years before, he casually mentioned the opportunity for profit afforded by operations into Cambodia.

Bob Kelly was out of Viet Nam. He had been hired by USIA and assigned to Thailand. After several months, Ev told me in a letter, Kelly decided that repetitive overseas assignments were not for him. He resigned and returned to Michigan. Bob Montague was also away from Viet Nam and, as far as I know, never returned. He was eventually promoted to brigadier general, but his further advancement was obstructed by military bureaucrats (yes, there are military bureaucrats) whom he offended during 1966–69. Robert Matteson, disillusioned with the war, had returned to Washington. Jerry Dodson was a graduate student in Massachusetts who was making frequent trips to Washington to lobby against the war. Gordon Huddleston was still in IV Corps, working with special teams, but he found it difficult to maintain quality: "I have hired 70, released 40, and have about 15 that don't get lost."[10]

Vietnamese friends had not fared as well as I had hoped. Nguyen Be, commanding the Vung Tau National Training Center, was basically coopted. Tran Van Phien, formerly chief administrative officer in Quang Ngai, and seldom consulted by Americans, who usually connected to the province chief or 2nd Division commander, felt basically sidelined. Dam Van Quy, whom I used to see in Djiring, was killed in May 1968. Nguyen Viet Thanh, commanding the 7th Division, referred to by soldiers as one of "the four honest generals," died in a helicopter collision a few weeks before I returned to Viet Nam. General Lam Son, once commander of Special Forces, brave and candid, was unassigned and drinking excessively. Nay Luett was ethnic minorities service director in Phu Bon province. Ton That Thien, brilliant intellectual, advocate of civilian governance and reform, briefly worked as minister of information in 1968 but was now dean of social sciences at Van Hanh University.

Bac Sau was in detention on Con Son Island. He had been arrested in late December 1969, following the August capture of an SVNLF courier with a document originated by my clever friend. Uncle Sau, aka Nguyen Van Sau, real name Bui Van Sac, was skillful. He never overplayed his hand, always claiming to be a nationalist, and effectively sheltered in Gen. Nguyen Chanh Thi's house. Over time he became a source for a few Americans, including embassy officers, and ipso facto *they* became his sources. I know that in early 1969 he even introduced two senior COSVN intelligence officers (Sau Dat and Tam Rau) to Ev Bumgardner, not as who they really were, but as good friends who wondered whether Americans were serious about negotiating for withdrawal. I think Sau was in a different category from the better-known Pham Xuan An, who was born in the South (Bien Hoa) and gradually grew into his role, whereas Sau had to

relocate himself from the North to Phnom Penh and then to Saigon, man-
ufacturing cover along the way. He was very good at working sources as
friends. Ev referred to him later as "the Viet Cong Sam Wilson." Although
he proved to be an opposition agent, I couldn't think ill of him. That's how
good he was.[11]

Tran Ngoc Chau had been arrested, tried, and convicted and was held
in Chi Hoa Prison. He was entirely different from Bac Sau, who was a
national communist and agent, albeit personable, of the party's cause.
Chau was a national noncommunist with almost naïve faith in elections,
representative government, and the principles of commitment and financial integrity that he identified in his closest Vietnamese and American
friends. Moreover, in Kien Hoa and later at the national level he applied
himself wholeheartedly to anticommunist operations while coincidentally
educating others as to what needed to be done. We who best knew him
never believed there was real documentation of Chau's being a communist
or supporting the party. We did understand that he played at a high-stakes
table, and he lost. Soon after my arrival I visited his family and offered to
make arrangements for the eldest daughter to study in the United States,
but the family decided they would all stay together and wait for Chau's
eventual release. I called on Director of National Police Tran Van Hai and
asked him (understanding I was not there to debate guilt) to assure that,
within the limits of what might be possible, Chau would not be mistreated.[12]

Jeffrey Woods wrote that by early 1967 coordination of the American
counterinsurgency and pacification effort had reached its apex.[13] Given
the initial friction encountered by Bob Matteson in II Corps and Lathram
team grumbling, the coordinative apex was really reached in late 1967,
disrupted in the first half of 1968 by two communist offensives, and then
revived in late 1968 by adoption of the accelerated pacification campaign.
Organizationally, the CORDS model of 1970 was superior to that of three
years earlier. Advisory responsibility for RF/PF, earlier ambiguous, was
clarified by the CORDS Territorial Security Directorate's taking responsibility for RF/PF and PSDF (People's Self Defense Force). Phung Hoang,
operations against the communist political apparatus, had its own directorate. War Victims, another directorate based on reorganization of the
previous Refugees Office, was institutional recognition of the destructive impact of the big-unit war (including PAVN and SVNLF) on rural

communities. Evaluation reporting, previously a branch office, was now the Pacification Studies Group, more closely connected to the assistant chief of staff for CORDS (Jacobson) and appreciated by Colby for relevance, accuracy, and timeliness.

In late 1967 the GVN organized its own "pacification" and rural development bureaucracy so that not only would plug-ins by MACVCORDS and USAID be eased, but also at a central point the GVN would be apprised of US planning and operations.[14] The November 1967 Central Revolutionary Development Council was chaired by the prime minister and included the most important ministries.[15] The minister of rural development was secretary-general of the council. This first attempt at grafting the American concept of a central planning and coordination entity onto Vietnam's bureaucracy was not successful. The prime minister, Nguyen Van Loc (friend of Nguyen Cao Ky), possessed insufficient force of personality and political authority over all the ministries. Gen. Nguyen Duc Thang resigned as minister of revolutionary development just before the January 1968 communist Tet Offensive. Spring/summer 1968 disarray in the rural areas and competition between Nguyen Cao Ky and Nguyen Van Thieu caused the GVN to puzzle over what ought to be done next. The first reorganization after the Tet and May Offensives was a Central Recovery Committee that in an emergency setting was more forceful.

Komer and Colby, supported by the creative thinking of Bob Montague and organizational expertise of Clay McManaway, saw that where the SVNLF suffered enormous personnel losses there was an opportunity to fill the consequent vacuum with reorganized and revitalized RD Cadre teams and RF and PF. This effort was tardy but announced in October, and finally the Accelerated Pacification Campaign was launched in November 1968. Recommitment to a government counterpart link for CORDS resulted in establishment of a Central Pacification and Development Council (CPDC), with Prime Minister Tran Van Huong chairing in principle, but with First Minister Huynh Van Dao as secretary-general and his assistant, Buu Vien, playing an important part in day-to-day operations.[16]

Huong was respectable but slow-moving, a conservative figure without much patience for the effort required to lead, persuade, manipulate, or force others to implement policy. Tran Thien Khiem was brought back to Viet Nam in May 1968 to be minister of interior in the Huong cabinet and had the profile of a prime minister in waiting. While retaining his own ministry, Khiem functioned as deputy prime minister for pacification and then took over as CPDC secretary-general. In August 1969, Tran Van Huong, in some disagreement with President Thieu, was maneuvered into submitting his resignation. Tran Thien Khiem replaced him in September, and at the same time Gen. Cao Hao Hon, who had already been in the Prime Ministry, was promoted to be special assistant to Prime Minister Khiem and chairman of the CPDC. The immediate impact of Bob Montague having worked with Hon beginning in the spring of 1969, facilitated by their past history in Bac Lieu, meant that CORDS planning and the next CPDC annual plan would have congruency. CORDS had what it long desired, a parallel GVN structure that could leverage performance from the ministries.[17]

The village level of government was the conceptual focus for recovery operations from late 1968 onward. Vietnamese who might have advocated the hamlet as the basic building block of rural society were not in positions of influence. Commitment to applying resources at the village level evolved from a planning and resource advantage supposed to result from calculating for about two thousand village entities instead of twelve thousand or more hamlets. Lack of understanding on the part of Vietnamese generals, who were either born to urban families or left the rural environment at a young age, plus American lack of knowledge and imprecision of translation between the languages, allowed general acceptance of the notion that the village was the traditional level of local government. It was not understood that the village was really the traditional (on the part of royal and subsequent French administrations) *supervisory* level of government, while the hamlet was the basic community. Lacking understanding of rural sociology, confused linguistically, and coping with resource limitations, we were falling into the same pattern: apparent ease of control and influence through the village instead of the hamlet: "The hamlet chief acts for the Village Chief in the hamlet, carrying out his responsibilities according to the plan and under the control of the Village Chief."[18]

An obvious anomaly was that, although the village was our (US and GVN) primary point for resource planning and applying government control, we still recognized that hamlets were where people lived and made their basic commitment (to family), and hamlets were the point of entry, or concealed presence, for communist military and political operatives. So the measurement of success was (HES) hamlet-based. Therefore, the 1969 plan (and later the 1970 plan), although focused on villages, also addressed wresting away hamlets from communist control or influence. In order to make that effort expeditious, RD team strength was roughly halved to thirty-man teams, and most PF platoons were reduced in strength so that authorized personnel spaces could be used to activate additional units. In practice, the RD teams were expected to make activity against Viet Cong infrastructure their principal focus. Although there were other tasks, such as organizing PSDF (People's Self Defense Force) and helping to establish local administration (to represent the government), when province officials came to check progress, the RD team leader had better be prepared with a VCI list, a map indicating homes of sympathizers, and a plan for "census grievance" to follow suspect families.[19]

15
Headquarters MACVCORDS

What did William Egan Colby expect from me? When we sat down to discuss specific responsibilities, he began by saying he prized flexibility. While duties would be specialized, my view of the Viet Nam scene should be catholic, and he expected me to identify problems. "Don't concern yourself with whether or not I agree, just give me your best thinking. If we were always thinking the same, I wouldn't need you." He said my position would be executive assistant, as Bob Montague and Ev Bumgardner had been before me, but that since he didn't require much personal assistance, he would be surprised if I were in the office every day. If I would be away from the office for more than a few hours, just let his secretary know my location.

My first responsibility would be counseling the GVN and JUSPAO with respect to the "people's information" program intended to support the CPDC annual plan. I interjected that my first impression was that there was faint political content to the CPDC plan, so "people's information" was marketing a stale product. He smiled and replied that conveying this view to the information committee wouldn't hurt, and in any case monitoring people's information was like having a hunting license. Because information cut across all operating categories, it meant I could look at anything of interest.

The second general area for continuous attention would be maintaining the files on corruption and inept performance that Bob Montague and Ev Bumgardner previously activated and preserved. When advisors forwarded a complaint to our office, it would be my responsibility to appropriately record the allegation. I had already acquainted myself with the files and assured him that, when Americans made complaints, specificity would be required. When, in my judgment, a situation merited action, I would bring the case to him for discussion with the prime minister, and it would be well documented.

He added that following up on developments at the National Training Center, helping to hold Colonel Be on the reservation, and staying informed as to the work of the Pacification Studies Group would be useful. I should, he advised, come in and talk whenever information had immediacy. Written reports ought to be brief and direct to the point. There was, he said, no pause in headquarters paper flow, so he would expect most of my reporting to be oral rather than by memorandum.[1]

Ambassador Colby inquired as to my interest in the continuing Phung Hoang program,[2] saying explicitly that "this is not a project or short-term operation, it is an ongoing program, including sentencing and detention, that the government will implement over years." I responded that when I mentioned, in January 1969, fundamental disagreement with the way we operated in Viet Nam, evolution of ICEX to Phoenix was one of my reservations. He appeared surprised and said he understood I was involved with something similar years before in Quang Ngai. I explained there was both exaggeration and misunderstanding with respect to what Bob Kelly and I had applied during 1964. We did expect units to develop such good relations with people in hamlets that identifying individuals and families involved with the SVNLF would be easier, but identification was for two purposes: to let them know they were identified (the infamous black eye logo) and to provide such enhanced *beneficial* attention that comrades outside the hamlet might suspect their loyalty. The goal was to isolate those people, to neutralize them in place, not to "neutralize" by killing them—unless it was as the consequence of ambush and exchange of fire outside the hamlet.

I was familiar with counterterror theory, and I thought it wasn't effective and in fact contributed to the rural pathology that communists exploited. Colby was a patient and attentive listener. His very posture conveyed interest in what a discussant wanted to convey, even when he disagreed. I was experiencing the interpersonal skill that was central to his success as recruiter, manager, and leader. He asked what, specifically, troubled me about Phoenix.

As ICEX, in the first stage, was conceived, I welcomed and even on the margin encouraged organization of a national system for managing intelligence related to the communist administrative and support apparatus. But in the next phase, organizing units specifically directed to go after individuals identified through DIOCC records and interrogations, we appeared to echo what had transpired in the denunciation campaign of the late 1950s combined with the French *ratissage* approach applied in Algeria. Now it seemed to me, since my return and recent conversation with friends in the provinces as well as in MACV, that there was inadequate distinction between persons accused—suspects, detainees—and offenders. The categories (ABC) appeared reasonable, but I suspected conservative province committees would not understand that a farmer could not avoid paying tax to ascendant local communists, at least by night. Ambassador Colby understood my reservations. He agreed, with no disputation, that there were inequities, but CORDS had assigned an officer to work toward assuring a legal basis for the arrest and detention system.[3] He concluded that, as previously with Ev, this subject would not be part of my portfolio, but if I happened to spot a problem, bring it to him, and if I encountered a Phung Hoang advisor who was uncomfortable with the process, I should bring that to his attention as well.

Colby's immediate office staff also included Executive Secretary Tina Kapazinas, Tony Allitto (special assistant for reports), Col. Don Metcalf (assistant for territorial security and liaison to the Phung Hoang directorate), a specialist in data processing, and two administrative NCOs. Additionally, Clay McManaway,[4] Gage McAfee, and Lee Braddock (heading the pacification studies group) were frequent visitors for discussion with Ambassador Colby. Ambassador Colby had as close to an open door as one could imagine for a senior official.[5] Tina was sentry at the portal, and one was wise to check with her before presuming to enter the boss's office, because she knew his schedule and had a sense of what the pressure and priority of the day would be. Tony Allitto had experience-based understanding of the CORDS operation from district up through province. Colonel Metcalf had minimal background knowledge of Viet Nam but satisfied the requirement for having a senior field-grade officer in the office. Harry Johnson and Jean Sauvageot had a special relationship with us because they were at the Prime Ministry to serve as permanent liaison with the prime minister, General Hon, and CPDC.

Ascension of Tran Thien Khiem in September 1969 meant there would be a Vietnamese prime minister more receptive to CORDS advice than had been Tran Van Huong. Ambassador Colby and Ev Bumgardner had therefore decided to push a program to link citizen and government that would work through CPDC and around the stale Ministry of Information. The result was the Political Mobilization Decree of 28 October 1969 that would assure distribution of accurate information by monthly booklets through province political mobilization committees. A typical GVN bureaucratic response was to focus on process and procedure vice action, so setting up committees, discussion, and debating the topic of the first booklet required several weeks. The national committee, with input from the province committees, had to (1) prepare a national political mobilization plan, (2) set up a general program for both political and psychological warfare, (3) provide guidance on political indoctrination for military personnel, cadre, and civil servants, and (4) coordinate government and private efforts. National Political Mobilization Guidelines would be drafted, based on presidential and other leadership statements, to prepare the masses for political struggle against the communists. Central to the Colby/Bumgardner concept was the necessity for leaders at all levels, civil and military, to be responsible by personal involvement rather than delegating political communication to a staff member. Periodic seminars at all levels, with required attendance, would groove the message to be carried to the citizenry. Public attitude and reaction should be reported back to higher authority. A major emphasis was expected to be on local problems and issues. The monthly booklets, to focus discussion, would be forwarded to provincial committees and corps commands by the national committee. Each ministry would prepare a plan for participation. But little was accomplished that winter, and on 6 April 1970 the name was changed from Political Mobilization to Mass Information (Thong Tin Dai Chung).[6]

I looked into this spongy bureaucratic mess that Ambassador Colby expected me to energize. Prime Minister (in name) Khiem chaired the Central Mass Information Committee. Minister of Information Ngo Khac Tinh served (in name) as secretary-general. They had the titles but chose not to take personal responsibility for implementation. Instead, the actual (marginal) results were achieved through a standing office (*ban thuong truc*) chaired by the deputy chief of CPDC, Nguyen Xuan Liem.[7] The Standing Office, with representation from the Ministry of Interior, Ministry of Information, Ministry of Chieu Hoi, and Central Political Warfare Directorate, agreed mass information would be a priority for 1970 Phase II pacification and development from July through October. But by August only four topical booklets had been sent to the field, and only a total of fifty thousand copies of each title. A few talking papers were issued by the Standing Office, but only three copies of each were sent to ministries and provinces.

I attended the next meeting of the Standing Office (which, however labeled, formally or informally in Vietnamese, functioned as a permanent committee), and, speaking in rough but serviceable Vietnamese, stressed four points. These were command responsibility, substance not theory, need for shaping generalities to local specifics, and no fancy equipment. I said our goal, although we might fall short, should be spiritual mobilization (*dong vien tinh than*) of the quality that communists sought to instill in their best cadre. I suggested we add an intelligence representative to keep the Standing Office apprised of communist mass information activity. Lieutenant Colonel Viet was designated as my contact. I hoped (as opposed to expected) that the Standing Office would enliven itself and would go to provinces, districts, and even hamlets to set an example of desirable practice. Later that day Colonel Viet met with me and described a letter the prime minister would sign to energize the mass information campaign. Regrettably, it was a reformulation of previous stale practice.

I understood the Standing Office was not going to meet the standard of cadre operations we had witnessed from 1964 through 1966 and that could still be found in the CORDS Pacification Study Group, but I thought I ought to provide General Hon and Ambassador Colby with a glimpse of reality. I prepared a paper for Ambassador Colby stating that the "program is not effective today" and describing the lack of coordination and absence of command execution. I recommended a permanent staff for the Standing Office (that at best met once a week), a staff that would make decisions and get into provinces and districts to check implementation. My actual intended recipient was General Hon, so the paper was translated and provided to him "as a courtesy" on 6 August 1970.[8] On 7 August a staff was appointed and began work. The next day DEPCORDS/MACV Colby sent a circular letter to senior American officials describing "People's Information" and the expectation that American advisors would encourage their counterparts to take active roles.[9]

The real test was whether the GVN would commit—would execute. Even that question ignored the continuing lack of motivational political content that would inspire a messenger. Ambassador Colby and I discussed this on a few occasions. I pointed out that Thomas Paine and Martin Luther King amplified the dream of their times, but that the dream was so powerful it would have been advanced by others even if Paine and King had not. The communists had their dream, to unify the country, replace the old ruling elements, and expel foreigners. What was our dream? Consolidate President Thieu? Build the Nhan Xa Party?[10] The other side's rallying cry was "Bao Ve Mien Bac! Gia Phong Mien Nam!" (Protect the North! Liberate the South!), while we had no emotive equivalent.

In early September I reported by memorandum to Ambassador Colby that the Ministry of Information still had not assigned a full-time representative to the permanent staff established four weeks earlier.[11] In the provinces there was little to no people's information activity. Subsequent memoranda during the remaining months of 1970 portray a repetitive pattern of lack of energetic implementation. The Ministry of Information finally assigned a full-time representative to the permanent staff, but that person explained that the Ministry of Information would not print material for other ministries. CPDC recommended eliminating hamlet information cadre in 1971 and instead forming mobile teams to operate in their home areas, something like what Ev and I had organized in Binh Dinh at General Freund's request in late 1965. But well-connected Minister Ngo Khac Tinh made sure that guidance back to CPDC from the president's office was to maintain hamlet information cadre. I felt as though I was trying to jump-start a truck by pushing it uphill.[12]

I reject the simplistic suggestion that Bumgardner, Kelly, and I were Lansdale acolytes, but it is true we had significant areas of agreement independently realized. Perhaps our consensus sine qua non was the absolute value of elections. Even if elections were, regrettably, infuriatingly, rigged, we still believed there was value to creating an election "habit" with expectation that eventually citizens would demand fair process, observers, and independent certification. The 1966 constituent assembly elections struggled for by Vietnamese of diverse persuasion, but above all by the central Viet Nam Buddhists, delivered the April 1967 Constitution and a schedule for executive and bicameral legislative elections in September 1967. Following those elections, it was appropriate to refer, once again, to the Republic of Viet Nam (RVN), and from this point onward (having reminded myself) I will do so. But it is significant that almost all US documents from September 1967 onward continue to use the appellation GVN.[13] Although the constituent assembly wanted to include a constitutional stipulation for election of province chiefs, that was vetoed by the ruling military chiefs, who used national security as pretext for holding on to lucrative appointive authority. Hamlet and village elections also were arranged and carried out from 1967 onward. There were obvious problems. Intimidation and rigging scarred the ballot exercise at the highest level. In the countryside, district chiefs were required to assure that hamlet and village candidates were acceptable. That meant candidates were frequently selected, not just vetted, by local authority. Nguyen Be, still running the National Training Center at Vung Tau, was responsible for courses organized to encourage and train elected hamlet and village officials.[14] He acknowledged that the government continued to feel inadequate to meet the need for effective presence and work in hamlets, so village-level administration was both a coordinating and a controlling mechanism. Countryside elections were far from open and truly democratic, but like me, Be believed those elections were better than none at all.[15]

On 30 August 1970 half of the senatorial seats, in the upper house of the bicameral legislature, were up for election. Three years earlier the Buddhists, in general disgust with blatant government manipulation, had abstained from the elections, although some deputies, such as Kieu Mong Thu, received local Buddhist support for their candidacies to the lower house. Now, despite indicators of repression, the An Quang–inclined Buddhist coalition entered a slate of senatorial candidates in the contest. That list, headed by Vu Van Mau, obtained more votes than did the other two winning slates.[16] An embassy assessment noted that the list had balanced geographical representation, that participation meant An Quang Buddhists were moving from protest politics to legislative politics, and that President Thieu had not tried very hard to squeeze them out.

I wrote a rebuttal memorandum for Ambassador Colby based on looking at the results province by province. I called attention to the strength of Vu Van Mau's slate, even in provinces far from central Viet Nam and where the list did not include a native son. Since the Mau list was not one of the three favored and supported by the government, and since it was well known which lists were and which were not, then the total of votes for other slates (the Mau list above all) could only be understood as a rejection of the president and his government. Referencing this paper, I prepared another one addressing what the election signified for President Thieu and the Second Republic if it were entering a period of political competition with the Communist Party. My opinion was not completely negative, because I believed that if the choice were between a "reformed" Thieu and communists, then voters in general would not choose communists. But I did urge reformation, cutting connections to the corrupt and ineffective past, and selection of a respectable vice presidential candidate for the 1971 presidential contest. I was surprised when Tina Kapazinas saw me the next morning and said she had collected all copies of the second paper advocating political reform. Ambassador Colby felt I had strayed onto embassy political pasture.[17] This was the first of only two occasions when something I wrote was expunged.

The office files on corrupt and incompetent RVN civil and military officers were extensive. What began during the Komer-Montague 1967 initiation of CORDS seemed to have grown exponentially since then. Ev told me that when he had the files, he felt there was insufficient focus on the problem at the highest RVN levels, even though Ambassador Colby discreetly referred to this specific duty as "follow-up on individual recommendations to the government with respect to the performance of various Vietnamese officials."[18]

The issue of corruption was complex and addressed hypocritically. We Americans vacillated between excusing corruption as "traditional" in Asian societies and demanding a degree of civic cleanliness rare in our own country. While the Viet Nam economy was inflating yearly, official salaries never squared with expenditures. Furthermore, family expectations, in competition with other families, fueled the temptation to "squeeze" for personal benefit. Consequently, wives, even those of officers who cultivated an austere image, became cogwheels in the machinery of public office for private benefit.[19] Fictive assignment to a draft-exempt position, or if in the military to a safe position, was a service that, as Ton That Thien once said, "Khong duoc mien phi." (I translate that as: "Cannot be without compensation.") Americans could usually be fooled, saying to others, "My counterpart, General X is honest to the bone, but his wife takes advantage of her position." Rather than directly approach an officer with a bribe for favorable consideration, a favor-seeker could make an arrangement between wives, thereby preserving the fiction of spousal probity. Other officers had bagmen who could make arrangements on their behalf, and occasionally a deal would even be handled by the principal himself. The chain of command was also a chain for exchange of favors and kickbacks. When I found miserable CIDG food in a Special Forces camp in mid-1966, the commander told me that he had to squeeze money to move his monthly quota up the chain, eventually to the corps commander. Advising creatively, I suggested that he siphon away from civic action, psychological operations, or even intelligence funds rather than degrade the food for camp defenders.

Once Wilbur Wilson called me from Can Tho with a complaint concerning the Ke Sach district chief in Ba Xuyen province. I explained that my standard for bringing a charge to Ambassador Colby's attention was persuasive evidence that malfeasance had such an effect on performance that RVN rural development was endangered because continuation in office would benefit the communists. Documentation arrived from Wilbur a couple of days later. I combined what he submitted with notes already on hand, then prepared a talking paper for Ambassador Colby to raise the matter with Prime Minister Khiem. We both knew the artificiality in discussing the issue of a culpable major, who would only be reassigned, with the prime minister, against whom there were more serious allegations.

During the time I worked this issue for Ambassador Colby, and I worked the problem to a greater extent than did any other officer, I think we were really only occasionally pulling or transplanting a weed. Over the next two years, in each case in which we either advised against an appointment (Le Duc Dat as commander of the 22nd Division in March 1972) or sought removal of a senior officer, we were not (to my knowledge) successful. Moreover, there were always inconsistencies in our approach to this problem. John Vann, who in 1972 would urge making the most of what I thought was a circumstantial case against Dat, tolerated Ngo Dzu in IV Corps and later II Corps because John believed he could manipulate Dzu to a level of acceptable performance.

The atmosphere of deals and arrangements was not limited to Vietnamese. Ambassador Colby was approached with an improper offer while I worked for him. He made that conversation the subject of a memorandum and cut off contact with the person involved. A few months later, my wife and I were invited to lunch at Pham Van Dong's house, where he introduced me to Hong Kong businessmen who sought my assistance in obtaining a PX concession, with benefit for myself. Angry and disappointed that Dong believed I was corruptible, I immediately told him that we were leaving and I would never meet with him again.[20] An American general officer asked Jean Sauvageot to interpret for a wealthy businessman from Hawaii, whom the general met when stationed there and who was sniffing around Saigon for possible ventures. I resented my friend's being placed in that position.[21]

Nguyen Be, now a colonel, during discussion at the National Training Center in Vung Tau said that RD Cadre teams were no longer the cutting edge of RVN pacification and rural development. The new emphasis, given what was understood in 1970 to be an environment favoring the RVN, was on administration and governance. Although some RD Cadre teams were reorganized at province level, and occasionally in Vung Tau, the National Training Center increasingly concentrated on courses for village and hamlet administrators. When they graduated, the president and prime minister addressed them. Overall, Colonel Be considered this a positive development. However, he cautioned, the apparent RVN advantage was based on communist overreaching and vigorous RVN/American response in 1968. Now, with the American military withdrawal, we should not expect the beneficial balance of 1970 to endure. I asked him to look into the future and share what he foresaw. He replied that, looking far out, there were "alternative futures" depending on choices we would make in the next year. Expecting to determine the future by defeating the communists militarily was foolish.[22] Without American forces and lavish supply (and he expected extraordinary air operations to vanish when no longer in support of American units), ARVN would not be able to withstand a combined PAVN-SVNLF push. So, he continued, the alternative would be to use the negotiations in Paris to shape a political competition over time. He believed that, if the RVN adopted a reform agenda, an outcome more desirable than battlefield defeat might be possible. Be cautioned me not to attach his name to the case he had just made. I had never known him to be so circumspect and asked why. He said that President Thieu already distrusted him, and now his wife and children were with him in Vung Tau. He was feeling family responsibility.

I traveled in provinces and districts, talking with Vietnamese administrators and an occasional American advisor. Rather than dilute my perception by looking at every province, I went to a few: Chuong Thien, Kien Hoa, Long An, Hau Nghia, Binh Dinh, Quang Ngai, and Quang Nam. I would always begin by asking about rural administration. Village chiefs were not familiar with specific tasks of the 1970 national plan, and, when they did come close, their reference was vague and unrelated to their own locale. Most village officials expressed degrees of reliance on district offices for supervisory as well as logistic support. There seemed to be an overall sense of administrative isolation from the hamlets, where people lived. I felt, not everywhere, but definitely in some districts, as though it were 1963 all over again: there was a government presence in district and village apparatus, and then people in the hamlets were prepared to accommodate.

I was also interested in rural security. There was some improvement. Although skeptical of the HES report for any specific month, and knowing why hamlet chiefs would accommodate or sleep elsewhere rather than in a C hamlet, I did think the trend shown by HES reports over several months had validity. Convergence of RD team operations and significant Popular Forces improvement, combined with beneficial aspects (placing aside problematic impact on noncombatants) of US maneuver units, had resulted, in 1969–70, in a countryside with less overt communist presence. There were still incidents in restless areas where communist presence had long been a political fact of life,[23] but in a few provinces it almost seemed as if the war were over.

I attributed PF improvement in some measure to regularizing salary and equipment. While inflation hurt, at least now pay was constant and reliable. Equipment issue was not the extracting-wisdom-tooth kind of problem that I had encountered in 1965. Talking with PF soldiers and American advisors persuaded me that the Mobile Advisory Team (MAT) approach, implemented in 1967 and significantly expanded in 1968 and 1969, had made the difference more than any other single factor. The concept might have grown from the seed that we planted with MACV and RF/PF headquarters in 1965, but the 1968–70 version was much improved. Whereas we had two or three Americans with a cadre team that would go from platoon to platoon (and in the case of CIDG more like company to company), a full MAT consisted of five Americans, including an assigned medic. This concept and implementation was close to the encadrement that my friends and I had advocated in 1965, that we welcomed as US

Marine CAP practice, and that should have been applied with ARVN. Now, in late 1970, the American drawdown resulted in phasing out MAT presence. But when I spoke with Popular Force soldiers, they almost uniformly expressed warm regard for the Americans who had lived with them. The only problem they mentioned was language difficulty. They missed the Americans and knew that absent the MAT, medical evacuation (medevac) would be *much* less likely.

CORDS, specifically Ambassador Colby, pushed implementation of the People's Self Defense Force (PSDF) against an initially reluctant RVN. The intention was to involve the general population in defense of their own families and homes. Remembering the 1966 Roles and Missions Study's judgment on "people's self defense" as an unrealistic goal, I was at first doubtful that PSDF in 1970–71 would serve any useful purpose. [24] I was wrong. There was quite a difference in the environment compared with 1966, and PSDF were not expected to be assertive militia seeking out and confronting SVNLF units. Instead, PSDF was more emblematic of low to moderate public involvement with the RVN. PSDF maximum participation grew from an estimate of two million persons in 1969 to a generous supposition of four million persons around the end of 1970. Yes, there was some appearance of dumping weapons into a political vacuum, but, unlike 1963–65, when US ordnance was immediately useful for new SVNLF trainees, in 1970–71 there was much less risk of PSDF weaponry having employment value with communist units that were already well provided with the AK-47, Chinese carbines, and other Communist Bloc issue. I did find some PSDF more fictive than actual, with weapons being held at the village or at PF outposts rather than being in the hands of people, but I also spoke with some in hamlets who comfortably described themselves as members of the PSDF. Even as a low-level symbol, this was better than nothing and potentially could be meaningful in local political competition with communists if we had a post–cease fire environment such as the one Colonel Be thought possible.

In late September John Ehrlichman and George Shultz came to Viet Nam as a White House Executive Group. Ambassador Colby brought them to IV Corps for firsthand exposure to the Mekong Delta. Maj. Jean Sauvageot and I were along to assist with explanation and interpretation. Ehrlichman and Shultz separated when it was time to visit a district and a hamlet, and by toss of coin Jean accompanied the former, while I spent part of the day with Shultz. Afterward, I made a special trip to Can Tho for conversation with John Vann. The reason I went back to see John was because, although I believed the overall situation in the countryside was far better than it had been in 1965–69, the briefing packet prepared for the two visitors presented an excessively optimistic description.[25]

John and I discussed my strong feeling that C-category hamlets were not "relatively secure" and, although the HES system might have that as the definition, we should not be fooling ourselves. We agreed that B-category hamlets were actually the "relatively secure" ones. So, realistically, it was 72 percent of the Mekong Delta hamlets that were secure or relatively secure, not 90 percent as presented in the handout. We also agreed that our consensus of 72 percent represented significant improvement over previous years. But then, when the VC manpower base was considered to be derived only from the population that communists controlled, I felt we were underestimating potential recruitment from areas where they had access rather than control.

Looking at the Chieu Hoi Program and Phung Hoang results reported in IV Corps, I suggested to John that when figures in the briefing handout indicate 40 percent of Hoi Chanh "presumably go back to the rice paddy," we ought to assume that they are back in touch with their friends surviving in "mini-base areas." Most interesting was the handout's acknowledgment that "the Phung Hoang program has not yet succeeded in neutralizing the VCI faster than the VC can replace them, but it has made it increasingly difficult for the VC to develop experienced and aggressive leaders." Which side would outlast the other?

Our conversation extended for most of the night. We talked, of course, about Tran Ngoc Chau, his arrest and prison term. I asked John to describe his most significant difficulty in IV Corps. "Getting the Vietnamese leadership to perform!" He was just becoming comfortable with Ngo Quang Truong, but he felt that with the Delta Military Assistance Command (DMAC) between him and Truong, General McCown and General Cushman were going to have greater access. My sense was that Truong would prove more capable than his predecessor, Ngo Dzu. But Vann responded that "Ngo Dzu was shapeable, I had influence." John was hoping a way would be found to be placed in charge, command, of the American effort in IV Corps. He had allies in Washington who worked to make that happen.[26] John thought that if his preference for IV Corps "command" could not be realized, then it might be possible to transfer up to central Viet Nam, II Corps, in the spring, and he asked whether I would consider going with him as deputy. I responded that, although Ambassador Colby and I did not have the same kind of friendship, I had already made commitment to Colby and would not break my assignment.

John told me our friend Gordon Huddleston, in Chau Doc as a Vann troubleshooter, was "worth his weight in gold."[27] I told John to consider taking action on some of his input. Otherwise Hud might feel that the effort and risk were unappreciated. My example was his reporting on Regional Forces' repetitive use of the same ambush sites and approach routes: "Lien Doi 4/67 has been extremely fortunate in not being ambushed enroute to the semi-permanent positions."[28] Corrective action was required.

Naturally, we also talked about the personal, our family circumstances. John knew I was married now. He kept shaking his head, as if puzzled. On my part I knew more about John's personal life than anyone else, except possibly Jake and Wilbur Wilson. Once the father of a young girl sought me out and asked me to persuade John to leave his daughter alone. I tried and failed. Now, almost four years later, they had a daughter, and John somehow juggled time to include visits with them and with other women. John asked whether I was seeing someone in Saigon, and I responded no, because it would not be fair to the woman, my wife, or my son. And, I reminded him, with my wife in Taiwan, the family separation provision allowed me to travel there to see her every two months.

Thinking about the personal dimension of our conversation, I realized John's behavior differed from that of many other Americans only by an almost driven appetite for seduction. I incline to being Francophobic, but as with my nontheist affection for certain biblical phrases, there are expressions in French that really are *le mot juste*, and one of those is the phrase *droit du seigneur*. Although its root meaning and degree of historic practice are debatable, in common usage it signifies a lord's right to do as he wished with property or even the lives of those he presumed less worthy. By 1970 a sort of *imperium maius*, rule over an allied but dependent tribe, unquestioned from the capital (Washington), was the license for many Americans' privileged behavior. Colonel Be spoke with me about rumors that a senior American official spent time with the prominent wife of a Vietnamese gentleman. He mentioned the story as an example of how people could confuse American conduct with that of an earlier generation of French colonialists. I raised the matter, in exactly that context, with the American who was the subject of the rumor. I had to wait a few days for a least awkward occasion to make a short presentation of the need for every American to avoid even an inadvertent appearance of colonial behavior. As for myself, yes, I had women friends, but there were always boundaries.[29] If anything in my own conduct might offend Vietnamese, I would expect friends to call it to my attention.[30]

Ambassador Colby called me to his office one day and asked whether I would be agreeable to having my wife and son join me in Viet Nam. American dependents had not been allowed residence in Viet Nam since 1965, so it had not occurred to me that having family in Saigon was possible. Sa Yun came once in the fall for a visit. I introduced her to friends and so was sure she could be emotionally comfortable in Viet Nam. WEC, as we referred to him in the office, explained that on a couple of occasions he had wanted to point me onto a problem but then had learned I was about to depart on a family visitation trip to Taipei. He didn't want postponement, but at the same time he felt deprived of the use he would have made of me. The solution, he said, was to move papers approving her residence in-country. His push worked. Sa Yun arrived with David Philip in January 1971.

Both were tired from half a day of flying and Hong Kong transit. David, not yet two years old, was restless and cranky. We warmed some semi-baby food, calmed him, and got him to bed. There we were in the apartment sitting area, each looking at the other, and the doorbell rang. When I opened, John Paul Vann absolutely swept in, fresh pizza in hand, saying, "I just had to meet the girl that Frank Scotton married!" And, with a bow, he took Sa Yun's hand and placed a kiss on the back of it. I was dumbfounded by John's unusual courtly manner. But then I realized, as easily as that, John had won an ally. From then on, no one could be critical of John within Sa Yun's hearing. When he once mentioned the need for a place in Saigon where he could rest in privacy, she assured him (before I could respond) that we would always have a guest room for him. That was the "John Vann room," with special peppermint-striped sheets. The women who occasionally joined John for private rest were welcomed as his friends, so I had to be off my high horse and refrain from provoking John about his continuing indiscretions.

The "health" of ARVN divisions (twelve, including Airborne and

Marines[31])—that is, their psychological health as well as operational readiness—was extremely important to the outcome of negotiations. Each of the twelve represented value at the table. Negotiating strength depended on maintaining at least the appearance of ARVN unit integrity, responsible command, and combat performance. Although CORDS did not have advisory responsibility for those ARVN units, I told Ambassador Colby we should be aware of morale. The easiest way was to examine the monthly desertion figures for each division. As with HES, one could spot trends. One conclusion was obvious. The units experiencing the most intense combat (Airborne, Marines, 1st Division) did not have the worst rates of desertion. Higher desertion rates were found in units that had the least capable leadership. Occasionally I would visit a unit that had good figures and another that did not, then discuss my observations with WEC.[32]

The 1st Infantry Division was the backbone of I Corps defense. Pham Van Phu was division commander. He was originally from Ha Dong in the North and an early convert to Catholicism. He began his military service as an interpreter with the French and later commanded a company in the 5th Vietnamese Parachute Battalion. He continued airborne service and was suspected of involvement in the November 1960 coup attempt, which caused him to be detained from 1961 to 1963. Following the November 1963 coup and assassination of President Diem, he was briefly chief of staff for Vietnamese Special Forces. We had last met in 1967, almost four years earlier, but I remembered his interest in collecting swagger sticks and so brought him an unusual one made of Ha Tien tortoise shell, lacquered wood, and silver trim.[33]

Phu had taken command of the 1st Division several months earlier. I was impressed by the relatively low desertion figures for the division. He replied that division morale benefited from attachment to a stable operating area over years and a succession of commanding officers committed to defense of Hue city. But, he went on, that spirit was about to be tested by the major operation launched into Laos. He looked at me expectantly. I was mystified.[34] He paused, then explained that Chien Dich Lam Son 719, a multidivision operation, would drive across southern Laos on Route 9, raiding communist base areas and supply routes and seize Tchepone (Xepon). I asked about US participation and could tell by the look on his face that Phu only then realized I was uninformed. But he shrugged and continued. My memory of the conversation is that his emphasis was on US forces being limited to the 5th Mechanized and 101st Airborne Divisions, which would be charged with opening Route 9 westward past old FSB Vandergrift and as far as Khe Sanh, with that base revived as the support platform for the ARVN operation some forty or fifty kilometers into Laos.

He said ARVN airborne and armor units would make the thrust along Route 9 to Tchepone, with airborne and ranger battalions screening the northern flank and his own 1st Division having responsibility along the southern flank. After a month or two, depending on success, withdrawal would be eastward on Route 9 or southeastward through A Shau. For consideration of his feelings, given the enormity of what he had described, I steeled myself to avoid any outward sign of the wave of pessimism cresting within. I asked about command relationships on the Vietnamese side and between Vietnamese and supporting Americans, and the role Americans played in planning the operation. It is an American plan, he assured me.[35]

The command line of authority for the operation, as he talked, seemed more like a spider web than a chain. Hoang Xuan Lam, I Corps commander since May 1966, would have overall authority.[36] But he was outranked and disliked (*ghet*) by both Marine Lt. Gen. Le Nguyen Khang and airborne Lt. Gen. Du Quoc Dong, whose forces were charged with major, absolutely critical, roles. Phu told me Lam received command from Nguyen Cao Ky after suppression of the 1966 struggle movement, but in the next year, politically clever, Lam supported Thieu over Ky for president. Phu described Lam as mild-mannered and subtle on the surface, but superstitious and always calculating for personal benefit. I asked whether Lam had a past record of command achievement. He responded that when Lam had the 23rd and later the 2nd Division, he was passive (*bi dong*), *passif*, he emphasized in French to be sure I understood. Obviously, the play of personalities worried him. Phu offered to get me up to Khe Sanh for a look. Not wanting to be thought passive, I accepted.

Khe Sanh was a beehive. I had not seen such concentric, focused aerial activity since the Air Cav established its base at An Khe in 1965. The airstrip didn't seem ready for major fixed-wing use but was being worked on, and helicopters were shuttling back and forth. Most of the crews were American and seemed to have come from all over Viet Nam. I knew there was, since December, some congressional prohibition on US entry into Laos, but obviously the legislation was not being applied against air elements. The US helicopter crews were curious and, figuring me for a reporter (roughly dressed but not in fatigues), asked me who I was with. I replied that I was on my own.

"Want a lift?"

I wasn't sure if I did or not, but there it was. Just a bit farther. The crew told me they were going to touch down at an ARVN LZ, and expected ships would be constantly in and out for supply. So far, they said, there was little resistance, but some antiaircraft activity. For fear of showing fear, we can sometimes put ourselves in fearful situations.

Approaching the already secured LZ, we took fire. The sound of rounds striking, something like a screwdriver puncturing tin can, chilled my innards. We hovered, touched down, and I jump-stepped off. It seemed automatic, past instinct, natural. I moved around within the LZ perimeter. I think these were the 39th Rangers, first seen when commanded by Son Thuong at Duc Pho during 1963.[37] They had been in place, they said, only two days; another ranger battalion was a few kilometers to the south. I gazed beyond to the mountainous terrain enfolding this small position. We were several klicks north of Route 9. It seemed a very isolated spot and was already receiving fire as PAVN pushed back against patrols. I felt the enemy coiling for overwhelming reaction. These Vietnamese rangers were brave men, but bravery might not be enough. It was a fearful place. I boarded an incoming helicopter when it briefly touched while kicking off supplies, then I was off and on my way by stages back to Saigon.

Ambassador Colby was away from the office, so Tina Kapazinas had time to type my short memorandum describing what I believed was imminent disaster for the Republic of Viet Nam. I presented my reasoning and concluded that initiating and supporting Lam Son 719 was a MACV failure. A few days later, when we discussed the subject, WEC told me that my memorandum had been erased because it intruded on advisory responsibilities that were not CORDS's.[38] He rebuked my spur-of-the-moment look into Laos by reminding me that I was "over thirty," with family, and expected to act my age. When I defended myself by commenting that I thought the prohibition on entry into Laos only applied to military personnel, he responded that while I worked for him facile rationalization ought to be avoided. He obtained a promise not to discuss my observations with anyone else.[39]

The US military had a problem with public perception of operations in Viet Nam, particularly with respect to their impact on noncombatants, and whether some conduct could be considered war crimes. The Schell brothers (Jonathan and Orville) had written accounts from Ben Suc (III Corps) and Quang Ngai–Quang Tin (I Corps) that portrayed rural devastation. The Son My massacre conducted by American soldiers of the Americal Division in 1968 was investigated and became public two years later. Special Forces Detachment B-57 (focused on Cambodia) tortured and executed a suspected double agent in June 1969. About the same time, John Vann called my attention to the 9th Division "bloody rampage" through the Mekong Delta. Moreover, there were reports of drug abuse and racial tension in many units. General Metaxis, deputy commander of the Americal Division, told me with considerable emotion that there were unprecedented discipline problems in the division.[40] My impression was that these problems varied in degree from unit to unit, might have been more prevalent in rear-area commands, and were less frequently observed among US Marines. As for crimes against civilians or prisoners, a blanket indictment would be foolish and unfair. Special Forces, CAPs, and MATs, all integrated with local forces, were more unlikely (another advantage of encadrement) to abuse civilians. Units operating in unpopulated areas, ridges west of Dak To or south of A Shau, would not negatively impact a civil population. Treatment of prisoners, even in the heat of combat, was significantly dependent on the quality of command and unit discipline.

The embassy had a continuing concern about American public reaction to news reports highlighting these problems and supposed they would have deleterious impact on support for the war.[41] I never witnessed murder or rape. When I did see torture or prisoner abuse, I intervened.[42] But observing destruction in Binh Dinh and Quang Ngai, the result of casual application of firepower from 1965 through 1967, and talking with Vietnamese in remnant hamlets and refugee camps all convinced me that crimes of rape and murder were committed in those provinces.[43] Mutual misunderstanding between Americans and Vietnamese was linguistically and culturally unavoidable. Americans, frustrated by failure to communicate, referred to Vietnamese as "gooks" or worse.[44] Soldiers, practicing the ancient art of scrounging, would steal, ridiculously, from Vietnamese hamlets, and Vietnamese envious of relative wealth would opportunistically take what they could from individual Americans, unattended vehicles, or depots. By a peculiar syllogism (people like us don't live like animals: Vietnamese live like animals: therefore, they aren't people)

Vietnamese were too often considered subhuman. Only a rare American combatant would recognize the sophistication of Vietnamese culture and its relationship to the environment and conclude, "*We* were the gooks."[45]

Ambassador Colby called me to his office. He asked what I was thinking about in terms of onward assignment after CORDS. I had not been concerned about my next assignment, because he had brought me back to Viet Nam and then arranged for my wife and son to join me. He appreciated that acknowledgment and personal commitment but said he would not be staying more than a few more months.[46] "There seem to be a couple of options," he continued. "John spoke with me about taking you as his deputy. I won't discuss it. That's not in the ballpark. I won't approve."

The second option would be transfer to JUSPAO to head up one of the divisions at the level of assistant director. WEC explained that the chief of the Program Liaison Division for JUSPAO had died a few months earlier.[47] JUSPAO Director Ed Nickel, who had replaced Barry Zorthian in 1968, approached Ambassador Colby and asked to have me transferred into that position because we were entering a period of political sensitivity prior to RVN elections. We met with Ed Nickel. He agreed to my continuing to be available for special tasking at MACV or at embassy request and having a loose leash, beyond the position description, for looking into subjects of interest. As easily as that, almost a handshake deal, I was assigned to JUSPAO effective 1 March 1971.[48]

16
Adjustments

My JUSPAO experience a few years earlier had been field-focused and punctuated by significant friction with senior officers who knew little of Viet Nam and resented my (relative to them) initiative and freedom of action. Now I had to cope with the opposite situation. I was an assistant director responsible for coordinating ten Americans and, directly or indirectly, twenty Vietnamese. I knew more about rural Viet Nam than they did, including the Vietnamese, who were urban and technically oriented. It would be necessary to lead with sensitive but consistent direction. It did help, significantly, having a reputation, benefiting from the Colby imprimatur, and they all knew Ed Nickel had asked for me. Still, I had the impression that a couple of senior officers were, with curiosity, observing whether I would stumble. And it was interesting to see orthodox senior officers making an adjustment to me.

One point of organization sensitivity had to be addressed right at the start. I was, by the Foreign Service system of the time, a class 5 officer supervising (higher) class 4 and 3 officers who were all older than I. One of them, a spokesman (I understood), Nick Ruggieri, came in to see me on my first day. We sat down together.[1] He told me some of his friends, other senior officers, expressed a sense of regret that he was not made assistant director, and he wondered whether I could suggest an appropriate response. Judging from his expression and reputation for sincerity, I believed Nick was not challenging me. He really wanted a discussion about how we would work together and a useful explanation that would be responsive to queries.

I began by pointing out that until now PLD (Program Liaison Division) assisted the Ministry of Information and other RVN elements with funds, equipment, products, and distribution as if there were no tomorrow. "Today *is* tomorrow. We are charged by Ed Nickel, Ambassador Colby, and the Mission Council with delicate and diplomatic, but definite, disengagement from the ministry so there will be no basis for supposing that JUSPAO is running this year's RVN get-out-and-vote campaign." In order to achieve that objective within four months, I told him, we needed to understand in detail what recent practice had been. Unfortunately, as I reviewed files provided by our secretary, it appeared most of the necessary information had not been retained. So I would depend on him to be my navigator. "You can tell friends that I might be difficult, or anything else you wish, but that I also acknowledge needing your advice and having you beside me at every step."[2]

While disengaging from the Ministry of Information, we needed to help ministry officers through this major adjustment, assist them to manage inventory, match funding to procurement, and respond to field requests either from the provincial Vietnamese Information Service or from other RVN elements through the CPDC. Addressing these three categories of activity was time-consuming, and we encountered resistance in some corners of the ministry. It was difficult to break from a pattern of dependency. The USIS Motion Picture Center had begun doing newsreels for the First Republic about fifteen years earlier, then followed with taped radio programs, print media products, and, more recently, television technical and program support. JUSPAO had two dedicated military aircraft during 1965 through 1966 to move leaflets, publications, and other material for the ministry, and in 1971 it was still using Air America for that purpose and for VIP flights.[3]

I spoke with Senator Dang Van Sung, who chaired the Senate Foreign Relations and Information Committee.[4] He suggested working closely with Maj. Dao Tran Lam, director of research and plans in the Ministry of Information. A few months earlier they had argued during a budget hearing for the ministry, and Senator Sung advised me that Lam's influence definitely extended beyond research and plans to issues of procurement. I mentioned to Major Lam that Senator Sung described him as the most important officer in the Ministry of Information and requested his support and time for working together to compile a ministry-wide inventory as a basis for budgeting procurement. In that way a potential obstacle was circumvented, and we began to dig into ministry warehouse and storage closets. Ha Quoc Buu (our JUSPAO liaison representative) and I worked with Major Lam to list what was held in the ministry headquarters. Nick Ruggieri was responsible, with others from PLD, for assisting with inventory of the main warehouses. We were not surprised to find a lack of systematic storage and to learn that some items had deteriorated beyond any possible use, but we were entertained when discovering the ministry still preserved dozens of hamlet information radios, in yellow plastic cases marked with red lettering, "Ap Chien Luoc." They still worked, but they had outlived their political time. Major Lam said it would have been embarrassing to send them out to hamlets after 1963. I suggested that they be offered to ministry civil servants just to clear the records and shelf space. Based on our real-time inventory and review of requests from the provinces, Major Lam examined the ministry budget and developed a procurement plan that was flexible enough to allow for contingencies. That was sufficient for me. Implementation would be up to the minister and his Nhan Xa Party cabal.

Ambassador Colby was in Washington on consultation when he met with Congressman Paul "Pete" McCloskey, a Republican who opposed President Nixon's war strategy. Congressman McCloskey was leaving for his second trip to Viet Nam and asked for assistance in getting specifics on Phung Hoang and other operations impacting the countryside, especially in I Corps, where the US Marines had operated for six years.[5] His trip was politically sensitive because of his opposition to presidential policy and possible entry in forthcoming state presidential primaries. WEC sent a telegram to the mission recommending I be assigned as escort and facilitator for McCloskey and his party. A separate back-channel message advised me to be assertive during briefings, even to interrupt, if necessary, but under no circumstance to tolerate lack of cooperation or evasiveness.

The party, including Congressmen McCloskey and Waldie (Democrat, California), two staff assistants, three other members of the group, Colonel Hogan (MACV), and me, flew to Danang on Friday, 9 April. Jake saw us off at Tan Son Nhut and provided background commentary while we were waiting for the aircraft. The group was surprised by the intensity of his personal commitment to "holding the line" in Viet Nam. When Congressman Waldie remarked that Jake must be a believer in the domino theory, Jake replied almost belligerently, "Yes, I am."

Our travel provided intensive exposure to the contemporary situation in I Corps and Binh Dinh province. The two members of Congress were already well informed. They knew what they wanted to see. The degree of self-direction, departure from planned itineraries, and avoidance of social events was unusual and bothered a couple of senior officers. We had an initial fuss when the deputy for CORDS in I Corps (John Gunther Dean) described himself as holding an assimilated rank as general officer. I was surprised (but refrained from comment) because I understood that assimilated rank required specific procedure, and I was not aware paperwork had been prepared for any of the regional CORDS deputies. Congressman McCloskey was immediately irritated, because, he told me later, Marines take a dim view of "assimilated rank nonsense." Dean's initial responses to requests were typically, "We'll try," and "We'll see." During a break over coffee I told him privately, quietly, that on this trip I spoke for Ambassador Colby, and my guidance was that his reply to every congressional request should be, "Yes, we will." Although aggravated by the intensity of my instruction, Dean was thereafter positively responsive.[6]

A major focus of the congressmen's interest was operation of the Phung Hoang program. When appropriate, I represented Ambassador Colby's perspective, that there were deficiencies but we were working to address problems. I cited the tangled body of domestic security law and regulations and mentioned there was a legal officer in CORDS working on the problem.[7] There was no immediate need for me to present my own fundamental doubts about the effectiveness and moral principles of the program. I thought by their own observations and questions Congressmen McCloskey and Waldie would spot the problematic aspects of Phung Hoang. The two congressmen spoke with one provincial security committee member, who made it obvious that presentation of cases was procedurally flawed, and every vote was so weighted in favor of security agencies that conviction was assured. Congressman Waldie had extensive discussion in Quang Ngai with the Phung Hoang advisor and two men who worked with the province interrogation center (PIC) and Vietnamese Police Special Branch. He ascertained that these two were CIA employees and were treated differently in CORDS than were other advisory elements.

So, by the time we were in Binh Dinh province, the two congressmen were primed to probe more deeply. In Qui Nhon, honest responses by American advisors revealed operational vagueness and a complicated chain of command for those working in the Phung Hoang program relative to others connected to the PIC and prison facility. Congressman Waldie found the lack of precision so aggravating that at one point he burst out, "Then what the hell do you do when you advise?"[8]

There was more spirited discussion on the subject of Phung Hoang ethical and procedural issues. Both congressmen were surprised to learn the Phung Hoang advisor in this important province had not taken the relevant course at Vung Tau. Congressman McCloskey obtained acknowledgment from two advisors that the program was a denial of the American tradition of due process. When he asked why American officers did not go to the PIC, one answered, "It isn't appropriate for an Army officer." In this way the two congressmen learned more about the Pacification and Security Coordination Detachment that reported to the Pacification and Security Coordination Division (PSCD) of the Territorial Forces Directorate in CORDS.[9] We did see the PIC, where the province interrogations officer joined our group. He revealed that not all detainees' cases were placed before the Province Security Committee, and he did not know what happened to those people.

The delegation's extensive scrutiny of Viet Nam reality in April 1971 (in the aftermath of Lam Son 719) was not limited to Phung Hoang. We looked at ARVN and US units and a Marine CAP and went in and out of FSB Charley 2 and FSB Alpha 4 (Con Thien), so McCloskey (especially) comprehended the inevitable weakening as American forces continued to draw down. When Colonel Townes (1st Brigade, 5th Mechanized Division) described the effort required to reopen Highway 9 (for Lam Son 719) to Khe Sanh and Lang Vei, it was hard to imagine that ever happening again. Congressman McCloskey asked an experienced advisor in Quang Nam what would happen if all US forces pulled out in the next six months. "Probably ultimate collapse," he responded. In Binh Dinh recent communist prisoners of war were described as "healthy young boys," and the province senior advisor stated that following departure of the US 173rd Airborne Brigade and Korean forces, deploying all four regiments of the 22nd ARVN Division would be required.[10]

We went to about eight districts, speaking with RVN officials, American advisors, and Vietnamese encountered while walking. We learned that MATs (for RF and PF) were scheduled for termination in June, Marine CAPs would not be far behind, district advisory teams were reducing in size preliminary to phaseout, and VCI eliminations were usually "accidental." All of the advisors, in response to questioning from Congressman McCloskey, acknowledged there was no documentation for an incoming advisor as to history of a province or district prior to his own arrival. Each district we visited presented a snapshot of the destructive impact of our kind of war on Vietnamese rural society.

We were in Duc Duc about ten days after an attack on the district headquarters in Phu Da hamlet. Before the war this district listed forty-five hamlets; now HES scored twenty-two. The other twenty-three had been abandoned. Of the twenty-two recognized as continuing hamlets, only one was scored B (and that was Phu Da). The others were C or D. In Dai Loc district, where previously there were seventy-five hamlets, now the RVN recognized only twenty-nine, with forty-six abandoned or consolidated with other communities. The resident population on Go Noi Island, in Dien Ban district (scene of intense US Marine operations), had decreased from more than thirty thousand people to fewer than three thousand.

Hau Duc district of Quang Tin province had abandoned many hamlets, and the road to the next district, Tien Phuoc, was traveled under convoy discipline only. An old road to Tra Bong in Quang Ngai province was impassable. The entire area was HES-rated no better than C or D. Twenty-four of sixty-three abandoned Quang Tin communities were located in Tam Ky district despite the nearby province capital. One resident, asked by Congressman Waldie who had destroyed all the houses in the area, replied that government bombing had destroyed those homes.[11]

While speaking with the province senior advisor in Hue (Thua Thien province), Congressman Waldie asked whether we kept track of homes and buildings destroyed by US units in the same way that we recorded VC terrorism. "I am interested to see that we have copious records on VC destruction, yet none on our own. Wherever we fly, all the houses are flattened." On our way to Phong Dien district we flew over Thanh Tan hamlet, previously destroyed and abandoned, and later at a resettlement site we met people from that area. Under the observant presence of the district chief, they told us the Viet Cong had destroyed their hamlet, and they voluntarily moved with the help of Americans. That fairy tale was shattered when a local force (PF) soldier stepped forward and insisted that wasn't what had happened. He told us how a US Marine battalion destroyed houses while he was assigned to guide them on operations.

Tra Bong (Quang Ngai province) was overrun several months earlier, in September 1970, after the Special Forces camp was converted to a local ranger command. Even in 1963 and 1964, access by road was a risky proposition, and now movement was by convoy discipline. I knew this district was Viet Nam's primary source of cinnamon, so I asked one of the district officers how they moved it. He told me that buyers came to Tra Bong, bought the bark product (primarily from Co tribal people), and then contracted with General Toan, the 2nd Division commander, for running a convoy.

The traveling group was determined to get to the Son My area, scene of atrocities committed by a unit of the US 23rd (Americal) Division. We flew to Chu Lai, formerly a Marine base but now US 23rd Division headquarters. We needed to refuel but also make a courtesy call on the 23rd Division. There was some discussion of the recent attack on FSB Mary Ann,[12] but the congressmen had other interests and did not want to embarrass the 23rd by probing that disaster. Officers were disconcerted to learn that we planned to land at Tu Cung hamlet to see the 1968 crime scene. One officer suggested the area was insecure and not cleared for congressional travel. I interposed that the area was reported secure by province, and arrangements were already in place for Major Kiem, the Son Tinh district chief, to meet us on-site.

As we circled before landing, I realized that this was the hamlet closest to where Bob Kelly and I had paused in 1963 for iced beer and where I had spent a day with a People's Commando platoon in 1964, and that it was part of the 1966 Return to Village Program. RF and PF soldiers occupied the ruins one day before our arrival so we could safely wander paths among the remains. No one could see those walls with bullet and fragmentation damage and deny something terrible had happened. I felt chilled when Major Kiem brought us to a drainage ditch and showed where more than a hundred bodies had been recovered.[13]

From Quang Ngai we flew to Bong Son in northern Binh Dinh province. Ed Long, deputy for CORDS in II Corps, and Colonel Mendheim, the Binh Dinh province senior advisor, accompanied us. We landed at

LZ English, located about five kilometers north of the town.[14] The district advisors from Tam Quan, Hoai Nhon, Hoai An, and Phu My were waiting for us. They recounted recent action in those districts and described ARVN as much improved and NVA prisoners as young without strong motivation, although some of the "old hands are still very eager." We traveled to a couple of hamlets in Hoai Nhon district. Congressman McCloskey asked what the overall effect of the past five years had been in that province. I told him that in 1963 the province planned for more than nine hundred strategic hamlets. In 1971 it would be surprising if there were as many as six hundred.[15] We flew up the abandoned An Lao Valley over ruined, barely recognizable hamlet sites. I told him how idyllic the valley had been, by comparison, eight years earlier. Turning southward, we passed over the Go Boi plain and river delta area north of Qui Nhon Bay. The scene below revealed some hamlet activity, compared with An Lao, but one still noticed the effect of intense war from 1965 through 1968 and continued conflict at reduced level in recent years.

When we were back in Saigon, and before we parted, the two congressmen asked for my reaction to what we had seen and been told. I told them my thoughts were personal, and maybe not pertinent, but I believed they conducted themselves exactly as I would hope my own representative might while looking into a matter of importance to me.[16]

I spoke with Ambassador Colby, and later with Jake, about my observations. As CORDS chief of staff and probable successor to Ambassador Colby, and given our shared history and friends, Jake deserved the same consideration I would provide John and Ev.

1. Based on Qui Nhon discussion, I felt that conducting an advisory activity (interrogation and special branch) without province senior advisor input was organizationally and ethically flawed.

2. Five years before, the 1st Air Cavalry believed they were grinding the PAVN 3rd Division to oblivion, but the principal enemy force in northern Binh Dinh was still the 3rd Division.

3. We were told, in effect, by General Toan that what would happen after US forces were gone would depend on the enemy, and American advisors said that ARVN would hold if there was no enemy buildup, *but* there was nothing in the history of this country, and Communist Party history in particular, to presume there would not be another buildup and offensive.

4. I thought we had been climbing a mountain in persistent fog.
We were at the edge of a precipice and didn't know it.

When WEC and I later discussed the congressional party, I expressed surprise that his instruction was to intervene (when necessary) to assure that congressional query was not thwarted. His response was that, in our system of governance, the worst thing an officer could do would be to deceive an elected representative of the people. "And," he added, "it does not matter what you personally think of that particular representative." When Jake and I spoke separately, his perspective was slightly different. He had received feedback from advisors who were understandably nervous. Jake concluded that I had pointed the party in directions that were not helpful to the American effort. I was not able to convince him that the two congressmen were their own bird dogs.

Turning back to the Ministry of Information, I continued to observe the inventory and procurement process, but without interfering. In previous years, contracting for supply offered the opportunity for kickbacks. Major Lam had his hands full trying to break with the past. Irregular response from ministry to province information services had caused JUSPAO in 1966 to initiate a "parallel request" channel. Discussing this situation with first Ed Nickel and then Ambassador Colby, I advocated eliminating the parallel request practice because the RVN needed to exercise its own procedure to support the field, and JUSPAO was pulling back from placing a representative in each province. Because the Mass Information Program was supposed to be applied across ministries and in support of their programs, and the prime minister's office and CPDC had established a standing office with a permanent staff, I suggested a different kind of parallel channel. Copies of a request for support could be sent to CPDC for the Mass Information Standing Office. The difficulty with opening a channel direct to CPDC was, again, that Minister Ngo Khac Tinh believed that would infringe on his authority. Rather than have a permanent staff for the Interministerial Standing Office begin to exert pressure, Minister Tinh established a special task section in his ministry to coordinate all people's information programs. Nguyen Xuan Hue was appointed chief of the Special Task Section. Major Lam, designated director general for propaganda (Phu-Ta Tong Giam Doc Tuyen Van), was made responsible for coordinating twenty-three mass information programs. This Ministry of Information special mass information section held its first meeting on 1 April 1971 and reported to Minister Tinh that coordinating (*phoi tri*) mass information functions would be difficult due to already lacking systematic coordination (*phoi hop*) and liaison (*lien he*) with other directorates and services.[17]

My absence from CORDS left a small gap, particularly with respect to monitoring corrupt or ineffective officials. Ev Bumgardner was underemployed in Washington and agreed to return for a few months. We were each other's allies in trying to breathe life into the RVN mass information effort by nudging CPDC and the ministry. I tried working with Nguyen Xuan Hue, chief of the Special Task Section in the Ministry of Information, and responded to his request for thoughts about mass information and implementation problems. I always copied Ev on my memoranda and other RVN papers, and he would do the same for me. Our effort through CPDC and the Ministry of Information resulted in consensus at the top. However, there was never an effective push at the level of the rice paddy or urban ward. "Most district chiefs, chiefs of provincial services, village chiefs simply pay lip service and give little emphasis to informational work. Their dozens of other routine tasks simply outweigh everything else at the operational level."[18]

At the end of April 1971, JUSPAO held a program review for all divisions and offices. My presentation made just a few points. We were fundamentally changing our relationship to the Ministry of Information and would complete transfiguration well before the scheduled late August (National Assembly) and early September (presidential) elections. We reviewed USIS/JUSPAO support to the ministry and assisted in conducting the first comprehensive inventory. That inventory was now the basis for ministry development of need-based procurement. The parallel request system (JUSPAO field advisory and province VIS) needed replacement on the RVN side. The ministry from this day forward would be responsible for its own transportation of people and products.[19]

Several days later, Ambassador Colby and Ed Nickel cochaired a meeting in Can Tho to review information, psychological operations, and rural development in the context of the continuing American drawdown. Sa Yun came with me, and we stayed in Wilbur Wilson's quarters, because he was out of country.[20] Before the conference opened, John and I had a chance to talk with Ambassador Colby about the overall situation, political and military. John was about two weeks from relocation to Pleiku in command of the II Corps advisory effort. This would be a new position, director of the Second Regional Assistance Group, tailored especially for him. Although he would have an army brigadier general as deputy for military affairs, John would definitely be in charge. Tom Barnes would be John's deputy for CORDS. Tom had a solid reputation in the field, dating from service in Hue as consul about ten years earlier and more recently as the province senior advisor in Binh Long.

I asserted that II Corps would be the most important of the military regions during the next couple of years. John made one more attempt to bring me with him. He said, "I'll place you as senior advisor in Binh Dinh, or make you deputy for special projects, and you can just do whatever you want." WEC looked at me and awaited my response. I knew that, even if I did reach back to the past and commit to John, WEC and Ed Nickel would immediately disapprove. I would still be in JUSPAO, but compromised. I shook my head, but then WEC spoke up and said, "You can't have Frank on assignment, but he can go up for a few days and give you a feel, familiarization, for that part of the country. I'll square it with Ed, but you better understand Frank comes right back."[21]

Ambassador Colby presided over the opening session of the review meeting with an overview of planning for 1971 and beyond and then summarized the situation in each of the military regions. The three priorities were Phung Hoang, Nhan Dan Tu Ve (Peoples' Self-Defense), and information. "The expansion phase is over, and now we face protracted warfare."[22] Summarizing each of the regions in a sentence or two, Colby began with the fourth military region because that was the location for our review meeting, and then he continued in order geographically northward.

MR 4—RVN retains the initiative, although there are still incidents and outpost problems.

MR 3—War has almost stopped except where traditional resistance centers (Trang Bang) function. Have to improve our systems to move ahead.

MR 2—Couple of areas where RVN is stalemated. Binh Dinh, Phu Yen, Pleiku. This is the core problem now, because it is an indicator of whether the RVN can hold momentum.

MR 1—RVN still holding momentum, despite Quang Ngai and
Quang Nam, which aren't so good. East of the railroad is OK,
problems are to the west.

A couple of perpetual difficulties were cited and discussed. On the
Vietnamese side, problems were raised from the field and then not answered. Overall commitment, at least equivalent to that of the communists, needed to be realized through patient persuasion. But in terms of
mass information (*thong tin dai chung*) there was a gap at the top, and no
one was held accountable. John Vann, in exasperation, cried out, "What is
the information product? I have not seen anything which fires the imagi-
nation of government cadre."

Ed Nickel explained that information and psychological operations
might soon be limited by declining resources. He described the impact
of congressional attitudes and budget legislation on a nervous USIA: "We
can expect domestic criticism to increase over the next several months
and the pace of Vietnamization will have to be accelerated. USIA plans
to withdraw the last of province field advisors in the fall of 1972 and have
only two officers in each military region by early 1973. We might have
to accelerate this plan." Print support to the RVN would be reduced 25
percent by July, just two months on, with another 25 percent reduction in
September, and the remainder stopped by the end of 1971.[23]

The attending military representative stated that MACV would not fill
the gap, because the pertinent budget category was already short by one
million dollars; there was a policy decision to *not* produce what RVNAF
could do, and pressures to expand Rice River operations in Cambodia and
Ho Chi Minh Trail operations in Laos would eat up the remaining funds.
In terms of personnel, the planning was for district advisory teams to dis-
appear in FY 1973 and province S-5 slots to close out 1 July 1973.

The conference mood was not celebratory.

Soon John and I were together for a few days in northern II Corps.
We went in and out of districts by helicopter, spoke mostly with Vietnamese, extracted a badly wounded Jarai Regional Forces soldier from an
overrun outpost in Phu Bon, and night and day continually discussed the
special characteristics of II Corps and what he needed to change. John did
an orientation tour of II Corps in mid-1963, but relative to his III Corps
and IV Corps experience, central Viet Nam, highlands and coastal, was

like a different country. John, as many will attest, usually dominated any conversation, promoting his point of view.[24] But he could be a perceptive listener, too.

We talked about central Viet Nam having a different sociology than the south (with the hamlet rather than village as the basic community), a different history (the Tay Son brothers, greater feelings for Hue than Saigon, An Quang Buddhist connections), revolutionary identity (the Ba To uprising, Pham Van Dong birthplace, Salvation and then Struggle Movements), and Quang Ngai–Binh Dinh linkage due to shared Viet Minh Inter-Zone V history. The highlands issue, basically an ethnic collision between Vietnamese and non-Vietnamese tribes, was a critical problem, because without tribal cooperation there would be little human intelligence concerning communist maneuver units.

That was a lot, but John and his regular LOH pilot also needed adjustment to differences of physical environment between the center and the south. In the south there was one monsoon (rainy and stormy) season, basically spring and summer. In the center there were two monsoons: one in the highlands, spring and summer (like that of the south), and one along the coast, roughly late summer through the fall and into winter. So there would always be challenging monsoon flying. Topography would require adjustment of flight habit. In the south John often flew on the deck, popping over tree lines. In central Viet Nam, ridgelines, narrow valleys, and seasonal mist made nap-of-the-earth flying much more risky. I told them they would encounter a kind of ground fire, disciplined and intense, not recently experienced in the Mekong Delta.

John accepted my not staying with him. "You're going back to Saigon, with your wife, in some bullshit office assignment. *But if* you were staying up here, what would you push?"[25]

I had already given a lot of thought, beginning in Can Tho several days earlier, to what to recommend. I began by telling him that in the long run, but bearing in mind there may not be a long run, only dramatic beneficial change for the hill tribes would provide him with eyes-and-ears intelligence. Otherwise, the RVN would be a blind man fumbling in the area west of Highway 14 all the way to the border and beyond. The communist forces, even without support from the tribes, have an advantage, since they always know where RVN units base and operate. "I know you can't solve this right away, but as long as people persuade you that 'this is a long-term problem,' nothing will ever be done. It might already be too late. That's why change has to be dramatic. I mean Rhade, Jarai, Bahnar district and province chiefs, a real compromise with FULRO and a new FULRO division, the 77th or 99th, some auspicious number. I know you can't make it your first push, but never forget that this is what you most need, because without change, the highlands will be lost, and then all will be lost." I urged him to get to know tribal leaders like Y Dhuat Nie Kdam (Rhade), K'sor Rot (Jarai), and Nay Luett (Jarai) just as he previously befriended Hoa Hao leaders in IV Corps.[26] The RVN accepted a Hoa Hao solution for Chau Doc and Long Xuyen. Vietnamese needed to get past their ethnic bias and apply the same formula in the highlands.

Immediately, and relatively more achievable, John needed a change of command in II Corps and the two assigned divisions. I knew that he was obligated to Ngo Dzu, who asked for him in II Corps, and I knew that he thought Ngo Dzu could be manipulated to competency, but I described Ngo Dzu as soft metal, something of a hypochondriac, who when bent too often would break. I reminded him of the night we had dinner at Tran Ngoc Chau's house, when the talk turned to how ARVN morale and performance could be improved, and Ngo Dzu seriously suggested reinstituting the French practice of mobile field bordellos. The 22nd Division, which ought to be entirely shifted to Binh Dinh rather than split between there and Kontum, was commanded by Le Ngoc Trieu, whose previous assignments had been blandly on the staff side. The 23rd Division, commanded by Vo Van Canh, a middling officer, would not be up to handling any 1971–72 challenge. John was committed to Ngo Dzu but asked what kind of officer he should have in mind for division command replacements. My suggestion was to look to the Airborne Division and Ranger Command, because the airborne had low tolerance for ineffective battalion and brigade commanders; he would surely need airborne reinforcement at some point, and there were many ranger units throughout the region. I suggested Nguyen Trong Bao (airborne), Le Quang Luong (airborne), Nguyen Khoa Nam (airborne), and Tran Van Hai (ranger). Eventually, I urged, Ngo Dzu would have to be replaced. He would need a brave officer, a smart officer, and a top-quality person to make a deal with FULRO. I recommended Nguyen Duc Thang, even though he was in political eclipse, or Nguyen Van Hieu, who knew the region better than most.[27]

I thought there were really two fronts in II Corps. One was the frontier zone, west of Route 14, and the other was in northern Binh Dinh spilling over into Quang Ngai. Even HES portrayed a concentration of C (and I never considered C as "relatively secure"), D, E, and V communities south and west of Pleiku and another similar cluster in central and northern Binh Dinh.[28] Adequate, maybe barely adequate, ARVN presence would require the entire 22nd Division in Binh Dinh and the complete 23rd for Pleiku and Kontum. That would mean an additional division for II Corps was necessary to operate in Quang Duc, Darlac, Phu Bon, and Phu Yen. The only way to raise and organize that new division would be with FULRO, or by consolidating some ranger and RF elements that might still be a shadow FULRO force. One way or another, effective RVN presence would have to recognize the reality of FULRO, just as the Hoa Hao were acknowledged. I suggested he arrange transfer of our friend Capt. Gordon Huddleston from IV Corps to a point in Binh Dinh from where he could observe and independently report truth to John, as he had done from Chau Doc.[29]

John and I discussed the countrywide tendency to preserve isolated bases that were previously easier for US forces to supply and reinforce but now more vulnerable. I shared what Phil Werbiski and I reported to Colonel Bennett in 1965 with reference to remote fixed-position Special Forces camps. I thought the same considerations applied to isolated ARVN or RF outposts. They were subject to being either avoided or enveloped and eventually overrun. When small posts were under pressure, intense enemy fire would inhibit helicopter evacuation of the wounded, and accumulating casualties would lower morale. Mobile operations were the answer, but I was not sure ARVN and VNAF were capable of altering established habit. We flew north to the 22nd Division forward command post at Tan Canh for a situation briefing. The information conveyed was vague and the tone pessimistic. They expressed doubt whether the forward positions (Fire Support Bases 5 and 6) on the ridge to the southwest could be maintained.[30] When we asked who had recently been there, the response was silence. John said he thought we would make FSB 5 our next stop. We were urged not to go.

While John went to the latrine, I walked out from the bunker to talk with our pilot, WO Rob Richards. We ought to check his map for FSB 5. Rob asked why. I answered, "Because John was just advised not to go."[31]

Sure enough, John emerged with the pronouncement that we needed to get into Firebase 5. Our plan was for Rob to approach high, as if on flight elsewhere, then make an abrupt descent through broken clouds and do a touch-and-go while John and I would jump out as he lifted off before mortar rounds caught him on the ground. Rob would return at a predetermined time by making the same approach while we leaped aboard at touch-and-go.

Sometimes a good plan goes foul because of bad luck, and sometimes one that others call reckless is a home run. The PAVN besiegers were just as surprised as the soldiers on the firebase, who were not informed of incoming visitors. We talked with the commander, a tense captain, who (once past his surprise) candidly told us that he had inconsistent communication with his rear, the CP at Tan Canh. He was told to hold the position, but ammunition was low, there was no medevac, and Tan Canh promised reinforcement but gave no details. While John spoke with him, as the ARVN officer knew some English, I walked through the position talking with soldiers. Almost immediately I found the artillery pieces, prime reason for the base, already prepared for removal by helicopter sling. The mood of these soldiers was dour, more depressed than I had expected. They felt abandoned. Night listening posts beyond the perimeter were under such pressure that nobody wanted to man them. Bodies were stacked in one bunker, and wounded were collected at another bunker for medevac flights that never came. When I rejoined John and the ARVN officer, who by now seemed slightly cheered simply by our arrival and concern, we made a plan. It was obvious that without one this place would go under, as it almost had three months earlier.

We would arrange for an ARVN combat medic to come back by LOH the next day, leap off with supplies, and stay on the position until a relief column arrived to improve security and facilitate evacuating the wounded.[32] Meanwhile, John would urge faster movement of a relief element from reinforced FSB 6 (not yet invested) and would get ammunition brought in for the four 105 howitzers, "that by the way should be returned to firing position." We circulated with the ARVN officer while he explained the plan to his men. Their spirits lifted. I suggested to John that the only way we could be sure our plan worked would be for me to stay on FSB 5 until the LOH with medic returned the next day. He thought that was the dumbest idea imaginable. "Oh, sure, you're here, something goes wrong, and then I'm explaining to your wife and Colby why I left you on a hilltop surrounded by NVA. I might just as well stay here with you!"[33] Rob dropped in, almost like a rock, seemed to bounce, and we were on the run, onto the LOH, and out of there. I was on my way back to my wife and son and my bullshit office assignment.

Sooner than anticipated, I returned to I Corps and II Corps. Bill Buckley suggested to Ambassador Bunker that his friend and occasional contributor to *National Review*, Ernst van den Haag, travel to Viet Nam to rebut charges that Americans committed war crimes. Presumably van den Haag would make firsthand observation for persuasive denial. Ambassador Colby insisted that I make arrangements, accompany the visitor, and interpret as necessary. Ernst was, on the spot, disconcerted by what he was shown and told. In Quang Ngai we spoke with members of a LRRP unit. When asked whether they knew of any atrocities or war crimes, one responded, "Wadayathink, the war's a fuckin' atrocity!" A couple of soldiers showed van den Haag their personal collection of ears cut from bodies as trophies. At the US 173rd Brigade near Bong Son we were told about an active case still under investigation. The charge was that Vietnamese were tortured and made to walk through a probable minefield. Ernst asked if the accused was available to speak with us. A lieutenant was brought forth, and when asked whether he had done as charged, he responded that in fact he had, because "the people were obviously VC."

We took lunch in Nha Trang, where I figured on placing Ernst in contact with people having Phung Hoang experience, but he decided that he didn't need further field exposure. He was much more interested in our waitress. We returned to Saigon, where he requested Lee Braddock assist him in changing to a more "open" hotel so that he could get a better feel for the people.[34]

Ambassador Colby departed Viet Nam for Washington and reassignment.[35] During the intermediate transitional period, while MACV was doing a headquarters reorganization, Jake appeared to be the functional DEPCORDS, but he was reporting to General Weyand (deputy commander, MACV) rather than to General Abrams. In October, General Weyand, on the recommendation of General Abrams and Ambassador Bunker, formally added the DEPCORDS responsibility to his role in MACV. Jake continued as chief of staff for CORDS. About that same time, Ev Bumgardner stopped spending time in-country on extended TDY. We had come full circle from the 1967 Komer formulation for CORDS: that it include military resources and personnel but be directed by a strong civilian officer. Now the late 1971 model included civilian resources and personnel but was directed by a military officer.[36]

I was not personally affected by the Colby departure. He had already arranged my transfer to JUSPAO in a way that provided transition while retaining my availability to him for other tasking. He was always accessible and, like Ev, enjoyed argumentative (but civil) discussion. We did have points of disagreement, candidly discussed between ourselves but not shared with others. One was Phung Hoang implementation. The system of interrogation, sentencing, and detention, all accomplished with no consideration for the accused, was flawed because the people apprehended or denounced were almost all low-level cooperators rather than higher-level operators. Another subject of incongruent opinion had to do with Buddhists, particularly those from central Viet Nam usually referred to in mission reporting as the "An Quang faction." When I was providing him with post-1970 election analysis concerning the Vu Van Mau Buddhist–supported ticket, during our discussion Ambassador Colby bizarrely (I thought) referred to the Buddhists as a reactionary antimodernizing movement in comparison with President Diem and President Thieu. I thought that interpretation did not historically account for the Buddhist push in 1966 for elections that in fact led to the Second Republic.[37] We never discussed the Tran Ngoc Chau case except once in passing. I do not believe WEC was part of the Bunker-Shackley arrangement, but he stood aside and allowed it to proceed. And I do think he was much later artfully vague on the subject whenever he was asked.[38]

Thinking and writing about Bob Komer and Bill Colby, I acknowledge that my personal involvement with them was fleeting, only a few months with Komer and barely a few more with Colby. Others had a closer relationship with them. But the impression they made is indelible.

Komer was bluff, hearty, a keen organizational warrior. What you saw is what you got. He forcefully sought out the most relevant information and the most useful people. I cannot imagine anyone else who could have brought MACVCORDS from conception to implementation. Colby, engineer for the machine passed to him by Komer, I thought was a more complex character. It is interesting that the bridge between them was Col. Bob Montague. Bob's skill in planning and energizing CORDS was fundamental to their enterprise from 1967 through 1969. Neither one, Komer or Colby, was particularly hierarchal (witness their use of nonorganization personalities like Vann, Bumgardner, and me), but they did believe in a structure wherein every officer understood what others were responsible for and how one's own duties fit into the whole.[39] Komer was, relatively speaking, a fast gun for hire and could as comfortably operate from CIA, the White House, RAND, or even an academic institution—on his own terms, of course. Colby was more organizationally loyal and more institutionally tuned to the CIA as offspring of his World War II OSS. Komer directed, with firmness, sometimes loudly, all those who worked for him. Colby inspired, taught, and led by example. Komer denied my 1967 request for field assignment because of organizational concern. Colby deflected me from a 1971 field assignment because of regard for my family circumstances, when it would have been just as easy to see me off with John Vann.

When Bill Colby visited Fort Bragg in 1990, I understood there was still something of the young OSS officer in him. He engaged in lively conversation with Special Forces officers in our home. He provided items for the Special Forces Museum and copies of his 1945 memorandum recommending an organization for future special operations forces.[40] He wrote to us a few weeks later expressing pleasure at having been with the new generation of special operators, and he provided additional material for the Special Forces collection.

Komer was loud and assertive, but one would be mistaken in assuming bluster compensated for insecurity. He was usually, with Bob Montague and Richard Holbrooke assisting, pretty sure of what needed to be done and how he intended to do it. Colby was self-effacing, modest, and generally soft-spoken, but if he thought it necessary, a sharper, steel-edged tone would get your attention.

17
Elections, Governance, and the 1972 PAVN Offensive

JUSPAO in the summer of 1971 was still a sizable organization. We had unplugged from the Ministry of Information, other than technical advising for television, and distancing ourselves precluded even an appearance of involvement in the August and September elections. But we still had active field operations at the province level, and total JUSPAO personnel probably consisted of about one hundred military, fifty civilians, and around five hundred Vietnamese employees. Ed Nickel departed Viet Nam about the same time Bill Colby left. The new JUSPAO director was Robert Lincoln. When I moved from MACV to JUSPAO, my family was provided a house in a compound of five residences. The one across from us was for the JUSPAO director, so there was opportunity for informal discussion. Bob Lincoln was charged by USIA with downsizing JUSPAO to resume a regular USIS operation during his tenure.[1] I had already reduced the Program Liaison Division to the point where we no longer needed an assistant director or even chief of Program Liaison Division. Wilson Dizard was assistant director for Policy, Plans, and Research, but he was ready to leave Viet Nam. Bob Lincoln asked me to take that position.

Elections for the 159-member National Assembly Lower House were held in late August. An Quang Buddhist leaders suggested a boycott, but the turnout was impressive and cited by some in the mission as evidence of RVN acceptability and declining An Quang importance. An Quang influence was still strong enough to boost reelection prospects for some deputies such as Kieu Mong Thu and Le Tan Buu, who, despite his attachment to the Hoa Hao congregation, was affiliated with the An Quang bloc. The most important factor in voter turnout was citizen need for certification that one had, in fact, voted. Failure to have proof could create difficulty if legal papers needed processing by authorities or if not voting was equated to support for the SVNLF.

At least one deputy, Ngo Cong Duc, was targeted for defeat by government machination, and he did lose.[2] And there was one candidate who won election with my encouragement. Touneh Ton, road and field companion of 1964, approached me that summer. He was already an elected member of the Tuyen Duc province council. He decided to run for election to the National Assembly because being a deputy could provide opportunity to do more for highland tribes. He needed campaign funding, primarily to buy buffalos for sacrifice at rallies. I could not turn him down, so he became one of the 159 elected deputies. Touneh kept me informed of developments in the assembly, as he understood them, but he was his own man.

The presidential election was more farce than contest. There was the issue of whether Nguyen Cao Ky would be a candidate. Duong Van Minh was also a possibility. President Thieu might have been disadvantaged if both Ky and Minh had opposed him, so he maneuvered to have Ky disqualified. Then Minh calculated he was being made a sacrificial lamb. He decided to withdraw.

The prospect of an uncontested election was uncomfortable for American policy makers. Ambassador Bunker consulted in Washington, returned to Saigon, and attempted to persuade Minh to stay the course. Minh considered his options carefully, including the possibility of American financial assistance for his campaign, and finally decided to make his withdrawal unequivocal. President Thieu then thought it would be better to have some opponent rather than none, so he directed that the corrupt process by which Ky was disqualified be reversed so that Ky could run after all. A few days later that gentleman decided there would be no point in sacrificing himself for his rival's benefit, so he also definitely withdrew. The Supreme Court ruled 8–1 for approving a one-candidate process. Meanwhile, Tran Van Huong, deposed as prime minister two years earlier so that Tran Thien Khiem could ascend, was persuaded to stand for vice president beside President Thieu in the no-contest contest.[3]

The presidential election was such a mess that even chronic opportunist Huynh Van Cao was opposed to ballots for one man. Ton That Thien commented to me, "If Nguyen Cao Thang were still alive the same steps might have been taken, but more smoothly." Tran Van Lam, foreign minister, was circumspect but not enthusiastic about the playing out of the 1971 elections. He expected the president would convince himself that he had accomplished, by his reelection, what was necessary for the national interest: "But when President Thieu makes appointments, personal loyalty will count for more than ability." When the government announced in October that Vice President Huong would have responsibility for eliminating corruption, many people were skeptical, particularly when little followed.[4]

Nguyen Van Bong, at the National Institute of Administration, had an interesting perspective on the election. He suggested that the addition of Tran Van Huong as vice president could make it possible to appoint more civilians to significant office, including province chiefs. I would say that he was hopeful rather than expectant, but he was one of the few who were encouraged by Huong's having been announced as responsible for investigating corruption. The Communist Party had also taken note of some potential for positive political development (however slight), and in early November it assassinated Bong. This act represented, because assassination was just one of their tools of trade, a striking instance of how they understood the multidimensional nature of revolutionary/national liberation warfare. For them, removing Bong as a potential impediment was like dropping a bridge on Highway 19. The political atmosphere in Saigon was so poisonous that many Vietnamese suspected government involvement. At one stroke the communists removed a rival and caused the RVN to appear worse than it actually was.[5]

Most Vietnamese friends despaired of obtaining change sufficient to secure a southern (and central) identity necessary for competition with the communists during negotiations and a probable ceasefire jostle. Now, many of them would remark, we are stuck with an unopposed president and have to wait until October 1975 for another chance. Four more years. Although JUSPAO allowed me to range where interest pulled, and I was unrestricted, some officers noticed my tendency to make non-JUSPAO sorts of contacts. Deputy Director Bryan Battey, with whom I had a good relationship, suggested more focus on "contacts of organic interest to JUSPAO's concerns, rather than to the area of purely political concern."[6]

In our discussions he told me his real worry was that Deputy Ambassador Sam Berger or Political Counselor Josiah Bennett would realize someone was trespassing on their preserve and then insist I either cease or leave the country. I felt pretty sure the mission at highest level was so self-focused and numb that my personal meandering would always be off their scope.

Away from the political arena, the war between ARVN (assisted by fewer US elements) and communist forces seemed to have momentarily paused.[7] Howard Walters (promoted to lieutenant colonel) was assigned to the Phung Hoang office in Nha Trang. Based on his awareness of SVNLF organization in Phu Yen and Binh Dinh, 1962–63, he told me the greatest threat to senior VCI members was old age. Vulnerable Special Forces camps that had previously received attention from the 5th Special Forces Group and had not converted to RF were switched in 1970–71 to Border Defense Ranger battalions (Biet Dong Quan Bien Phong).[8] The communists had not yet followed up their repulse of Lam Son 719 with increased pressure in I Corps. This wasn't really "the pause that refreshes," but it did allow for wishful thinking on the part of American leadership.

A new ARVN Infantry Division, the 3rd, was organized in October 1971 to help fill the vacuum left by departing Americans. I was surprised when told by Nguyen Van Hieu (assigned to I Corps after being replaced as 5th Division commander) that the new division would headquarter in Quang Tri while pulling together its three regiments, composed of a few veteran battalions drawn from the 1st and 2nd Divisions, combined with new battalions that would include RF and PF inductees. It seemed madness to place a new division, still on shakedown, at the DMZ just a few months after the shambles of Lam Son 719. They could be the best soldiers, led by the finest officers, and it would still take time for a new unit to jell. I went to see Jake because I couldn't think of any other point of entry for registering strong disagreement.

Jake listened, but not with pleasure. We were not as comfortable with each other as we had been five years earlier, and Jake was not in as strong a position in the MACV hierarchy as he should have been. When I finished, he said, "Frankie, you're pushing against the tide. The shoulder patches are already on 3rd Division uniforms, and they say 'Ben Hai.'" The Ben Hai River was the most conspicuous terrain feature marking the boundary between North and South Viet Nam, so Jake was emphasizing that the DMZ area would definitely be the 3rd Division's area of responsibility. My response was that the tide was probably going to be a PAVN onslaught next spring, and the 3rd would be like a sand castle on the beach. We looked at each other. There was a divide between us. Jake said I ought to know that MACV had already reported improvement in RVNAF leadership and unit capability to Washington. I asked for examples. He told me the MACV assessment included "outstanding" commanders in I Corps and IV Corps and "acceptable" commanders in III Corps and II Corps. Jake said MACV graded all ARVN division commanders as good to excellent except for the 22nd, where steps would be taken to obtain a change of command.[9]

I was stymied. Jake, while not exhibiting warmth, was still being pretty candid and patient. He even asked for my reaction. I told him it was clear that ARVN, and RF and PF, had improved, improved significantly, since 1964–68. There really never had been anything wrong with the courage and endurance of the basic soldiers, experienced noncommissioned officers, and junior officers. The problem was inadequate leadership higher up the chain of command, due in part to senior officers who chose to support French policy in their own country rather than fight for independence, then saw France defeated by others who had made a very different choice. That was complicated in the next generation by deaths in combat or helicopter crashes of some of the best officers, who led from the front. Beginning in 1965, the communists distributed basic arms (AKs and B-40s, later RPGs) that were superior to what we provided, and our ally failed to develop a viable "southern" political ideal for which men would risk dying.

I continued my running comments for Jake: "Now where are we? The field soldiers are still as capable on their own as the enemy. Issuing M-16s and M-79s has almost matched what the enemy fields. Our problems are still inadequacies at higher command levels, and we lack a motivating ideal. Right now the divisions in the Delta are not facing the kind of pressure that will probably develop farther north. So the 21st, 9th, and 7th are at least adequately led for their operating environment, and in the case of the 7th, that general is so good that I wish he were in II Corps.[10] The 5th and 18th might be all right, although I am much less sure of them than the 25th. I told John months ago that the 23rd and 22nd need change of command. In I Corps General Toan ought to be replaced as 2nd Division commander because he was part of the Son My coverup, was blatantly corrupt, and was of questionable competence.[11] The 1st Division is the right fit for Phu. I think that Vu Van Giai has what it takes to command the 3rd, but that division should never be placed in Quang Tri while it is still organizing. If Abrams can't see that, then he should be replaced."

Jake waved his arms to signal that was enough, more than enough, but I was on a roll and continued: "Just think about those corps commanders. The best one is in IV Corps, the least vulnerable region. We can't really tell about Minh in III Corps yet, except that we do know he's Dang Van Quang's nominee. John is propping up Ngo Dzu in II Corps because that suits his own purpose, and I Corps commander Hoang Xuan Lam was proven not capable of mastering a complex battlefield last spring."[12]

Jake gave me a long, weary look and said, "When you think you know more than everyone else, it just means you've stayed around too long. You're John's friend and my friend. You've been a problem-solver and troubleshooter for Komer and Colby. But take care you don't start to look like a troublemaker." We were both unhappy. Jake thought I knew too much to ignore, but resented my bringing bad news. I now understood he was comfortably inside the command walls while I was trying to undermine them. I thought my assessment of RVNAF problems was correct; I would personally (distinct from professionally) rather be proven wrong, but how?

US troop strength continued declining according to schedules set by Washington. On 13 January 1972 President Nixon announced that a further decrease of seventy thousand would drop total US military in Viet Nam to sixty-nine thousand by the end of April. There were no US Marine maneuver units in I Corps. The drop would include removal of the 101st Airborne Division and result in only two combat field brigades remaining: the 196th (near Danang) and the 3rd of the 1st Air Cav in III Corps. MACV SOG would, truncated, serve in a headquarters advisory role to Nha Ky Thuat (Strategic Technical Directorate) for special operations. The fall 1971, post–Lam Son 719 appearance of equilibrium could not last. HES measurement showed the same areas of weakness in II Corps: south and east of Pleiku and northern and central Binh Dinh.[13] The combination of accelerating American withdrawal, determination to keep the RVN reacting to communist initiatives, denying the RVN time to catch its breath and develop politically, and interest in breaking the impasse of the Paris negotiations led (with some internal discussion) Communist Party leadership to opt for another major offensive.

There were some indicators from late 1971. Aside from increased traffic on supply routes, defector and prisoner reports, and communications intercepts, in January 1972 communist leaflets in Quang Nam claimed comparison of forces between themselves and RVN had turned to their advantage, opening the opportunity for attacks against the RVN in three strategic zones. Leaflets in Thua Thien from the same period made specific reference to withdrawal of the 101st Airborne as proof that America was losing.[14] Conditioned by the 1968 SVNLF/PAVN offensive keyed to the lunar New Year, RVN and American attention was focused on the mid-February holiday period. Although there was some pushing and shoving by both sides in February, by late March RVN and American leadership felt a major communist offensive was not imminent.

When I spoke with John, his principal concern was how best to overturn the appointment of Le Duc Dat, who was given command of the 22nd Division on 4 March.[15] That appointment was made without, as far as I knew then and now, consultation with MACV. John had bad history with Dat dating from 1966 and 1967, when Dat was province chief in Phuoc Tuy, and he raised hell with Jake, who then asked me to examine whether a case could be made for Dat's quick removal and replacement. I prepared a memorandum for Jake pointing out that aside from innuendo dating to alleged corruption and sale of pharmaceuticals to the SVNLF when Dat was in Phuoc Tuy, we could only make it clear that there was nothing in his record to persuade anyone that Dat could command a division under pressure on two widely separated fronts (Highland Plateau and Binh Dinh province).[16] My recollection of that period is that Ambassador Bunker and General Abrams departed Saigon for Easter holiday family visitation. We were surprised, not that a communist offensive was possible, but by the timing, scope, and intensity.[17]

The Spring Offensive (Chien Dich Xuan He), also referred to as the Nguyen Hue Campaign (named after one of the Tay Son brothers), had four principal fronts. The first (DMZ–Quang Tri–Thua Thien) was opened 30 March by a thrust over the DMZ, then one eastward down Route 9 and another from A Shau toward Hue. The second was a push into northern Binh Dinh province out of the An Lao Valley and Quang Ngai border area, beginning in the first week of April.[18] The third was movement into Binh Long province from Cambodia, beginning 6 April. The fourth was initiated with general attacks north of Kontum, beginning 12 April.

The ARVN 3rd Division should never have been placed in Quang Tri while it was still organizing. The division shattered when the 56th Regiment surrendered a position that could have been held. Communication difficulty and interference and restrictions (by corps and Saigon) fouled 3rd Division commander Vu Van Giai's attempts to coordinate the 2nd and 57th Regiments to respond to a rapidly changing situation. Withdrawal became a rout. I Corps commander Hoang Xuan Lam was incapable of coping with the rapidly deteriorating situation. Although the 1st ARVN fell back under pressure from the west, it made a fighting withdrawal, and Phu performed effectively. The 2nd Division was overextended in Quang Tin and Quang Ngai but held together. The last remaining US Army brigade did not engage.[19] Hoang Xuan Lam and Vu Van Giai were relieved of command at the beginning of May. Lam's removal was overdue and should have been done a year earlier after Lam Son 719. But Giai was meanly sacrificed to protect the continuation in office of those, especially Cao Van Vien, Dang Van Quang, and President Thieu himself, who fixed the 3rd Division where it should not have been placed.[20]

Naming the offensive Nguyen Hue had special resonance in Binh Dinh, homeland of the Tay Son brothers, where one of the communist 3rd Division regiments was called the Tay Son Regiment.[21] Northern Binh Dinh at the end of April looked a lot like it had six years earlier. Pressure was so intense that two districts (Hoai An and Hoai Nhon) were overrun. The 12th Regiment of the 3rd Division blocked Route 19 for two weeks, and it took B-52 strikes and (piecemeal) application of Korean forces (generally passive throughout the previous year) to reopen the An Khe Pass. Although many people took the refugee option out of areas of intense combat (air and artillery), most chose to remain in their hamlets even when communists assumed control. The acting province senior advisor summarized by writing that in order to avoid repetitive failure, we should reorient on *what needs to be eliminated*: "The soldier's monthly contribution to his commander, the buying of positions and assignments, the reluctance to relieve (not transfer) the inept, the reluctance to assign the able because of lack of schooling or position, the concern for self and not for one's men, the blatant theft of government and private property—these and other injustices, corruption and inattention bred the reluctance or refusal of the soldier to fight, the NCOs and junior officers to lead, and the senior officers to command. This, above all, must be remedied."[22]

More than anything else, prospects for collapse in Binh Long alarmed the RVN and American mission. Divisions attacking from the Cambodian border seized Loc Ninh. And when An Loc was surrounded and could have fallen, in Saigon the immediacy of communist maneuver units was a reality not sensed since 1968. Three communist divisions, the 5th, 7th, and 9th, well equipped and supported by artillery and tanks, failed to overrun An Loc. The difference there, compared with Quang Tri, was basically that by surrounding An Loc the communists precluded any possibility of panic retreat. Furthermore, they didn't seem to understand how to employ armor and infantry in an effective mix. Although Route 13 was interdicted (and the roadblock never broken), active involvement by American advisors who stayed with their counterparts, around-the-clock air strikes, frequent resupply by air, and reinforcement, especially by the 81st Airborne Ranger Brigade and 1st Airborne Brigade, inhibited a gnawing feeling of abandonment. Still, it was a close call. ARVN senior commanders bunkered themselves, while the street-to-street defense of the town was in the hands of junior officers and soldiers fighting for honor and their lives.[23]

The offensive in Kontum demonstrated PAVN and ARVN deficiencies. It was directed against what John thought was the strongest point of RVN defensive positions in the highlands. But the ARVN 22nd Division fractured, in part because, during the confusion around Tan Canh and Dak To, commanding officer Le Duc Dat disappeared. II Corps commander Ngo Dzu had a failure of nerve. Nguyen Van Toan, previously removed from the 2nd Division, was sent to Pleiku to replace Dzu.[24] The 22nd Division command was given to Phan Dinh Niem, and the two regiments in the highlands (the 42nd and 47th) were pulled back to Binh Dinh to join the 40th and 41st Regiments. Ly Tong Ba, commanding the 23rd Division, brought his regiments north to combine with airborne and ranger survivors of the Dak To collapse to form the defense of Kontum.

The possibility of a highlands collapse, the loss of Kontum and then Pleiku, was real. Similar to the An Loc situation, if the communists had achieved a more effective mix of armor and infantry, if the offensive had been firmly pushed at Kontum right after the loss of positions on the ridge southwest of Dak To, and then Dak To itself, Kontum would have fallen and panic could have made Pleiku untenable. By the time PAVN did attack Kontum in force, an ARVN defense had been organized, and US air strikes, including B-52 missions, brought hellfire onto the concentrated communist units. The defense held, but at enormous cost, and John Vann was killed on 9 June while flying at night to Kontum. It was in bad weather. Sa Yun and I were sleeping when Jake called and told me that John was gone.

I sat numb on the edge of our bed. I had no illusion there might have been a mistake, that somewhere John was emerging, cursing, from wreckage to organize a defensive position and care for survivors. Jake would not have made the call if he were not sure. Jake and I had developed some different opinions during the past couple of years, but affectionate respect for John was still a strong bond. I probably sat there for an hour or so, having an enormous empty feeling. John and I were linked from 1962 onward through Ev, Phil Werbiski, Doug Ramsey, Tran Ngoc Chau, Dan Ellsberg, Gordon Huddleston, and, less intensely but still significantly, many others. Chau was in Chi Hoa prison; Doug was a prisoner in the Cambodian border region; Ev, Dan, and Hud were in the United States; and first Phil and now John were killed. I still had Vietnamese and American friends, but, sitting in the dark, even with my wife beside me and our son David in the next room, I was irrationally lonely.

My feeling about loss of friends (and many were lost) is so personal, painful, that it is difficult to articulate. John in particular led a complicated personal life. I knew that he was working toward providing a future for his Vietnamese wife and daughter, because he had asked Ev and me for advice. Subsequently, we found he had taken the first steps, but in typically so convoluted a manner that everything had to be retraced for validity.[25]

John is sometimes described as morphing from counterguerrilla to conductor of B-52 missions, implying that the change was insane. I thought he was counterguerrilla when that was called for and "Captain B-52" when there was no other option at Kontum. He would often adopt the role of positive morale–building team leader while seeking to rally the rank and file, but when speaking privately with me, he was realistic and inclined to pessimism. In 1972, John Heilman (associate director for USAID) chaired a mission task force to study CORDS in the context of a changed environment. It was meant to be a reprise of the 1966 Jacobson Roles and Missions Study. I was the only person who was a member of both. John appeared before the team, shortly before his death, to provide his sense of the future. He said that the United States had been the propulsion for a heavy RVN aircraft. The flight path looked stormy, the engine was cutting out, and at best we could only lift the RVN to the highest possible altitude so that a glide path would allow for a crash landing rather than a crash. When asked the difference, John replied, "More survivors in a crash landing."[26]

Unlike when Doug was captured, I did not feel driven to reimmerse myself in field operations. Still, I did get into provinces and ARVN units to develop an understanding of what the 1972 offensive meant for the future. Speaking with officers of the 5th and 21st Divisions in Lai Khe,[27] it seemed there was no sense of commitment to the announced objective of recovering Binh Long province. A staff officer told me that the actual mission was to block any approach toward Saigon by the enemy, and when that threat diminished, he expected the 21st Division would return to Bac Lieu and Chuong Thien.

Deputy Chief of Mission Charlie Whitehouse was easy to speak with because we had known each other two years earlier when he was III Corps DEPCORDS.[28] I told him the immediate situation on the ground was not a foundation for optimism. The communist regiments and divisions paid an enormous price to achieve new lodgments in I Corps and the II Corps western highlands and Binh Long. Hue, Pleiku, and Saigon were safe—for now. But ARVN had also suffered a blow to its self-esteem, and there was a massive loss of equipment. We Americans lost John Vann, the little engine that could. We could not do anything for ARVN morale, and there would never be another John Vann, but immediate resupply was necessary to demonstrate US steadfastness to both sides. Delay would signify abandonment. President Thieu ought to be counseled to take an inclusive approach to governance and refrain from any appearance of insecure dictate.[29] No one was comfortable with bad news, but Charlie expressed appreciation for sharing my opinion. He said his door would always be open for discussion and expressed the expectation that I would continue to be available for special needs. I replied that I was sure Bob Lincoln would be responsive.

After a few days' travel in what remained of I Corps, and a conversation with new corps commander Ngo Quang Truong, I looked more carefully at ARVN equipment losses and shortages.[30] An immediate problem was that RVNAF J-1 and J-4 systems couldn't cope with the scope of the crisis. US advisors had to provide loss calculations. MACV used those figures to make estimates of need for JCS action. Project 981 would be a massive effort to bring in the equipment authorized to the end of FY 72 as soon as possible. The criticality was such that MAP funding could not cover all requirements. The US Army budget had to cover the gap. ARVN units needed equipment and personnel reconstitution for a counteroffensive, but legally certifying combat loss required an RVNAF signature with serial number. That was not easily obtained in the May and June environment.

ARVN lost 142 M41 tanks, 65 M48 tanks, 275 armored personnel carriers, and 634 two-and-a-half-ton trucks. Artillery losses were 232 pieces of 105mm and 75 pieces of 155mm. Generally speaking, half of the losses in each category took place in I Corps, attributable to collapse of the 3rd Division and its disastrous retreat from Quang Tri to the My Chanh River. The personnel situation was not good. There was an especially severe shortage of qualified noncommissioned officers. I was still sure the most significant personnel deficiency was at the highest level. It was clear to everyone that JGS, theoretically subordinate to the Ministry of Defense, in fact (just as during the First Republic) worked directly for the president, who looked upon JGS as his personal staff. President Thieu personally assigned general officers and made other important assignments. This was not an opportune moment for General Abrams to depart, but the April–May period of potential disaster had passed, so at the end of June 1972 the MACV baton was passed to General Weyand.

In mid-June JUSPAO was dissolved and USIS revived from the remaining parts. The mission established a North Viet Nam Task Force to review the impact of the communist offensive and develop ideas for applying pressure on Hanoi. The task force comprised some embassy officers and me. We knew each other and were determined that our recommendations would be practical and principled. After we were up and running, Doug Pike was assigned TDY from Washington. Doug refrained from adopting the attitude of a lead expert, listening carefully to everyone's analysis before speaking. Although he didn't contribute anything not already under consideration, his methodical endorsement added some credibility to recommendations submitted to the mission and Washington.[31]

The three most important conclusions we reached were: (1) the United States should *not* target irrigation and flood control dikes in North Viet Nam; (2) we should use immediate field intelligence by radio broadcasts to portray PAVN mounting casualties, hardship, and suffering; and (3) we should print leaflets that would appear to be Hanoi currency, but with a propaganda tab, for drops over the north. We understood there would be inevitable unintended damage to dikes due to attacks on antiaircraft batteries mounted on or near the earthen ramparts, but deliberately hitting the hydraulic system would produce a human catastrophe that could in the long term unify the population and Communist Party while tarnishing America.

For the first time immediate field intelligence would be openly broadcast to North Viet Nam. I brought raw but dependable items of field intelligence to Tom Polgar, station chief, for vetting to ensure that a source was not compromised. There was no chance of that happening, but procedure had to be followed. Each time I brought material to his office for clearance, I was asked to wait while he busied himself at his desk, then with a weary sigh he pushed papers aside and crossed the room to examine my package. It was as if he were doing me a personal favor. Occasional contact with previous station chiefs had not prepared me for that level of pomposity. Working with Colonel Doan Van Nu for the same purpose during this period was entirely different. He was always accessible, his staff was quick to provide general information and intelligence, and the STD (Nha Ky Thuat) that he commanded continued to jab aggressively at communist rear areas.[32] Specific items describing decimation of identified PAVN units, supply failure, and lack of medical support were incorporated with other material into programs for North Viet Nam.

A Hanoi resident who occasionally visited Saigon provided me, through an intermediary, with some Democratic Republic of Viet Nam currency in denominations of 5, 2, and 1 *dong*.[33] Almost exact copies, but with an end-tab propaganda message, were printed at our USIA regional service center in Manila and airdropped over the north. The intent was for people to pick up and read a message attached to what appeared to be money. Of course we knew some wily recipients would snip off the tab and pass the leaflet as if it were real currency. That was just part of the price that the Communist Party would have to pay for maintaining a "maneuvering army" in the South. The DRV figured out what was going on and quickly protested. Our own government is extraordinarily sensitive to anything that implies condoning or justifying counterfeiting currency. So our special leaflet operation was canceled after several successful missions.[34]

The Republic of Viet Nam conducted counteroffensive operations on all four fronts from midsummer onward. In each case ARVN made significant progress but could not roll communist forces back to their point of departure. In I Corps, Quang Tri city was recaptured on 16 September, and that was important to void any SVNLF/PRG (Provisional Revolutionary Government) claim to occupying a province capital. Further south, an area around Fire Support Bases Bastogne and Veghel was retaken. In II Corps, Kontum city was secured, but ARVN could not reach Vo Dinh. The last remaining ranger camp (old SF and CIDG) was Dak Pek, with the assimilated 88th Border Ranger Battalion. ARVN was able to clear Route 19 and National Highway 1 in Binh Dinh province, and Bong Son and Tam Quan were back in government hands while the communist 3rd Division pulled back into the An Lao Valley and associated base areas. In III Corps, temporary presence of the 21st Division really served as a blocking, not An Loc relief, force. Highway 13 remained closed, and Loc Ninh close to the Cambodian border was now a PRG-administered town.

In effect, compared with 1971, there was a new late 1972 western frontier zone well within Viet Nam's border. This part of the RVN was now administered by communists and utilized by them as a supply corridor. It would be the new forward operating area from which attacks could be launched for the next offensive. Despite that change, President Thieu, JGS chairman Gen. Cao Van Vien, and National Security Advisor Dang Van Quang believed ARVN overall (other than the 3rd and 22nd Divisions) had performed at a satisfactory level, and some units (the 1st, 23rd, Airborne, and Marine Divisions) were excellent. They thought that with the United States taking a tough position at the Paris negotiations, and with continued US air support and generous logistics, their administration could cope with renewed communist offensives.

I was, again, a skeptic. It seemed to me that even with the best leadership, overdue reorganization, and reformation, RVNAF simply could not carry the load previously assumed in large measure by ten (or more) US divisions, two Korean divisions, and other Free World contingents. The 1972 fighting revealed the consequence of continuing to indulge the same leadership problem (favoritism) that plagued the First Republic. American field advisors, particularly US Marines at Quang Tri and Thua Thien and US Army advisors everywhere, made up for command and staff deficiency, but they, like our maneuver formations, would eventually depart. Moreover, another consideration was congressional practice to authorize funding for support to US forces in the field. Remove the US forces, and I doubted that much funding (and congressional patience) would be available for B-52s, other air force and navy air operations, and necessary unlimited ARVN artillery rounds.[35]

Communist casualties were greater than those of RVNAF—small comfort—but it appeared to me that PAVN/SVNLF could continue to manage manpower sufficient to maintain offensive capability. I noted this point, and the following, in a summary memo I prepared for USIS Director Bob Lincoln:[36]

1. Enemy supply situation is not as critical as we thought.

2. RVNAF desertion increased each month in 1972 (through June).

3. The 22 August Decree (No. 120/SL/NV) abolished not just hamlet elections, but also elections for village officials other than the screened and approved village chief. A supplementary message told province chiefs to dismiss those who are unqualified, negative, or have bad behavior.

4. The economy is stagnant. Credit is down, savings have increased, wholesalers are reluctant to invest in stock, and people will not spend because they doubt the future.

5. Psychologically, our evaluation of conversations reported by staff and Major Sauvageot indicate that people are pessimistic.

6. The June rural PAAS showed 40 percent of respondents stating that ending the war is the most important problem for the country. That increased to 54 percent in July and 56 percent in August. In June 5 percent of respondents stated VCI were more effective than last year. That increased to 19 percent in July and 21 percent in August.

I always had an inclination to point myself in the direction of Binh Dinh and Quang Ngai, but in October I very deliberately decided to take a look at provinces in III Corps and IV Corps. The problems there were different from those encountered where ARVN divisions were under pressure from PAVN. Typically, I found residual positive influence of the RD Cadre program. Many village and hamlet officers were former RD Cadre or rural teachers. Temptation to abuse one's position by charging fees for service was inhibited by previous training and responsiveness to local opinion. Unfortunately, the picture was less positive higher up the administrative ladder.

There was practically no coordinated planning between civil and military services. The major fault, I thought, lay with generally weak province chiefs, who were appointed for reasons other than administrative competence and command presence. Since village chiefs were reduced to regime figureheads, and other rural officials at hamlet and village levels would be appointed, province and district officials now had enormous patronage power. Posts on village administrative committees (draft exempt) could be purchased. In some provinces former RD Cadre told me National Police, responsible for Phung Hoang, extorted money from people. There was especially frequent abuse of the F-6 program authority. It seemed to me that the more insecure a province (Hau Nghia and Chuong Thien), the more pervasive was RVN malfeasance.[37]

18
Negotiations, Ceasefire, and Land Rush

I am rarely diplomatic, even less a diplomatic historian, but I think of those long, drawn-out DRV-US negotiations in Paris as having three distinct periods.[1] The first one aimed at achieving a post–Tet 1968 arrangement prior to the US presidential election of the same year. The second phase, for almost another four years, traded rhetorical body blows from intransigent positions but finally in August 1972 arrived at a point where each side had renewed incentive to make a deal: the DRV because they had just gained significant territory, albeit painfully, and the United States because we needed a framework for departure before the next swing of the axe brought everything down while we were still halfway up the tree. The third period proceeded from a high-speed stall in October, when President Thieu threw a wrench into the Kissinger machine, through most of January 1973 until signatures were applied to the Agreement on Ending the War and Restoring Peace in Viet Nam.

The negotiations began in May 1968 with a relatively open process in which Xuan Thuy represented the DRV and Governor Harriman headed an American delegation. Following the fall 1968 negotiations train wreck, discussions resumed with a new American president sending Henry Kissinger to engage with Le Duc Tho. From late summer 1972 onward, talks between the DRV and United States were conducted secretly. The Republic of Viet Nam, ally through years of shared pain, was not fully informed concerning progress and substance. In early October, Le Duc Tho dropped communist insistence that Nguyen Van Thieu be removed from RVN administrative authority. The United States was prepared to accept continuation of PAVN elements within RVN territory. Washington, in delirium, was sure that President Thieu need only to be informed of this "good deal" obtained on Viet Nam's behalf, and then Americans could leave with honor.

In late October 1972, Henry Kissinger arrived in Saigon, accompanied by Assistant Secretary of State Bill Sullivan; General Abrams, army chief of staff (presumably present as a friend of Viet Nam to humanize the edict delivered from Washington); and staff. On the following day Ambassador Bunker and DCM Charlie Whitehouse went with them to meet President Thieu, Foreign Minister Tran Van Lam, Vice President Huong, Tran Kim Phuong (RVN ambassador to Washington), and Hoang Duc Nha. It was a stormy meeting.[2] A point of contention was that the meeting was based on Kissinger's professorial presentation, absent a Vietnamese text. President Thieu had some intimation that the United States had concluded a deal with the DRV, but receiving confirmation from the duplicitous American national security advisor was both painful and infuriating.[3] The RVN would not initial the deal made on their behalf. Consternation. Frustrated Kissinger. Aggravated President Nixon.[4]

At the end of the month, Hanoi broadcast the agreement text as it had stood prior to Kissinger's rollout in Saigon. When the two sides met in Paris a month later, the United States presented changes to what the DRV had previously accepted as text in early October. Understandably, the DRV countered with some suggestions of its own. Impasse. The negotiations were recessed. President Nixon decided to "bomb the hell" out of North Viet Nam. The public explanation was that force would drive the DRV back to the negotiating table. The actual purpose was to sweeten the package for President Thieu by implying that Big Brother B-52 would always be on call.

President Thieu and his supporters had cause for uneasiness, and not just because of the behind-the-back nature of US arrangements with Hanoi. Nguyen Tuy, now a lieutenant colonel and still assigned in Binh Dinh, visited us in Saigon in late October, prior to the Kissinger visit and presentation. He told me that a prisoner had disclosed that a ceasefire was imminent, there would be an international control commission, and "patriotic forces" should prepare to seize and defend important areas. Tuy was especially concerned that the RVN needed to deny access to coastal ports, because if one would be taken by the communists, they could make the case for a point of entry to supply northern Binh Dinh and even the area north of Kontum.[5]

Despite the summer/fall RVNAF counteroffensive, the trend-indicative HES rating for hamlets in November and December 1972 revealed persistent communist presence in rural Republic of Viet Nam. In November (reporting 12,207 hamlets) 7,117 were A or B, but 5,490 were C or less (including 885 V). A month later (December reporting 12,071 hamlets), and more reflective of some RVN counteroffensive success, 8,010 were A or B, but 4,061 still were C or less (including 743 V).[6] The only chance for the RVN to recover those lost hamlets and territory held by PAVN would be if a cease-fire agreement required withdrawal of PAVN to the North, or if sustained RVN effort over time were to receive *undiminished* American logistic and air support.

When our embassy in Saigon received messages from Paris, including text of the cease-fire agreement as amended by January 1973 argumentation, it was obvious that the first (and preferred) course would not apply. Ambassador Bunker had me look at what was transmitted from Paris. There were few alterations, barely enough for the United States to claim (unconvincingly, I thought) that the changes represented significant DRV concession. But the most telling indicator that this agreement was a disguised US surrender was that PAVN units were still not required to withdraw.

We planned to take the final text, as received from the Kissinger team in Paris, and print bilingual (Vietnamese and English) copies that would be an authoritative reference for the ICCS teams deploying to monitor and supervise. Bill Ayers, USIS officer, was at Tan Son Nhut ready to fly the text to our USIA regional service center in Manila for production. I was making one last check to assure consistency between both language versions when Bill Gausmann, USIS North Viet Nam analyst, told me that he had the text as broadcast by Radio Hanoi. He asked if I wanted to see it. My immediate reaction was that it wouldn't be necessary. I already had the text as the embassy had received it from Paris. But then I thought, why not?

Well, there were some textual differences, not major, but differences. I called Eva Kim, Ambassador Bunker's secretary, and told her that I needed to see him right away. When I sat down at a table in his office, Ambassador

Bunker looked over my shoulder while I indicated the differences between what he had received and what Hanoi had broadcast. "Well, I'll be god-damned!" he exclaimed, then, immediately, "Excuse me, Eva." That was gentleman Ellsworth Bunker's expression of disappointment on learning that right to the last, even the American Embassy in Saigon was not fully, and correctly, informed. We made quick rectification, and so the USIS "cease-fire and restoring peace" booklet was based on the text from Hanoi.

When PRG and DRV representatives to the Four-Party Joint Military Commission (established by the agreement) arrived in Saigon, Jim Yellin (embassy officer) and I were at Tan Son Nhut to witness a historic moment in Vietnamese history. Not only was the premise of the Agreement on Ending the War and Restoring Peace in Viet-Nam (that the signatories committed to ending the war) false, but also the protocols and clauses were written vaguely for the purpose of having a text that all parties could sign. Now they were subject to different interpretation. When PRG or DRV personnel prepared to deplane in Saigon, Republic of Viet Nam officials informed them that they would have to fill out customs and arrival forms, as though they were foreigners. They refused to comply. Hours and hours passed while the temperature rose inside the aircraft. A few uniformed Americans on the scene actually enjoyed the spectacle. Jim and I, on the spot, acted as embassy representatives, communicated circumstances to the embassy, and advised providing water to those stuck on the aircraft. Eventually, after persuasive reasoning on the part of the embassy with RVN leaders, communist delegates were allowed entry without following immigration procedures. This was a two-day exercise, since the DRV team and the PRG representatives arrived separately on different days.

While Henry Kissinger was discovering, during his 10–14 February 1973 Hanoi meetings, that the Hanoi appreciation of the agreement was very different from his own, I was witnessing misunderstanding on the ground in Loc Ninh on 12 February. Most of the US prisoners of war were aviators held in North Viet Nam and would be released there. Loc Ninh, serving as the PRG administrative center, was designated as the release point in the South. I was one of the escort officers on the recovery team and would be responsible for specific returnees on the UH-1D to which I was assigned. Doug Ramsey was listed to come out of Loc Ninh with me. The night before recovery, we briefed at HQ MACV. The helicopters were provided by the downsizing but still active operational 1st Aviation Brigade. General McClellan, chief of the reception party, expected we would be on the ground for less than one hour.[7]

We left Tan Son Nhut about 0730, refueled at Lai Khe (as contingency) and touched down on the ramp of the old Loc Ninh strip about 0830. Approaching Loc Ninh from the south, we flew over hundreds of persons dressed in light blue trousers and shirts, seated in orderly groups but obviously excited by our arrival. Since we knew there would be twenty-seven Americans, those others had to be ARVN. So the American supposition of a smooth process, that we only needed to fly out fellow Americans, grounded on the shoals of Viet Nam reality. PRG and PAVN representatives awaiting our arrival in an administrative tent expected that release of the twenty-seven Americans would be part of a larger exchange, including delivery of some of their people held by the RVN and release of hundreds of ARVN prisoners. The immediate American reaction, including that of General McClellan, was to assume bad faith, even treachery, on the part of the communists.[8] General McClellan, frustrated and irritable, suggested we might just return to Saigon until the issue could be resolved. I had my annotated bilingual copy of the protocol concerning return of captured persons and pointed out that the wording in Vietnamese and English did not state exchange would be simultaneous. But the wording was so nonspecific that it could be inferred mutuality would apply. Furthermore, I added, most important, somewhere out of sight our Americans were gathered. They knew we were on the ground. If they were to see our helicopters lift away without them, it would have a devastating impact on morale. We couldn't do that. We had to stay on the ground while the issue was resolved in Saigon by the Four-Party Commission, the US Embassy, and the RVN.

We were in Loc Ninh about eleven hours. The eventual solution, based on agreement by parties in Saigon, was to fly in the first of several C-130s with communists for release to the PRG/PAVN representatives, then that C-130 would carry out as many of the ARVN prisoners as feasible. Before that happened, the pierced-steel planking of the landing strip had to be cleared of debris and some jagged points hammered back beneath the surface. SVNLF soldiers and cadre brought baskets of bread around to the helicopter crews. Despite instructions during the previous evening briefing to "not become engaged in conversation or contact with representatives of the enemy forces," in the prevailing situation all of us were dependent on young enemy soldiers for bread and water.[9] They began talking with us and we with them. I saw that interpreters provided by our opponents were excellent, surely better than I, so I was freed to do some walking around and conversational exploring.

The PRG and DRV personnel were polite and trying to be friendly. The PRG (SVNLF) soldiers wore an odd assortment of uniforms and crude sandals, but their weapons were clean. Their comments demonstrated determination and resolve to accomplish "liberation" of the remainder of South Viet Nam. They expressed pride in being part of a liberation army. Of course they were coached in how to present themselves to us, but I thought their spirit was genuine and formidable. "The Liberation Army does not have helicopters, but we can march everywhere. Take away your planes, stop bombing the people, and then you will see us all around you. Now it is hard for us to be friends, but come again and leave your gun at home. Then we will see."[10]

At 1918 hours we received confirmation that Americans would be released; they were brought forth, happy beyond measure, and with quick greetings we loaded the helicopters and were off. Then another, singular complication required creative response. Halfway back to Tan Son Nhut, one of the returnees, Richard Waldhaus, asked about our plan. I explained that a medevac aircraft was waiting to bring everyone to Clark Field for medical screening, initial treatment, if necessary, and then family reunification. Richard surprised me by responding very determinedly, almost fiercely, that he did not want to leave Viet Nam and would refuse travel anywhere. I asked what he expected to do. He answered that when he was captured in 1971, he had been looking for his girlfriend.[11] Now, before leaving, he wanted to find her and propose marriage. Using the headset that allowed me to monitor communications, I got patched through to the operation command center at Tan Son Nhut. I informed a surprised command group that we had one returnee who did not want to leave Viet Nam.

"Well, make him!"

I responded that we should not treat a returnee as he had been treated in captivity, and the image as reported by the planeside media of an American being forced up the ramp against his will would not be what President Nixon would want to see in the newspapers the next day. After a short silence I was told to manage the situation as I thought best. Doug

Ramsey was an interested observer while I made a deal with Richard. I said he needed medical evaluation, and if he would promise to follow my guidance, we would arrange for his examination and initial treatment at the 3rd Field Hospital.[12] Then we would try to locate his girlfriend so they could meet. But if I made that commitment, I needed one from him. He had to agree that if we could not find the young lady, or if the meeting were not what he hoped for, then he would definitely return home. His promise received, I instructed our pilot to touch down in the shadow of a C-130 much further back from the other helicopters. Doug wished us luck, then he, Fritz, Newingham, and Rollins walked away and over to where the official welcoming party waited. Rich Waldhaus and I took a circuitous route to the USIS car and driver that were waiting for me.

I brought Rich to the 3rd Field Hospital and, by explanation to the staff, obtained an entire ward on the top floor dedicated solely to him.[13] The hospital MP detachment was enlisted to assure he would be secure and not approached by anyone without my authorization. Rich really wanted to come home with me, but he needed a checkup, and Sa Yun (pregnant and made nervous by my frequent absence) needed serenity. Rich suddenly looked lonely, but the friendly and concerned MPs became his new friends.

The next morning I went to the embassy to explain the situation to Charlie Whitehouse and seek assistance from political officer Jim Nach. Deputy Ambassador Whitehouse asked if I knew what I was doing. I replied that we would find out, but I knew what I did not want to do, and that was to force a returned POW. Charlie said, "Okay, Frank, but it's your responsibility, and keep me informed. No surprises!"

Jim Nach was immediately responsive. Jim lived in the small villa behind the one occupied by Sa Yun and me. We had been in the field a couple of times, and I knew Jim was daring (when called for) and an excellent speaker of Vietnamese. We returned to the 3rd Field Hospital and spoke with Rich, who was comforted by seeing that our end of the bargain would be kept. Rich provided us with the girl's name and the location of the hamlet where he knew her. In two days, with support by Air America helicopter, even entering an area occupied by PRG cadre, Jim found the young girl.[14] When we spoke with her in my office, we learned that she cared for Rich but thought he should return home; if he came again to Viet Nam, then they could talk about a future. I arranged for the daily Pan

Am flight to delay departure while we all went to the hospital to speak with Rich. Wayne Peterson, a USIS officer, agreed to escort Rich as far as California, where family would meet him. Our discussion at the hospital was intense. Rich was so frustrated that he struck the young lady by mistake and shoved me while insisting she ought to leave with him. Finally, after about an hour, Rich decided to return home. A fast trip to planeside, and he was on his way, having been treated with the consideration that a returning POW deserved.[15]

Soon after, the 3rd Field Hospital was closed out. The advisory program, expanded over the years, evaporated in a few weeks to meet the agreement's sixty-day time frame for withdrawal of US military. CORDS was erased on 27 February 1973, with a vestigial field advisory apparatus now directed by Jake, who was functioning as special assistant to the ambassador for field operations (SAFFO). I never liked the term *advisor*, but whether as counselor or discussant, maintaining an engaged liaison function should have been recognized as even more important during a ceasefire environment of political and rural security competition. Jake would be all right, maybe just right, but he would have fewer horses to work with, and much would depend on a new ambassador.

The Four Party Joint Military Commission (Four-Party JMC), ostensibly existing to assure implementation of agreement protocols, held regular meetings. Jean Sauvageot was interpreter for the American side, and his engaging personality and ability in Vietnamese quickly made him the interpreter of choice for all the delegations. Jean and I frequently discussed what was happening around the country and within the Four-Party JMC discussions. United by our concern for a noncommunist Viet Nam, but convinced there was no honorable, no realistic, alternative to ending the war, we hoped (not the same as expected) a period of political competition might provide for the crash landing that John Vann had postulated a year earlier. The greatest problem, it seemed to me, was that two of the parties (DRV and PRG) arrived with some confidence that the agreement would work for them. Le Quang Hoa (DRV) was a politically wired general officer, and Tran Van Tra (PRG) was one of the outstanding field commanders of the war. The other two parties (the United States and the RVN) were suspicious and defensive. General Woodward (United States) brought to the table unconcealed antagonism for the communist adversaries. General Ngo Dzu, the RVN representative, who had been removed from II Corps command for inadequate performance, must have been an indicator to the communists that President Thieu was not serious about making the agreement work.[16]

The United States understood the Four-Party JMC primarily as an administrative umbrella for obtaining release of all detained Americans and providing verification that the US military was withdrawing from Viet Nam in accordance with the agreement. To those ends the US delegation even facilitated logistical support for the PRG and DRV delegations. The DRV/PRG side, perhaps not wanting to be entirely dependent on American support, also used transport by Aigle Azur. They were familiar with Aigle Azur because it previously had held the contract for the International Control Commission established in 1954 by the Geneva Accords.[17] The agreement required all parties to submit lists and other documentation according to a schedule. At one point, with Jean Sauvageot interpreting, the DRV representative reported that they could not make timely submission because a list had not arrived from Hanoi as expected. General Woodward was incensed and accused the DRV representative of obstruction. Sauvageot followed up with Le Quang Hoa and learned that the problem was mechanical difficulty with an Aigle Azure Boeing 307. He informed General Woodward, but a message had already been sent to Washington mischaracterizing the situation. General Woodward was not willing to send a correction, so angry but misinformed Washington leadership temporarily pulled back from the obligation for removal of harbor and waterway mines that was part of the Paris Agreement.[18]

As weeks passed, even in strain, an unanticipated Stockholm effect operated. One day, while riding in a staff car, General Woodward commented to Major Sauvageot, "I think old Hoa [meaning Le Quang Hoa] is just a regular soldier like me." Sauvageot thought to himself, "Sure, if you were editor of Stars & Stripes and a member of the Republican National Committee."[19]

The ceasefire period of pushing and shoving to make claim on terrain was sometimes referred to as a time of land-grab offensives (by both sides), but I thought it was more analogous to the Oklahoma land rush. Although the ICCS did not play an important role (despite the agreement), and although the probability was unlikely from the beginning, both sides (in their own self-interest) had to behave as though the ICCS might be a significant umpire. Just as Oklahoma Sooners would jump the gun to stake claims to land, so communists and the RVN claimed governance of rural areas by raising competing flags. In some instances the PRG/PAVN forces retained important lodgments; in other places they overextended and RVNAF was able to recapture important areas.[20] At the same time, expanding the extent of RVN control in nonstrategic territory meant that eventually RVNAF would be on the defensive with significant sacrifice of mobility.

I traveled extensively in the four military regions from March through May. ARVN seemed to have caught its breath in Binh Dinh, but the impact on rural communities was, again, devastating. I had an opportunity to speak with Gen. Cao Van Vien, who expressed confidence that RVN forces, with continued American air and logistic support, could repulse any communist offensive. He added that everyone doubted that the enemy would abide by the peace agreement, so all would depend on whether the United States lived up to the commitments made to President Thieu. Several days later in I Corps, General Truong (corps commander) and Gen. Le Van Than (commander of 1st Division) took care to walk a noncommittal tightrope, neither optimistic nor obviously pessimistic.[21] They were both, like Vien, skeptical of communist ceasefire motivation, they acknowledged that RVNAF lacked an immediate national strategic reserve, and they expected continued US support at previous levels.[22] With friends, I drove through the Mekong Delta and spoke with Le Van Phoi, Hoa Hao commander, in Tinh Bien (Chau Doc province).[23] Phoi realistically expected Hoa Hao could preserve security in home districts, but he said that what happened elsewhere would determine the outcome on a national level.

Charlie Whitehouse hosted a dinner for several embassy field reporters. At the end of the evening he asked each of us for our estimate of RVN longevity. Some allowed that need for the Communist Party to reorganize and revive political apparatus in the South, while repairing damage in the North, could provide the Republic of Viet Nam with a few years' breathing space. There was no reason to expect that it would be used wisely. I flat out predicted Saigon governance would not survive beyond 1976. Consensus coalesced at about 1976 or 1977, with the only debate being whether the end would be a slide through coalition or battlefield collapse. Charlie was surprised. We in turn were all surprised that he would have believed there was a chance for anything else.

Bob Lincoln, who had morphed JUSPAO into USIS, was leaving. We had worked together fairly effectively. Our only difference of opinion was a consequence of his asking me to organize staff seminars to provide new officers (we would have almost 100 percent turnover) with orientation to Viet Nam history and sociology and communications problems. I visualized the sessions as being problem-oriented, but Bob was concerned morale might be degraded. He asked me to arrange for each problem topic to be followed by a positive discussion or speaker. That was not easy. When I mentioned this to Ton That Thien, he asked to be told about any positives in the Republic of Viet Nam's situation.[24]

Some friends, such as Jean Sauvageot, were required, by being military personnel, to depart in conformity with the agreement. Jean understood and convinced me that a new period of Vietnamese-American relations was under way, and for people like him and me there could only be heart-break if we thrashed around to find some way of staying.[25] Ev Bumgardner emerged from a sort of USIA Washington purgatory to assignment in the East Asia Office as Indo-China desk officer. He telephoned to advise me that I ought to accept return to Washington to be China affairs officer for USIA. He sweetened his counsel by promising, on behalf of the area director, that I would be his backup for Indo-China. That would make it possible to stay connected, share information with him, and even get back to Viet Nam once a year.

Our daughter was born on 14 May 1973 in the Adventist Hospital that had been the 3rd Field Hospital and, before that, an American school. Her birth certificate is Vietnamese, and the "place of birth" entry in her American passport will always be Viet Nam. Six weeks later, on 28 June, Sa Yun took infant Barbara Sayun and young David Philip to Taipei for a few days with her family while waiting for me. I followed a week later, after making some other arrangements and personal farewells. Col. Nguyen Be and others were at Tan Son Nhut when I left. It was an emotional parting, because we could not be sure of meeting again.

Reflection, 1973

You are on your own when returning for a domestic assignment, unless a friend helps you through reentry. Ev Bumgardner was always our friend. He met us at Dulles Airport, took travelers home to relax with Odette, Ginny, and Gene, and advised me to get off to a fast start on China issues. Otherwise, he said, some would claim I was a Viet Nam operator who could not adapt. He said that was the accusation aimed at him by a new breed of USIA officers, organizational "communications theorists." Ev also counseled us on purchasing a home and guided us toward a new house in North Arlington that was behind his parents' place. And that was where, a little more than two years later, Ha Thuc Can and family, Nguyen Be, and other friends found sanctuary.[1]

I did concentrate on tasks associated with being the USIA China affairs officer. I applied relationship lessons learned and practiced in Viet Nam. Don't just be approachable (although always that is a minimum), but be outgoing and forthcoming. Do not be constrained by protocol and hierarchal sensitivity, but don't be insistent if a person of interest is status-oriented. Whenever possible, make a direct approach rather than ask for an appointment. Catch unexpected opportunities. Help others accomplish their tasks. Give credit for success to the people who work with you. Protect the people who work with you.

We were successful in obtaining approval for Chinese officials in the Washington liaison office (not yet an embassy) and the China mission to the United Nations to participate in USIA invitational travel programs within our country. We also overcame the resistance of Voice of America (VOA) Radio to increasing the hours of English language–study broadcasting, based on the text series English 900, and provided books in response to letters mailed to our postal box in Hong Kong. About every other month I chaired a small, informal working group of officers from other US government offices with interest in the developing US-China relationship.

I was also the desk officer for USIS posts in Malaysia, Hong Kong, Singapore, and the Republic of China (Taiwan). I took those duties as seriously as the exciting contact work with the People's Republic of China, because no post should feel its needs and concerns have low priority in a home office. I maintained correspondence with the USIS directors in each of those countries and visited each post. We were especially concerned to assure USIS Taiwan that they were not being cast adrift.[2]

In late 1966 and again in late 1967, when I had spent some time in Washington, it seemed everyone wanted space on the Viet Nam bandwagon. Civilian careerists jockeyed for appointment to senior administrative positions in Viet Nam because an assignment might be rewarded by promotion.[3] Now the opposite pertained. Viet Nam service, which earlier might have been a stepping-stone, was now a millstone. The price was too steep, the burden too heavy, the hardship intolerable, and Henry Kissinger in frustration portrayed South Viet Nam as less friend than albatross.[4] The South was an aggravation, and the North was still the enemy. The deal that provided for US military departure along with released prisoners of war, in return for the DRV's maintaining troops inside the RVN while tolerating President Thieu in office, was a Faustian bargain for southern Vietnamese. Just when friendship and consultation would be most needed, we were reducing field representation, and we would soon cut other forms of assistance.[5]

Ev used a term that was unfamiliar to me, *zeitgeist*, in telling me that the 1973 Washington zeitgeist was rationalized self-interest. There was no more suave practitioner than Henry Kissinger, who in 1968 wormed his way into consultancy for the early Paris negotiations, under President Johnson, despite his affiliation with Rockefeller (Republican). Ev told me he was sure Kissinger played a devious role in the shadows while the Nixon campaign encouraged President Thieu to withhold cooperation because a better deal would be available if Richard Nixon were elected president.[6] The description Ev provided was painful for him because he was deeply Republican by party affiliation, personally acquainted with Richard Nixon (having been on the vice presidential trip to South America), and still had some contact with Rose Mary Woods. He was uncomfortable with his own conclusion: that President Nixon and Henry Kissinger perpetuated the war and rationalized that by asserting a need to gird American credibility.[7]

On my part, I supposed that Kissinger, through General Haig, promoted or at least endorsed the 1971 Lam Son 719 operation that ripped the carefully constructed image of ARVN competency. Influenced by his academic fascination, I think, with the Congress of Vienna, and supposing world powers could steer a lesser nation, Kissinger believed that Viet Nam could be nudged by the Soviet Union and China toward a settlement acceptable to the United States. He did not understand that, for Viet Nam, their country was the world, and the Communist Party had bitter memories of the Geneva settlement, in which so-called friends had urged settling for less than what they had earned on the battlefield. So, yes, they would sign on to withdrawal of the American military from Viet Nam, but not removal of their own military from the South. An observer could only conclude that Kissinger's rampant hubris was an element in the late 1972 miscalculation that delivered, three months later, disguised surrender. This was rationalized self-interest triumphant.[8] How was it that executive and legislative branches followed a delusional policy advocate? They were ignorant themselves, and anxious, desperate, to be quit of the war.

Since fall 1967 I had been convinced the United States could not win a war, as we were fighting it, in Viet Nam. I thought our goal should be withdrawal, preferably by negotiated agreement, as quickly as possible. Making that tough decision and implementation should not have required five, almost six, years. So in 1973 I was not someone who would argue against withdrawal, but I did feel that dishonesty—pretending that "Vietnamization" worked, reducing liaison personnel (advisors) when they might be most needed, and cutting funding for supply and operations—was dishonorable. We ought to have had an honorable policy. We should have informed the RVN that we could no longer station Americans in Viet Nam but would provide financial and logistical assistance as long as they wanted to continue their struggle for a distinct identity. My preferred course would have been difficult, but not more tortuous than the one we followed.

I thought it peculiar that, in the mid-1973 Washington atmosphere, General Abrams was considered a hero too late placed in charge, while General Westmoreland was treated with some lack of respect. I did think General Westmoreland misstepped by not insisting on joint or combined command and only infrequently accepting limited application of encadrement. But CINCPAC and Washington (other than Gen. Harold K. Johnson) did not provide the national command push that was needed. The post-1968 reaction to the war was so pronounced that the "bad war" image created by the media implied that the general commanding must have been a bad general. General Abrams harvested the benefit of being the "un-Westmoreland." This was illogical, because crediting Abrams with initiating a one-war approach, as though he applied a PROVN template, was unreal. Moreover, the so-called Abrams one war never included a political factor, while for the communist one-war effort, political intent was the core. Abrams's single war was simply the consequence of coping with the resource tide running out and the need to support the Komer-Colby CORDS operation in place. Abrams never got his hands around the ARVN assignment and promotion process any more than Westmoreland did, which is to say, not at all. And the Abrams sign-off on Lam Son 719 (while Westmoreland in Washington was doubtful) reveals abysmal ignorance of the situation. If those RVNAF soldiers and Marines lost in Laos had been American boys, the Abrams reputation would have had no luster.

Ev and I had quite a discussion about insurgency and counterinsurgency, because he wanted to believe that CORDS had defeated the insurgency, and then the Communist Party changed the game from insurrection and guerrilla warfare to PAVN invasion. But I asked, had we not changed the game ourselves when we introduced American units in 1965? My opinion was that, by the time CORDS shaped up in late 1967, the nature of the war had already changed from insurgency to maneuver warfare. The cumulative impact of Phung Hoang and other formulae was as part of a total effort, including not only CORDS (RD Cadre, RF, and PF), but also the operations of ARVN, US, and other allied forces. It was whining to complain that the game was changed by the PAVN offensive. Even as many were turning away from Viet Nam, some asserted, "We never lost a battle." Saying so did not make it true. The case could be made that a few small engagements were lost, but debating the issue was meaningless. The purpose of war is to bend the opponent to your will. Our goal from the beginning was to perpetuate a southern entity and prevent the North from unifying the country on communist terms. After years of strife we signed an agreement allowing the northern army to maintain itself in the South. We left because our own will bent. We lost.

I thought then, and still do today, that our general thinking about in-surgency is hobbled by imperial perspective. Our emphasis is on how to organize and apply measures, inducements, and tactics to treat symp-toms. It would be best first to identify the motivating reason for the insurgency and then consider whether we can meet, satisfy, or acqui-esce, and by so doing, provide insurgent leadership with an immediate nonviolent path for success. If, like King George III, we are not willing, then we must ask ourselves if we are better prepared than he and his government were for years of bloodshed, mounting casualties on both sides, and misapplication of national resources better used in other en-deavors.

Early in the Viet Nam War we Americans failed to appreciate that the one war (the one I believed existed—not the war and the "other war") was polysided and multidimensional. It was polysided in that the Viet Nam Communist Party, RVN French derivative leadership, An Quang, Hoa Hao, and FULRO all had different objectives. It was multidimen-sional because the tactics and strength of contending forces varied over time and region. Only the Communist Party and its armed com-ponents (PAVN and SVNLF) demonstrated national consistency and unity of purpose throughout.

We also misunderstood the relationship between hamlet and village, particularly as they existed in central Viet Nam. When, even years later, Americans would say or write that the hamlets were "not a traditional organ of administration," that was true only because the village (for the emperor and for French colonial rule) was an administrative organ to control the hamlets, where the people lived. Even in the Mekong Delta, where the village did have a traditional social role, it came to be used as a point for collecting taxes and checking citizen loyalty.[9]

Some of the men I respected still looked back on the Diem period with appreciation for its relative stability. I thought this was a nostalgia-induced illusion that Diem had been more effective than was the case. When Bill Colby and I talked on his boat one day after the war, my po-sition was still that, absent 1963 reform, a change of government was probably unavoidable, but the means should have preserved at least the appearance of constitutional transfer of authority. The favor retrospec-tively accorded Diem was (irrespective of any role in his overthrow and murder) to Nguyen Van Thieu's benefit. Whereas Ev understood that a "second coming" in the person of Thieu was highly unlikely to produce a healthy result, Bill Colby was more optimistic.

Sink or swim with Ngo Dinh Diem.
But maybe win with Duong Van Minh?
Then, strange sign for Nguyen Khanh.[10]
An Quang would rather Nguyen Chanh Thi.
Troi Oi! It's Nguyen Cao Ky.
So see it through with Nguyen Van Thieu.

I realized in the fall of 1973 that my own understanding, appreciation, and insight for Viet Nam history, society, and the war itself would be less relevant than it had been in the past several years. Until 1968 PAVN was auxiliary and supplementary to SVNLF. Since then, and especially from 1972 onward, SVNLF (PRG) was auxiliary and supplementary to PAVN. It was still one war for the communists, led by one national (not northern) party. CORDS did not defeat the insurgency, but CORDS exploited the impact of US forces that knocked the insurgency phase of the communist game plan back to a subsidiary but important supporting role. The concluding phase would be PAVN divisions supported by local forces against RVNAF divisions and RF/PF.

I thought a lot about warfare and American presidential responsibility. Unlike Grotius, looking for natural and universal principles, I began from the personal and minute particular. It seemed proper to consider my own acts of violence from 1963 through early 1966. I concluded that when I fired upon an opposing combatant or armed cadre, it was legitimate within the context of our government supporting another that was endeavoring to establish an independent identity. Geneva Accords aside, there was nothing inherently wrong in the attempt. But it should have been obvious from late 1967, or at least 1968, that our good-faith effort would be insufficient. Ending our involvement in the war should not have required five more years. If we were not going to cut (permanently) PAVN's route through Laos in 1966 or 1967, then we had no business urging RVNAF to make the attempt in 1971.[11]

There are unavoidable wars of national defense. The one in which my father was killed, World War II, was one. There are smart wars. The Korean War, simply because we could not allow in 1950 a militarized communist united Korea pointing like a dagger at occupied Japan, was one.[12] Despite my personal commitment, I could not characterize our war in Viet Nam as either necessary or smart. Within the international environment of the mid-1950s, assisting Vietnamese to secure an independent political identity from Quang Tri southward was worth a try. But despite the sacrifices of Vietnamese, Cambodians, Laotians (combatants and non-combatants), Americans, Australians, Koreans, New Zealanders, and Thais, the Viet Nam War, particularly from 1968 on, has to be considered a mistake.

Any president's national defense responsibility should be to ensure that armed forces are representative of our society at large and prepared for war. This means selective service and total citizen engagement in wars of national defense.[13] The president must absolutely distinguish between smart (but painful) and mistaken wars and, once mistakes are identified, make quick corrections. When I arrived at those simple conclusions in 1973, it did not occur to me that one day an American administration would adopt a preemptive strike policy and deploy an army abroad with even weaker rationale than that applied to Viet Nam.[14]

The Last Chapter: Deterioration and Collapse of the Second Republic

We all know how the story ends. There are good descriptions of the 1974 and 1975 events. I am particularly impressed with the accounts presented by William Le Gro, Frank Snepp, and Tran Van Tra. I would not attempt to duplicate their excellent first-hand observations. Instead, here follows my sense of how the situation seemed to degenerate, based on my Washington perspective and travel to Viet Nam in 1974 and 1975. Although I concentrated on China program responsibilities, Ev shared his Viet Nam messages with me so I could cover for him when he was absent.

Because Ev and I worked on Viet Nam developments, some others in the office thought of us as "the last true believers," when we really believed that disaster was coming. I found it irritating that more people seemed concerned about the Washington Redskins than the country from which we had just withdrawn, and damn few were bothered by America's reducing support to Vietnamese to whom we had commitments. It bears repeating that no one had more reason than I to conclude that the United States should withdraw, and I had reluctantly reached that conclusion in late 1967; but we should not have short-changed Vietnamese efforts for making a stand on their own. Following withdrawal of US units there were no inhibitions against Congress' reducing assistance to Viet Nam. Just before our family arrival in Washington, the Senate passed a resolution that opposed bombing North Viet Nam, even if the cease-fire agreement failed. In August 1973, bombing in Cambodia was prohibited. These steps foretold absence of direct air support in the South as well. And, even more ominously, in August 1974 the US Congress reduced planned assistance by 30 percent, from one billion to seven hundred million dollars.

Uninformed persons might have supposed in 1974 that South Viet Nam appeared strong. It was a sweet mirage. The military conundrum for President Thieu and the Republic of Viet Nam was that the obligation to defend all points recovered during the 1973 land rush resulted in overextending the RVNAF and increasing the number of isolated outposts. The equally severe political pinch was that the president had already, since 1970, deliberately foreclosed the option of an opening to elements that were not intransigently deeply conservative or reactionary. In early 1974 even some conservatives openly criticized the president and his administration for corruption that compromised the national effort.[1] The result was further isolation for the president. Simultaneously, the civil economy in central and southern Viet Nam was decaying. Military families were affected because the cost of basic items and services outstripped income.

The appearance of governmental rot and family deprivation was an accelerant for corruption, despite public outcry. When Ev and I traveled, separately, to Viet Nam in early 1974, we both noted a *cho chieu* (evening market) atmosphere. Good friends, including some in government such as Chau Kim Nhan, told me that they struggled to maintain personal ethical standards of conduct, but their hands were tied when it came to enforcement on others. I was not under illusion as to the military situation, but I remember orienting my trip report toward emphasis on the fragile, fractured economy and the desperate situation for soldiers and civil servants.[2]

PAVN/SVNLF circumstances were not as problematic. They had no responsibility for the southern economy, and in the North everything was, enforced by the party, subordinate to the war. On the battlefield they had slowly taken back much of what was lost in 1973. A test appeared under way in April 1974 at an ordinarily insignificant base, Tonle Cham, about eleven or twelve kilometers west-southwest from An Loc, manned by the 92nd Ranger Battalion. The base did not really block communist movement between Zones C and D, since constriction was so tight the opposition could easily move around it. The communist side could determine the quality of RVN response—to reinforce and maintain, preserve with air support (strike and supply), or successfully evacuate. The RVN could evaluate US reaction to a threat in III Corps. The result demonstrated ineffective

RVN response and lack of interest on the part of the United States. Tonle Cham was abandoned through no fault of the ranger defenders.

But overall in 1974, ARVN III Corps was proving resilient. Pham Quoc Thuan directed a major spring offensive into the Cambodian Svay Rieng border salient that disrupted the PAVN 5th Division. A multiregiment ARVN operation in Binh Duong (successively involving regiments of the 18th, 5th, and 25th Divisions) through the summer and fall recovered terrain and frustrated the PAVN 7th and 9th Divisions. Tran Quang Khoi, commanding III Corps armor, and Le Minh Dao, commanding the 18th Division, proved energetic, successful battlefield leaders.[3]

In other regions, especially the western highlands, communists held the initiative. Dak Pek was finally seized in mid-May, and a PAVN logistics center operated in Duc Co. Communist equipment supply was purposeful and consistent, unlike our own for the RVN, and extension of a petroleum pipeline further south signaled continued commitment to their cause.

In 1974, Frances FitzGerald visited North Viet Nam. When she and a couple of companions returned to the United States, they were invited to attend a luncheon at the Foreign Service Association. I was persuaded to attend and went with the intention of listening, and learning, in silence. But Frankie, in her remarks, told the audience she had the impression that the DRV would be patient and could live a long time with something like a coalition or reformed government in the South. That was at such variance with my own understanding that I had to ask, "From whom do you obtain that impression?"

Frankie casually responded that it was derived from conversation with, among others, Hoang Tung and Le Quang Hoa. I replied that we have good cause to be skeptical of the veracity of our own officials, but what makes us believe that those in Hanoi were any less deceptive?[4] I pretty loudly declared, for all present, that I believed communist commitment to unification at any cost was undiminished, that I would rather be wrong than right, but I found no evidence to support wishful thinking.

President Thieu changed three of the four corps commanders in late October 1974. Ngo Quang Truong remained in I Corps. Du Quoc Dong replaced Pham Quoc Thuan in III Corps. Pham Van Phu replaced Nguyen Van Toan in II Corps. Nguyen Khoa Nam replaced Nguyen Van Nghi in IV Corps. From my bleacher seat at 1750 Pennsylvania Avenue, I was puzzled. Leaving Truong in I Corps and promoting Nam to IV Corps command made sense. But, although replacing Toan in II Corps was overdue, bringing Phu to Pleiku was questionable. I believed Phu two and three years earlier had been a solid 1st Division commander, but most recently he was placed in charge of the Quang Trung Training Center after sick leave. I did not see the case for replacing Pham Quoc Thuan in III Corps, particularly because he had just proven capable in the Svay Rieng operation and Binh Duong campaign. He should have been left there and Dong sent to Pleiku. Ev told me the shuffle had something to do with President Thieu's wanting to appear responsive to the anticorruption movement, but, other than with Nguyen Van Toan, I didn't see conspicuous relevance.

Declining American support, and lack of units comprising a strategic reserve, caused President Thieu to emphasize conserving supplies in 1974 and 1975 while holding in place. He, and almost everyone else, to be fair, expected that the greater need would be in 1976. In this respect we were prisoner of an expectation that our communist opponent would act on the (1968–72 and presumably 1976) four-year cycle that we assumed was his inflexible fascination with American elections. Instead, communist on-court footwork was more responsive to changing conditions than we anticipated. And another test was applied in Phuoc Long province.

The communist command began with feints in Tay Ninh and Long Khanh provinces that distracted RVN III Corps, then in mid-December overran three districts in Phuoc Long. The remaining government positions, Don Luan (Dong Xoai) and Song Be (also referred to as Phuoc Binh or Phuoc Long city), were lost (after a valiant fight) on 26 December and 5 January, respectively.[5] The struggle was costly for both sides. PAVN casualties were high. ARVN committed and lost two companies of the 81st Airborne Rangers, virtually the only reserve element available to JGS. Until now RVN had lost district towns, even districts, but not an entire province, with little expectation of recovery. The communists derived two significant conclusions: The United States of America would not intervene, and the RVN truly had no reaction forces for responding to communist initiatives. Accordingly, there was tremendous incentive to launch a major offensive.

Ev made his official travel to Viet Nam in the middle of January 1975. As usual, he focused on observing the Mekong Delta situation. He had expected, he told me after returning to Washington, that IV Corps would be unaffected by RVN setbacks in other parts of the country. Instead, he learned that security in parts of the Delta had also deteriorated and that RF and PF morale was collapsing. I was already scheduled to stop in Viet Nam in late March as part of travel that would bring me to Beijing and Taiwan. Ev suggested that it might be a last chance to see the Viet Nam we knew and loved. I had not seen him so pessimistic since early 1965.

New president Ford was advised of deteriorating RVN morale and decided to seek a supplemental congressional appropriation for Viet Nam to restore some of the reduction previously applied.[6] A congressional delegation was formed to examine the situation in Viet Nam preparatory to reporting recommendations. Assistant Secretary of State Habib asked me to be one of the field-experienced officers to travel with the delegation in late February 1975. Congressmen McCloskey and Bartlett traveled to Saigon separately, and the rest of the delegation—Representatives Abzug, Fenwick, Flynt, and Fraser; Assistant Secretary Habib; and staff—joined them on 25 February.

My impression then, refreshed by recollection today, is that, with the possible exception of one (Fenwick), the representatives had each already formed an opinion and would seize on evidence that could support their point of view. Anyway, I believed that the US mission should make the most accurate presentation possible of a developing grim situation. Therefore, the initial embassy briefing conducted by Ambassador Martin surprised me. I did expect that he would, out of consideration for the delegation, preside over the briefing, but I had not anticipated a deceptive presentation. The ambassador's supporting chorus (principally DCM Lehman, Political Counselor Bennett, and Station Chief Polgar) amplified the theme of a pending NVA offensive that would be thrown back by a resilient RVN if Congress would just approve funding. Political dissent, corruption, and recent military setbacks were categorized as having only marginal relevance.

My personal belief was that prospects were unfavorable for the RVN, but denying support while South Vietnamese struggled to determine their own future, on and off the battlefield, would be callous and dishonorable. That said, presentations for congressional representatives ought to be scrupulously candid and honest.[7] Instead, the embassy conference room reeked of deceit. Jake, now Ambassador Martin's special assistant for field operations, coordinating the residual sliver of CORDS, was in the chorus. We spoke later and had an argumentative discussion. Jake accused me of "probably" poisoning the congressional well. I told him Habib's guidance was to avoid instructing the representatives, just facilitate their seeing and hearing for themselves. I would limit myself to that role, but I hated to see friends dancing in a smoke screen.

I knew the mission officer most knowledgeable about PAVN, and well informed as to RVN problems, was my friend Frank Snepp. When Congressman McCloskey asked my opinion of the briefing, I told him the person who should have been part of the presentation was absent. I suggested he request an opportunity for discussion with Frank but avoid mentioning it was my idea. The next day Congressman McCloskey told me that speaking with Frank was "illuminating," and he wished others could meet with him, too. I called Frank and asked whether he would, at risk of his career, be willing to meet with "friends" (meaning other representatives) the next morning for breakfast. He agreed and shared a candid analysis with two of the other representatives and traveling staff. Frank's presentation was within the margins of US policy, but it was informative without obfuscation. I was appreciative, because I knew in that embassy few officers would be as responsive.

Ambassador Martin decided to accompany the delegation back to Washington and boarded the special aircraft at the last minute. During the flight he sought me out and charged that I had exceeded my role by making unauthorized arrangements.[8] I stood up from my seat so that he would not be looming over me. Habib intervened and led Ambassador Martin away.

While I was in Viet Nam with the delegation and facilitating examination of the situation pursuant to Habib's instructions, I had opportunity to meet with friends in and around Saigon, including a fast trip to 7th Division headquarters and Long An province. I would have gone up to II Corps, but time did not allow for my travel preference. Now, back in Washington during the first week of March, and exchanging impressions with Ev, we shared our understanding of RVN vulnerability. There was already some mention of "light at the top and heavy at the bottom" as a rationale for redeployment, but I persuaded Ev that the immediate problem was "softness in the middle." Whereas I Corps fielded five divisions, and III Corps and IV Corps three each, II Corps (the largest) had only two. And, perpetual problem, there was no strategic reserve force.[9]

•••

Applying deception and communication discipline, the first heavy PAVN blow was struck at Banmethuot on 10 March. I promised to avoid painting over the excellent portrayals already on the record, so I am self-restrained to make just a few points:

> 1. Years of disparaging tribespeople and considering FULRO as an enemy equivalent to the communists left the RVN deaf and dumb with respect to human intelligence in the highlands.

> 2. Banmethuot might have been retaken if 22nd Division regiments or the still-forming additional airborne and Marine brigades had been thrown into the breach. Breakdown of order in the 23rd due to concern for family members ought to have been anticipated.[10]

> 3. The decision 12 March to pull the Airborne Division from I Corps and subsequently fragment it brigade by brigade not only broke I Corps but also devalued the Airborne Division's battlefield impact.

> 4. The meeting at Cam Ranh on 14 March when Thieu, Vien, Quang, and Phu decided to abandon the highlands and chose Route 7B as the corridor for withdrawal doomed the RVN.[11] This was the only strategic decision during the war that was made solely by the RVN. Americans were uninformed.

> 5. Subsequent interventions by President Thieu, as during Lam Son 719 in 1971, made the situation progressively worse.

While the situation evolved from crisis to catastrophe, I was returning to Asia on planned travel to a number of countries, including Viet Nam. Before I departed I saw Habib, and he told me to "use your head" but let chiefs of mission know we were probably in the end game.

I was in Taiwan in late March, spending a Taichung evening with Bill and Pat Ayers, when Ev telephoned me at their house. He had a "serious directive" for me and was instructed to make sure my compliance would be absolute. Then he spelled out that Ambassador Martin refused to allow my return to Viet Nam in any capacity. Ev asked if I understood. I replied that I knew why he was selected to pass the message. Then I explained that since my schedule was already fixed, I would use the time originally planned for Viet Nam to instead stay in the mountains beyond Wulai with my wife's family. "They don't have a telephone, so I will be out of touch for a few days." Ev said he understood.

Then I went to Viet Nam.

Circumstances were chaotic. Undocumented travel into Saigon was still easy. Respectful of Ev's circumstance as conduit for the ukase, I avoided official Americans. Instead, hoping realistic evacuation planning would account for Vietnamese with whom we had cooperative relations, I sought out people who would surely be on their own, urging them to make plans for departure and providing them with points of contact. Some, like Ngo Ba Thanh and Buddhist lay leaders, said they would stay to work for a better Viet Nam. Some, like Trinh Cong Son, said that they could leave but needed to bring extended family with them. Ha Thuc Can, typical of many, hoped for a coalition of patriots that would share authority with the communists. To all who expressed those dreams, I asked how anyone could believe a fuel pipeline and T-54s were within hours of Saigon just so, at the moment of victory, power would be shared with others. Most, despite loving their country, decided to seek means to depart.

I telephoned Jake, who I thought was the only person with some authority for evacuation planning who would take my call without revealing I was in the city. "Jesus Christ! Don't tell me you're in Saigon."

"Okay, look, I'm not going to be a problem for you. I just want to ask that you make a special effort to include our PSG cadre in your plans for departure. They've risked a lot with us over the past ten years. Do everything you can to take care of Nay Luette, Nguyen Be, and Tran Ngoc Chau, too. It will go especially hard for them if they are left behind."[12]

Jake was irritated but said he would do what he could.[13] I left Viet Nam and continued travel onward to other countries. I spoke with chiefs of mission and conveyed the sense of end game. In Beijing, George Bush remarked that official reporting held out some hope for holding a new defensive line buttressed by a reorganized ARVN and American resupply. I told him official reporting was not reliable and should not be credited. "The Republic of Viet Nam is like an ice cube in a hot cup of coffee; it's disappearing fast."

Back in Washington I joined Ev (who for thirty years never inquired about my stay with relatives in the Taiwan mountains) and others in an informal group that began to push for realistic evacuation planning and quick execution. Inertia, insane regard for the feelings of Ambassador

Martin, and archaic points of organizational protocol, all radiating from senior government levels, slowed the process. When we were informed that some flights were even departing Saigon empty, I checked unofficially with reliable friends in the mission. They conveyed this sense of a desperate situation, ambassadorial incompetence, and lack of focus by the station chief. Ev and I passed the plea for intervention to Colby, at first through Clay McManaway and later directly. We were rebuffed.

Eventually, by fits, and painful realization that Americans had to flee or stay with bitter Vietnamese who had been abandoned at the last, a desperate helicopter pullout was conducted around the clock through the final hours. I was in the State Department Operations Center. Senior officers, including Dean Brown and Larry Eagleburger, were there, and I was cursing (in a vile manner) the disgusting lack of performance and shameful behavior that made the final effort so troubled and had abandoned so many for whom we should have provided exit. No one asked me to control my temper or moderate my language.

I walked back to my office on Pennsylvania Avenue with an indescribable feeling of pain and loss—so many friends gone, and now only memories. The best part of my life was over. Yes, I know, shamefully self-centered, a fool I was, but it is how I honestly felt.

Appendix A

Long An Hamlet Survey Guidelines

Organization

1. Three seven-person teams. Six from province and one USIS.

2. Each of the province cadre will have a revolver for personal self-defense.

3. The revolver will be concealed at all times unless used for self-defense.

4. Each of the USIS cadre will have an automatic weapon, discretely slung.

5. We will work in three adjoining hamlets, one team in each hamlet.

6. Speak with at least one adult member of each household.

7. At night all teams will group in one of the three hamlets for mutual support.

8. When the three hamlets in a set are surveyed, we will meet in Tan An for review, and preparing report, including sketch map, for each hamlet.

Conduct

1. Our approach and attitude will be conversational not interrogatory.

2. Our behavior will be friendly and always polite, even if provoked.

3. Treat everyone fairly and equally, including persons in families that are suspected of supporting the SVNLF.

4. Touch nothing, pay for food except tea, treat women respectfully. Any violation will be punished.

5. What is the past and recent history of the hamlet?

6. How do people think their lives can be improved?

7. Be thankful for information about the SVNLF, but don't demand it.

8. Ask people with SVNLF relatives what might be the best way to bring them home.

Appendix B

The Nature of Irregular Warfare

Irregulars

Choose the circumstances of conflict and battle.

    a. Require support of significant part of the civil population.

    b. Derive intelligence from the population.

    c. Train for superior motivation.

If one side operates and fights more skillfully as a politically driven army in Viet Nam, then that is the side that will win. The American Continental Army fought for independence almost two hundred years ago, but would find SVNLF troop motivation, use of propaganda, covert political activity (communications and supply), very familiar.

With Apology to Chairman Mao

Everyone knows that when doing something, if one does not understand its circumstances, characteristics, and relation to other things, then one cannot know how to do it and will not do it well. A revolutionary national war has its own special circumstances and characteristics. Without understanding them we cannot operate appropriately.

Vietnam's revolutionary war is waged in the special environment of Viet Nam, and so compared with other wars it has its own special characteristics. If we do not understand them, we cannot win.

Even when irregular warfare is further developed and organized into mobile unit warfare, revolutionary armies do not entirely abandon irregular warfare, and if circumstances require, irregular warfare will be preeminent again.

Taking the initiative means doing the proper thing at the proper time in the political field as well as on the battlefield. Sometimes slipping away is the appropriate manner to retain the initiative.

GVN and Advisory Difficulty

Employment of our conventional forces is characterized by alternating search for guerrilla forces by "sweeps" and "drives" with subsequent withdrawal at conclusion of frustrated effort. Assuming a position of barbed wire and bunker before lunging out again attaches us to a war of attrition in which the enemy is permanent presence in the countryside only occasionally troubled by us. Area saturation (oil spot) strategy without political content is a waste. Garrisoning forces in an area of communist activity with expectation that our physical presence will deter SVNLF activity is insufficient to resolve the problem. SVNLF units may submerge, but political action will continue undetected.

SVNLF recruitment and training of cadre, activating units, and driving support from the population proves that there are serious basic problems within the national society. The real objective of the SVNLF is not just to take outposts or decimate battalions, the real objective is to destroy the social, economic, and political potential for an independent South. Unless the government achieves political ascendancy over the SVNLF by persuading the people that there will be extensive change and reform, the communists will win.

Positive, even dramatic, action by the government for political, socio-economic, and psychological reform programs, beginning in the hamlets, and publicizing those measures, is essential to any chance for success against insurgents. They are the only building blocks on which victory can be constructed.

Advisors have to recognize that the war against the French in Viet Nam 1945–1954 was a war for national independence. Some good people who fought against the French are now fighting against the South Viet Nam government. We must take care in every way that we do not appear by action or attitude to be simple replacement for the previous colonial ruler.

Special Role of the Quang Ngai Biet Kich Nhan Dan

Absent a national political content impressively and consistently carried into the field by an army of divisions, regiments, and battalions, the special units that we are training in Quang Ngai will have to have their own political nature. We achieve this by assuring that members of each commando unit are local to the district in which they operate. They are all volunteers, and they have been motivated toward sensitive behavior with their fellow district and hamlet citizens. They do simple, bare handed, civic action; they talk with all the families in any hamlet where they operate; they posit themselves as representatives of the people; they are, in effect, a political message.

They are not intended to make ambushes their principal task. Rather than working from outside hamlets inward, they must work from inside hamlets outward. One of the toughest things to do in Viet Nam is entering a hamlet at night when there is an alert defensive force. Push the communists into that uncomfortable position. We will consequently kill some of them, but it will be a result of our operating politically.

Appendix C

Abbreviations and Terms

AC/S: Assistant chief of staff, usually for some particular function in a higher military headquarters.

Air Cav: 1st Cavalry Division (Airmobile)

An Quang: Shorthand reference to An Quang Pagoda, Saigon, a place of residence for Buddhist opposition leader Thich Tri Quang and other monks and Buddhist lay leaders who were often central Vietnamese and opposed to Saigon forms of government.

APA: Armed Political Action, paramilitary formation at the province level.

ARVN: Army of the Republic of Viet Nam.

AWOL: Absent without leave; absent without permission, suspect of desertion.

BAR: Browning automatic rifle, a weapon first designed and manufactured late in World War I. Durable, reliable, and uncomplicated, the BAR is surely still in service somewhere in this world.

C-5: A 5th Special Forces Group element created to conduct operations along and across the Cambodia–Viet Nam border; also called Sigma.

CAP: Combined action platoon, a Vietnamese local force (usually Popular Forces) unit encadred with US Marines in I Corps.

CIDG: Civilian Irregular Defense Group, intended to be local forces to be recruited and trained by US Special Forces to provide a local security and operations presence.

CINCPAC: Commander in Chief Pacific.

CG: Commanding general.

CMD: Capital Military District, comprising Saigon and adjacent districts.

COMUSMACV: Commander, United States Military Assistance Command, Viet Nam.

CONUS: Continental United States, often designated as point for ongoing assignment as opposed to a follow-on foreign area posting.

COSVN: Central Office for South Viet Nam (Van Phong Trung Uong Cuc Mien Nam), established by the Communist Party to be the regional coordinating headquarters for operations in the southern part of Viet Nam.

CPDC: Central Pacification and Development Council, intended to coordinate Second Republic of Viet Nam recovery and rural development programs.

DCM: Deputy chief of mission (deputy to an ambassador).

Delta: Special operations element intended to be a mobile reconnaissance and strike force operating independently of fixed camps and large formations.

DEPCOMUSMACV: Deputy commander, U.S. Military Assistance Command, Viet Nam.

DIOCC: District intelligence and operations coordinating center.

DMAC: Delta Military Assistance Command, formed to distinguish the US advisory organization focused on the RVN IV Corps from the IIFFORCEV, which focused on US operations and advisory responsibility in the RVN III Corps.

DMZ: Demilitarized zone between northern and southern Viet Nam established by the Geneva Accords in 1954.

F-6 authority: An alteration to Phung Hoang procedure wherein one accusation was sufficient to issue an arrest warrant.

Four-Party Joint Military Commission: Functioned immediately following the Paris Accords and was intended to implement the immediate post-ceasefire requirements, including repatriation of prisoners.

FSB: Fire support base

FSI: Foreign Service Institute, once located within the garage premises of the Arlington Towers apartment complex in Arlington (Roslyn) Virginia and now occupying almost campuslike grounds at a former US Army facility in Arlington.

FULRO: Front Uni de Lutte des Races Oprimées, a Central Highlands organization founded in 1964 to struggle for tribes' autonomy. It was somewhat derived from the earlier BAJARAKA tribal interests organization of the late 1950s. FULRO contained some who were willing to revolt against the GVN and others who aimed for accommodation on terms that would not place tribal people in subservience.

G-5: A staff position at the division level that analyzes requirements and solutions for a mission and works most closely with G-2 (intelligence) and G-3 (operations). Psychological operations were frequently tossed into the G-5 salad because no one could figure where else to place them.

GVN: Government of Viet Nam is the term that most accurately applies to the South Viet Nam government in the period from late 1963 until 1967 when there was absence of a constitution.

HES: Hamlet Evaluation System.

I Corps (pronounced *eye core*): The northern provinces of South Viet Nam.

ICC: International Control Commission, established following the Geneva Accords and intended to monitor implementation and adherence to the accords. As witnessed by the author in 1962 and 1963 in Qui Nhon, the ICC was ineffective.

ICCS: International Commission of Control and Supervision, established in 1973 by the Paris Agreement and not to be confused with the earlier ICC, although its effectiveness was about the same.

ICEX: Intelligence Coordination and Exploitation, the initial step toward the eventual Phung Hoang program.

IFFORCEV: 1st Field Force Vietnam, with headquarters in Nha Trang,

II Corps: The Central Highlands and coastal provinces of Central Viet Nam.

IIFFORCEV: 2nd Field Force Vietnam, with headquarters in Bien Hoa.

III Corps: Provinces south of II Corps and around Saigon.

Inter-Zone V: Viet Minh and later SVNLF command area of Central Viet Nam coastal provinces, including the two most important, Quang Ngai and Binh Dinh.

IV Corps: The Mekong Delta provinces.

J-1: US military element focused on personnel issues.

J-4: US military element focused on logistics.

JCS: Joint Chiefs of Staff (United States), coordinating interservice matters.

JGS: Joint General Staff (Republic of Viet Nam), in theory somewhat equivalent to the American JCS but in fact with much less autonomy from the presidency.

JUSPAO: Joint United States Public Affairs Office, established by agreement between the USIA and the Department of Defense to merge personnel and assets for an overall information and psychological campaign effort in Viet Nam.

Lam Son 719: The operation in 1971 by RVN that was intended to disrupt the communist supply corridor through Laos.

LOH (pronounced *loach*): OH-6 light observation helicopter, best for reconnaissance and even two-man insertions because it was about one-third the size of the UH-1 Huey, thereby presenting a much smaller target. It was familiarly called the Loach.

LRRP (pronounced *lurp*): Long range reconnaissance patrol, formed by regular units and usually comprised of rangers.

LZ: Helicopter landing zone, distinct from paratrooper DZ (drop zone).

M3: Light .45-caliber submachine gun.

M16: Basic US infantry rifle.

M79: Shotgunlike grenade launcher providing infantry with minimortar capability.

MAAG: Military Assistance Advisory Group, precursor to MACV.

MACV: Military Assistance Command Viet Nam.

MACVCORDS: Military Assistance Command Viet Nam Civil Operations and Revolutionary Development Support. I suggest just considering the *R* to stand for rural.

MACVSOG: Special operations organized to operate over borders in support of the war in Viet Nam. SOG initially stood for Studies and Observation Group but was more popularly and increasingly understood as Special Operations Group.

MAP: Military assistance procurement.

MASH: Mobile Army Surgical Hospital.

MAT: Mobile advisory team.

MP: Military police.

NCO: Noncommissioned officer, such as a sergeant.

Nha Ky Thuat: Technical Directorate, the RVN counterpart to MACVSOG.

NVA: North Viet Nam Army, the term Americans were instructed to use instead of PAVN.

OB: Order of battle.

OCO: Office of Civil Operations, the tardy pulling together of civil agency planning, personnel, and resources just before MACVCORDS.

OPCON: Operational control of one unit as it is attached (nonpermanently) to another.

OSA: Office of the Special Assistant, headed by the chief CIA officer.

PAAS: Pacification Attitude Assessment System, the psychological trends measurement counterpart to the HES measurement of hamlet security.

PAT: People's Action Team.

PAVN: People's Army of Viet Nam, the proper term for the main-force regular army of the Communist Party of Viet Nam.

PF: Popular Forces, district-level forces, Nghia Quan in Vietnamese, and earlier called Self Defense Corps (SDC), Dan Ve in Vietnamese.

PIC: Provincial interrogation center.

PIOC: Province intelligence and operations center.

PLA: People's Liberation Army (China).

POI: Program of instruction, a sort of basic manual shared by instructors to assure consistency of training.

PRG: Provisional Revolutionary Government, another fictive structure erected by the Communist Party of Viet Nam to posit an independent southern identity committed to overthrowing the Republic of Viet Nam.

PROVN: The short-form abbreviation for Program for the Pacification and Long-Term Development of South Viet Nam, produced by a Pentagon study group in early 1966.

PRU: Provincial Reconnaissance Unit.

PSCD: Pacification and Security Coordination Division.

PSDF: People's Self Defense Force, issued weapons to people willing to participate in local security and thereby indicate support for noncommunist government.

PSG: Pacification Studies Group, an element in MACVCORDS that produced special reporting on specific problem areas.

PSU: Provincial Support Unit.

RAND: A research corporation headquartered in Santa Monica, California.

RD: Revolutionary development, or rural development as it was more generally understood.

RD Cadre: The field component personnel organized as teams that were charged with bringing government programs to hamlets, identifying communist agents, and setting the preconditions for local governance and loyalty to Saigon.

RF: Regional Forces, Dia Phung Quan in Vietnamese, that were usually province-level companies and later increasingly used on a regional basis even as battalion formations. During the First Republic these were called Civil Guard, Bao An in Vietnamese.

RPG: Rocket-propelled grenade, particularly the RPG-7 that was supplied by the Soviet Union.

RVN: Republic of Viet Nam (Viet Nam Cong Hoa).

RVNAF: Republic of Viet Nam Armed Forces.

SACSA: Special Assistant for Counterinsurgency and Special Activities.

SAFFO: Office of the Special Assistant for Field Operations, established to coordinate field support activity after MACVCORDS was dissolved.

STD: Strategic Technical Directorate, American term for Nha Ky Thuat.

SVNLF: South Viet Nam Liberation Front.

TDY: Temporary tour of duty, as opposed to PCS, permanent change of station.

3rd Field Hospital: Originally built as a school for American dependents and subsequently converted to medical use in 1965, it was located almost adjacent to Tan Son Nhut airfield and so received medical evacuation flights by helicopter landings in the vacant field between TSN and the hospital. The facility was provided to the Adventist Hospital in 1973.

TO&E: Table of organization and equipment describes a unit's authorized personnel structure and issue of basic equipment.

TOC: Tactical operations center.

UH1-D: The ubiquitous Viet Nam War helicopter, usually called the Huey after its original designation, HU-1.

USAID: United States Agency for International Development, organized in 1961 to administer foreign economic assistance. It was a regeneration of the earlier Foreign Operations Administration (1953–55) and International Cooperation Administration (1955–61), both of which had been active in Viet Nam.

USIA: United States Information Agency, formed in 1953, operated during most of the Cold War to promote as positive an image of the United States as possible, and in some countries to assist host governments in conducting their own information programs. The agency was a sort of maverick within the Foreign Service and eventually was abolished in 1999 in a deal between Congress, especially Senator Jesse Helms, Vice President Al Gore, and Madeleine Albright while she was secretary of state. Cultural, educational, and media operations were transferred to the Department of State.

USIS: The overseas posts and personnel of USIA.

USOM: United States Operations Mission, the operating arm for American economic (and some police) assistance programs in Viet Nam before USAID was established in 1961. The acronym was still widely used instead of USAID even into 1963 and 1964.

VCI: Viet Cong infrastructure, being those generally nonmilitary but supportive political and administrative organs and personnel that enabled armed units to operate, analogous to that portion of the iceberg below the waterline.

Viet Minh: Viet Nam Doc Lap Dong Minh Hoi, usually translated as the League for Independence of Viet Nam and designed in 1941 by Ho Chi Minh and his fellow communists to be the umbrella for all patriots.

VIS: Vietnamese Information Service, the field activity and personnel of the Directorate General of Information, later the Ministry of Information.

Appendix D

Persons of Interest

The following list is in alphabetical order by last name. Readers should understand, though, that in Vietnamese names the "last" name as it appears in the list is in fact is the given name of that person, not the family name. In Vietnam, family names (as in China) precede the given name, and yet both professionally and among friends a person is always called by his given name and not by his family name. Non-Vietnamese names are listed in alphabetical order by family name, with the given name preceding the family name. The author follows this practice because only Sean Connery can convincingly say, "Bond, James Bond."

Creighton Abrams: MACV commander, 1968–72, whose reputation benefited from being the "un-Westmoreland" but whose sign-off on the 1971 Lam Son 719 operation demonstrated questionable judgment.

Tony Allitto: Previously Ke Sach district advisor (near Soc Trang) and 1970 special assistant (for reports) to Ambassador William Colby (MACV-CORDS).

Pham Anh: A senior ARVN officer who provided an early description of the significant history of Inter-Zone V.

John Arnn: Commander, Detachment B-42, killed in action in Chau Doc province, 1965.

Nguyen Be: Former Viet Minh officer, native of Quang Tri province, who in 1965, as an ARVN major serving as deputy province chief for security in Binh Dinh province, significantly altered the 1964 Quang Ngai (Biet Kich Nhan Dan [People's Action Team]) template to produce larger "recovery operations" units that were the basis for 1966 RD cadre teams.

Nguyen Duy Be: Former Viet Minh officer, native of Quang Ngai province, who submitted a request for assistance in forming a mobile self-defense force that resulted in training the first Biet Kich Nhan Dan (People's Commando) unit in Quang Ngai. He remained with the program in Quang Ngai throughout the war.

Charles Beckwith: Second commander of Delta Force in Viet Nam, seriously wounded in 1966 during an An Lao Valley mission.

John Bennett: Deputy commander, 5th Special Forces Group, in 1965.

Ngo Van Binh: Business and community leader in northern Virginia.

Nguyen Van Bong: Rector of the National Institute for Administration and emerging political leader when assassinated in 1971.

Malcolm Browne: Associated Press (AP) correspondent, died in 2012.

Everet Bumgardner: World War II veteran and USIA officer with field experience in Korea and Laos. He was leader and mentor for many of the Viet Nam generation of young officers and an important link between them and George Jacobson, John Vann, and Sam Wilson. He was the author's first supervisor and eventually more like an elder brother.

Ellsworth Bunker: US ambassador to Viet Nam, 1967–73.

Bob Burns: USOM Phu Yen province representative, 1962–63, and subsequently a business representative in Saigon.

Le Tan Buu: Hoa Hao army officer who rallied to the First Republic. He was in the Directorate General of Information, 1962–63, and subsequently elected senator with significant An Quang support during the Second Republic.

Ha Thuc Can: Former Viet Minh combatant and CBS cameraman with self-taught expertise in Viet Nam culture, becoming knowledgeable in the areas of ceramics, sculpture, bronze artifacts, and painting. He authored two books, one on Vietnamese bronze drums and the other on contemporary painters.

Huynh Van Cao: "Old-school" (French), politically cautious division and corps commander during the First Republic and a senator aligned with President Thieu during the Second Republic.

Tran Ngoc Chau: Former Viet Minh combatant who rallied to the first Vietnamese government allowed by the French and later held important positions during the First Republic. After exercising responsibility for the
national RD Cadre program in 1966, he expressed disagreement with
policy, was elected to the lower house of the national legislature, and was
subsequently charged with treasonous conduct, unconstitutionally tried,
convicted, and jailed. He lives in southern California. The author assisted
Tran Ngoc Chau in preparing his memoir, also published by Texas Tech
University Press.

William Colby: OSS veteran as a young officer during World War II and
author of an early proposal for establishing something like contemporary special forces. He was comfortable working with non-CIA resources
while still retaining institutional loyalty for that organization that had
replaced OSS.

Charles Collingwood: Began his broadcast career with Edward R. Murrow
during World War II and was highly regarded by competitors as well as
CBS colleagues.

Lou Conein: Legendary American field operator from World War II in Eu-
rope and Asia and through the postwar period, including adventure with
Ed Lansdale in northern Viet Nam. Lou was the liaison between the US
Embassy and ARVN generals as they plotted the coup that toppled the
First Republic in 1963 when President Ngo Dinh Diem was murdered.

Cao Dan: Local businessman as buyer of livestock from province to province and the author's advisor on road travel and facilitator for early off-
road travel. His family lives today in the house once used by the author
and others passing through Qui Nhon.

Phan Quang Dan: Popular opposition political figure during the First Republic who was unable to gain traction thereafter.

Le Minh Dao: Province chief in Long An 1963 and a few years later in Dinh
Tuong. Led 18th Division in its astounding resistance at Xuan Loc in
1975.

Le Duc Dat: Conspicuous instance of a mistaken division commander assignment.

John Gunther Dean: Self-promoting senior foreign service officer and eventual ambassador.

Peer de Silva: Chief of Saigon Station (CIA) who enthusiastically endorsed the armed parapolitical concept initiated in Quang Ngai province. Seriously injured in the 1965 communist bomb attack on the US Embassy.

Jerry Dodson: Perceptive and tireless field evaluator during the early MACVCORDS period. Semiretired investor strategist living in San Francisco with his wife, whom he personally rescued in 1975 from the turmoil of RVN collapse.

Pham Van Dong: Significant military officer during the First Republic and for a few years afterward, but who compromised his integrity with business schemes.

Bui Thuc Duyen: Originally a mathematician and educator, Binh Dinh province chief until late 1963.

Ngo Dzu: Ineffective ARVN general who was propped up by John Vann despite awareness of Dzu's deficiencies.

Daniel Ellsberg: Brilliant senior Pentagon analyst who sought and obtained inclusion on Lansdale's 1965 team. First sought ways to optimize chances for some kind of victory, but later believed that the American war in Viet Nam should end.

Charles Fisher: A communications technician with previous experience in Laos who much later adopted a career in medicine.

Charles Francis: Senior US officer at Qui Nhon airfield, 1966, who facilitated the author's occasional special aviation requests.

George Forsythe: Robert Komer's first military aide while shaping the new CORDS format. Forsythe later commanded the 1st Cavalry Division (Airmobile) and much later was instrumental in launching the all-volunteer US Army.

John F. Freund: A Naval Academy (Annapolis) graduate who opted for an army commission. JUSPAO deputy director after a II Corps advisory assignment, and thereafter commander of the 199th Infantry Brigade.

Stan Frileck: Physician with a private humanitarian medical team in Quang Ngai, 1964, who made a long drive with the author to Saigon and insisted on returning to Central Viet Nam by the same route, despite experiencing an attempted road ambush on the first leg of the round-trip.

Bill Garrison: Deputy commander, US Army Special Forces 1989–90 while the author was assigned at Fort Bragg and who subsequently led operations in Mogadishu after commanding Delta and JSOC, now retired and living in Texas.

Jack Gibney: Outstanding army advisor and unit commander during several tours in Viet Nam, particularly with the 1st Cavalry Division (Airmobile), now retired and living in the Seattle area.

Phil Habib: Senior Foreign Service officer who habitually sought out junior officers for their observations.

Tran Van Hai: Career ARVN ranger officer and onetime Phu Yen province chief and commander of the 47th Regiment who much later was National Police commander. Hai committed suicide in 1975 following the surrender of the Republic of Viet Nam.

Paul Hare: One of the young astute and flexible architects who reshaped OCO to CORDS at Komer's direction in mid-1967. Paul much later was a US ambassador.

Nguyen Van Hieu: Outstanding combat strategist and tactician with an independent personality that isolated him from the typical ARVN circles of influence.

Dick Holbrooke: Brilliant and assertive field-experienced junior Foreign Service officer who, as a close friend of Bob Montague, was an indispensable member of the Komer team in Washington in 1966 and subsequently in Viet Nam in 1967. Decades later Dick was forceful formulator of the Dayton Accord that ended armed conflict between Bosnia and Serbia. He died in 2010.

Cao Hao Hon: Mild-mannered chief of the CPDC who had worked closely with Montague and Holbrooke in the Mekong Delta during 1963.

Gordon Huddleston: Korean War noncommissioned officer who was a Special Forces lieutenant and later captain during the war in Viet Nam.

Talbot Huey: USIS officer responsible for the Can Tho branch post in 1963. Later, Talbot was a China language officer with further USIS assignments until he decided to resign and follow a career in higher education.

Tran Van Huong: Old-line southern Viet Nam politician of honorable personable behavior who was persuaded to be vice president to Nguyen Van Thieu during the latter's final term of office.

George "Jake" Jacobson: Had two decades of service in Viet Nam from initial assignment as army officer to the final days of the US Embassy, Saigon. Good friend of Ev Bumgardner, John Vann, and Sam V. Wilson.

Darryl Johnson: Former Peace Corps volunteer in Thailand, China language officer at FSI Taiwan, and traveler to Viet Nam with the author in 1969. Darryl was later US ambassador to Thailand.

Ralph Johnson: A long-serving intelligence officer in Southeast Asia who provided some significant logistic support during the early period of the Biet Kich Nhan Dan project in Quang Ngai province.

Temenggong Jugah: Iban ethnic community leader from World War II onward who helped bring Sarawak into Malaysia.

Jusiu: ARVN captain, Jarai tribal leader, and deputy to Capt. Nguyen Tuy while Tuy led the 4th Psychological Operations Company in northern II Corps, 1962–64.

Bob Kelly: Fought in New Guinea during World War II and first arrived in Viet Nam 1963 to be G-5 (psychological operations) advisor to the ARVN 25th Division in Quang Ngai. His thirst for area knowledge and relevance soon made him obvious choice to be MAAG sector advisor in Quang Ngai province. And the same outstanding profile persuaded USOM to take him as USOM province advisor. His local relationships and courage were fundamental to initiating the Biet Kich Nhan Dan project in Quang Ngai, 1964.

Francis J. Kelly: Commander, 5th Special Forces Group, June 1966 to June 1967.

Nguyen Khanh: ARVN general with a reputation for command ability but whose political ambition was thwarted by 1964 turmoil.

Tran Thien Khiem: Senior ARVN general with an instinct for more than just survival, but who (with his wife's assistance) also attained financial accumulation and administrative advancement. Once friendly with Pham Ngoc Thao, Khiem was finally prime minister for Nguyen Van Thieu.

Tran Xuan Khoi: USIS field representative resident in Qui Nhon who frequently accompanied the author on special missions or in support of special projects in Quang Ngai, Binh Dinh, and Phu Yen provinces. Khoi now lives in California.

Robert Komer: Organizer and hard-driving initiator of MACVCORDS, and in so standing up something new in place of the moribund OCO, definitely irritated many who were habituated to old formats.

Nguyen Cao Ky: Commander, VNAF (Viet Nam Air Force), once friendly with Nguyen Chanh Thi but who in 1966 while prime minister directed suppression of the Buddhist-based Struggle Movement in Central Viet Nam. Later, his personal ambition was thwarted by loss of key associates during the 1968 Tet period combat and comparatively adroit political maneuver by Nguyen Van Thieu.

Hoang Van Lac: First Republic "pacification" theorist who was substantially ignored after late 1963.

Hoang Xuan Lam: Politically connected I Corps commander first assigned to that region following suppression of the Struggle Movement. His initial loyalty was linked to Nguyen Cao Ky, but following the eclipse of Ky by Nguyen Van Thieu, Lam was able to relabel himself as a Thieu supporter. Proven incapable of managing a complex, multifaceted battlefield by the 1971 Lam Son 719 operation.

Tran Van Lam: A seasoned and conservative successful southern businessman and politician whose personal comportment was honorable, so he occasionally bemoaned the ethical misbehavior and inability of the Second Republic.

Lu Lan: Young and capable 25th ARVN Division commander, 1963–64, in Quang Ngai, where the 25th was first organized.

Ed Lansdale: Dynamic field operator on a number of levels, primarily in Asia but with an occasional role elsewhere. He excelled at mixing solicitous questions with sympathetic listening that would draw others into his confidential circle.

Wade Lathram: OCO (Office of Civil Operations) director for the brief period that OCO existed as predecessor to MACVCORDS.

Bob Lincoln: The final JUSPAO director who winnowed personnel levels to the point that it was easy to convert back to a USIS template.

Kim Loan: A local-force SVNLF guerrilla leader in Long An province, 1961 through 1967, when she was killed.

Vinh Loc: A burly senior ARVN general who had a lofty opinion of himself but whose lack of competence was obvious by 1967.

Henry Cabot Lodge: Twice US ambassador to the Republic of Viet Nam.

Gary Luck: Commander, US Army Special Forces, 1989–90, during the period the author was assigned to Fort Bragg. General Luck was subsequently commander, XVIII Airborne Corps, and later commander in Korea.

Nay Luett: Jarai leader who understood that all of the tribal forces in the Central Highlands needed an accommodation with the Second Republic as the preferred alternative to coping with any unified national communist administration.

Phan Manh Luong: Originally from Hue, and like many of his generation a member of the Boy Scout movement in Central Viet Nam, he had Viet Minh organizational and training experience that he introduced into training for the early special units in Quang Ngai. Today he is a Buddhist monk in southern California.

Ung Van Luong: Administrative assistant to Everet Bumgardner, and so responsible and proactive that Ev was freed from office tasks and able to travel widely as a roving trouble spotter, fixer, and mentor.

John Lybrand: First arrived assigned to 5th Special Forces and later detailed to MACVCORDS as an experienced field evaluator.

Le Xuan Mai: Director of a special training facility outside of Vung Tau. Today lives in California.

Graham Martin: Final US ambassador to the Republic of Viet Nam.

Robert Matteson: Seasoned public servant from Minnesota who volunteered for a Viet Nam assignment and was placed in II Corps as CORDS regional director.

Vu Van Mau: Foreign minister during the First Republic and senator during the Second Republic.

Paul "Pete" McCloskey: Republican congressman from California who challenged President Nixon on Viet Nam policy. McCloskey was awarded the Navy Cross for action as a US Marine during the Korean War.

Bill McKeane: Commander, 5th Special Forces Group, July 1965 to June 1966.

Billy McKeithe: Member of the Delta team that took heavy casualties when inserted into the An Lao Valley in 1966 and who subsequently accompanied the author on field operations, especially in the Vinh Thanh Valley, where we survived a helicopter crash.

Clayton McManaway: USAID officer originally with OCO who transitioned more smoothly than many others into MACVCORDS.

Dick Meadows: An underage volunteer to the US Army during the Korean War, when he began a legendary special operations career. He received a direct commission while with MACVSOG and was team leader for the Son Tay raid. He was introduced to me by Phil Werbiski.

John Mecklin: Director, USIS Viet Nam preceding arrival of Barry Zorthian. He had extensive correspondent experience in the old Indo-China.

Duong Van Minh: Titular head of the conglomerate of ARVN general officers and senior colonels who came together in late 1963 to overthrow the First Republic and murder the president.

Bob Montague: Shared extensive field experience in the Mekong Delta with Richard Holbrooke and Cao Hao Hon in 1963, and after working on the MACV staff in Saigon was eventually brought in to Robert Komer's Washington office by Holbrooke. Colonel Montague was the untiring and indispensable executive assistant for Komer and later William Colby.

Jim Nach: Member of US Embassy political section with determination to plumb the depth of any puzzle placed before him.

Hoang Duc Nha: Confidant and relative of President Thieu who had observed the United States and Americans during academic study.

Chau Kim Nhan: Logistics and budgeting expert originally in the Ministry of Defense and later finance minister during the Second Republic.

Do Minh Nhat: Originally from the north and enlisted by Ev Bumgardner into his small but expanding USIS field office in 1962.

Nguyen Van Nhung: By all accounts the person who murdered President Diem in 1963. Although it may never be known precisely who gave the order, the author believes all those generals involved are culpable, because not one firmly stated that killing the president would be unacceptable. Nhung was the sole casualty of the next coup, being found hung.

Ed Nickel: Replaced Barry Zorthian as JUSPAO director.

Richard Noone: Tracker and anticommunist paramilitary organizer in Malaya during the 1950s. After a brief venture into Viet Nam, served on the SEATO staff in Bangkok.

Doan Van Nu: Energetic airborne officer who was both a friend of Nguyen Chanh Thi and on good terms with Tran Thien Khiem. Colonel Nu was the last Strategic Technical Directorate (STD) commander.

Paul Payne: Original member of Delta in Viet Nam, later a special instructor in Virginia and assigned in the same office while the author was at Fort Bragg, 1989–90. Paul is retired in Fayetteville, NC.

William Peers: World War II veteran with unconventional (OSS 101, northern Burma) experience. In Viet Nam commanded the US 4th Infantry Division and later headed the official inquiry concerning what happened in Son My (Quang Ngai province) in 1968.

Nguyen Xuan Phac: Deputy camp commander to Le Xuan Mai. He is son of a prominent medical specialist and political leader. Today he lives in California.

Tran Van Phien: Native of Nghia Hanh district in Quang Ngai, Phien was the chief of province administration and committed to serving citizens rather than himself or family members. His personal support was vital for launching the first special units in Quang Ngai during 1964.

Le Van Phoi: Hoa Hao battalion commander in the An Phu area of Chau Doc during 1965; several years later commanded in the Triton area just after the 1973 Paris Accords.

Pham Van Phu: ARVN airborne officer with experience dating from Dien Bien Phu. Exceptionally capable commander of the 1st Infantry Division but later worn out and physically ill in 1975 when II Corps commander in Pleiku.

Nguyen Van Phuoc: Chairman, Binh Dinh province Buddhist Association.

Tom Polgar: Final chief of station in Saigon. Officious in personal comportment, generally ignorant of Viet Nam background, he seems to have been danced by the Hungarian ICCS team.

William J. Porter: Deputy ambassador when Ambassador Lodge was doing his second stint, approachable and personable during the period in which he had oversight for "pacification" but so stretched beyond reason by traditional DCM tasks that he could not get his hands wrapped around what needed to be done.

Dang Van Quang: Trusted advisor of President Thieu and executor of the president's requirements, he was often considered blatantly corrupt, but the author thought Quang was really more fascinated by patronage and influence than with accumulating wealth.

Dam Van Quy: Outstanding regimental commander who undoubtedly would have been effective at a higher level but who was killed in 1968 by an errant US helicopter gunship strike.

Doug Ramsey: Foreign Service officer recruited by Ev Bumgardner to leave embassy halls and join his expanding field operations team. Ev later introduced Doug to John Vann, so Vann enticed Doug to join him in Hau Nghia as deputy provincial representative. Vann was devastated when Doug was captured in early 1966. After enduring more than seven years as a prisoner, Doug resumed a Foreign Service career. He lives in Nevada today.

Rob Richards: Not only John Vann's trusted frequent LOH pilot, but he even taught John the basics of flying the helicopter. Richards was not with John when he crashed and died in June 1972.

Bui Van Sac: Real name of the skilful agent who inserted himself into South Viet Nam while reporting to COSVN. He used the fictive name Nguyen Van Sau and was referred to by Vietnamese and American friends as Bac ("Uncle") Sau.

Bac Sau: See Bui Van Sac.

Dang Van Sau: Regrouped to the North in 1955 as a young Viet Minh and was trained to be a medic. Returned to the South as a member of SVNLF, as company commander and combat medic. Separated from SVNLF and recruited to join a US Special Forces political cadre team, then later worked in OCO and MACVCORDS as a field evaluator. Now lives in Georgia.

Jean (Andre) Sauvageot: US Army officer self-taught (with assistance of Vietnamese friends) in the northern dialect of the Viet Nam language.

First a district advisor in Dinh Tuong province, and subsequently a field evaluator specializing in rural attitude assessment, he became a valued member of the Komer-Colby operation, eventually with an office in the Prime Ministry as their liaison with Tran Thien Khiem.

David Scotton: Physician, the author's brother, who served on active duty with the 3rd Special Forces Group (Airborne), retired and living in Maine.

Sa Yun Scotton: Married to the author from 1970 until 2012, now living independently and dividing her time among Florida, Virginia, and Taiwan.

Ted Serong: Senior Australian army officer with background in counterinsurgency who coordinated early attachment of Australian personnel to US elements in Viet Nam. Remained as a consultant in Viet Nam after retirement.

Dave Sheppard: First in Saigon as the USIS motion picture officer (with attention to the weekly newsreels produced for use in Viet Nam film theatres), and beginning in 1963 was USIS deputy director to John Mecklin.

Frank Snepp: Had two tours of duty in Viet Nam and during his second was the principal "order of battle" officer (analyst of opposing forces) and briefer in the US Embassy. Frank authored *Decent Interval*, portraying his observation of the collapsing Second Republic.

Lam Son: A veteran ARVN combat officer who could have been the Viet Nam equivalent of Wilbur Wilson but whose problem with alcohol consumption meant that he was at his best only from late morning to early afternoon.

Trinh Cong Son: Folk song writer and singer who also occasionally painted, he was the most popular cultural figure among young Vietnamese in the South. He was unable to leave Viet Nam in 1975 or thereafter. Thousands attended his funeral after he died in 2001.

Charles Spraggins: Deputy commander, 5th Special Forces Group, in 1965.

Dang Van Sung: Dai Viet political leader and publisher of *Chinh Luan*, probably the most politically sophisticated newspaper in Saigon. He was an elected senator during the Second Republic.

Tran Ngoc Tam: Senior ARVN general officer whose genial comportment seemed to ease his acceptability to whoever was heading the government at any time.

Nguyen Van Tat: Quang Ngai province chief until late 1963.

George Taylor: Air America pilot, 1962–63, when AA aircraft could just about be counted on the fingers of one hand—or at most, two hands.

Maxwell Taylor: US ambassador, 1964–65, who did not have a clue as to what was occurring and how to engage constructively with Vietnamese.

Ian Teague: Australian army officer in the first contingent brought to Viet Nam for special-purpose assignments, some with US Special Forces. His specific assignment was in Quang Ngai province, and he became supervisor of the later (pre-PAT) phase of the Quang Ngai Biet Kich Nhan Dan project.

Nguyen Duc Thang: ARVN general officer in the artillery branch with a solid background in mathematics. Thang was politically affiliated with Nguyen Cao Ky, so when Ky was eclipsed by Thieu, Thang was nudged to the side. The unfortunate result was that the Second Republic failed to utilize one of its brightest honest generals.

Ngo Ba Thanh: Lawyer who was definitely sympathetic to the SVNLF and who some considered a secret member of the Communist Party. The author remembers her, political views aside, as personable and solicitous of his health while she was present on an occasion when he experienced some discomfort during intense discussion following a couple of days with little sleep.

Pham Ngoc Thao: Clever manipulator of persons and situations who may have been a secret communist during the First Republic and afterward until his death in 1965, or he may simply have been consumed by his own fascination with playing the game of intrigue.

Ron Theiss: US Army officer who replaced Bob Kelly as USOM province advisor (on detail from the army).

Nguyen Chanh Thi: ARVN airborne officer who supported President Diem in 1956 but became a leader in the 1960 abortive coup against the president. When Thi returned from exile (in Cambodia), he was placed in command of the 1st Division and later moved up a rung to command I Corps. He was exiled to the United States in 1966 following removal from command, an event that stimulated the Central Viet Nam "struggle movement," which was basic to elections for a constituent assembly later the same year.

Ton That Thien: Brilliant, somewhat acerbic intellectual who in his lifetime knew and sometimes worked for many of Viet Nam's leaders.

Nguyen Van Thieu: ARVN general officer from Central Viet Nam who married into a prominent Mekong Delta Catholic family and subsequently converted to the Catholic faith. Entrusted by President Diem with command of the 5th Division (adjacent to Saigon), headquartered at Bien Hoa, Thieu betrayed the president by joining with other generals in the 1963 coup. Later, Thieu outmaneuvered rivals from 1967 onward to take the Second Republic presidency for himself. He resigned the office and fled Viet Nam in 1975, residing first in England and finally in the United States. He died in 2001 in Massachusetts.

Kieu Mong Thu: Born in the Mekong Delta, a journalist, and later elected to the lower house of the Second Republic's National Assembly with significant support from An Quang Buddhists. She was supportive of Tran Ngoc Chau when he was dragged from the Chamber of Deputies and taken to prison preliminary to trial.

Pham Quoc Thuan: ARVN general officer who was perceptive of enemy intentions, who was willing to exchange views with US officers, and who fought a smart campaign in III Corps during mid-1974 just before being relieved for reasons still unfathomable to the author.

Charles Timmes: Last MAAG chief before MAAG was absorbed by MACV. He subsequently returned to Viet Nam to report on ARVN developments for the US Embassy.

Nguyen Van Toan: Senior ARVN general whose personal conflict with Nguyen Chanh Thi made him appear attractive to others who needed to appoint persons reliably hostile to Thi.

Touneh Ton: Recruited as a USIS employee in II Corps to be traveling companion for the author. Later, with some modest financial assistance, he was elected to the Second Republic's National Assembly.

Tran Van Tra: Charismatic SVNLF general officer whose battlefield competence and sense of strategy were perhaps unrivaled on the communist side. He authored a review of the 1975 campaign that was suppressed by the party, and he lived the remainder of his life as an honored but subdued "old veteran."

Do Cao Tri: Senior ARVN general officer of a southern family whose ambition and personal conflict with other generals, especially Nguyen Khanh,
were basis for exile until he was allowed to return by President Thieu and
made III Corps commander. Died in a helicopter crash.

Tran Huu Tri: Former 40th Regiment soldier under command of Dam Van
Quy who was recruited to work with USIS in parapolitical/paramilitary
projects and who subsequently worked with US Special Forces, OCO,
and MACV. Lives in the Atlanta area.

Jim Tull: USIA officer and friend of Ev Bumgardner who volunteered for
service with OCO and, after the OCO metamorphosis (Komer-induced)
to MACVCORDS, assigned to Chau Doc as senior advisor in that province.

Lam Quang Tuoi: Young airborne officer who was district chief in Tan
Binh (Gia Dinh province), where the first special mobile PF platoon was
trained under USIS/MACV auspices in late 1964.

Le Trung Tuong: First met by the author when Tuong was with the 25th
Division in Quang Ngai, and later more frequently when he was the
province chief in Binh Dinh province before being reassigned to II Corps
headquarters in Pleiku. Tuong was the commander of the 23th Division in
Banmethuot in 1965 when that widely dispersed unit was overwhelmed.

Nguyen Tuy: Recipient of training at Fort Bragg and supported by wise
counsel of Capt. Howard Walters, Tuy commanded the 4th Psychological
Operations Company in 1962–64. He later worked with MACVSOG and
finally was the Binh Dinh provincial security commander.

Le Quang Tuyen: USIS employee with considerable facility in the English
language and a talent for organization. Although Tuyen and the author
had disagreement concerning training and operations in Quang Ngai
during 1964, later Tuyen was an important contributor to setting up USIS
cultural drama teams.

Joe Vaccaro: Special Forces veteran of an early tour out of the 1st Special
Forces Group. After being wounded, Joe continued to work in Viet Nam,
especially in Central Viet Nam, 1963–66. He was in the embassy in 1975
as all collapsed.

John Vann: One would not say that a book could be written about John, because in fact one was. This author suggests further reading in Neil Sheehan's *A Bright Shining Lie: John Paul Vann and America in Vietnam*, a book that portrays the complexities of character in the man, who was a good friend and influential American participant in the war, 1962–72.

Cao Van Vien: Chairman of the Joint General Staff, loyal supporter of President Diem, commander of the Airborne Brigade (before its expansion to a division) beginning November 1960, and stalwart supporter of President Thieu.

Nguyen thi Kim Vui: Became the most popular singer and actress in Viet Nam during the late 1960s and early 1970s. Always gracious, today she cares for a tropical orchard in California and is writing her own memoir describing coming of age during the post–World War II period of French colonial defeat and then the First and Second Republics.

Nguyen Van Vy: Opposed future president Diem in 1955 and 1956 and so fled to France. Returned to Viet Nam after the 1963 coup and held a number of positions including, briefly, minister of defense in 1968. Widely believed to be guilty of, and charged with, gross corruption.

Richard Waldhaus: POW released at Loc Ninh in 1973 who initially refused repatriation via Manila to the United States. After a few days of respectful consideration for his concerns, he was persuaded to depart Viet Nam.

Howard Walters: US Army captain with extensive psychological warfare background who was advisor to Capt. Nguyen Tuy in Phu Yen and Binh Dinh provinces, 1962–63.

Phil Werbiski: Young advisor to a battalion of the 7th ARVN Division, later with the 5th Special Forces Group and various special activities including C-5 (Sigma). Killed in Laos, 1969.

William Westmoreland: Replaced General Harkins as commander, MACV. I believe Westmoreland was a fundamentally decent man whose background entirely inclined him toward visualizing the Viet Nam conflict in conventional terms. He was far from the only general officer stuck in that box, and his part in losing a war that might never have been ours to win was only one among many.

Fred Weyand: Onetime deputy to General Abrams in MACV and good friend of John Vann who prior to departure also assumed CORDS responsibility when George Jacobson might have been the better choice.

Charles Whitehouse: III Corps deputy for CORDS, then took a Washington assignment and followed by serving as deputy ambassador to Ellsworth Bunker.

Len Wiehrdt: Air America pilot who frequently flew the author and teams in and out of provinces in Central Viet Nam and the Mekong Delta. Len was a World War II veteran flier and once commanded the USAF test pilot school. He was killed in Laos when his plane crashed.

Earl Wilson: USIS director, Malaysia, when the author was briefly assigned to be branch post officer, Kuching (Sarawak), in 1969.

Samuel V. Wilson: World War II veteran of the Burma campaign who continued thereafter with unconventional assignments, some uniformed and others nonuniformed. Sam was a Russian language officer and so personable that many discussants would find themselves sharing their most private thoughts with him. He was good friend of George Jacobson and John Vann.

Wilbur Wilson: May have been the crusty old colonel most respected by US Army general officers. An early military advisor noted for being outspoken in his assessment of situations, Wilbur was later returned to Viet Nam by USAID at the behest of John Vann.

Frank Wisner: Effective staff liaison between OCO remnants and the new CORDS, respected by all with whom he interacted. He served a tour as province senior advisor in Tuyen Duc during the Tet 1968 period. Following Viet Nam service, Frank was ambassador several times.

Walter Wong: Captain and leader of teams formed from Sarawak Rangers, whose mission was to represent Malaysian government activity in remote areas of Sarawak (Borneo). The author traveled the upper Rajang River area with Walter and benefited from his guidance and candid description of ethnic social and political elements.

Mai Huu Xuan: A pre–World War II member of the French Sûreté who joined in the post–World War II attempt by France to restore control over Indo-China. He was an important senior ARVN officer during the First Republic and for a couple of years after.

Barry Zorthian: World War II combat veteran (US Marine) who organized JUSPAO from its USIS core with military accretions into an important joint entity with several sections all aimed at stimulating an improved information/psychological environment into which US maneuver forces were being introduced.

Notes

Preface

1. I have in mind *weiqi*, called *go* in Japan and the United States.
2. In late 1972, while speaking with Tran Quoc Lich (acting commander of the 5th Division and previous commander of an airborne brigade) in Lai Khe, I realized what he told me varied from information already reported by retired general Charles Timmes. I asked whether the situation had changed. "No," he replied, "but we [*chung ta*] already know General Timmes reports to the embassy, and from there it may get passed to the prime minister or even president, resulting in some misunderstanding."
3. Another incentive to protect confidentiality was that American senior officials took a proprietary attitude toward contact with senior Vietnamese or particular ministries, and they would have regarded my reaching out as poaching.
4. For example, *sacrifice* can be spelled *hy sinh* or *hi sinh*.
5. *Atlantic Monthly* editor Robert Manning suggested in 1967 that I consider writing under a pseudonym, and after I responded with a carefully considered and polite demurral, he wrote in January 1968 that he still hoped we might talk in the future about an article, articles, or even a book. Manning to Scotton, January 16, 1968, Ngo Van Binh Collection.
6. Descriptions of the development of parapolitical forces in 1964 Quang Ngai and Binh Dinh, as in William Colby and Peter Forbath, *Honorable Men: My Life in the CIA* (New York: Simon and Schuster, 1978) and Thomas L. Ahern, Jr., *Vietnam Declassified: The CIA and Counterinsurgency* (Lexington: University Press of Kentucky, 2012), are partial and not accurate. Even books that have contributed to my own understanding have deficiencies: confusing national and interprovincial route numbers; mixing place names (Binh Gia and Ba Gia)

although they are separated by hundreds of miles and in different provinces; and referring to Zone C as Zone D. One writer cited interviews with me when in fact we had not met and those interviews were with another person. Seeking original interpretation, an author may advance a thesis without good supporting evidence. Cleverness substitutes for fact-based analysis. Historians writing to popularize history risk producing mush. All that said, despite best intentions, I may also commit errors within the following pages. I apologize in advance.

7. In 1989 USIA held a meeting in London for European-area USIS officers. Most of us anticipated changes in Eastern Europe, but changes of degree, not of kind. Patrick Hodai described the factors in Poland's changing situation—Solidarity, a Polish pope, illegitimacy of the Polish Communist Party, insecurity of a Russian army of occupation (the Warsaw Pact notwithstanding)—and then predicted the imminent collapse of communist Poland. Moreover, he said, within a year or two that change would be an accelerant for the fall of other East European communist governments, because Czechs, Hungarians, East Germans, and others would be asking themselves, "Are we less daring, less deserving, than the Poles?" Hodai understood the environment, dispassionately analyzed the operative factors, and identified probability that was the basis for prediction.

8. Colby and Forbath, *Honorable Men*, 261–62.

Chapter 1

1. United States Information Agency (USIA) was established in 1953 to conduct information programs in other countries. In 1978 it was briefly renamed United States Information and Cultural Agency (USICA) and absorbed cultural and educational responsibilities, but in 1982 the agency resumed its previous name. USIA was abolished in October 1999, and most of its functions were absorbed by the Department of State.

2. Beginning several months after arriving at a post of assignment, a newly appointed junior officer was required to submit by "operations memorandum" three progress reports to comment on work performed related to training. My three included scathing reviews of Washington training but made recommendations for improvement. I recommended that, rather than lectures, discussions led by specialists to stimulate trainee participation should be the rule. I retained copies for reference (Binh Collection) but never received a response.

3. United States Information Service (USIS) was the USIA operational arm in countries outside the United States.

4. The full name of that organization announced in December 1960 is Mat Tran Dan Toc Gia Phong Mien Nam Viet Nam, usually abbreviated in English (but I think inaccurately) as National Liberation Front, or NLF. I will use SVNLF rather than NLF or the pejorative term *Viet Cong* (an early Diem administration term for Vietnamese Communist). *Viet Cong* was often used by Americans and by RVN/GVN officials, and my occasional use of it and the abbreviation *VC* will be in that connection. The SVNLF emphasized political struggle, direct action, or military operations according to location and phase of the war.

5. The Directorate General of Information was reorganized as a ministry in 1964.

6. Ev told me much later that a tank town was one that had a water tower or tank to service railroad steam engines.

7. The main road from Saigon proper to Tan Son Nhut airport was at that time named for the eldest brother of President Ngo Dinh Diem, who was killed by the Viet Minh in 1945. After President Diem was overthrown and murdered, the road was renamed Cach Mang (Revolution), and then the name was changed again after 1975 to Nam Ky Khoi Nghia to commemorate the 1940 southern uprising. The most recent change for the portion from Cong Ly Bridge to the airport boundary is Nguyen Van Troi to memorialize the young man who was executed near Ben Thanh Market in Saigon because he attempted to assassinate Secretary of Defense Robert McNamara. I am obliged to friend James Nach, who caught me up on name changes.

8. Ev provided other exercises, once dropping me off to spend a few days with a ranger battalion in the Plain of Reeds (Kien Tuong province), but that was, he said, a check on my adaptability and language learning, not a tutorial.

9. Renamed Truc Giang during the early Diem administration.

10. Ev was present as a photographer for *Free World* magazine.

11. A few years later, Nguyen Chanh Thi told me that President Diem intended spending each Christmas Eve midnight in a remote location meditating and praying. An airborne detachment would provide security. The locations were in 1956, Phu Phong; 1957, Tri Ton; 1958, Ka Tum; and 1959, Dong Xoai. Diem discontinued the practice in 1960 due to the attemped coup late that year.

12. Viet Minh is abbreviation for Viet Nam Doc Lap Dong Minh Hoi, which was founded in May 1941 as an organization (controlled from within by the Communist Party) for attracting a broad coalition of people to struggle for independence. The Communist Party itself (founded in 1930) dissolved (fictively) in 1945, the better to conceal its dominance of the Viet Minh, but it resurfaced in 1951 as the Dang Lao Dong (Workers' Party). In the same year, the Viet

Minh organization was absorbed into a new structure, Mat Tran Lien Viet, but people generally continued to use the term *Viet Minh*. Although still another communist entity, Dang Nhan Dan Cach Mang (People's Revolutionary Party), was brought forth in 1962 to appear as a Southern party, in fact this PRP was another deception. All along there has really been one Vietnamese communist party, a national party, not simply a northern party, and in 1976 the PRP was combined with the Dang Lao Dong to reconstitute the Dang Cong San Viet Nam (Viet Nam Communist Party).

13. Ev, as I learned to appreciate over coming months and years, indulged in original sprightly phrasing, and *stumblebumming* was among the mildest.

14. Ong Buom was a Vietnamese nickname for Ev that was something like the first syllable of his last name. *Buom* with the appropriate diacritical marks means "butterfly," and maybe that was also a wry take on Ev's appreciation for a pretty face.

15. He was referring to Pham Ngoc Thao.

16. This was when Huynh Van Cao was 7th Division commander.

17. Examples of challenging placement are Thanh Thoi in Kien Hoa, My Phuoc Tay in Dinh Tuong, and Duc Hue in Long An.

18. Bumgardner wisdom: Your weapon should always have a folding stock for concealment and easy use from a vehicle.

19. Ev taught that advance notification of travel by road was not wise.

20. I think USOM provided these vehicles.

21. Chien Khu D in Vietnamese.

22. Since Phuoc Thanh was congruent with a former Viet Minh base zone, the province was continuously on the SVNLF barbecue spit. Phuoc Thanh was pushed together in 1959 from parts of adjoining provinces. The rationale was to facilitate administration of tough territory by providing focused funding and resources. Increasing intensity of combat made that optimistic expectation invalid, and in July 1965 Phuoc Thanh was dissolved and its parts redistributed to neighboring provinces.

23. Noncommissioned officers (sergeants) are the backbone and frequently brains of our army.

24. Vanguard Youth was a patriotic movement organized in the South during World War II to participate in the eventual struggle for independence. Communists exercised control of the organization and its activity. Pham Ngoc Thach, a respected physician and eventual minister of health for the Democratic Republic of Viet Nam (DRV), was one of the principal organizers.

25. The Caravelle Petition was drafted in support of the November 1960 coup attempt led by Nguyen Chanh Thi and a few other paratrooper and Marine officers. The intellectuals and political figures that signed the petition were all arrested after the coup failed.

26. A new IV Corps was organized in late November 1962 to include all provinces southwest of Saigon. Subsequently, the four corps boundaries changed in October 1963 when Quang Ngai was shifted from II Corps to I Corps, some provinces were shifted to II Corps from III Corps, and four provinces (including Long An and Kien Hoa) were transferred to III Corps. In October 1964 Kien Hoa was returned to IV Corps.

27. This division was composed largely of northern ethnic minorities, particularly Nung, and Pham Van Dong continued to have influence within the Nung community many years later.

28. A few months later, when Huynh Van Cao was made first commander of the newly organized IV Corps, Bui Dinh Dam took command of the 7th Division.

29. I heard this phrase from time to time in 1962–63, and at first it was a bit jarring. It wasn't clear whether the intent was to signal loyalty to papal doctrine or make a statement of personal identity. Over time I understood this was shorthand for "I am Catholic and so loyal to the president."

30. When working with a new language, "Where is the toilet?" is an indispensable phrase to learn early.

31. When I thought about this later, it made sense that clandestine political operators would use public transportation to move around the country. During the years that I was in Viet Nam there may have been attacks against a ferry, but I never heard of one. On the other hand, in central Viet Nam the railroad was a prime target because it had no utility for the SVNLF and was a symbol of government presence.

32. I made one more nighttime visit to the ferry landing area, accompanied by Do Minh Nhat, one of our field representatives. We avoided the police post (since we knew they would be inside, not outside) and moved around in the groves behind shops and homes. We observed shadowy figures entering the area from the southwest, conversing with people, and then departing before dawn. We supposed they were SVNLF but could not be sure. We avoided them by being still and silent. We spoke with Vann and confirmed my previous report. The ferry landing excursions were the beginning of a bond with John until his death ten years later.

33. As I recall, the correct order of the sprockets was red, white, and blue, so it was impossible to be confused, reassuring for me.

34. Tom Dooley was a naval physician in North Viet Nam when refugees were organized to move south in 1954. After resigning from the US Navy, he moved his personal medical relief effort to northwestern Laos. He received assistance from private and government sources. The aircraft mentioned was transferred to Saigon after his death in 1961.

35. This was my first trip to Phan Rang. Later I made a second flight with David Engel, a political officer in the US Embassy. We shared the same landing experience: George's buzzing the strip to clear cattle before landing.

36. Thap Cham is a fifteenth-century brick sanctuary constructed by one of the residual Cham principalities around the time northern Champa was conquered by Vietnamese. It is on a small hillock overlooking the plain where Phan Rang Air Base was constructed in 1966.

37. His claim was debatable, but argument with him would have inhibited full disclosure of his thinking.

38. But it was not the only fault line; others were the divisions of ethnic minority/ethnic majority and regional origin.

39. Operation Hai Yen (Sea Swallow) in Phu Yen province from 1962 through mid-1963 was intended to "pacify" the area by expanding strategic hamlets step by step. USIS produced a Phu Yen–specific edition of *Kien quoc* in support of the effort.

40. Ev Bumgardner's source was Lt. Col. Le Tan Buu (alias Ky Son), who, although Hoa Hao Buddhist by faith, was assistant to the director-general of information. In 1955, when the new South Viet Nam government of Ngo Dinh Diem was suppressing the Hoa Hao movement, Hoa Hao officers had to decide whether to go underground or acquiesce and join the government while preserving Hoa Hao belief and maintaining links. Le Tan Buu was one who followed the latter path.

41. The 47th Regiment was an independent regiment responsive directly to II Corps. It operated primarily in Phu Yen and occasionally in Binh Dinh. In late 1963 it was made part of the 23rd Division until two years later, when it was again briefly independent before attachment to the 22nd Division in mid-1966.

42. I think Pham Anh was actually thirty-three years old in 1962. I learned later that he had previous assignments in the Military Security Service (MSS), and perhaps that accounted for the interrogative approach during our meeting.

43. A year later, Pham Anh was briefly Phu Yen province chief, and he served thereafter as province chief in Long An. In 1967 he was minister for Chieu Hoi, the program that was supposed to offer former SVNLF members a chance to participate in the republic. Since I did not have any involvement with the national program, I do not know his views during that period.

44. The 1963 plan was prepared in late 1962.

45. Typical branch posts required managing USIS programs and lots of paper-work.

46. I had already observed the Research Office during orientation. Some of its product was our own propaganda (*Tam anh hung my hoa*, for example). Translation and analysis were really done by the Vietnamese research assistant. He received little credit and recognition from the American who benefited from his work.

Chapter 2

1. Yugoslav forces entered the Trieste area on 1 May 1945, and British Common-wealth units entered the city the next day to take the surrender of German troops. The area is ethnically mixed, and a tense situation prevailed. Eventually the UN Security Council established a two-zone administration with peace-keeping forces. The arrangement worked because the Soviet Union was not directly involved, and it was in the best interest of Italy and Yugoslavia to prevent war. In 1954 the two zones were peacefully absorbed by Italy and Yugoslavia.

2. The Jarai are one of the Central Highlands tribes, concentrated in Pleiku and Cheo Reo, but also with some presence in adjoining provinces.

3. Once in 1964 friend Charlie Fisher woke to the blood-curdling scream of a pig as its throat was cut. He emerged from the guest room clutching pistol and hand grenade, prepared to defend our position. I had neglected to tell him about early-morning market preparation.

4. Before 1965, trucks were usually called *xe* (classifier for vehicle) *camnhong* (Vietnamization of the French *camion*), and after 1965 the term became *xe truc*, reflecting the encroachment of English in popular, or at least soldier, vocabulary.

5. The 9th Division was formed in Binh Dinh during 1962. I would not have described it as very aggressive, but merely by its presence there was some displacement and discouragement of SVNLF activity.

6. Viet Minh policy in 1945 and 1946 was to destroy public buildings and fortifications that might be used by the French if they returned. A former imperial rest house on a hill overlooking the sea just south of Qui Nhon received the same deconstructive attention, but it was still possible in 1962 and 1963 to find interesting tile shards on that site.

   Although Go Boi was actually in Tuy Phuoc district in 1963, this particular hamlet on the connective road was located in An Nhon district.

The publications were *The gioi tu do* (Free World), and a Binh Dinh edition of the *Kien quoc* newsletter.

7. Although I am a nontheist, there are certain biblical terms that succinctly capture the essence of a moment, and this was such an instance.

8. Rural family clothing in the Mekong Delta provinces was typically black, and this was often true in central Viet Nam, but in Binh Dinh dark purple was common, and older gentlemen sometimes wore white when not working.

9. I seldom, I think never, used the term *Viet Cong* when speaking with Vietnamese in the countryside, but when with Americans or Saigon government officials that term was almost mandatory lest one be thought out of sync or peculiar.

10. In April 1962 the principal post in that district was attacked and overrun, and the district chief was killed.

11. The more frequently noted Deo Mang Yang farther west brings the traveler from the An Khe plateau to the higher Pleiku elevation.

12. An American company—my recollection is Piper Johnson—was contracted in 1959 to regrade and hard surface Route 19 from the Highway 1 junction to An Khe. From An Khe to Pleiku the road was regraded and bridged but not hard surfaced.

13. I believe that at this point in early 1963, Malaya had not yet been combined with Singapore, Sarawak, and Sabah to form Malaysia.

14. This was a basic training handbook developed and printed by USIS. Copy in Binh Collection.

15. Soon after our meeting in An Khe, the team was withdrawn due to lack of agreement with the Republic of Viet Nam on recruitment and operations. A few years later I saw Dick Noone in Bangkok, where he was a SEATO counterinsurgency consultant. When I was briefly assigned in Malaysian Borneo in late 1969, Norman Herboldt was running a copra plantation in Sabah. Although the An Khe meeting was brief, the challenge they raised had considerable impact on my personal conduct during the next few months.

16. The road continued even farther north from Phey Srunh toward Lac Thien and Banmethuot.

17. The Rhade, like the Jarai and Bahnar, were another important hill tribe. The first Civilian Irregular Defense Group (CIDG) was established with a Rhade community. Research materials elsewhere describe the concept's origin and the conversion to fixed camps.

18. If the French that I provide as a quotation sounds peculiar, that is simply an indicator of my lack of facility.

19. The term *moi* disparagingly means "savage."

20. As I wrote this account, I could not remember the exact name, but I checked my old maps and this seems to be the right location, and the place name has a familiar echo.

21. I have mentioned Cham towers in Phu Yen and Binh Dinh. Actually, vestigial monumental remains, statuary, and irrigation works were in all the coastal provinces from Quang Tri through Binh Thuan. There were still remnant pocket Cham settlements in Ninh Thuan and Binh Thuan. Once a powerful league of principalities, occasionally in alliance with Viet Nam against China, but usually in a struggle to the death with Vietnamese to determine which ethnicity would dominate, the Cham states succumbed one after another from the twelfth through sixteenth centuries while the ethnic Viet Nam frontier advanced southward.

22. There were basically two classes of provincial hotels. A *khach san* (guest inn) was usually fairly clean and would have a toilet and cold-water shower and sink with your room. Second class was a *phong ngu* (sleep room), which provided a communal toilet and shower or large tub of water on each floor, not desirable but sometimes the only facility available in small towns.

23. It was possible still to see stone statuary and terra cotta figures on many of the towers in Binh Dinh.

24. My judgment of the man was not entirely rational, but I wondered then and occasionally since what personality trait leads one to employment in a political prison.

25. "Long Life to President Ngo!" It was an affectation of President Diem that, to match Ho Chi Minh, at least by political nomenclature, he would use his family name as part of his official title.

26. When I did, later in the afternoon, he knew my meaning right away, smiled, and said, "You're not the first to see a resemblance."

27. Nguyen Huu Tho was well known in the south as an attorney who was opposed to foreign intervention and bifurcating the country. Following his escape, he took office as chairman of the SVNLF.

28. He obviously paid SVNLF tax and knew people on both sides. I always expressed appreciation for his advice and assistance. Once I asked why he helped when there might be risk to him. He responded that it was oddly interesting (*ky*), and I was his tenant (*nguoi nha thue*), so he felt some responsibility.

29. Service Geographique de l'Indochine, 1:100,000, Reissue 1953. The French maps available in 1962–64 were not very good, but better than no map at all. Like echoes of the past, those old French maps indicated remote militia posts that no longer existed.

30. I think his expression was, "Chuc may manh!"

31. The US Army 8th Transportation Company based in Qui Nhon flew H-21 helicopters and Caribou supply aircraft. I loved the Caribou for its short-field capability but had no affection for the underpowered H-21. The 8th was later redesignated as the 117th, subordinate to the 52nd Aviation Battalion head-quartered at Pleiku.

32. Pham Van Dong was prime minister in Hanoi of the Democratic Republic of Viet Nam. The province chief could not approve Kelly's proposal because he felt President Diem would not agree to providing resources for a communist leader's hamlet.

33. Kelly delighted in making scatological points during discussion. Among the mildest of his expressions were "dumber than hammered shit" (a poorly con-ceived plan), and "he's got shit in his neck" (describing someone lacking nerve). Actually fairly sophisticated, Kelly enjoyed playing roughneck with people who didn't know him very well.

34. In addition to the 1st Battalion, USOM provided civic action funding, VIS as-signed an information team, USIS assisted with printed material, and the USAF 1st Air Commando Squadron provided OV-1 Mohawk photo reconnaissance and L-28 leaflet drops. Frank Scotton and Howard Walters, "After-Action Re-port on Clear and Hold Operation in An Lao District," April 1963, Binh Col-lection.

35. I have drawn the capsule geographical description and condensed history from the after-action report I coauthored with Howard Walters and cited in the previous note.

36. Binh Dinh province and An Lao district assigned civic action personnel to work with the 1st of the 47th in developing the two strategic hamlets.

37. People were encouraged to stay in the valley but not cooperate with the com-munists. Three years later, US 1st Air Cavalry operational intent was the oppo-site: people were told to leave the valley for refugee camps.

38. Dan Ve in 1962–63 were armed district militia, poorly trained, poorly led, un-derequipped, underpaid, and often used as security for landowner and village tax collection. They later were renamed Nghia Quan.

39. Four years later, with John Vann one evening, he asked whether I had ever

done anything that I felt ashamed of. I thought carefully for a few moments and then replied, "No, but I am not proud of all that I've done, either." And first of all, I thought to myself, was having taken that life in An Lao Valley.

40. Our ideas were that a CP should always be well forward of the LOC, thus forcing the rear to push forward in support; that a ranger-reconnaissance element be available to exploit intelligence obtained with respect to trails, transit stations, and bases; that an armed civic action presence be retained in the area long-term rather than withdrawn after announced success; and that additional combat-qualified psychological operations companies be organized.

Chapter 3

1. The Can Lao Party was organized by the president's brother, Ngo Dinh Nhu. It featured an obscure philosophy, operated secretly, and was structured somewhat like a communist party.

2. According to both of them, Buddhist organizations and families were forbidden to show the Buddhist flag on the date commemorating Buddha's birthday, although days earlier Catholics had flown the Vatican flag to mark the anniversary of the ordination of President Diem's brother, Ngo Dinh Thuc, who was archbishop in Hue. Previously a Buddhist venerable had been allowed to address believers on the government radio station in Hue at every yearly celebration. This year, as demonstrations continued, the invitation was withdrawn. People rallied at the station to protest what was considered suppression of Buddhism. Soldiers and police ordered them to disperse. Shots were fired into the crowd. Mr. Phuoc told me nine people were killed. Dr. Nhung had eight as the number of fatalities. Contemporary research provides additional detail, but the account here is as presented to me by two Buddhist lay leaders within forty-eight hours of the incident.

3. Vinh Tuy had pronounced residual Viet Minh loyalty. During the war against the French a small arsenal there produced explosive devices.

4. Two years later Ba Gia was the site of a fierce battle when the 1st SVNLF Regiment beat up the ARVN 1st Battalion of the 51st Regiment (2nd Division). I Corps commander Nguyen Chanh Thi reinforced with the 39th Ranger Battalion, but armor commanded by Nguyen Van Toan precipitously withdrew, resulting in additional casualties. It was a stunning defeat for ARVN.

5. Kelly had World War II experience that I, son of a soldier killed in action in 1944, deeply respected. That he would tolerate abrupt dismissal of the Vinh

Tuy effort by someone so junior to himself says much about his good character.

6. The Chieu Hoi program was initiated in April 1963. General Timmes, MAAG chief, was in Quang Ngai to look at the recently established, and still forming and training, 25th Division. Military Assistance and Advisory Group (MAAG) was a formation activated in a number of countries where the United States provided military assistance. In February 1962 Military Assistance Command Vietnam (MACV) was established, theoretically to support MAAG, but in May 1964 when General Timmes completed his tour, MAAG was deactivated and its advisory functions were absorbed by MACV.

7. In Viet Nam there were two local beers. One was named Bia 33 because the bottle contained 33 centiliters, and the other was Bia LaRue, but popularly called "Bia Lon" (*lon* meaning "big") because the bottle was larger.

8. The Vietnamese language is literary, poetic, allusive, and seeded with cultural referents, to almost all of which I was ignorant. Therefore, my translations are often inadequate, or wrong.

9. CONUS is a US military term meaning Continental United States. Howard and I next met in fall 1966 when I visited West Point while he was an instructor, and much later when he was in Nha Trang on a second Viet Nam assignment.

10. Jarai and Bahnar territory overlapped, and there was traditional conflict. While Jarai would often speak well of Rhade, complimentary notice of Bahnar was rare.

11. His facility with a map surprised me as much as his candor. My experience with soldiers in Tuy's company was that they did not have a feel for map representation, even of familiar terrain.

12. *My-Diem* was a term of disparagement used by the Hanoi government and the SVNLF to insultingly refer to the Diem administration in harness with Americans.

13. By that time I had spoken with more than thirty prisoners or ralliers.

14. A few months later I shared this insight while attending a Saigon meeting with other Americans. I was told my observation was not relevant, because we were not French, Vietnamese would understand the difference, and we would be supplying modern weaponry.

15. I refrain from providing the actual place and personal name on the chance that family members might still be at the same location.

16. The monk was Thich Quang Duc. Thich ("venerable") is the form of address for an ordained monk. His Buddhist name, Quang Duc, I translate as "Great

Virtue." There is abundant material elsewhere that describes his life of service and scholarship.

17. Little more than a year later some of these same fishermen landed their boats on the north side of Qui Nhon as reinforcement for the virtual takeover of the city by the antigovernment Hoi Dong Nhan Dan Cuu Quoc (People's Salvation Movement).

18. Bat Trang is a kiln site located in North Viet Nam, but production was exported widely through Southeast Asia.

19. An Giang in the Mekong Delta was the most populous, but although the government had a major problem there, the difficulty was not with communists but instead with Hoa Hao Buddhist congregations.

20. The photographs have survived. I offer what is remembered from Kelly's note.

21. *If* is so important a qualifier in any language that it should be learned early.

22. The captured weapon was identified as a French MAS-36 carbine.

23. Much later I learned there was disagreement between the RVN and the Noone Mission as to how to work with the tribes. Political difficulty, especially in central Viet Nam, that summer made resolution impossible.

24. On this occasion communicating indirectly through Phuoc was not entirely due to language difficulty. It seemed natural to speak through an intermediary who knew how to phrase a political question to one ordained to follow a meditative path.

25. Given the circumstances of this conversation, it did seem politic to use the pejorative term *Viet Cong*.

26. Whenever I returned to Qui Nhon, I always offered my respect to Cao Dan. In 1996, when I was stopping there after more than twenty years' absence, his wife and I reminisced while she showed me the family photo album of his funeral ceremony. She guessed I was more than just a tenant for her husband, she said, because he always referred to me as brother when talking about the past. I will surely never forget him.

Chapter 4

1. There is no shortage of research material on Ed Landsdale. I did not meet him until the summer of 1965, so it is an exaggeration to suggest (as some have) that my friends and I were Lansdale disciples. By the time he returned to Viet Nam on assignment in 1965, our own thinking and tactics were already well established. We simply recognized and respected him as like-minded. There was

one person during 1962–63 in the Lansdale mode, Rufus Phillips, who directed USOM Rural Affairs. Phillips in turn influenced many USOM field representatives, but I did not know him. His book, *Why Vietnam Matters: An Eyewitness Account of Lessons Not Learned* (Annapolis, MD: Naval Institute Press, 2008), describes the ad hoc and dynamic effort led by Lansdale during 1955–56.

2. Several years later this house was reconfigured to be the USIS Viet Nam office.

3. Earlier that afternoon Ev told me that Lou Conein was in liaison with ARVN at the highest level. I knew Lou better from 1965 onward and, although we were not close friends, I liked him and respected his special background. He shared knowledge of episodes and personalities going back to Berlin Station, but it was not easy to distinguish actuality from a good story.

4. In fact, Ev was confirming the rumor shared with me in Qui Nhon. Washington and Saigon had already made the decision. Relocation, with division headquarters placed at Sadec, was accomplished between late September and early October.

5. Three months later in Pleiku, Tuy told me that the An Lao district officer told him about the incident, and then Tuy told Howard and Jusiu.

6. I avoided mentioning the special enthusiasm my previous road companion brought to the job.

7. Blao and Djiring were place names later Vietnamized to Bao Loc and Di Linh. Dam Van Quy was a Protestant Christian, half ethnic Tho, from Cao Bang in North Viet Nam. He was openhearted, did not conceal emotions and opinions, and was one of the most interesting, courageous, and honest officers I knew. Unfortunately, he was killed in May 1968 by errant US helicopter fire.

8. Inter-Zone V included Quang Tin, Quang Ngai, Binh Dinh, and Phu Yen.

9. Although originally from Khanh Hoa province, I think Thich Quang Duc had affiliation with this pagoda, as did Thich Tri Quang.

10. In subsequent years, even in 1996 when on official travel, nothing prevented me from returning to the same street for that Hue specialty.

11. Ha Thuc Can was a member of a prominent Hue family, former Viet Minh, and had friends on both sides of the civil war. He generously taught me what he had learned about Viet Nam ceramics and Cham sculpture. Through Can I met Vuong Hong Sen, former director of the National Museum; Trinh Cong Son; Nguyen Van Minh, an artist who worked in lacquer; and others—singers, writers, artists, students—too numerous for mention here. They introduced me to Cai Luong and Hat Boi. In long discussions over coffee, they were always patient with my frequent questions.

12. Nguyen Tuong Tam (pen name Nhat Linh) was a popular writer in North Viet Nam before World War II. He became politically active, with both Dai Viet and VNQDD connections. In 1945 he was briefly foreign minister in the first Ho Chi Minh government and participated in the abortive Dalat negotiations with France. In 1963 he was arrested and endured "enhanced interrogation." He committed suicide on 7 July 1963 and actually died the next morning. In his note he wrote: "Only History judges me. I do not allow anyone else to judge me. The arrest and persecution of opposing nationalists is a crime that will cause loss of country to the communists. I oppose those acts and so kill myself, as did Monk Quang Duc, to warn against those who tramp on liberty."

13. There is extensive documentation and commentary on this complicated period of American-Vietnamese relations, so I present only what I was told by Ev Bumgardner.

14. National Day commemorated the day in 1955 when, following a national referendum, Ngo Dinh Diem abolished Bao Dai royal rule and took office as president.

15. I recall two French sisters owned the restaurant. The menu for each evening was fixed according to what they had purchased in the morning market. Walls in the dining area had dated autographs of French officers from their war with the Viet Minh.

16. I of course was not going to do that.

17. The coup was launched midday, 1 November, and the two brothers were detained and murdered the next morning.

18. Ordinarily I liked "loose," but considering the stakes, the absence of clarity made me uncomfortable. If there was persuasive description of our policy on that day, it was so camouflaged as to be invisible. I knew nothing of the policy discussions taking place in Washington.

19. One of President Diem's last acts (administratively) was to establish Hau Nghia in mid-October. It was his reflex to make problem areas into provinces in order to focus resources. About two years later, John Vann told me that you had to live in Bao Trai to appreciate it. I replied, "Relative to what, Duc Hanh?" (Duc Hanh was a notoriously insecure and generally unfriendly hamlet on Provincial Road 8.)

20. Hau Nghia was primarily formed from the northwestern, most insecure part of Long An.

21. Additionally, on this short day's drive I had left my folding-stock carbine back at the USIS office in Saigon, so I had only a pistol beneath a loose-hanging shirt.

In fact, as soon as I was on the road to Bao Trai from Cu Chi, I had a feeling that I was under-armed for the neighborhood.

22. Invitation retained in the Binh Collection.

23. The generals lacked internal consistency of purpose. They were a conglomerate of competing interests (their own individual self-interest above all) and presided over by Duong Van Minh (died in 2001), who was most comfortable as a figurehead.

24. C-123 aircraft were sometimes slanged as the "dollar twenty-three"; later, the C-130 was naturally the "dollar thirty," and the "dollar nineteen" was still around.

Chapter 5

1. Years later I worked with other creative and open-minded supervisors— William Colby in MACVCORDS, Patricia Byrnes in Burma, Gary Luck at Fort Bragg, and Stapleton Roy in China—but Ev set the standard I would try to emulate when people worked with me.

2. Given his wife's Mekong Delta origin and proximity to Saigon, he was understandably oriented in that direction. His wife told me a couple of times, not exactly as a complaint but with a sigh, "He goes away for a few days, comes back with two or three country people from My Tho or Long An, and leaves them with me while he takes a shower. I have to talk with them, and remember what they said—while he goes to sleep."

3. Ev was my supervisor from 1962 to 1964 and thereafter friend and elder brother and like an uncle to my children.

4. Le Minh Dao six years later was province chief in Dinh Tuong (My Tho). In 1972 he commanded the 18th Division, and in 1975 he stayed with his soldiers at Xuan Loc.

5. Anticipating the need, I did bring one M3 "grease gun" with me from II Corps. Ev provided two Thompson submachine guns with stick magazines.

6. Coincidentally, some of my principles were the same those Tran Ngoc Chau applied in Kien Hoa with his census grievance approach to recovering contested areas. Years later we discovered that our practices, without either of us knowing what the other was doing, were similar.

   The guidelines are reprinted in Appendix A. For a couple of years I kept the original handwritten draft to refresh my thinking prior to initiating new training or operational projects. When the original became ragged, I had the notes renewed with Thermo-fax copies in 1965. I thought new technology would be preservative, but I was wrong. The next time I pulled out the guidelines for review and modified application, the thermosensitive paper was so faded that my administrative NCO at Fort Bragg, Sgt. Tanya Watlington (airborne ranger, mother of two) had to retype the eight points all over again.

7. Hamlets were polarized when both sides mistreated families identified as supporters of the opposition. The SVNLF benefited from the consequent social pathology.

8. I had my folding-stock carbine, and Nhat chose to take a revolver. The CIA station provided all the revolvers through Ev.

9. Governments would rise and fall, but Captain Meo seemed a permanent presence in Long An. He was one of those who not only knew where the bodies were buried, but also had put some of them there. He was assassinated in 1966.

10. Hamlet and village are two distinct levels of governance and socioeconomic relationships, and although the previous constitution and administrative decree accorded primacy to the village level, hamlets were the center for most people's lives. This was especially the case in central Viet Nam, where communities had been established by wavelets of Vietnamese migrating southward in the wake of armies that successively defeated Cham principalities. In that part of Viet Nam, village government was fastened onto a cluster of hamlets for easing administrative direction by higher authority. South of Saigon, formerly Khmer territory and taken much later by the Vietnamese, the pattern of settlement was different. Large tracts of land were available, and often by royal grant the grantee could make some of that land available to settlers. Some members of the noble family would live in the principal settlement and provide leadership, patronage, sponsorship of community pagoda and meeting hall, counsel, and (often) loans. Satellite hamlets would have economic and social relationship to the principal settlement, and this web became the pattern for village sociology and economics in the greater Mekong Delta. There were some exceptions to the two geographic norms, but in every case the terms *village* and *hamlet* should not be used interchangeably. Countrywide, village administration was often viewed as an undesirable intrusion into hamlet life. I am far from a cultural anthropologist or rural sociologist, but that is what I observed in the field. It is interesting to note that the current government of Viet Nam continues the practice of using *xa* ("village") as an intermediate level of administration (for

coordination and control) between *huyen* ("district") and *ap* ("hamlet"), even though the communist movement was hamlet-based and often directed against the village.

11. Similarly, General Abrams told John Negroponte and me several years later that just before the 1970 cross-border operation into Cambodia, General Davison called him to report Do Cao Tri wanted to postpone the operation by two days because he was advised by his astrologer that the planned day was not a good one. The date was accordingly adjusted.

12. Many Vietnamese (except those from Quang Ngai) believed people from that province were rough and capable of anything. Sophisticated Saigonese would never have thought me part Vietnamese, but in hamlets, even years later, country people would often suppose that Sauvageot and I learned Vietnamese from our mothers. We would sometimes acknowledge we were "nguoi My, ma nguoi My Tho!" The jest is best appreciated in a remote hamlet surrounded by good-natured oldsters.

13. *Ap* means "hamlet." Nguyen Huynh Duc is the person for whom the hamlet was named.

14. Nguyen Huynh Duc worked with Le Van Duyet in the early nineteenth century to suppress the Tay Son revolt. Both were instrumental in restoring the Nguyen dynasty to power with assistance from the French.

15. Generally, when fencing was removed the SVNLF left the section facing the road undisturbed, allowing the government fig-leaf comfort while gaining unimpeded access for themselves.

16. I increasingly used the term *cadre* for our people because it conveyed the committed backbone role they filled. We bought local candy and cigarettes in the Tan An market.

17. In 1967 I learned Kim Loan entered the Chieu Hoi program, but she returned to the SVNLF a few months later. A family in Vinh An hamlet told me she was killed the same year by artillery fire.

18. Wilbur Wilson was an old warhorse of an army officer not promoted to general but respected by many who were.

19. Significantly influenced by the Mekong Delta family into which he had married, Ev was always claiming that everything was somehow more truly Viet Nam southwest of Saigon. I would usually make the counterargument for central Viet Nam.

20. Ev did implement those two recommendations. I think Peter Hickman was selected to be survey liaison officer.

21. USIS produced a summary report on the next sixteen hamlets surveyed with Do Minh Nat as leader. He sent a copy of the report via USIS Dalat that eventually reached me in Qui Nhon. That report erroneously stated that SDC (Dan Ve) had accompanied the original survey of the first phase of fifteen hamlets, and Nhat explained that that was a mistake by the American who drafted the report. Some SDC were used in the second phase, and the drafting officer assumed that had been also true in the first. The report described problems similar to those noted in the first phase. The most disturbing point was that government personnel returned to the first fifteen hamlets and chastised people for having spoken so candidly (Binh Collection).

Chapter 6

1. This was daily Flight 719, which in the morning flew Saigon, Nha Trang, Tuy Hoa, Qui Nhon, Quang Ngai, and Danang and then in the afternoon reversed those stops back to Saigon. A couple of years later Phan Rang and Cam Ranh were added.

2. Nay Luett was a Jarai leader. He told me that while a young man, Nay Muon adopted him in Cheo Reo, and he subsequently married one of his adoptive father's daughters. This was common practice when a family wanted to add a son. He was Catholic and educated in Dalat at the Lycée Yersin. Nay Luett was involved in the BaJaRaKa movement for highland autonomy, arrested in 1958, and jailed in Hue. In 1962 he was allowed into a parole program and trained at Hoa Cam for paramilitary service. He served as a company commander until December 1963, when, after the coup, he was released from parolee status and allowed return to Cheo Reo. He was exceptionally admired and respected by other tribal leaders.

3. Tuy remained with the 4th Company in the highlands. He was subsequently with CCS (SOG) at Banmethuot. In 1968 he was heartbroken when his daughter, Nhung, was killed during the Tet Offensive. In 1970 he was sector commander in Binh Dinh, and in 1975 he was last sector commander in Khanh Hoa. We saw each other in March of that year, but then he disappeared in the April debacle along the coast.

4. The International Voluntary Service (IVS) was structured similarly to the Peace Corps and worked with USOM to engage young Americans in foreign rural development.

5. Vo Trang Nhan Dan, usually translated as "Force Populaire" in non-Vietnamese

accounts of the war, was a paramilitary organization unique to central Viet Nam. Sponsored by Ngo Dinh Can, the reclusive brother of President Diem, Vo Trang Nhan Dan effectiveness was questionable, and it disbanded after the overthrow of the Ngo family's First Republic.

6. Nguyen Duy Be's background is derived from his autobiography, which is an attachment to my report of October 1964: "A Report on an Indoctrination and Motivation Program for Special Commando Units in Quang Ngai Province," Binh Collection.

7. In Quang Ngai one could hardly find anyone between sixteen and sixty who had not fired weapons. Almost all young men had some previous experience from 1945 onward, and that allowed for a shorter period of training than might be necessary elsewhere.

8. Joe Vaccaro was a former Special Forces NCO previously wounded. He was working in Quang Tin while Kelly was in Quang Ngai. Joe was always prepared for adventure, could be relied on in every respect, and exercised contacts and relationships to assist us before our program was on any organizational book.

9. A less self-assured supervisor would have requested a written proposal for submission to the USIS director and the embassy. Ponderous gears would have ground slowly, with nothing accomplished.

10. The original "Tu Nghia Training Program," on blue IVS memorandum sheets, is in the Binh Collection. Where the word *LOCAL* appears in it, it means we would have a province officer address the topic. Reference to thirty-two men total is because of the number of people Nguyen Duy Be originally said he could provide. My first draft confused explanation of organization, and it would have been better and simpler as three ten-man squads, each with a leader and assistant and with a leader and a deputy for the combined three-squad unit. After the Nha Trang meeting I wrote a better outline. The "Soldiers Handbook" referred to in the report is *Nguoi linh chien*, the illustrated booklet of simple tactics prepared by USIS for ARVN and militia basic training.

11. Kelly was 25th Division G-5 advisor when I met him in 1962 while working with Howard Walters to draft the 25th Division's psychological operations plan. His next assignment was as Quang Ngai MAAG sector advisor before USOM took him on detail as province representative. My understanding of Viet Minh training was based on information from friends like Phien, Be, and others previously trained by the Viet Minh and from some conversations with prisoners and ralliers.

12. Once in 1962 another USIS officer, while trying to persuade me to consider a nonfield assignment, said: "If you aren't careful, you'll wind up being another Ev Bumgardner." That was like telling a kid from Boston that he risked being another Ted Williams.

13. The older NCO who responded to our request for submachine guns had asked whether we wanted "Chicago typewriters or grease guns." Chicago typewriters, he explained, were the Thompson submachine gun, .45 caliber, and grease guns, of course, were the M3, also .45 caliber. I opted for the latter.

    When Kelly and Bob Day were unloading the crates from a C-47, curious American onlookers asked what was in them. The crates were stenciled, "M3— 12 each" so Kelly explained that they were "model 3 hamlet development calculators, twelve to a crate."

14. The leaders of the cabal that terminated the First Republic and murdered President Diem were toppled themselves on 30 January 1964 by a coup led by Nguyen Khanh. So in less than three months we had our second military government. The sole casualty this time around was Nguyen Van Nhung, who had stabbed President Diem and his brother. His death was reported as suicide, but that was as believable as the earlier claim that President Diem had killed himself.

15. One summed up opinion by saying, "Anh Pham khong co vui" (Pham being a phonetic for Frank, chosen by Vietnamese friends). It could be taken as an intended witicism or an unintended irony because of multiple possible meanings. And I acknowledge that overall my life has been more sad than happy. Noi that, doi buon nhieu hon vui.

16. *Ba xi de* is a rice wine, ubiquitous in the Mekong Delta but extremely rare in the central coastal provinces due to lack of surplus rice for home fermentation.

17. Almost a year later, Doug Ramsey accompanied me on a visit to the same family. When we walked into their yard, just about in the middle of Vinh An, we saw several young men seated and eating at tables. They had a surprised look on their faces as we appeared, but even before they could get to their feet, one of the brothers was loudly welcoming us as family friends. The other two brothers, speaking urgently, but low, were at the tables calming their guests. Two Vietnamese Special Forces cadre had accompanied us, and they stood back by the path, nervously prepared for the worst. Throughout, the young men at tables, with weapons at their feet, seemed as tense as we were. Small glasses of *ba xi de* materialized for everyone. We made apology, saying we had to depart,

and carefully exited the scene back to the road. Later, Doug described the event as a classic example of Vietnamese conflict avoidance, and we were damn glad it worked.

18. Before satellite systems, tropo communications bounced signals off the troposphere that were recovered by giant antenna receptors resembling tilted outdoor drive-in movie screens. Connections were made, like rungs on a ladder, from one to another: "Puma, give me Tiger; Tiger, give me Advon; Advon, give me American Embassy."

19. Issue of corruption aside, the deputy province chief's comment would make a fine Buddhist epitaph: "He achieved good results despite not being perfect."

20. So when, midway through training the Tu Nghia commando unit, Deputy Province Chief Phien told me he learned the 25th Division would soon be transferred to the Saigon area, and when Kelly and I confirmed this with Division Commander Lu Lan, I could scarcely believe that the same dumb mistake was about to be made again.

21. Project initiation chronology is documented by my memo to Barry Zorthian (for Peer de Silva and Ralph Johnson, copy to Sam Wilson) dated 25 November 1964, and Frank Scotton, "A Report on an Indoctrination and Motivation Program for Special Commando Units in Quang Ngai Province," October 1964, Binh Collection.

In late 1963, Quang Ngai sector was transferred from II Corps to I Corps. But in April 1964 the shift didn't seem to have taken hold, perhaps because the I Corps commander, Ton That Xung, was somewhat passive relative to dynamic Do Cao Tri in II Corps. I could have resolved the situation as easily as Ralph, but he felt seniority was necessary in speaking with a corps commander, a consideration never important to me.

Another factor was that Ralph supported a so-called counterterror team that Kelly told me drove down Highway 1 in a Dodge truck, entered hamlets, and abused people while sweetly smelling of American PX soap.

Ev's guidance was "make haste slowly," whereas Ralph wanted full speed ahead. I think the difference was that Ralph reflected his desperation to get something working as soon as possible.

My constant reference to "Kelly" is not at all from lack of respect. It is simply that when we first met, he said, "Just call me Kelly." In fact, I can't recall anyone who didn't. We were more like older and younger brothers than just good friends.

22. It was frequently assumed that rural militias were ignorant and incapable of comprehending political discourse. While it is true that literacy was often a

problem, people in hamlets were perceptive and articulate. This was especially so in provinces such as Binh Dinh and Quang Ngai, where people were either circumstantially or intentionally politicized from 1945 onward.

23. Quang Tin was another province formed due to area insecurity and belief that problems could best be addressed by establishing a sector with its own identity and resources. Quang Tin was formed from southern Quang Nam in mid-1962, and it corresponded to the northernmost part of Viet Minh Inter-Zone V.

24. Europeans previously called the town "Faifo," giving rise to a popular joke, not vulgar like the one concerning the Paul Doumer Bridge in Hanoi, about foreigners who cannot speak Vietnamese.

25. The expression used was *ac qua*, and that could mean fierce or even cruel.

26. And that's pretty much what we did in Viet Nam, in Washington after his exile in 1966, and later in Pennsylvania, where he died in June 2007.

An identifiable accent difference of the south is a soft *s*, so that it becomes *sh*, and Saigon is pronounced Shygon, Sadec is Shadec, Sa Huynh is Sha Huynh, and so on.

27. Dr. Frileck was a volunteer physician with Medico, a branch of the international relief organization CARE. He offered to accompany me on one long drive from Quang Ngai to Saigon. In the vicinity of Sa Huynh, as we slowed to navigate some road cuts, our vehicle was targeted by SVNLF shooters on the ridge west of the railroad. Stan Frileck returned fire as I drove. His insisting that he wanted to make the return drive a few days later really showed courage and daring. He did come with me. The trip was uneventful, but he could not have supposed that it would be.

28. Months later I realized this was exposure to pre-uprising FULRO thinking. In late September 1964 the tribal (primarily Rhade) Civilian Irregular Defense Group (CIDG) rebelled at some Special Forces camps. But at the time we spoke in Cheo Reo, I only thought that making a case for limited autonomy was wishful thinking and most probably not acceptable to any Vietnamese government.

29. I regret that my path did not cross Jusiu's again. He was captured and executed in 1975. Nay Luett was made minister for ethnic minorities in June 1971. He did his best but was frustrated by bad faith on the part of other government officials. In 1975 he should have been one of those we most determinedly tried to evacuate. Instead, he was captured and cruelly treated, and he died soon after his release. Y' B'ham was principal FULRO leader from 1964 onward, returned to Banmethuot briefly in 1968 for negotiations, and later took refuge in Cambodia, where he was killed in 1975.

30. Phac was a brother of Lieutenant Giai, whom I met in Washington more than two years earlier. Their father was Dr. Nguyen Xuan Chu, oncologist and significant political figure, who died in 1967. He was briefly in 1964 (30 October until 5 November) chairman of the High National Council.

31. I did prepare a report in August on training and operation of the first unit. I wrote that success of the pilot project was the result of cooperation among USOM, USIS, and OSA. Although I do not have a copy, updated, it was the basis for the October 1964 summary.

32. I was skeptical of report numerology and also recognized that the 25th Division was, after the Do Xa operation, retracting and planning for movement to an area northwest of Saigon. This characterization of the division is speaking in general about the period 1962–64.

33. Reviewing the first Tu Nghia unit biographies, we saw that about a quarter of the men had previously received Viet Minh or Vo Trang Nhan Dan (Ngo Dinh Can's paramilitary) training. Most of the others had some Dan Ve or hamlet militia experience. We expected the same situation in other Quang Ngai districts.

   I knew Luong had extensive Viet Minh experience beginning with the Boy Scout movement organized by Ta Quang Buu. Luong was courageous, an independent thinker, and frank in expressing his opinion. We shared adventure, hardship, and an occasional small glass of Kahlua. Today he is a Buddhist monk in California.

34. Expelling foreigners and unifying the country, in the flow of Vietnam history, was an appealing political platform for the communists, never mind what might come afterward.

   Kelly was the critical link to key people in Quang Ngai, Tran Van Phien, or Nguyen Duy Be. He was on the spot, knew them well, and could communicate effectively. We were always "on the same page" for training and operations methodology. Phien was the most important province official, without whose approval expansion would have stalled. I thought of Ralph Johnson (CIA) solely in terms of financial and logistical support.

35. Of course another, just as important, reason for delay was that if I gave him the POI, he would have to submit it up his channel to OSA, and some higher-grade, nonfield functionary would screw with what we (Phien, Kelly, the USIS cadre, and I) were doing.

36. I did see Ron again about a year later when he was with the US 1st Infantry Division.

37. Australia provided special warfare personnel through a program headed by

then colonel Ted Serong. Some were detailed with US Special Forces and some to other projects, such as the one birthing in Quang Ngai.

38. I never even heard the term *Vo Trang Nhan Dan* used in Binh Dinh, but Nguyen Tuy (a Hue native) suggested that I inquire in Quang Ngai.

39. R. W. Komer, "Organization and Management of the 'New Model' Pacification Program—1966–1969," RAND Document, 7 May 1970, p. 19.

Chapter 7

1. Frank Scotton, 6 July 1964 Memorandum, "I Corps and Quang Ngai Activity," Binh Collection.

2. Le Quang Tuyen, 6 July 1964 Memorandum, "The 2nd Training-Course for SDC at Quang Ngai Province," p. 3, Binh Collection.

   When USIS reorganized, combining with military personnel to form JUS-PAO in April 1965, a new section organized cultural drama teams to perform in the countryside. Ev Bumgardner told me Tuyen's contribution in that program was outstanding.

3. Scotton, 6 July 1964 Memorandum. The Vietnamese American Association was a binational forum for cultural programming, English teaching, and educational exchange with its own staff and separate building. Ed Silvis, the cultural officer, was dedicated to his work but not naturally field oriented.

4. Destroying the railroad was not that militarily important for the SVNLF, nor did it significantly impede ARVN movement of personnel and supplies, but it did represent elimination of a longtime symbol of government presence in the central Viet Nam region and was also reminiscent of Viet Minh policy, 1945–55.

5. Appendix B is a re-creation of that paper. I have not located a copy of what I passed on to others, but my primary notes on yellow sheets are in the Binh Collection.

6. Bao An and Dan Ve were two levels of militia, originally the former at province level and the latter at district. They were most often rooted in outposts, inadequately trained, underequipped, and correspondingly ineffective. In April 1964 Bao An were redesignated Dia Phuong Quan (Regional Forces) and Dan Ve redesignated Nghia Quan (Popular Forces). The new terms were gradually coming into use during the summer of 1964, along with the practice of using Bao An as a regional rather than strictly provincial forces.

7. Scotton Personnel Evaluation Report, 1 July 1964 to 6 May 1965, Binh Collection.

8. The move, as modified, was officially complete in October.

9. The meeting produced what became known as the "Vung Tau Charter," by which Nguyen Khanh, exploiting a perception of political crisis, received endorsement from other generals to assume complete power. Balloting was secret, and there may have been a couple of abstentions. Days later in Dalat I was told there had been one vote for Do Cao Tri. General Khanh was aggravated, and this was the beginning of a career dip for Do Cao Tri, as he departed a few weeks later on extended travel to France and Hong Kong until July 1966. He did not have another military assignment until mid-1968, when he was appointed III Corps commander.

Ambassador Maxwell Taylor had replaced Lodge on 7 July.

10. This was another of the 1:100,000 Service Geographique de l'Indochine sheets.

11. When US maps were available around late 1965, whether 1:50,000 or 1:250,000, the indication of a wall along the foothills was not picked up. Despite recent reports from Viet Nam, I have not seen a definitive research paper in any language that conclusively explains the wall remnant extending from An Lao to the Tra Khuc River. I would like to see one.

12. We did not know that during an August meeting in Hanoi the Communist Party decided to send the first PAVN (Quan Doi Nhan Dan; Peoples Army Viet Nam) regiments, distinct from fillers or returnees, southward to fight in central Viet Nam and the highlands. There has been a lot of discussion about that step. Some historians believe it was taken to ensure control over southern cadre; others think PAVN wanted to be on the ground in case of US large-unit intervention. I think that, first of all, there was no chance for the south's going separatist, except possibly in the dreams of a very few nonparty SVNLF persons whose origin was in Saigon or points farther south, and the Mekong Delta was not sufficient to go it alone. The Communist Party in 1960–75 was a truly national party, not a northern regional party, and the dominant leadership (Ho, Pham Van Dong, Vo Nguyen Giap, Le Duan) was central Vietnamese. As those party leaders looked forward to the probable 1966 collapse of South Viet Nam (absent greater US intervention), they believed it would be best to have some PAVN on the ground to accelerate developments and obtain credit for having a role in unification.

13. The Qui Nhon situation was eclipsed by confrontations in Danang and Saigon, where demonstrations turned violent and resulted in Buddhist-Catholic property destruction and killing.

14. I did not realize what a novel and daring approach it was to express, just short of advocating, acceptability of communist participation in elections.

15. The Huey was originally designated HU-1, and although that was changed to UH-1 in late 1962 (consistent with B, C, and the famous D models), the nickname never changed. It became the real pickup truck, ambulance, and jeep for soldiers and Marines.

16. Immediately after the coup, planners and enablers were arrested or dismissed, Thieu was assigned to command IV Corps, and his friend Cao Van Vien took III Corps. When Thieu returned to Saigon in January 1965, he was considered one of the military council's steady leaders. Dang Van Quang replaced him in IV Corps. During the next ten years, Vien and Quang were Thieu's most important advisors and dependable supporters. They were with him during the crucial 1975 meeting at Cam Ranh.

17. Tanham was an insurgency analyst who wrote an early book on the subject while at RAND. Samuel Vaughn Williams is one of the most interesting Americans who served in Viet Nam. Smooth, articulate, decorated for combat with small-unit irregulars during World War II in Burma, Sam was in Berlin early in the Cold War, learned Russian, was always on one interesting assignment or another, and in Viet Nam worked with USOM and later as mission coordinator. His career extended into important Washington assignments. Sam was a close friend of John Vann and George Jacobson. Ev once explained to me that Sam, case officer that he had been, could make anyone his new best friend.

18. I never liked the term *pacification*. It has a colonial flavor or an image of a device jammed into a child's mouth to preclude noise. Occasional use of the word was unavoidable because it had such currency, but from 1963 onward I tried to use the term *recovery operation* because we were concerned with areas recovered from the SVNLF, and in a clinical (medical) sense, special attention would be required for full recovery. I was also uncomfortable with the term *advisor*, because Americans, for a variety of reasons, were not really effective advisors. But it was part of the basic vocabulary, and when I tried to refer to Americans as liaison officers (*lien lac vien*), I only confused fellow countrymen.

19. From the announcement of New Life Hamlets on through spring 1965, just before and into the beginning of the US buildup, I was in a lot of hamlets day and night, especially in Quang Ngai, Binh Dinh, Gia Dinh, and Long An. I witnessed no evidence of Ap Tan Sinh program activity, much less effectiveness. Granted, I was in the less secure areas, but I should have come across some program presence of a major government initiative. It just wasn't there.

20. My guess was confirmed almost two decades later when I read a 1982 interview wherein William Colby said, "In 1964 and 1965 we looked around for some vestiges of some of the programs that had existed in earlier times, and we

found up in central Vietnam a vestige of a program that we had supported of Popular Youth or Popular Force, whatever it was called, which was teams going into villages." That inaccurate account is probably based on reports submitted by Ralph while Colby was director of the Far East Division in Langley. William E. Colby, transcript, Oral History Interview II, 1 March 1982, with Ted Gittinger, Internet copy, Lyndon Baines Johnson Presidential Library, Austin, Texas.

21. The POI and other material provided to Ralph is substantially what I presented in "A Report on an Indoctrination and Motivation Program for Special Commando Units in Quang Ngai Province," Binh Collection. My feeling was that the POI should never be finished. It should evolve. If one looks at what we applied in Quang Ngai, modified with PF platoons in Gia Dinh and the Mekong Delta, and later with CIDG, some changes will be evident, although there was core consistency.

22. This may read more harshly than in fact was the case. Even as I left his house, I understood Ralph showed more consideration for my feelings than I had for his during the previous six months. Ev disagreed and said Ralph probably enjoyed giving me bad news, but I chose not to believe that.

Chapter 8

1. This Saigon-area effort was named Hop Tac, meaning "cooperation." It was initiated in September and supervised by a joint Vietnamese-US council. MACV had a special planning office for it. General Westmoreland took an interest, but my impression was that on the Vietnamese side attention, other than pro forma, lagged.

2. The advantage of employing people with SVNLF experience was that they understood the concept of training by small groups in the field. Separately, more than a year later, our instructional cadre increased in numbers and morphed into other special-purpose projects. We were never betrayed in the field.

3. Roughly comparable to present-day Ho Chi Minh City.

4. Following the aborted Vung Tau Charter stretch for absolute power in August, and the September failed minicoup, Nguyen Khanh relinquished authority to civilian chief of state Phan Khac Suu in late October but managed to confirm himself as armed forces commander-in-chief. Constant intrigue on his part, and plotting by his opponents, was wearing on everyone's patience, hence Ev's pessimistic prognosis.

5. The Browning automatic rifle was a decades-old design, but a military classic.

Major Thoi had two older brothers who were already colonels and eventually generals. Lam Quang Tho (armor branch) was then 5th Division chief of staff, and Lam Quang Thi (artillery) was deputy commander of 7th Division. The family was from Bac Lieu. I don't think the two brothers had enough influence to place their sibling in this important (and lucrative) district. I assumed instead that the assignment had something to do with Thoi's being an airborne officer (the Airborne Brigade headquarters was at Tan Son Nhut).

6. Born 1919 in Thua Thien, Phan Dinh Phu (Lam Son's real name) was in France when he was captured by Germans in World War II. He escaped and then served first with British Special Operations Executive and later with the Free French. While with the British, he was given the cover name of Williamson, which he later Vietnamized to Lam Son, which providentially is also the name of the fifteenth-century resistance base for struggle against China.

7. Mai Huu Xuan's background was not appealing to younger officers on the rise. In May 1965 he was persuaded to take retirement. He became a businessman.

8. At night one could see the illuminated horizon to the east at Tan Son Nhut airport; that's how close we were to metropolitan Saigon.

9. Barry brought his own candidate to head up field operations as USIA prepared to assign more American officers to provincial duty. Ev was marginalized and unhappy, but he never stopped providing me with wise advice. I respected Zorthian, but Ev had my soul. I regretted the two of them did not bond as a team.

10. I confess that I am one of those who, in late 1964, underestimated Nguyen Van Thieu's political ambition and cleverness. I thought that he was genial and bland and would be a stolid executor for some more charismatic leader (I had no one in mind).

11. Civilian Irregular Defense Group (CIDG) units, derived from an early experiment in Darlac province, were paramilitary forces that operated from isolated US Special Forces camps.

12. This tough neighborhood was Nhi Binh, a group of hamlets at a bend of the Saigon River roughly opposite Lai Thieu in Binh Duong province. The area was a tangle of sugarcane fields and heavy foliage at the nexus of trails from Cu Chi to Lai Thieu and Ben Suc toward Saigon. Many of the volunteers for this unit were from Nhi Binh, so assignment to mobility within this area was in accordance with our concept. Major Vy was killed in action in late 1966.

13. Tom Donahue, in particular, was always available and never denied a request for equipment issue.

14. Nguyen Be was born in Quang Tri and spent much of his childhood in Lao

Bao. Like many of his generation, he joined the Viet Minh to fight against the return of French colonialists after World War II. He stayed with the Viet Minh until 1951, rising to battalion commander. In 1951, while visiting his parents, he was accused of being a communist, arrested, and imprisoned. In 1952 he was offered release if he would join the new South Viet Nam Army. We had met after November 1963, when he was briefly a staff officer for Vietnamese Special Forces. At that time I did not appreciate what an extraordinary person he was.

15. Be read the note and told me that sincerity compensated for mistakes of language. I asked him to help me make corrections. "No, as it is, no one can doubt that you wrote it yourself, and he will understand."

Nguyen Huu Co replaced Do Cao Tri as II Corps commander in September 1964. Tuong was a 25th Division officer commanding the 51st Regiment in 1963 and was Quang Ngai province chief in spring of 1964, transferring to Binh Dinh in September.

16. He was a straight-talking brother. A few months later I mentioned that a friend proposed I join the Cercle Sportif club. Be commented, "If you join, you will have many friends, but I will not be one of them." Then followed a short discourse on the image of what he called the "circle coloniale." I never joined.

17. We could tell in a few days whether a candidate would make it as a "living-in-the-field, on-the-go" instructor. Since we screened each one for background experience, if they could live our methodology, then each new cadre would be paired with one of our most experienced. We expanded like tree rings, from the core outward.

18. Nhat did tell me later that he flinched because he had never seen so many stars before, more than twelve altogether, beginning with four on each collar, four more on General Westmoreland's cap, and a star over his master parachutist badge.

19. Usually translated as Forest of Assassins.

20. Tran Huu Tri was born in Chau Doc province, but his family moved to Saigon later.

21. These former SVNLF were Chieu Hoi returnees and others with different backgrounds.

22. MACV was not prepared to fully support initiation of an ad hoc effort, so USIS was paying all instructor/operator cadre salaries and some other expenses. CIA generously provided important equipment support.

23. Our success in expanding the body of talent allowed for a positive response.

24. Khanh's travel was described as being that of an "ambassador at large," and he

did go to the United States and then Europe. Raymond was his French name.

25. My response to Colonel Spragins, indicating increasing commitment to elected representative government rather than support to a military caretaker, is in the Binh Collection.

26. JUSPAO was the first joint civil-military organization, and as such a precursor for MACVCORDS.

In response to one problem, inadequate supply, I submitted a report stating that training would shut down until the situation was corrected. CIA had been bridging until MACV was funded but could not continue to support PATs and our own expanding program. Barry Zorthian raised this problem directly with General Westmoreland and got an immediate solution.

I had already upgraded my carbine to an M2, but the AK (although heavier) was superior.

27. William R. Peers was a World War II Burma Campaign OSS veteran who later commanded the 4th Division in the Central Highlands.

28. Late in the summer of 1965 I affiliated with a Hoa Hao congregation, but that had not been even on my horizon in the spring.

29. Right then, and later, I understood Dr. Dan to be a decent, very good person who would always be taken advantage of by more aggressive, less principled competitors.

30. Several years later a friend asked me why I did not try to keep in contact with Thieu as he rose above others. The simple answer is that I felt he was not approachable, at least by me. He was, even in relations with Vien and Quang, self-contained and not at ease with others.

31. In fact, we never had half a dozen. Andre Jean Sauvageot is sui generis.

32. Dang Van Sung was a Dai Viet politician and prominent publisher of *Chinh luan* newspaper. The quote was: "Man is so made that he never wholeheartedly risks his life fighting for a lesser evil; but he will willingly die for an illusion." I thought the first part was most important because it meant that we needed to establish ourselves as dramatically different and better than the SVNLF arm of the Communist Party.

33. I expressed the opinion that a three-year pilot project was loony, given that we were running out of time, but John and Ev said Washington didn't realize that, and suggesting three years would get our foot in the door so that application could be accelerated later.

The paper was titled "Revolutionary Warfare and Motivation Training" (2 June 1965, copy in Binh Collection). The second edition was in Washington by late July, and the PROVN Study Group had it on 10 August. (Colonel Hanifen Memorandum for Lieutenant Colonel Day, copy in Binh Collection). A third edition, dated 10 September, sometimes cited by researchers, was intended by John to be persuasive in discussion with General Westmoreland and Ambassador Lodge.

34. General Tam was born in My Tho in 1926. He was an engaging conversationalist and subsequently represented Viet Nam with Free World Assisting Nations and served as ambassador to Thailand.

35. When mobile PF assistance/advisory teams were formed a few years later, it was an instance of a good concept applied too late while the US forces were already withdrawing.

Reflection 1965

1. Order of Battle Study No. 66-1, MACV Combined Intelligence Center, 18 February 1966.

   When Inter-Zone V (Lien Khu Nam) was reestablished in 1961, its boundaries corresponded to those set earlier during the Viet Minh period: roughly from the DMZ area south to Nha Trang and including the highlands. In mid-1964 the highland provinces were split from Inter-Zone V to constitute a separate command and control region. In 1965 the Western Highlands Front was designated B-3, while Quang Tri and Thua Thien were separated from Inter-Zone V and designated something like the Tri-Thien Front. These command and control alterations were clues to PAVN movement south, but I think we did not read them in a timely manner. And even if we had, we might not have paused or halted our own escalation.

2. "Southern" in this context included the southern portion of central Viet Nam.

3. I thought Phu Yen might have been an exception, but even there, emphasizing local hamlet leadership would have been an improvement.

Chapter 9

1. Just one year later, there was quite a difference. But in the early summer of 1965 our country at large seemed somnolent.

2. I had forgotten that when General Westmoreland was appointed, Phil Werbiski and I asked Gordon Huddleston what kind of MACV leadership we could expect. Huddleston, who had served in the 187th Regimental Combat Team when Westmoreland commanded that unit, replied, "Boys, General Westmoreland is possibly the finest regimental commander this army has produced." Phil asked,

"Okay, but what kind of MACV will we have?" Hud smiled, and replied, "I repeat, General Westmoreland is possibly our finest regimental commander."

3. Hank Miller was former USIS Director in Laos and a Lansdale friend since their assignment together in the Philippines.

   I hasten to note that I would not have been one of Lansdale's team. In the summer of 1965 I would have scorned any Saigon assignment. But Ev, John Vann, and Sam Wilson could have provided him with excellent recommendations.

4. A friend in the station told me about the message but would not let me read it.

5. The French have a couple of oft-quoted maxims: *toujours l'audace* and *surtout, pas trop de zele*. I usually followed the former, not always to good effect.

6. "Program Proposal for a Motivation Project Sponsored by JUSPAO and Fifth Special Forces Group (Airborne)," included in a thin hardbound volume titled *Indoctrination* (in Binh Collection).

7. This habit on the part of Vietnamese and Americans was so grooved that, a year later, a district chief who knew me as "major" was told by our cadre that I was already a colonel. In 1989, when I was assigned to Fort Bragg, the protocol office assigned me the courtesy equivalency of a two-star general to appropriately place me at the table and in the parking lot. But I trust Gary Luck, Bill Garrison, Mac Dorsey, Juan Chavez, and Paul Payne will confirm that I never confused military courtesy and protocol with command authority.

8. Communists assassinated the first Hoa Hao teacher, Huynh Phu So, in 1947. That inoculated Hoa Hao against any sympathy for the party's cause.

   Through conversation with Le Van Phoi and others, I affiliated with Hoa Hao Buddhism. Phil Werbiski joked that I had found my perfect faith, one that allowed killing, but after we had sharp words, he dropped the subject and didn't mention it again until five years later. Factually, Le Van Phoi taught that killing is only allowable for self-defense, and the act has (cause and effect) consequences. Buddhism is not a religion, as commonly supposed, because understanding the four truths and trying to follow the eight-fold path is not deity-dependent. I am an inadequate practitioner, but a better person than if I were to make no effort at all.

9. Our combined genius provided for searchlights, loud hailers, and small boats manned by CIDG.

10. Recalling the AK-47 that we had been shown a few months earlier, I doubted the night traffic was entirely commercial.

11. I did not suggest elections as a means to control corruption because I supposed that might give cause to oppose elections.

A few months later, after we were out of Chau Doc, Major Arnn and Sergeant Torello were killed near Ba Chuc, close to Nui Dai in the Seven Mountains area. USAID Province Representative Tony Cistaro was severely wounded.

12. For the Communist Party itself the war would quickly become total, in that it would require complete national effort with all else subordinate.

13. The percentage of the population living in communist-controlled hamlets increased dramatically. SVNLF companies expanded to battalion size, and regimental commands were formed to control even larger formations. In January 1965 at Binh Gia, south of Xuan Loc, ARVN forces were committed piecemeal and were skunked.

14. This occurred when he responded to General Westmoreland's request and loaned me to MACV.

15. John Bennett was just replacing Colonel Spragins as deputy group commander. They were both lieutenant colonels, but by traditional practice a lieutenant colonel is usually referred to as colonel, just as a second lieutenant is usually referred to simply as lieutenant.

16. Recently promoted, General Freund was an unusual army officer in that he was an Annapolis graduate. He had a part in defusing a dangerous situation in one of the Special Forces camps during the FULRO uprising. After Viet Nam he was briefly SACSA, and then he retired after controversial travel to the Philippines.

17. Brother Werbiski later told Gordon Huddleston that my radio call sign ought to be Horse Dentist.

18. PAT stands for People's Action Team. The CIA representative fumed but eventually was limited to coordinating logistical support.

19. Hon Con was a prominent hillock west-northwest of An Khe and was usually pronounced Hong Kong by Americans.

20. A few days later Colonel Tuong told us that in one hamlet, after receiving sniper fire, Korean soldiers lined up residents and selected some for execution. We asked Colonel Tuong if he had reported the incident, and he responded affirmatively, to General Vinh Loc at corps. But he doubted any action would be taken, because "General Vinh Loc will not jeopardize his own position."

21. Route 19 from Qui Nhon port would be the principal supply LOC for the 1st Air Cav.

22. And the 1st Air Cavalry Division followed up with its own operation in the same area from early October to mid-November.

Chapter 10

1. Others suggest that Thi was biding his time. I simply report what he told me. I think people who posit the notion of Thi waiting in the wings were actually themselves attracted to the "strongman" notion. Thi did wait, and he was beginning to appoint civilian province chiefs. I thought his inclination to civil government was sincere.

   Abrupt greeting was typical of Thi's personality. More than thirty years later, when I went to his home in Pennsylvania, he burst out the front door, asking why I had not come to see him sooner. Explaining that I had been on assignment in other countries was barely sufficient.

2. Plei Ta Nangle was closed in May 1965. Kannack survived under 1st Cav cover until January 1966.

3. A coordinating and supporting Special Forces B Team was established in Qui Nhon. The team in Tuy Phuoc relocated to Vinh Thanh that November. Another team was retained in Bong Son until June 1967. It was the most isolated of the ad hoc district efforts because in 1965 the railroad and Highway 1 were closed north of Tam Quan, and to the south Route 1 was often interdicted, especially at the pass north of Phu My.

4. Frequently we had to explain to other Americans that those home bunkers were not Viet Cong shelters or fighting positions. They immediately suspected that bunkers indicated enemy or support to the enemy. So farm families were at risk without a bunker and at risk if they had one.

5. For years I would occasionally encounter someone who knew how a few old women had outsmarted me, so I know Ev enjoyed recounting the tale of Thanksgiving dinner 1965.

6. Battle accounts are often partial, because they are told from the perspective of one sector in a complex battlefield. In the case of this October–November sequence, my understanding is that the PAVN 33rd Regiment attacked Plei Me beginning in mid-October but was beaten back by camp defenders and the arrival of Project Delta elements with part of the US-organized 91st Airborne Ranger Battalion (Mike Force). The 32nd (sometimes identified as the 320th) PAVN Regiment intended to ambush the relief force (ARVN Task Force Luat) coming south from Pleiku, but the movement was so slow that the ambush was unsuccessful, and as the 32nd withdrew westward, it was engaged south of Duc Co by an ARVN Airborne task force commanded by Ngo Quang Trung. The 32nd was shattered by 26 October.

   The 66th PAVN Regiment, which had just arrived in the area in early November and still lacked its full table of equipment, engaged battalions of the 1st Air Cavalry Division in mid-November, and these distinct, violent encounters at landing zones and along ridges became well known as the Battles of Ia Drang and Chu Pong. Actually, the battles with the Air Cav were one part of a larger PAVN operational concept that failed—failed, but served notice on both sides that there was one hell of an opponent in the field.

7. Establishing an accurate order of battle for SVNLF and PAVN formations was especially difficult in 1965–69. Divisions moving south had *cong truong* (worksite) cover designations, sometimes they would be worn down then be reorganized and redesignated, and prisoners would provide faulty information.

8. Rural demographics were impacted by absorption of young men by the SVNLF, ARVN, and Regional and Popular Forces.

9. A Shau Valley is an example. In the summer of 1965 there were three camps: A Luoi, Ta Bat, and A Shau. In December 1965 A Luoi dissolved and Ta Bat was abandoned, and A Shau was overrun in March 1966. The indigenous population was of the Katu tribe, and the CIDG were foreign to the valley.

10. The stratification of JUSPAO at this point, from my perspective looking upward, was: Carl Gebuhr, my immediate supervisor; Bob Delaney, deputy assistant director of field services; General Freund, assistant JUSPAO director for field services; and Barry Zorthian. Ev was not then in my direct chain. I knew from Ev (after he returned to Saigon) that Delaney and Gebuhr resented our having tasking direct from Zorthian and General Freund, and that behind our backs they called us the "gold dust twins." I assumed that had an Arcades ambo connotation.

11. As the day and night passed, Gordon Huddleston was a silent, albeit amused, witness.

12. Tran Ngoc Chau, first in the youth resistance in central Viet Nam, was a Viet Minh officer from 1945 through most of 1949, when he joined the new South Viet Nam Army. His advancement was retarded by his Viet Minh background and unwillingness to participate in Can Lao Party activity. President Diem, however, appreciated Chau's capabilities and assigned him special duties, including that of province chief in Kien Hoa and later mayor of Danang. When Chau was first in Kien Hoa he pioneered a "census grievance" approach to pacification that stabilized some contested areas. When he returned to Kien Hoa to serve as province chief again, he revived that program. In December 1965 he was appointed director of RD Cadre, to include supervision of the training center in Vung Tau.

13. What I wanted to call "recovery operations" was usually termed "pacification" by Americans. Ambassador Lodge prefered "revolutionary development," later changed to "rural development," while most Americans still talked about "pacification." By whatever name it was called, the ministry was located in an old colonial-era edifice that was previously occupied by Nguyen Ton Hoan, a Dai Viet whom Nguyen Khanh had brought home from living abroad to be deputy prime minister for pacification. When Khanh lost power, so did Hoan, but he was never relevant anyway.

14. This was not at all unusual. Colonel Le Van Tu was deputy chief of staff for pacification from January 1966 until March 1968, and although he had been a district chief in Sa Dec and province chief in Phong Dinh and Hau Nghia, he could not articulate what needed to be done in the hamlets. Unlike Chau, Be, Phien, and Tuy—and perhaps other junior or field-grade persons—general officers talked in generalities that revealed lack of specific knowledge and ideas. When they did so with Americans who were as ignorant as they, the result was a mutual admiration society that masked numbness and ineffective performance.

15. Doug's multifaceted genius included special talent for electronics and for playing the piano at concert level. In his small house he had two corner speakers from floor to ceiling and a grand piano. Phil was about to transfer to C-5, an element complementary to Delta and SOG.

16. "In case of need": Tet, the lunar New Year, was beginning on 20 January, and our intent was to benefit from the cease-fire atmosphere to try to negotiate a humanitarian release. We would only fire if fired upon.

  Nguyen Thanh died in November 2009, and as of this writing, Do Dinh Duyet lives in Virginia.

17. I did not see Doug again until January 1973, when our prisoner recovery team brought him and twenty-six other Americans away from the Loc Ninh release site.

18. Huddleston came for a few days every couple of weeks. He and Phil told me a few months later that they had some of the same concern for me that I expressed about Vann.

19. I place in parentheses the parts of those districts usually referred to by Americans. The Kim Son Valley was also familiarly referred to as the Crow's Foot.

20. There is some controversy between the cavalry and Delta concerning the matter of coordination and support. I provide a sketch based on what one of the survivors, Sgt. Billy McKeithe, told me while we were together in the Vinh

Thanh Valley in March and what Major Beckwith expressed when I spoke with him in the Qui Nhon Army Hospital.

21. The most extreme example is probably the 1968 massacre of civilians in Son Tinh district (Quang Ngai), known by the GVN but not raised as an issue with the United States.

22. The source here is my rough notes from various dates in early February (Binh Collection). Harry Johnson was with the advisory detachment for the 9th ARVN Division, 1962–63, and he returned in 1965 as the Phu Cat district advisor. Following medical evacuation and recuperation, he returned as the sector RF/PF advisor.

23. As noted earlier, Korean operations were especially rough on civilians. The Binh Khe district chief told me on 14 February that two days earlier a Korean unit had encountered sniper fire and grenade booby traps, resulting in five killed and nineteen wounded. He said the Koreans grouped people and machine-gunned them. Forty-five civilians were killed (notes, Binh Collection).

24. Billy had temporary care in Qui Nhon but wanted return to Nha Trang. I brought him to the army airfield and got him on a C-130. When we next met, he told me the C-130 went to Pleiku and then Nha Trang. The crew invited him to ride up front. The plane lost an engine between Pleiku and Nha Trang. Billy said that, even with his arm in a sling, he grabbed a parachute and was struggling to harness into it. When the crew reminded him that a C-130 would fly even on two engines, he unmistakably told them that if they lost another engine, he was out of there. From An Lao to Vinh Thanh, Billy had a rough couple of months. He served twenty-seven years and now lives in Louisiana.

25. There was subtle irony implicit in this recommendation, because a year earlier Nguyen Be had been in dispute with the province CIA representative over utilization of PAT units.

26. Nguyen Chanh Thi described the following sequence of events to me in Washington several months later: There was a Directorate meeting on 2 March that Thi did not attend. On 3 March Nguyen Cao Ky flew to Danang and warned Thi that "other generals" were losing patience with his lack of cooperation. On 9 March Chairman Thieu called Thi and asked him to attend a meeting scheduled for the next day. At that meeting Nguyen Huu Co, minister of defense (and former II Corps commander), Ky, and Thieu spoke to lack of confidence in Thi. The Directorate voted to remove Thi from command. The resulting Buddhist-led riots were so extensive that Thi was allowed to return to Danang to help stabilize the situation, although he was not restored to command.

27. I believe Colonel Vong was a cousin of General Vinh Loc's wife.

28. Can introduced me to people in Saigon and taught me about Vietnamese ceramics and art; now I returned the favor by introducing him to Binh Dinh friends, who showed him a couple of Cham kiln sites.

29. There may have been nuances to the dispute, but this is my recollection of John's description of the problem.

30. Dai Viet was one of the political movement parties dating to the 1930s that included competing factions based on regional associations. Several prominent political figures were Dai Viet of one kind or another. Phan Huy Quat, Bui Diem, and Dang Van Sung were northern in origin, and Ha Thuc Ky and Nguyen Ton Hoan were central and southern, respectively. John thought Camp Director Le Xuan Mai had a northern Dai Viet affiliation. Deputy Director Nguyen Xuan Phac may have had Dai Viet inclination based on the leadership of his father, Dr. Nguyen Xuan Chu, of the Viet Nam Ai Quoc Dang (Viet Nam Patriot Party) in North Viet Nam before World War II.

My reaction on listening to John's summary was that we failed by not being a bridge between diverse Vietnamese personalities who were patriotic, lived an austere life, and wanted to contribute to cadre operations. I had personal regard and respect for Mai and Phac as well as Chau and believed we could have worked toward a cooperative endeavor.

31. A performance rating report prepared by these two officers, covering my work during the period November 1965 through June 1966, makes their feelings abundantly clear (Binh Collection).

32. Lt. Col. John Bennett retired from the army as a major general. He was briefly an assistant to Alexander Haig in the White House during the Nixon audio tapes imbroglio. He died in an Alaska plane crash in 1980.

33. C-5 was established by 5th Special Forces Group to be complementary and supplementary to MACVSOG. SOG was primarily operating against the trail system in Laos, so C-5 would begin by focusing on Cambodia. C-5 subsequently divided into B-56 (Sigma), B-50 (Omega), and B-57 (Gamma). Later, the C-5 elements were absorbed by SOG and formed much of CCS working out from Banmethuot.

34. The Trinh Minh The Bridge was named after the Cao Dai officer who was persuaded by Lansdale to fight in support of Diem against the Binh Xuyen in April 1955. He was killed right there during the fighting.

35. General Freund took command of the 199th Infantry Brigade operating

around Saigon. Thereafter, he was SACSA, and much later he commanded the Connecticut National Guard.

36. Vinh Loc was related to the former royal family (his father was a cousin to Bao Dai), so an appointment with him was in the nature of an audience.

37. General Sang was relieved of command several weeks later and replaced by one of South Viet Nam's outstanding generals, Nguyen Van Hieu, whom I had met in 1964 when he was II Corps chief of staff. Hieu was honest and self-disciplined, and he believed in the possibility of reforming the army and government. He was murdered or committed suicide in April 1975 at III Corps headquarters in Bien Hoa. Lieutenant Colonel Vong was later arrested, tried, and convicted on the charge of corruption. Vong was jailed, but he escaped execution because of his family's relationship with Vinh Loc. Gen. Vinh Loc retained command of II Corps until after the 1968 Tet offensive, when he was shifted to JGS with training responsibilities.

38. Do Cao Tri had not yet returned from political exile.

39. Subsequently there was discussion between General Vinh Loc and Tran Ngoc Chau that resulted in Chau's requesting Be's reassignment to his staff. When the Vung Tau command issue was settled, with Major Mai assigned to liaison with Korean forces and Captain Phac placed with the tribal cadre program in Pleiku, Colonel Chau obtained approval for Nguyen Be to be the new training center commander, replacing Colonel Le Van Thinh, who had been briefly in charge after Mai departed.

40. Nguyen Cao Ky made vague reference in January to providing a draft constitution in October and national elections sometime in 1967, but he gave no timetable. The Honolulu Conference in February also endorsed democracy, but with no schedule. Even in March and April there was still contention over whether an elected constituent assembly would have legislative power. Eventually Ky made it clear that the military would only accept a two-step process: first, a constituent assembly, with elections a year later for an assembly that could legislate.

41. Accounting for regiments assigned to SVNLF and PAVN divisions is difficult. Regiments did move and then attach to other divisions. I mention the regiments that I think were part of the 3rd Division during most of 1966. Subsequently, the 2nd may have moved into Quang Ngai, and at some point the 12th joined the 3rd. In the south (Nam Bo), the 7th PAVN, 5th SVNLF, and 9th SVNLF Divisions also had some changes of regiment components, and after 1969 (due to replacement of casualties) the two SVNLF divisions were PAVN in all but name.

In 1975, still active, the 3rd Division played an important role in taking over Binh Dinh province during the final communist offensive. Throughout the war Binh Dinh was as important a battlefield area for the communists as any other. General Doan Khue, commander in Binh Dinh, was eventually (decades later) promoted to defense minister of the Socialist Republic of Viet Nam.

42. General Westmoreland's mention of nuoc mam in his book is a case in point. I don't know why Americans perpetuated this myth. I admit a nuoc mam factory might be located by smell, and *mam* or *mam chua* (but not to be mistaken as nuoc mam) might tickle the nostrils. But nuoc mam has barely any scent.

Chapter 11

1. Nguyen Chanh Thi was arrested on July 5 by Directorate decision. My friends told me that Thieu, Co (minister of defense), and Dang Van Quang played the key roles in orchestrating votes. On 9 July the Ministry of Defense announced that Thi would be confined for sixty days and retired. He was exiled to the United States on 31 July.

2. All the candidates, their positions, and campaign symbols were reviewed by military authorities. There were some disapprovals.

3. Bilingual readers might have noted an oxymoronic aspect to the chapter 10 heading, in that Binh Dinh translates as "to pacify" or "pacification." Aside from the war itself, there was initial criticism of the pacification program as Nguyen Be developed and applied it in Binh Dinh.

4. Actually, I knew much more. When John and I were attempting Doug Ramsey's retrieval in January, John gave me his September 1965 correspondence with the PROVN group, so I read Colonel Hanifen's response to "Harnessing the Revolution," the PROVN study schematic, the seven-page PROVN study outline as approved by the US Army chief of staff on 17 August 1965, the seven-page annex describing essential elements of analysis, the PROVN group organization chart, and the PROVN Study Group Production Schedule, Binh Collection. A general officer chaired the study, but the actual driver was Colonel Hanifen.

5. PROVN ("A Program for the Pacification and Long-Term Development of South Vietnam") was completed in March 1966 and then had a bumpy rollout with very limited distribution. The initiator was Army Chief of Staff Harold K. Johnson, who had reservations (in spring 1965) about MACV strategy. When the study was complete, it had to be first briefed "upward" with the Joint Chiefs, then the secretary of defense. MACV was provided a copy for comment.

CINCPAC and then MACV were formally briefed in late May. The response was tepid, at best. I do not know how Jake obtained a copy.

6. It has been suggested that President Johnson's early February comments in Honolulu were PROVN-influenced. That is highly doubtful, because the study was not finished until March, and someone's head would have been mounted on a pike if a copy had arrived at the White House before the Joint Chiefs and secretary of defense had been briefed.

7. To this day I have not read the complete study.

8. Among ourselves we referred to the project as RAMJET: Roles and Missions Joint (or Jacobson) Evaluation Team.

9. The situation in Binh Thuan worsened after our departure. SVNLF forces overran the hamlet that we visited, so an area in the process of recovery by the GVN was abandoned. David James note to Frank Scotton, 6 August 1966, memorandum with attachment describing Dai Thien hamlet, Binh Collection.

10. I did not, and could not, have imagined that, less than two years later in 1968, members of the same families were to be massacred by Americans in Tu Cung and My Khe Tay.

11. Jake, like Lansdale and Ev Bumgardner, had an unconventional pre–World War II background. He once told me that before entering the army he was in vaudeville; as you observed him chairing the contentious group debates, you could imagine him as master of ceremonies before a tough audience. Two of his favorite expressions were: "He's just a zero with the rim knocked off," and "Dumber than a mashed potato sandwich." Jake and Esther later married. Jake made himself an indispensable senior administrator. He replaced Bill Colby as chief of staff for CORDS after Komer departed, and, following the 1973 ceasefire, when the US mission reconfigured, he was special assistant to the ambassador for field operations (SAAFO). He arrived in December 1954 and stayed through the final scene in 1975. Jake died in May 1989.

Deputy MACV Commander General Heintges strongly implied we were not competent to make judgments concerning the effect of military operations on pacification. I sharply disagreed, and Jake had to intercede in our argument.

12. Vietnamese leaders perpetuated themselves in positions of authority so as to maintain control of the existing order with levers of corruption and patronage.

13. Inter-Agency "Roles and Missions" Study Group, US Mission Viet Nam, 24 August 1966, Part II, "Some Other Major Problem Areas," pp. 26–27, Vietnam Center and Archive, Texas Tech University.

14. Colonel Serong previously coordinated Australians on special assignment.
15. Inter-Agency "Roles and Missions" Study Group." US Mission Viet Nam, 24 August 1966, Appendix A, "List of All Recommendations," p. 9, Vietnam Center and Archive, Texas Tech University.
16. Talbot was then the USIS BPAO in Can Tho.
17. Two other key staff persons were Dick Moorstein and Hans Heymann, both of RAND. I met them when they spoke with me in a Binh Dinh hamlet during April 1966.
18. A constituent assembly was elected on September 11. The new assembly was charged with writing a constitution that would restore civilian government through national elections in 1967. I thought it was still an open question how open and broad the next step would be.
19. Jake Jacobson to Frank Scotton, 8 October 1966, Binh Collection.
20. Thi and his wife had separated when he was exiled to Cambodia during 1960–63.
21. Maj. Frank Butler to Frank Scotton, HQ US Army Alaska, 5 October 1966, Binh Collection.
22. The Chao system today is regarded by Chinese teachers as an exotic curiosity.
23. About twenty-five years later Doolin was assistant secretary of defense for East Asia. He died in 2004.
24. Most accounts of the Great Cultural Revolution place its origin in the June 1966 announcement of Beijing Party Committee reorganization, but I believe the spark was struck in September 1964 when the Central Committee sent a "work team" to investigate Beijing University and determine whether it was a bourgeois or socialist institution.
25. The new approach for American rural operations, the Office of Civil Operations (OCO), was announced in late November.
26. Several months later, Dwight was killed in Quang Ngai province. With or without my encouragement, he was definitely going to Viet Nam. Still, his death personified for me the loss of volunteer young people on all sides in the Viet Nam war.

   On the way back, I stopped in Honolulu to meet Ev Bumgardner and Ed Lansdale at the Training Center run by John O'Donnell for USAID. We three provided discussion of problems associated with rural development. O'Donnell to Frank Scotton, 7 February 1967, Binh Collection.

Chapter 12

1. This work is summarized in KBC 3405 of 23 May 1966, issued jointly by Colonel McKean (5th Group) and General Doan Van Quang (Vietnamese Special Forces). In order to preserve security, there was no mention of using mobile instruction from camp to camp as a vehicle for identifying and recruiting volunteers to other projects. Loose-leaf folder marked "Frank Scotton, OCO/PED, U.S. Embassy," Binh Collection.

2. The models were Blackjack 21 and Blackjack 22. Consciously or unconsciously, this was the final turning away from the original Buon Enao concept.

3. I may be excessively opinionated and stubborn myself, but I have little concern for appearance of an office, either figurative or literal.

4. Documentation is contained in the loose-leaf folder previously cited, provided by Captain Gordon Huddleston (Binh Collection).

5. Prior approval of an American advisory element was not requested, and notification of travel was not provided, because those steps would compromise methodology and independent judgment. On departure from the area, a courtesy call and discussion opportunity would be appropriate. Bureaucratic feathers were often ruffled when regional and provincial advisors believed they were feudal overlords for the district or province to which they were assigned.

6. I don't mean to imply we always agreed (sometimes we are tempted to gauge another's intelligence by the percentage of congruence with our own opinions), but if you have a viewpoint different from Dan's, then you had better be prepared for serious intellectual debate.

7. The enemy order of battle also showed the 3rd, 21st, and 22nd PAVN Regiments in Quang Ngai, along with the reorganized 1st SVNLF Regiment. The 38th and 48th SVNLF Battalions were basically local, but experienced and tough.

    The intensity of conflict in I Corps increased to such a point that MACV in April directed the formation of Task Force Oregon (an army formation), commanded by General Rossen. Task Force Oregon, with significant brigade changes, eventually reconfigured as the 23rd (Americal) Division a few months later.

8. What we were discussing that day became a building block for ICEX a few months later.

9. Pham Van Lieu, Viet Nam Marine Corps officer, was chief of staff at Quang Trung Training Center when he joined the airborne officers' coup attempt in November 1960. He formed an attachment to Nguyen Chanh Thi and in February 1965 was named director-general of the National Police. In late April 1966 he was replaced when Nguyen Chanh Thi was removed from command

of I Corps. In March 1967 Lieu was commandant of the NCO academy in Nha Trang, but he was dismissed in September because of support to the Tran Van Huong candidacy for president. He was always approachable and easy to talk with.

10. Lt. Col. Bob Montague, on TDY from Komer's office, was the most indispensable officer during the period of transition from OCO to CORDS. In 1962 and 1963 he was in Bac Lieu as a member of the advisory team to the ARVN 21st Division. Dick Holbrooke was there at the same time as a Department of State officer on assignment to USOM. They worked together on the 21st ARVN Division plan for recovering an area from SVNLF control. From that point on they were as inseparable as Ev Bumgardner and I. Bob was a special assistant to General Westmoreland in 1964 and early 1965, and he especially worked on planning for the Hoc Tac priority provinces. We knew each other from 1963 onward.

The new II Corps regional director was Robert Matteson. Joe Vaccaro and I provided orientation for him in Binh Dinh province, and Vlad Lahovich (embassy political officer) joined us for discussion in Nha Trang. Robert grasped the essentials very quickly, and I think of him as one of the three best regional directors, the others being John Vann and (much later) Charlie Whitehouse.

11. My own preference for the general in charge, I told John, would be Ray Peers, who was commanding the 4th Infantry Division in the highlands. That I was even thinking in those terms proves remoteness from the highest-level discussion that soon brought Bob Komer to take charge.

12. Scotton memorandum for Ambassador Porter through Frank Wisner, 2 March 1967, and English translation of Nguyen Be to Nguyen Duc Thang, 8 February 1967, Binh Collection.

13. Deputy Ambassador Porter moved on to be ambassador to the Republic of Korea.

14. Montague to Scotton, 18 March [1967], Binh Collection.

15. Some accounts credit President Johnson or Ed Lansdale with persuading the GVN military to hold elections, but I think the real credit is owed to Vietnamese Buddhists and others who continued the spring 1966 struggle movement until the GVN committed to a constituent assembly in order to damp civil unrest sparked by removal of Nguyen Chanh Thi from I Corps command.

16. Scotton Performance Rating Report, January 7–June 15, 1967, Paul Hare rating, LTC Robert Montague reviewing, Binh Collection. Before retiring from the Foreign Service, Paul became, as his father had been, an ambassador.

17. Nonetheless, these systems technicians were very persuasive when conversing with other Saigon managers. Sharing the same "administrators language," they dwelled on a separate plane of existence from field advisory teams. McManaway was increasingly recognized as an administrative all-star, respected by Komer and Colby, and he served as ambassador to Haiti during 1984–86 and was Paul Bremmer's deputy (never mind that the Bremmer appointment was a foreign policy blunder) in Iraq decades later.

18. Le Nguyen Khang was a Viet Nam Marine Corps officer of northern origin, a high school (Chu Van An) and military academy (Nam Dinh) classmate of Nguyen Cao Ky. At this time he was concurrently CMD (Capital Military District) commander. He was relieved in mid-1968 when others supporting Ky were replaced by officers with greater allegiance to Thieu. Phan Trong Chinh was also northern by origin (Bac Ninh) and a fellow student with Khang and Ky at Chu Van An.

19. Up to then the province chief was able to disagree, and even argue, with General Chinh over issues such as the length of time cadre teams should spend in hamlets, but after 1 March the province chief, Lieutenant Colonel Nhu, was eclipsed.

20. Frank Scotton for Frank Van Damm, "Single Manager Effect on GVN Management," March 1967, Binh Collection.

21. "RD in Long An," Spring 1967, Binh Collection.

22. Ibid.

23. Holbrooke to Scotton, 15 April 1967, Binh Collection. See also Shubert to Scotton, 10 March 1967, Binh Collection.

24. Long Huu is an extensive island shaped roughly like a triangle, with an old French coastal artillery fort at the eastern point by the Saigon River, a major canal to the north, and the Vam Co Dong River to the west and then curving around the southern side and flowing northeast to meet the Saigon River. It was about ten kilometers long by a little more than six kilometers at its widest.

25. Although it was reported that government service representatives were active on the island, we neither saw nor heard of a single one during our trek in and around hamlets.

26. Actually at this point it was just Paul Hare and I who approved this procedure, but it became routine with occasional exceptions.

27. *Long Huu*, with comments by a former CP member SVNLF officer, 14 April 1967, Binh Collection. I appended my own two recommendations: that there should be no cable to Washington hailing Long Huu a success (although a

MACV press release of 16 April did) and that we should keep police out of similar operations because their past abuse of power compromised them.

I next saw Sam twenty-two years later while I was assigned at Fort Bragg. He was his customary good-humored, affable self.

28. General Abrams also arrived in the spring in replacement of General Heintges as deputy commander MACV, but at that point his connection to OCO-CORDS was minimal, as his principal responsibility seemed to be improving ARVN performance.

29. The draft paper would have built on the DIOCC approach pioneered, I think, by Bob Wall in Dien Ban district, Quang Nam province. ICEX was the first iteration of a comprehensive approach that several months later became Phung Hoang, which Americans translated as "Phoenix." Poor translation led to repetitive joking that naming a VCI elimination program after a mythic bird that rises from ashes only demonstrated an inevitable resurrection of the communist rural apparatus. However, in a Vietnamese cultural context, the *phung hoang* does no such thing. Instead, it symbolizes virtue and decency and even has the cosmological connotation of a "protector of the south." Phung Hoang as a program was not evil in intent, and although its effectiveness is debatable, I believe its performance in terms of identifying the opposition was outstanding, even though many of the neutralizations were incidental to non–Phung Hoang activity. Despite Bill Colby's assignment of Gage McAfee three years later to review the problem, I don't think there was ever adequate safeguard for persons accused under the "An Tri" detention procedures.

30. The tone of the paper is indicative of the frustration we felt in spring 1967. We also understood that the ultimate reader would be Komer, so our paper should be starkly severe, with compromise his option. The handwritten draft of sixteen pages on yellow legal-size note paper is part of the Binh Collection.

Warner, much later promoted to general officer, was a sharp-minded former province advisor who also participated in the PROVN study. Gibney, much later a colonel and brigade commander in Germany, was a West Point contemporary of Warner's and had also been a province advisor. In 1964–65 he worked on Hoc Tac planning with Bob Montague. He was just completing an assignment with the 1st Cavalry Division.

31. This condition would represent restoration (even strengthening) of the joint sign-off for province piaster funds that was casually cancelled by USOM Director Killen at the end of 1964. We recommended taking this revived concept right to the highest binational level.

32. Bob Matteson arrived in late February as OCO director in II Corps and held the same position for CORDS. I provided early orientation in Binh Dinh, and we kept in touch.

33. Bob Montague and I continued as good friends. He was instrumental in returning me to Viet Nam in December 1968 for a special project. I didn't see Komer again until we met, in a friendly way, at a social gathering in Bill Colby's house about ten years later.

Reflection 1967

1. Like many prominent and politically active Vietnamese, he knew Lansdale in 1955, so it was logical for him to approach someone who could provide reassurance or warning.

2. The Geneva Conference did not establish South Viet Nam as a separate nation, and the GVN of 1965 was a consequence of the assassination of the previous head of state.

3. Such as referring to our prime opponent, the Viet Nam communists, as "North Vietnamese leaders," when in fact most of them were central Vietnamese and members of a political party that was organized nationally.

4. The last term caused Ev to pun, "We think we're revolutionary, but we're really just revolting."

5. This concept, a more accurate understanding of what we were attempting, could have been *phuc hung* or *phuc hoi* in Vietnamese. It was always difficult to find good equivalencies in translation for the two languages, and that produced confusion or sometimes worse, such as the Phung Hoang/Phoenix mismatch. It would have been better just to introduce Vietnamese-specific terminology and educate Americans as to its meaning. Twitching, occasionally I had to use "pacification" or its "RD" variant in conversation and memoranda with Americans simply because that was the accepted vernacular.

6. When ARVN, egged on by Americans, made an attempt to cut the Laotian corridor in 1971, circumstances were different. We asked them to do what we had been unwilling to attempt three and a half years earlier. I did not ever consider an invasion, limited or otherwise, of North Viet Nam, because that would have been strategic insanity.

7. In fact, some candidates were disqualified and certain election symbols not allowed. Despite those inhibitions, one ostensible "peace" candidate (Truong

Dinh Dzu) obtained a significant percentage of the vote, and nongovernment senatorial tickets and independent deputies were elected. Dzu was subsequently arrested and jailed for advocating negotiation with the communists.

8. I avoid simplistic parallels with contemporary situations, but analogy to the botch-up in Iraq is clear. We are awfully good at deploying divisions and not very good at first (above all) constructing the concept (ideals and purpose) and operating political apparatus that troop engagement is supporting. So we wind up chasing the other guys all over their terrain before asking ourselves, "Should we be doing something different?" or "Should we be here at all?"

9. The problem was not that having distinct military and civil (recovery and development) components was wrong; the problem was that those two were still insufficiently coordinated and lacked a dynamic political component.

Chapter 13

1. I received more than sixty letters from summer 1967 through late 1968, and I retained those I believed most informative. From late 1968 through 1969 I was in and out of Viet Nam a couple of times and was less dependent on correspondents, so I saved fewer letters from that period. Excerpted letters and notes are part of the Ngo Van Binh Collection.

2. Final official results determined that Tran Van Lam's ticket of senatorial candidates did win the election. Tran Van Lam was a principled businessman, frequent elected official, and the last foreign minister of the Republic of Viet Nam.

3. Dodson was consistently one of the best field evaluators.

4. Don, one of my cousins, served with the US Marines.

5. Sau was the clever and personable intelligence agent who inserted himself into Saigon in 1964. The "dear friend" is Nguyen Chanh Thi. The address is for Thi's small house where Sau gained acceptance as a housekeeper.

6. Matteson was DEPCORDS for II Corps. He applied field practice suggested by Joe Vaccaro and me when we provided his field orientation in the spring.

7. When I left, Paul, heading Reports and Evaluations, was already back from Kien Hoa about three months, and the Vietnamese cadre evaluators were very comfortable with him. Now, while he was absent on vacation, they missed his understanding awareness of their capabilities.

8. John Lybrand worked with the Special Forces cadre program, so it was natural for those whom we brought into OCO/CORDS to share their concern with

him. The leadership difficulty referred to by Nhat and John was at the R&E branch level. John and I had some differences, but I never doubted his commitment to our Vietnamese friends.

9. There is some irony, but not contradiction, in that, given his liaison with COSVN (Central Office for South Viet Nam), Sau was surely informed that there would be a major offensive for the spring festival (Tet).

10. Tran Ngoc Chau, a significant member of the recently elected legislature, was traveling in the United States. So he was abroad during the first phase of the Spring Offensive. I assisted him with some appointments in Washington, DC, and witnessed his concern for declining American support for South Viet Nam.

11. I provided in the "Reflection 1967" section my reasoning for concluding that US policy in Viet Nam ought to turn toward achieving withdrawal. In September I was invited by friends working on the Pentagon Papers study to review reference material and their drafts. Previously, in Viet Nam, we had assumed that inane decisions made by the US government must have been based on faulty intelligence, especially during 1959–61. When Dan Ellsberg showed me his draft and documentation for early decision making, I was disturbed to learn that in fact the intelligence reporting during that period was outstanding. So then I understood that, even before 1962, our government ignored field reporting and analysis and repetitively wallowed in wishful thinking while deliberately deceiving American citizens.

12. A few of us thought the spring 1968 debacle might provide opportunity for Nguyen Chanh Thi to return as a field commander. Unfortunately he did a couple of untimely interviews, critical of the government's inept performance and corruption, that were played back to Saigon.

13. Lieutenant Colonel Lap was commander of the 51st Regiment (Quang Ngai) in 1965 and sector commander for Quang Nam in 1966. In 1968 he attended and graduated from the regular Command and General Staff course at Leavenworth. In his letter he identified a key aspect of the 1968 strategic situation, how American public opinion would react.

14. Tran Huu Tri completed his first enlistment with the 40th ARVN Regiment and then worked with the Special Forces cadre project before, with others, joining the OCO/CORDS evaluation branch. After Tet 1968 he rejoined the South Vietnamese army and, following an assignment to assist the US 199th Brigade, was detailed to MACVCORDS, where he continued special assignments.

15. The north-south highway was not the equivalent of a US interstate. It was just two lanes, and it wound through communities along the way. But the drive and

the opportunity to take a through-the-windshield look at small-town Taiwan was always fun.

16. Bob Montague later told me he offered the DCM a choice between kindly responding to a request that had necessary clearances or deciding whether he would rather take a call from Ambassador Colby, Ambassador Bunker, or General Abrams. The DCM, he said, made the smart choice.

17. I thought that was a bridge burned, but he invited me to lunch before I returned to Taiwan, and we met from time to time in subsequent years.

18. I did not know her brother, but I knew many like him, and by placing the girl within a family context that they understood, she became other than an object of lust, and I was understood as having an interest that was not claiming her for myself.

19. The Pacification Attitude Analysis System (PAAS), administered by Pacification Studies Group (PSG), did so organize, and like the Hamlet Evaluation System (HES), the significance was (1) specific information from individual reports, and (2) what could be interpreted as the trend over several months.

20. I did not assume a familiar relationship with him until invited to call him Bill early in 1971, so during this period I always addressed him as Ambassador Colby. When in conversation with Vietnamese, I would refer to him as Ambassador Colby or Mr. Colby.

21. There are other forms of spelling—Long Tieng and Long Cheng—but the one I have provided was the one most familiar to me. General Lam Son, our good friend, arranged for a medal for Phil issued by the RVN. I was in occasional touch with Phil's parents until first his father and then his mother died. I know where he is buried in Kankakee, Illinois.

22. Everet Bumgardner, note, 22 May 1969, Binh Collection. Actually, I was scheduled to complete the language program in late September 1969.

23. William Colby to Dan Oleksiw, 26 May 1969, Binh Collection.

24. Dan Oleksiw to Frank Scotton, 5 June 1969, Binh Collection.

25. Thompson had gone missing in 1967 while on vacation with Connie Mangskaw and Helen Ling and her husband in the Cameron Highlands of Malaysia. Dick Noone never solved the puzzle, and years later Connie and Helen told me they couldn't even imagine what could have happened that afternoon when "Jim just went out for a walk."

26. Issan (Northeast Thailand) is variously spelled Isan, Isaan, and the form that I use: Issan.

27. Hai described Thieu as "a little honest," indecisive, and conspiratorial. Hai also

told me about the capture of Tran Ngoc Chau's communist brother Hien and Hien's confession that implicated Chau.

28. Len, a retired US Air Force pilot who had led a P-47 squadron during World War II and once commanded the air force test pilot school, was later killed when flying a Pilatus Porter, shot down April 1972 in Laos.

29. Although many knew about suspect 9th Division statistics, Ewell received a third star and command of II Field Force in spring 1969; his deputy commander, Gen. E. B. Roberts, was given command of the 1st Cavalry in May 1969 (where he emphasized kill counts), and 9th Division Chief of Staff Ira Hunt was promoted to general officer (General Ewell took care of his boys). Figures supplied by Vann are reported in Frank Scotton, Operations Memorandum, For the Record, "Thailand and Vietnam Observations July 1969," 17 July 1969, Binh Collection. Additional material concerning the "Bloody 9th" is in a separate file folder in the Binh Collection. In 1971 an Army Inspector General Report made critical reference to 9th Division's 1968–69 operations. The Ewell perspective is provided in Julian J. Ewell and Ira A. Hunt, Jr., *Sharpening the Combat Edge: The Use of Analysis to Reinforce Military Judgment* (Washington, DC: Department of the Army, 1974).

30. Despite Tran Van Hai's mentioning Hien and Chau to me, I still had not made the connection (clear in retrospect) that it was Chau whom Vann wanted to help escape.

31. I believe through spring 1967, when we occasionally met in Saigon, Tran Ngoc Chau still believed in the possibility of independent regional (South Viet Nam) economic and political development. The book *Phuc hung lang xa* (in Binh Collection), which he published in Saigon in February 1967, was a description of how he believed struggle in the countryside could still be won. He campaigned, and won, on that premise in the 1967 election for Lower House. But when we met in Washington just at the beginning of the 1968 Tet Offensive, I could see he was profoundly affected. He decided that he ought to work for a political resolution to the war.

32. Decades later Darryl was US ambassador to Thailand.

33. President Thieu's determination, demonstrated through the following several months, to arrest Chau and unconstitutionally try, convict, and jail him was intensified by the embarrassing revelation that Huynh Van Trong, his special assistant for political affairs, was a real communist agent arrested in July 1969. Vu Ngoc Nha, a northern Catholic communist who cleverly attached himself to Father Hoang Quynh and then worked his way into Ngo family circles during

the Diem presidency, recruited Trong and assisted his placement into the Thieu orbit. I think they were both repatriated to the communist side at Loc Ninh in 1973, whereas Chau refused.

34. Scotton, Operations Memorandum, For the Record, "Thailand and Viet Nam Observations, July 1969," 17 July 1969, Binh Collection.

Chapter 14

1. My experience might have caused the Department of State to later insist that non-State officers must take the FSI consular course before confirmation as a consular officer.

2. "North Kalimantan People Rise Up, Overthrow Corrupt Alliance Government" was typical of such slogans. Painted characters were the simplified form popularized since 1949 in the People's Republic of China.

3. The Sarawak Rangers, Walter told me, were founded in 1862 as an Iban rural constabulary. They cooperated with the British SAS during the mid–1860s confrontation with Indonesia. Supported by the Royal Malaysian Regiment, stationed in Sarawak, they were in 1969 and 1970 the most effective force against communist insurgents.

4. When I met him in December 1969, that prop was no longer necessary, but the tattoo was still visible and part of his legend.

5. Although these few Borneo pages digress, they illustrate how my Viet Nam experience established the pattern of conduct (get into the country, learn from the people, analyze) that I repeated elsewhere. My impression is that Sarawak politics at the time of this writing are not very different (nor are our own) from those of forty or fifty years ago. A professional politician class takes large donations from entities with interest in legislation, votes itself generous salary and benefits, and all the while claims to represent and serve the electorate. It is the worst form of government, Churchill admonishes, except for all others.

6. A leader grant was invitational travel for a foreign person to visit the United States to attain improved understanding of our country and domestic and foreign policies. My judgment was questioned, but upheld, in the case of inviting a SUPP leader to accept a grant.

7. When I did read those comments in 1995, I realized that the author, being ten years or so older than I, probably born about 1928, imbibed social attitudes (from family and community) that reflected common prejudice of the very early twentieth century. I was more fortunate for being influenced by the

social-democratic practice of my own family. The Part II format, which allowed a rating officer to say behind an officer's back what would not have been dared face-to-face, was later discontinued.

8. There are similarities in affectations adopted by ambassadors and entertainment celebrities.

9. Seven years earlier, Tuy was the dynamic captain who (in concert with US Army Captain Howard Walters) taught me salient characteristics of the war in central Viet Nam. In 1963 and 1964 he had problems with senior officers because of criticizing corrupt practices. In 1968, while at Banmethuot with CCS (MACSOG), his daughter Nhung was killed on the first day of the Tet Mau Than Offensive. He was heartbroken. In March 1970 he was assigned to Binh Dinh as sector chief of staff.

10. Gordon Huddleston to Frank Scotton, 17 December 1969, Binh Collection.

In 1974, when assigned to Washington, I tried to contact Bob Kelly but could never catch him by phone. When I mentioned that to Ev, he said Kelly had told him two years earlier that he didn't want any contact with "the old gang" because he needed to focus on his family. I respected that choice, but missed seeing him again.

Brigadier General Montague, hired as director of the Special Olympics in 1974, died in October 1996. Robert Matteson left government service in 1972.

11. We learned that Sau was born in 1904 in Thai Binh and entered the Communist Party in 1950. He first operated in the north against the French and then in 1954 was sent to Phnom Penh to contact Nguyen Si Sau (Tam Rau). He operated a strategic intelligence cell, and at his trial he admitted having contact with a member of the SVNLF but claimed that person was a patriot and not a communist.

A dozen years later, Ev and I had lunch with Ed Lansdale in McLean. We mentioned our embarrassment at having been fooled so neatly by Sau. Lansdale replied that there was only one sure way to avoid that possibility: "Never leave your office. Just shuffle papers, and you can't be fooled. Of course you'll never get anything done, either."

12. When Tran Van Hai several months later was reassigned to be commander of the 44th Special Zone, I asked him to continue residual influence for Chau's welfare.

13. Jeffrey Woods, "Counterinsurgency, the Interagency Process, and Vietnam: The American Experience," in *The US Army and the Interagency Process: Histor-*

ical Perspectives, ed. Kendall D. Gott and Michael G. Brooks (Fort Leavenworth, KS: Combat Studies Institute Press, 2008).

14. The US mission pushed and prodded as well, because CORDS needed a counterpart.

15. "Central Revolutionary Development Council" is the name used by Americans, so for simplicity I apply it here, even though it perpetuated the difference in terminology between English and Vietnamese.

16. Tran Van Huong, a fundamentally decent and responsible political figure, was appointed prime minister in May 1968, replacing Nguyen Van Loc. This was his second time as prime minister, the first being briefly from late November 1964 to late January 1965, empowered and then deposed by Nguyen Khanh.

17. The paragraphs sketching the new CORDS and the evolution of CPDC are not based solely on my own observation, but are also derived from conversation with friends and from reviewing files inherited from Ev Bumgardner.

Clay McManaway was the CORDS officer responsible for consulting with CPDC on a regular basis, especially from early 1969 through July 1970. He was assiduous and so effective that his reputation for excellence in planning and systems management was enhanced during this period.

Gen. Tran Thien Khiem was politely exiled in October 1964 by being made ambassador to the United States, then being transferred to Taipei in November as ambassador to the Republic of China. He had a special relationship with Pham Ngoc Thao, now deceased, and a close relationship to Nguyen Van Thieu.

Cao Hao Hon was deputy commander and then commander of the 21st Infantry Division from November 1963 through mid-1964, when he was reassigned to command the 5th Division. While with the 21st Division, he had pacification planning counsel from Lt. Col. Bob Montague and Dick Holbrooke. This was the beginning of his reputation as a competent pacification planner and coordinator. He was mild-mannered and thrived in noncommand assignments, where he could prove loyalty and administrative competency.

18. "Village and Hamlet Reorganization," Prime Minister circular letter 093-TT/NV, 2 June 1969, Binh Collection.

19. Tran Ngoc Chau's original census grievance process, while expecting to discover information about communist operatives and plans, was also intended to draw forth complaints about the government and local needs that could be resolved in the province. I think multifaceted use of census grievance was infrequent by 1970.

Chapter 15

1. Colby subsequently noted that I provided information by oral commentary and conversation as well as an "occasional" written report. Frank Scotton Officer Evaluation Report, 16 March 1971, W. E. Colby, Binh Collection.

   Concerning Be, Colby probably had in mind the episode when Vice President Humphrey visited the Vung Tau center in 1967 and asked Nguyen Be what he, Vice President Humphrey, could do to help. Be replied that we needed to get rid of corrupt people in the government.

2. There are two spellings: *phuong hoang* and *phung hoang*. I saw them both used, sometimes in the same document. I am using that which was most often applied in US memoranda and organization charts.

3. He referred to rationalizing the accumulation of GVN internal security resolutions and decrees that from 1956 through 1965 and into 1970 dealt with administrative (nonjudicial) detention procedure. Collectively these were referred to as *an tri* (security administration) law. Gage MacAfee was the lawyer officer assigned to work this issue.

4. McManaway departed Saigon for one-year academic study soon after I returned, but he had a close trusted relationship with Colby that was demonstrated three years later when Colby was CIA director and asked McManaway to work for him on a special coordinating committee.

5. Colby's accessibility was rivaled by few and, in my experience, matched only by Komer and (decades later) Stapleton Roy.

6. Americans generally translated Thong Tin Dai Chung as "people's information." Although this was not awfully inaccurate, Vietnamese thought the phrase was best translated as "mass information." The information provided in this paragraph was derived from a translation of a GVN paper, "Political Mobilization," 5 December 1969, Binh Collection, and my "DRAFT NOTES: Mass Information (Thong Tin Dai Chung)," August 1970, Binh Collection.

7. Standing office was sometimes translated as *van phong thuong truc*, but informally (by members) it was referred to as a *ban*.

8. Frank Scotton, "Thong Tin Dai Chung Su Tien Cu," draft, Binh Collection.

9. W. E. Colby DEPCORDS/MACV, "People's Information," 8 August 1970, Binh Collection. The senior Americans were Ambassador Bunker, Ambassador (DCM) Berger, General (Deputy Commander MACV) Rosson, USAID Director Mossler, and JUSPAO Director Nickel.

10. The Nhan Xa Party was basically a Thieu-period revival of the Diem-era Can Lao Nhan Vi Cach Mang Dang, which is usually abbreviated to Can Lao.

11. The minister of information thought the permanent staff a diminishing of ministerial privilege. He was from Ninh Thuan, formerly an important Can Lao personality, current member of the Nhan Xa Party Central Committee, and, most important, one of President Thieu's cousins. Even the prime minister tiptoed around Ngo Khac Tinh.

12. Memoranda for Ambassador Colby, 5 September, 7 October; Memorandum for the Record, 2 November; Memorandum for Ambassador Colby, 10 November; Memorandum for Le Van Loi, Permanent Staff Mass Information (English and Vietnamese texts), all in Binh Collection.

13. There is a real difference. GVN signifies an administration. RVN implies a constitution, rules of the political game, and representation.

14. When we knew Nguyen Be in 1965 and 1966, he was a stimulant to our hope that honest, self-sacrificing GVN officers might still tilt the balance away from the SVNLF. Although sometimes more poetry than prose, his 1966 book *Chung thuy* (in Binh Collection) is an interesting portrayal of the personal idealism that attracted Bob Kelly, Ev Bumgardner, Phil Werbiski, Jean Sauvageot, and me. His second book, *Contribution to the Vietnamese People's Struggle* (in Binh Collection), written in October 1967 and published in 1967 in Saigon, still retained some fire by calling for elimination of corruption and new approaches to administration and education. In this period he sometimes referred to himself as *tuong van* (which could be translated as "literary explicator"), causing some Americans to erroneously think the honorific was part of his name. Three years later, as we resumed long discussions, he was something of an in-house devil's advocate, tolerated but not embraced.

15. Another problem was that in 1962 there were more than 16,000 hamlets (I cannot remember the exact number), but three years later the number was 13,211 (Captain Russel Stolfi, *U.S. Marine Corps Civic Action Efforts in Vietnam, March 1965–March 1966* [Washington, DC: Historical Branch G-3 Division, Headquarters, US Marine Corps, 1968]), and by 1970 the count was about 12,000. More than 4,000 hamlets had disappeared. That was a measure of the war's impact on rural Viet Nam, and it also made the election process much more complicated at that level.

16. Kieu Mong Thu was the pen and political name for Truong Ngoc Thu, a vibrant young woman originally from the Mekong Delta who was elected from Hue. She was also one of the many persons who supported Tran Ngoc Chau during his trial.

As examples of repression: Thich Thien Minh was arrested in February 1969, tried by a military court, sentenced, and held until his release in October 1969. Trinh Cong Son, folksinger and artist (introduced by Ha Thuc Can), was in hiding since late 1969. Tran Ngoc Chau was the victim of a fabricated petition for removal of his parliamentary immunity and then held in prison after the Supreme Court ruled his trial unconstitutional.

Vu Van Mau was minister of foreign affairs during the First Republic but he resigned and shaved his head in protest after pagodas were raided in August 1963. He had a law degree from the University of Hanoi in 1937 and passed the government service examination in 1938. He told me that, when he was a district magistrate in Phu Yen in 1944, he concluded that French colonialism could not be revived after World War II. He supported Tran Ngoc Chau's legal position during the March 1970 trial.

17. Most of the memoranda I prepared for Colby's attention were unclassified. However, this one was confidential, and I do not have a copy. It may have survived as part of MACV/JOIR documents, or all copies might have been shredded.

18. Frank Scotton, Officer Evaluation Report, 16 March 1971, W. E. Colby, Binh Collection.

19. In early 1966 I asked Nguyen Be why he had not brought his family to Qui Nhon from Quang Tri. He responded that he wanted to keep his wife away from the competition among wives for tailored *ao dai*, jewelry, and home furnishings.

20. However, in the summer of 1975 Dong called me in Virginia and asked for my assistance in rectifying his son's status with INS. I resolved the difficulty.

21. Favors are also arranged in Washington. When I met an NSC staff employee, on one of his visits to Viet Nam, it was explained to me that he was appointed because his father had been an early mentor to the national security advisor. Subsequently he remained with the NSC under four presidents, so one assumes he was effective, but the initial hire had the appearance of a personal favor.

22. I think he used the words *bay ba*, which could be interpreted as "extremely stupid."

23. See the Terrorist Incident Overlay for Quang Ngai province, 31 July through 30 September 1970, which portrays widespread communist assertiveness (Binh Collection).

24. Inter-Agency "Roles and Missions" Study Group, Part II, "Revolutionary Development—Concepts and Strategy," pp. 21–22, US Mission Viet Nam, 24 August 1966, Vietnam Library and Archive, Texas Tech University.

25. "Status Report on Pacification and Development for White House Executive Group," CORDS/DMAC, September 1970, Binh Collection.

Shultz was a considerate and observant traveler. On departing one location, in drizzle, he was asked by an enthusiastic American captain if he would like to look at the PF unit that the captain was advising. The colonel accompanying us was obviously irritated, but Shultz replied affirmatively. We went upstream by boat, along a canal, still in light rain, and spent time with the captain and his Vietnamese friends. Shultz got really involved, and I was able to interpret for him with some of the soldiers. On the way back to Can Tho, we ran into a wall of tropical downpour. Shultz was not at all put off by the drenching and later wrote: "It was a very unique experience. It really hits home when one goes to the field and sees the conditions firsthand." George Shultz to Frank Scotton, note, 3 October 1970, Binh Collection.

26. Everet Bumgardner to Frank Scotton, 15 and 22 January 1971, Binh Collection.

27. Gordon had already mentioned in a note to me that the deputy province senior advisor thought he "had been placed here by JPV as a personal spy. How can any one think that John Vann does things that way?"

28. Gordon D. Huddleston, District Senior Advisor, An Phu, "Lien Doi 4/67 Ambush Sites, 1–20 October 1970," 20 October 1970, submitted with attached sheets providing dates and coordinates, enclosed with Gordon D. Huddleston to Frank Scotton, note, 29 October 1970, Binh Collection. (*Lien doi* is a composite battalion equivalent.)

29. I am not being prurient or puritanical to note this problem. Historians should not be oblivious to the sexual aspect of American attitudes toward Viet Nam and the Vietnamese reaction. Once, while having a drink on the Continental veranda, I saw an acquaintance hurrying past. When I asked where he was going, he answered that a member of the Mission Council had charged him with procuring a girl for a visiting cabinet-level official. The atmosphere of Saigon depravity was so extensive that I knew he was not joking.

30. In fact, when I lost my temper with Ha Quoc Buu on a stairway in OCO, early in 1967, an American took me by the arm and asked, "Have you just made the situation better, or worse?" I thanked him and asked Buu to excuse my rudeness. Buu and I worked together about four years later, and he told me that he remembered my apology. The correction would not have been made if someone had been reluctant to confront me.

31. The 3rd Infantry Division was not formed until it was authorized in October 1971.

32. I do not have any of the one- or two-page memos that I prepared on desertion rates, but some may have survived in MACV/JOIR files.

Lt. Col. Tran Van Vinh, commander of the Airborne Training Center, reminded me that the Airborne Division benefited from recruitment based on volunteers.

33. Phu shared some of his history with me when we met in late 1963.

A swagger stick is a small staff carried by officers and senior noncommissioned officers to denote authority. It was frequently seen in British and French colonial armies, but (George Patton aside) it was considered an affectation in the American Army and today is almost unknown.

34. I was vaguely aware that Khe Sanh would be reoccupied, but planning for an operation into Laos was relatively contained, and although I was exposed to HQ MACV rumor, I was not specifically informed.

35. I knew that about four years earlier we Americans had developed a plan for a similar operation (El Paso) but had shelved the idea due to Washington's lack of commitment. Now we were asking the Vietnamese to take on what we would not.

36. Hoang Xuan Lam was an armor officer originally from Quang Tri, educated in Hue and then the Dalat Military Academy. His father, Hoang Trong Thuan, was a Viet Nam Quoc Dan Dang political figure, and he had an ear to the Dai Viet Party through Senator Hoang Xuan Tuu, a cousin. His wife had extensive active business interests.

37. The 39th Rangers were in the Ba Gia fighting during the spring of 1965, and they were the ARVN component at Khe Sanh in 1968. Son Thuong commanded that battalion when I met him in 1963. He was rough, merciless to prisoners, as close to fearless as anyone I knew, and shrewd, and he lived and fought beside the rangers he led. In 1975 he was captured in IV Corps and died in captivity. He was unforgettable.

38. This was the second of two occasions when one of my written efforts disappeared.

39. I made an effort to stay informed as Lam Son 719 proceeded. Within a week, PAVN concentrated three or four divisions, then isolated and overran the points that were supposed to screen a narrow Route 9 corridor (the 39th Ranger LZ was lost 19–20 February after fierce resistance). Phu had been correct in his depiction of ineffective command. To the extent that President Thieu involved himself, the result was only additional confusion. American losses were dozens

of aircrew personnel and large numbers of helicopters destroyed or damaged from February through March. Thousands (and I do not have an exact number) of South Viet Nam soldiers were killed, missing, or wounded. Loss of materiel, tracked vehicles, artillery, and helicopters was astounding. The greatest loss was compromising ARVN's image as a resolute force capable of defending and maneuvering on its own. I did another, mildly worded memo commenting on the domestic and international aspect of audiences witnessing the panicked withdrawal. That memo may have survived in MACV/JOIR files.

Separate from Lam Son 719, the capable (and culpable) General Do Cao Tri was killed (along with his staff and correspondent François Sully) in a Tay Ninh helicopter crash on 23 February. I always thought one could not be financially frisky and operationally effective, but Do Cao Tri was exceptional, and his death was a significant loss for the RVN.

40. I first met Brig. Gen. Theo Metaxis when he was a colonel and II Corps advisor to General Vinh Loc. Now he was in Saigon to meet with Ambassador Colby, and, while waiting in my office, he unburdened himself. We next met in Cambodia in 1971 when he headed the equipment delivery team.

41. Bob Kelly was directed to prepare a rebuttal for Ambassador Bunker (versus Schell Quang Ngai–Quang Tin reports), but Washington concluded that Kelly's report "was too critical of the GVN for publication." Bob Kelly to Frank Scotton, 4 January 1968 and 23 February 1968, Binh Collection.

42. Euphemistic terms (*extreme interrogation* or *rigorous interrogation*) are unacceptable.

43. One case of rape and murder in northern Binh Dinh was afterward the subject of a book and film.

44. Etymologically, use of the term *gook* originated during the Philippine Conquest, and like the origin of *barbarian*, it indicates those who do not speak "our language."

45. Discussion with author in Deland, Florida, 2009; name withheld on request, two tours (1969–70) with the US 25th Division.

46. Ambassador Colby's assignment would have concluded that spring anyway, but family circumstances, including his daughter Catherine's health, precluded extension. Mrs. Colby, Barbara, was also outspokenly against the Phung Hoang program and bombing in Cambodia. Everet Bumgardner to Frank Scotton, 22 and 25 January 1971, Binh Collection.

47. The Program Liaison Division consulted with, and supported, the Ministry of Information and generally maintained contact with other ministries and RVN offices. Paul Turner was division head until his death.

48. When I departed Viet Nam in 1967, the motivating trigger was incompatibility between my insistence on a field position and Komer's unwillingness to take a chance assigning me as a province senior advisor. Although the timing of my 1971 transfer to JUSPAO from CORDS could suggest that the Lam Son 719 report impaired my relationship with Bill Colby, that was not the case. He returned to Washington three months later, but while in Saigon he continued consideration for my family and, by agreement with Ed Nickel, occasionally issued special tasking. Much later we were in touch while in Washington. He reached out to us while transiting Bangkok a few years later, and when he visited Fort Bragg in May 1990 we hosted a dinner for him with members of the Army Special Operations Command.

Chapter 16

1. I don't talk with a visitor from behind my desk.
2. Nick was from Rhode Island. I did value his advice, and he made excellent pan pizza.
3. I bit on that bullet by responding positively to a request for Air America travel by Minister Ngo Khac Tinh to Banmethuot, with the provision that I travel in the party. During the return flight I expressed the conviction that in the spirit of national self-sufficiency our future air travel should be by Air Viet Nam or VNAF.
4. Dang Van Sung was the influential Dai Viet publisher of *Chinh luan* newspaper, someone John Vann and I had spoken with in the past, and we quoted him when finalizing our 1965 paper "Harnessing the Revolution."
5. Congressman McCloskey was a US Marine combat veteran (Purple Heart, Silver Star, and Navy Cross) of the Korean conflict.
6. Immediately on return I dictated a detailed sixty-four-page memorandum for the record and a separate three-page memo providing notes from my conversation with a wounded PAVN prisoner. "Congressional Visit to MR-1 and Binh Dinh Province," 13 April 1971, Binh Collection.

   More than eleven years later I worked at John Gunther Dean's direction when he was US ambassador to Thailand. He was prone to exaggeration (I heard him say during a Thailand Fulbright committee meeting, "I was the Marshall Plan."), a consistently successful promoter of his own advancement and assignments, and often manipulative and insensitive to those who worked with him. (In a Bangkok core country team meeting I witnessed him bring an embassy counselor almost to tears over an unimportant procedural matter.) But Dean could be really perceptive at identifying and defining elements in a problem, and when he harnessed his enormous ego to seek solutions, he might be successful when others would hang back.

7. That legal officer was W. Gage McAfee, the MACVCORDS legal advisor, especially warmly regarded by Ambassador Colby and one of the pallbearers at his 1996 funeral service.

8. The chairman of the Quang Nam province council told Congressman Waldie that the Province Security Committee met once a week for half a day and might review more than fifty cases with the accused absent and no defender. The intent was basically to determine the extent of punishment.

In March 1971 Binh Dinh reported thirty-one VCI in category A and B killed, but of those thirty-one, only three or four had been previously identified by dossier. Congressman Waldie pressed on this discrepancy, but it was never clarified. My own supposition was that it reflected RVN manipulation to meet a monthly quota.

The Phung Hoang advisor, an army major, had never been in the Province Interrogation Center, National Police Headquarters (province office), or the detention center. He was not sure of Province Security Committee composition. He thought that some who should have stayed in the system "fall out." That prompted Congressman Waldie to wonder whether "some should fall out who stay in." The Phung Hoang advisor also claimed that, of the sixty-two cases processed in March, some persons were released. Examination of the Vietnamese minutes showed instead that three cases were suspended (postponed), but there had been no releases.

9. Trying to comprehend this particular part of CORDS architecture (since September 1969) led to the arrival of the American who was the separate team PSCD chief (not reporting to the province senior advisor or Dep CORDS) supervising the "provincial interrogations officer" (not a Phung Hoang advisor). That produced more conversation with the PSCD chief about how long it took to break a detainee under blindfolded interrogation.

10. In spring 1971 the 40th Regiment was in Northern Binh Dinh, but the 41st, 47th, and 53rd (with OPCON from the 23rd Division) were all in the highlands. About a year later there was significant realignment following the communist 1972 offensive.

11. The province as a whole had 179 hamlets rated at A or B (mostly in the more secure lowland environment not far from National Highway 1), 50 C hamlets, and 31 at D, E, or V. Another 63 hamlets were abandoned.

A high percentage of bombing sorties would have been American.

12. On 28 March, enemy sappers penetrated FSB Mary Ann. American casualties were thirty-three killed and more than eighty wounded. The base was closed on April 24.

13. There is documentation of the crime and cover-up. In 1996, while in Viet Nam on orders for consultation with our Hanoi embassy and some offices of the Socialist Republic of Viet Nam, and traveling by road from south to north with USIS officer Bill Bach, we stopped in the same place. The curator of a small museum was hospitable, and some Quang Ngai high school students were merely curious about our speaking Vietnamese. Their casualness, very different from what Bill and I felt, made us realize that the awful event was part of their parent's past, not their new life.

14. LZ English was larger than I remembered from 1966. It could easily handle C-130s and was the principal base for the 173rd Airborne Brigade.

15. Later, Colonel Mendheim provided the figure of 588 hamlets.

16. In March 1975 I met Congressman McCloskey again during special congressional delegation travel in Viet Nam, just before the RVN collapse. Later, back in Washington, he asked whether I could be available to work with the committee addressing MIA issues with Viet Nam. I explained that I was already scheduled for assignment in Burma. He asked me to think about it, but the next day he called back to tell me that Gareth Porter (research critic of US policy) had told some committee members my name would be "anathema" to the new Vietnamese government. McCloskey suggested that, in order to limit damage to my reputation, I should speak with each of the congressional members involved. He made necessary appointments, so I did speak with Representatives Montgomery, Shroeder, and Gilman.

17. For an example of the Mass Information Program's intent, see Ministry of Interior Letter 177-BNV/NDTV/TH5, 31 March 1971, Binh Collection: "According to this concept, all PSDF activities and seminars will be within the framework of the People's Information Plan, so as to exhort people's voluntary and active participation in and support for all Government programs under the 1971 Local Community Self Defense and Development Plan." Concerning tasking, see Responsibility, Organization, and Operation of the Special Mass Information Section, Ministry of Information, 31 March 1971 (Vietnamese and English translation texts), Binh Collection.

The following year Major Lam was reassigned to the Ministry of Defense.

18. Frank Scotton for Nguyen Xuan Hue, "Mass Information Program," Appendix 6, memorandum, 22 April 1971; "People's Information Background"

(Bumgardner draft), 18 April 1971; and Mass Information Program: Second Semester 1971, May 1971 (Vietnamese and English translation), all in Binh Collection.

19. PLD Program Review, 27 April 1971, audiotape cassette, Binh Collection.

20. Accepting personal responsibility for being a husband and father was important, and while I made conscientious effort, my wife was adjusting to living in Viet Nam with a husband who was frequently away from home. This was a rare opportunity for her to see a different part of the country. Wilbur thoughtfully left a welcoming note.

21. William Colby had a talent for resolving stalemate by offering just a bit of what was requested, encouraging the other party to believe that the remainder might be delivered later. In this instance John got the something that was better than nothing. I was glad to have the opportunity for a few days in the field, while WEC actually strengthened the commitment previously made with Ed Nickel.

22. William E. Colby's comments and a summary of discussion by other participants are in notes from the meeting, Can Tho, 7 May 1971, Binh Collection.

23. Despite the reduction of print support to RVN, USIA planned to maintain printed materials describing American policies for distribution to Vietnamese recipients.

24. In 1966 I introduced John and Kelly. I liked and respected them both, and they knew that. I was disappointed afterward when each said of the other, "He talks too much!"

25. His delicate phrasing concerning a bullshit office position was true enough, compared to his field assignment, and he expressed it as only a friend could to a friend.

26. Y Duat was in Banmethuot, K'sor Rot was a 1970 reelected senator on the Vu Van Mau ticket, and Nay Luett was usually in Pleiku or Phu Bon, but in mid-June 1971 he was made minister of ethnic minorities.

27. Le Ngoc Trieu, from Nam Dinh, was commander of the Presidential Guard in 1958, had staff and deputy commander assignments, and in 1967 was commander of the Quang Trung Training Center.

   A Catholic from Quang Binh, Vo Van Canh was contemptuous of tribal citizens, had been mayor of Vung Tau with a shady record, and was an undistinguished regimental commander. The previous 23rd Division commander was Truong Quang An, an airborne officer (and nephew of Ton That Thien) killed with his wife (herself a former airborne brigade medic) in a helicopter crash near Duc Lap Special Forces camp in September 1968.

Nguyen Trong Bao was an outstanding officer whom I met near Bong Son in 1966. He believed a leader should command from the front rather than from the rear and was later killed in action in 1972 in Quang Tri. Le Quang Luong was commander of the 1st Airborne Brigade when Nguyen Trong Bao was chief of staff with responsibility for expanding the brigade to division strength. In 1972 Luong became deputy Airborne Division commander, and then division commander later in the same year. Nguyen Khoa Nam commanded the 3rd Airborne Brigade until he was assigned as 7th Division commander in 1970. Nguyen Trong Bao told me that Nam was a protégé of Cao Van Vien, but I still thought Nam was a better officer than many others. Tran Van Hai, a ranger, had been DG of National Police until he was replaced in January 1971 by Gen. Tran Thanh Phong, then Hai commanded the 44th Special Zone, but he could have been made available.

Nguyen Duc Thang remained shelved, an honest officer of good reputation, never trusted by Nguyen Van Thieu. In January 1972, Thang was placed on extended leave of absence.

Nguyen Van Hieu was 5th Division commander in 1971, had previously served in II Corps, planned the relief of Plei Me (for which Vinh Loc took the credit), and had even briefly commanded the 22nd Division. Soon after Vann and I spoke, Hieu was made the scapegoat for an ARVN failure (especially on the part of new corps commander Nguyen Van Minh) at Snoul in Cambodia, but I still think he had the right background and ability for appointment as II Corps commander.

28. HES Hamlet Map, MACV CORDS Reports and Analysis Directorate, 31 May 1971, Binh Collection.

29. John arranged for Huddleston's assignment to Advisory Team 29 in Phu Cat (Binh Dinh), and Hud provided John with useful information during the next several months until he married Khue in Can Tho and was reassigned to Fort Benning. He died in Colorado in late December 2009.

30. Even into 1970, American artillery occupied Fire Support Bases 5 and 6, then it was replaced by ARVN. On March 31 a ground attack on FSB 6 by the 66th PAVN Regiment resulted in abandonment of the position. An American five-man IOS (Integrated Observation System) team had two KIA, one WIA, one MIA, and one who later made his way to a friendly position. FSB 6 was reoccupied April 3, and the four destroyed artillery pieces were replaced.

31. Richards was John's most frequent pilot, a constant companion, and as daring as John. He understood John would be immediately motivated to go where he had just been warned not to.

32. A critical part of the plan was for the LOH to touch and go as we had, thus with no time to evacuate even one or two seriously wounded. But when John saw me days later in Saigon, he said that on the spot ARVN soldiers rushed two wounded toward the LOH, so the pilot hesitated, mortar rounds began to fall, and in the panic a soldier was struck by the tail rotor. That immobilized the LOH, and it was quickly destroyed by incoming. It took three more days to get the pilot out, but for now FSB 5 held.

33. John was especially irritable because one night, while he was occupied with a staff meeting, I used his name as leverage to get lifted out to Plei MN, which was home to WR, a 1963 travel companion. He was not there, but I spent an interesting night with his family and friends before getting picked up the next morning.

34. My trip report may survive in JOIR files. I never read any of van den Haag's pieces, but he was a caricature of a visitor who came to look at the war but really wanted to play.

35. Following two important interim positions, in early September 1973 he was named CIA director.

36. It is specious to suggest that Weyand had a great background in "pacification planning and operations" dating from 25th Division and field force command. Surely he was a better choice than Julian Ewell or Ira Hunt would have been, but otherwise a number of other military officers would have done as well, and Jake knew the mechanics, personnel, and substance better than Weyand. Vann would have been the best choice, but he was not tolerable by embassy, CIA, or MACV.

    Ev was, family aside, miserable in Washington, writing a few months later, "I am so identified with VN no one wants me assigned to them." And he advised me to extend in Viet Nam for another year. Ev to Frank, 14 February 1972, Binh Collection.

37. I thought that was a one-time off-the-cuff expression, but WEC years later repeated his description of Buddhists rejecting modernization in an oral interview, 2 June 1981, with Ted Gittinger for the LBJ Library. And in 1996, in his keynote speech for the 2nd Triannual Vietnam Symposium at the Viet Nam Center of Texas Tech University, he refers to Buddhists in 1963 "upset with the modernizing tendencies of the secular government." Had I been in the audience I might have respectfully questioned the extent to which President Diem's government was really secular, since it appeared Christian Catholic. I also would have expressed doubt whether Emmanuel Mounier "ism" represented

the modernizing philosophy most suitable for Viet Nam in the second half of the twentieth century.

38. Oral interview, 1 March 1982, with Ted Gittinger for the LBJ Library.

39. By contrast, I do think General Abrams was hierarchal and much more insistent on the chain of command. Resulting friction with Komer and other civilians was due to Abrams's view that "chain of command" encompassed "control of information."

40. William E. Colby, Major, FA, to Chief, Special Branch, Office of Strategic Services, Washington, DC, "Recommended Special Operations," 23 May 1945, Binh Collection.

Chapter 17

1. Bob Lincoln's plan was to slowly downsize JUSPAO by reducing support commitments to the RVN on the USIS side and not filling positions as military personnel completed their tours and departed.

   The JUSPAO compound was formerly property of a French rubber enterprise. The house in which we lived was taken over by a northern cadre family in the summer of 1975. A friend recently in Ho Chi Minh City told me the family now runs a small business from that address.

2. Ngo Cong Duc was a southern Catholic born in Tra Vinh and well connected to church hierarchy. He was controversial and, like many ambitious politicians, was frequently accused of the same corruptive practices that he charged others with practicing. In 1970 he supported Tran Ngoc Chau in his conflict with President Thieu.

3. Justice Tran Minh Tiet cast the dissenting vote. Previously, while he was chief justice (up to November 1970), Tran Minh Tiet ruled that Tran Ngoc Chau's 1970 arrest and trial were unconstitutional. Despite the ruling, President Thieu insisted that Chau remain in prison. Tran Minh Tiet was a southern Catholic from Hau Nghia and a former minister of justice. After 1975 he was jailed and "reeducated" by the communist government, eventually released, and allowed to depart Viet Nam.

   Huong was sixty-eight, with failing eyesight and high blood pressure, but still ambitious and susceptible to flattery. He was promised some responsibility for action against corruption, and his standing beside Thieu did persuade some voters that there was still a chance for reform.

4. Ton That Thien was referring to the political expeditor for President Thieu, who

died of a stroke in December 1970. Nguyen Cao Thang, a Catholic from Quang Tri, made a fortune in pharmaceuticals, was an influential Can Lao Party member and supporter of President Diem, then played the same role with President Thieu. He was especially adept at persuading members of the assembly to adopt positions in return for "other considerations."

Tran Van Lam's senate ticket had almost failed due to 1967 election irregularities. He was an honest businessman and political figure committed to developing a separate democratic southern identity. I first knew him in 1966, when he was chairman of the Commercial and Industrial Bank.

Gen. Nguyen Van Hieu, a notably honest officer of integrity, was not assigned as special assistant to the vice president until February 1972.

5. Nguyen Van Bong had a good relationship with Tran Van Huong dating back to 1964, when both were members of the Council of Notables. Bong was from Go Cong, a Buddhist, and born in 1929, so at forty-two he was a relatively young and dynamic personality compared with many other political figures. He was by original profession a lawyer, and he had a fascination for administrative philosophy and regulation. He was principal founder of the National Progressive Movement and seemed to me to have Dai Viet (Tan Dai Viet) inclination, but he was widely respected by other political movements, even the An Quang lower-house bloc. Two months after the assassination, his widow, Le Thi Thu Van, now solely responsible for three young children, was provided with employment at the Vietnamese-American Association. In May 1972, two members of a communist "special action team" confessed to the assassination.

6. Frank Scotton, Officer Evaluation Report, 16 June 1971–15 June 1972, Binh Collection.

7. The 173rd Airborne Brigade withdrew from northern Binh Dinh in August. In October the 101st Airborne Division withdrew from major operations. By the end of that month American troop strength in Viet Nam was less than 200,000, on the way to less than 160,000 by the end of December. In November, President Nixon announced further withdrawals that would bring the overall number to fewer than 140,000 by February 1972. As units withdrew, remaining soldiers were anxious to stand down. Maj. Joe Dye, a friend from my time with Special Forces, told me in October that an American unit on a Tay Ninh firebase refused to patrol beyond the perimeter.

8. Two ARVN Special Forces officers, one being Maj. Nguyen Van An (I regret not remembering the other's name), during a discussion of the process told me that most CIDG chose entry to Border Ranger battalions because there was no

alternative in remote locations. They seemed skeptical of long-term viability.

9. "Ben Hai" refers to the Ben Hai River, which flowed through a portion of the 1955 Geneva Agreement DMZ.

When MACV, according to Jake, reported that desertion was being addressed, the sweet perfume of wishful thinking should have been recognized. Desertion was *always* being addressed. The SEER reports (System Evaluating Effectiveness RVNAF), like the HES, might have helped make the case for improvement, but SEER validity was debatable. Senior American officers would also typically submit narratives, at least as end-of-tour submissions. Having seen quite a few, I was wary, because each Vietnamese counterpart was so positively described that you would wonder why there was ever need for change.

I do not know how determined an effort was made for change of 22nd Division command, but one did take place in early March 1972. It is questionable whether the change was for the better. Almost as soon as the new commander (Le Duc Dat) was named, American consensus (including Jake, influenced by John) was that a grave mistake had been made.

10. Nguyen Khoa Nam retained command of the 7th Division until November 1974, when he was assigned as IV Corps commander. Rather than surrender or run away, he committed suicide on 30 April 1975.

11. In 1969 Toan was cited by the inspectorate for corruption. In 1971, while in Tra Bong, I was told merchants had to pay him to open the road to the coast. In January 1972 *Song than* newspaper ran a detailed series describing how Toan worked through an associate (Madam Thanh) to procure young women for his pleasure. Toan was replaced later that month. (Translations of articles in Binh Collection.)

12. The best corps commander I was referring to was Ngo Quang Truong.

Nguyen Van Minh replaced Quang in command of the 21st Division in 1965, when Quang took IV Corps in replacement of Nguyen Van Thieu. As Quang rose in proximity to Thieu, so did Minh. In April 1968 Quang moved from minister for planning and development to assistant to the president, and two months later Minh was assigned as commander of the Capital Military District and governor of Saigon-Giadinh (a very lucrative position), staying almost three years until Do Cao Tri's death in February 1971.

13. HES Hamlet Map, MACV CORDS Reports and Analysis Directorate, 31 January 1972, Binh Collection.

14. Some sample leaflets and their translations are in the Binh Collection.

15. A couple of months earlier, at the beginning of January 1972, Ly Tong Ba was

put in command of the 23rd Division. John was completely satisfied with that choice, because he believed that his knowledge of Ba at Ap Bac and in Binh Duong province would enable him to energize aggressive performance.

16. Dat was briefly chief of staff for the 25th Division in 1968, but he never commanded a regiment.

17. There are good general descriptions of the 1972 offensive and some detailed accounts of specific engagements. I do not intend to duplicate what is already on the record, so I sketch only my interpretation of events.

18. The offensive in northern Binh Dinh was considered a diversion from Kontum. Actually, it was supplementary and as necessary to seizing and holding the Highland Plateau as any operation on the plateau itself. The pattern, established in 1965, seen again in 1972, and repeated once more in 1975, was to apply pressure in the highlands while simultaneously interdicting Route 19 to eliminate it as an avenue for reinforcement or withdrawal.

19. I recall that in an April embassy meeting it was reported that some soldiers of the 196th Brigade near Danang refused to patrol.

20. Colonel Nguyen Be claimed any division commander was at the mercy of JGS and the president, because no one had authority to make changes on the spot, therefore they could not respond to an immediate situation. He asserted that JGS approval was necessary even to shift artillery pieces. He also said, "When you hear us criticize JGS we really mean the President." Memorandum for the Record, Scotton draft, 8 May 1972, Binh Collection.

21. Although the regiment was not a direct descendent of the 1963–64 Tay Son company or battalion, the name itself was intended to resonate locally. Today the former RVN Binh Khe district in Binh Dinh is renamed Tay Son district.

22. Lt. Col. Willard B. Esplin, Acting Province Senior Advisor, Binh Dinh Province Monthly Report, Period Ending 30 April 1972, 2 May 1972, Binh Collection.

23. The 81st was the lineal descendent of the 91st Battalion organized by US Special Forces in November 1964 as the Project Delta reaction force and which had participated in relief of Plei Me in November 1965. It was reorganized in 1966 with additional, almost all Vietnamese, rather than tribal, companies and redesignated Lien Doan 81 Biet Kich Du, sometimes translated as brigade or group. Because of its origin with Delta, some knowledgeable PSG cadre still referred to it as "Mike Force."

CORDS/PSG had an independent reporting team in An Loc throughout the siege. By their eyewitness, the most consistently effective resistance was mounted by PSDF, rangers (particularly the 81st), and airborne. The team report (English translation) covering 4 April through 29 June is with the Binh Collection. A Vietnamese text is with Ngo Van Vu (team member) of Chantilly, Virginia.

24. It was thought that Dat might have been captured, but it now seems certain he was killed during the turmoil of withdrawal under pressure from PAVN armor and infantry. John told me that Dzu requested medical leave.

    Toan was assigned II Corps. It was thought that at least he had a fighting reputation, but many recalled that he had been dismissed by Nguyen Chanh Thi in 1965 when his armor unit retreated at Ba Gia, abandoning rangers who suffered more casualties as a result. Toan's career was revived by Hoang Xuan Lam when Lam was looking for anti-Thi officers to serve in I Corps after the 1966 "Struggle Movement," and he made Toan deputy commander of the 1st Division and later, in January 1972, commander of the 2nd Division. Nguyen Chanh Thi, exiled in Washington since 1966, attempted a return to Viet Nam on 23 February 1972. I was notified in advance and was on the tarmac to observe, but he was not permitted (nor was any other passenger) to disembark, and after three hours the Pan American flight had to leave. If Thi had instead proposed return (through the Viet Nam embassy) at the end of April or beginning of May (like Do Cao Tri in 1968), he might have been taken back for assignment and it could have been him replacing Dzu. But in February Nguyen Chanh Thi was too big a morsel for Thieu and Ky to swallow.

25. Almost immediately, Neil Sheehan began research for a comprehensive book on John and the American role in Viet Nam. When he approached me in Saigon, I told him I would not help, because it was inconceivable that a book could be written without taking a position on the war in Viet Nam. I thought John's life and death should not be a marker either for or against the war. My further, unexpressed reason was that I knew too well the dark side, and thought it best to be unresponsive across the board rather than lie about John's personal history. Three years later the war was over, Neil was still researching, and so when we met again I did agree to speak about some of what was shared in Viet Nam. When the book was published I was surprised to read that Neil had uncovered personal aspects that I would not have discussed. When I asked how he learned those unhappy details, he responded that family members had told him. I suppose talking with Neil might have been cathartic while coming to terms with personal/professional contradictions in John's life.

26. A copy of the "Heilman" Task Force Report may survive in some obscure collection of Viet Nam files, possibly USAID holdings. I do recall our findings were not popular.

27. The 21st was moved from the southern Mekong Delta (headquarters at Bac Lieu) to III Corps with the ostensible mission of reopening Route 13 to An Loc.

28. Whitehouse replaced Sam Berger. Charlie was a World War II veteran. He followed an unusual route, via the CIA, into the Department of State, and perhaps for that reason he was less hierarchical than many senior Foreign Service officers. In 1970 he was III Corps DEPCORDS, and I thought he was one of the best. In 1971 he was assistant secretary for East Asia in the Department of State before returning to Viet Nam as DCM.

29. I would be disappointed again. In June, President Thieu obtained senate approval to rule by decree, and in August, with that authority, he abolished hamlet elections and ordered province chiefs to appoint hamlet officials.

30. What follows is taken from my handwritten notes dated 29 May, supplemented by June conversations, all in the Binh Collection. There were refined and more accurate figures later, but the numbers first noted are indicative of the scale of difficulty faced by US logisticians right from the start. The later figures actually showed higher numbers in each category.

31. In 1972 Doug had an in-country reputation as the theorist created by USIA when he was sent to MIT for an academic year that resulted in a turgid tome on Viet Nam communist organization and operations.

    As decades passed, Doug maintained an important documentary research collection, first at the University of California at Berkeley and later at Texas Tech University. He significantly assisted the next generation of scholars writing about Viet Nam.

32. Col. Doan Van Nu was a career airborne officer who commanded the 1st Battalion of the Airborne Brigade in 1964. He was military attaché at the RVN embassy in Taipei while I was in Taiwan. He was brave, considerate of others, and responsible right to the end, leaving only because to stay would have surely meant execution.

33. The same source reported, early in June, that all indications were that the Hanoi population accepted the situation in North Viet Nam. People were calm and resigned and "seem grimly determined," and "Military [is] prepared to accept hardship to carry on." Handwritten notes in Binh Collection.

34. From 1966 through 1968 some "parody currency" leaflets were dropped over the North, but our 1972 issue was much more facsimile than parody. When we received samples of the 1 dong leaflet from the first press run, I found minor problems with the tabbed text, and that was corrected for subsequent printing. Samples are in the Binh Collection.

35. Avoiding restraint on RVNAF expenditure of artillery would be exceedingly important, because I had new appreciation for the quality of PAVN artillery. The excellent 130mm howitzer could fire five rounds a minute, and it outranged the American 105 and 155mm pieces, had a higher muzzle velocity, and fired heavier projectiles than the 105. The American 175 was in a different category, but there were not many, and they were not as mobile.

36. Frank Scotton, "Viet Nam Situation Update July/August," memorandum for Robert A. Lincoln, 8 September 1972, Binh Collection. I did not mention that in August, while in Binh Dinh province, I learned that B-52 strikes were placed on heavily populated rural areas to facilitate RVN operations. I went to see Deputy Ambassador Whitehouse and told him that B-52 missions against populated areas could be considered a crime against humanity. He took steps to assure restrictions.

37. "Chuong Thien" memorandum, October 1972, Binh Collection. F-6 authority was a late April 1972 alteration of An Tri detention procedure to allow province authorities to make arrests and detain on the basis of one accusatory report rather than three. The F-6 authority was suspended on September 10, I was told, but some people suspected that it was still applied when convenient.

Chapter 18

1. There are detailed accounts of the negotiations, and by comparison this summary only describes my understanding of what was involved. Any error illustrates how uninformed one can be when low on the policy totem pole.

2. Hoang Duc Nha was influential with President Thieu. I think he was a second cousin and, like the president, from Ninh Thuan. Nha studied in the United States from 1962 through 1967 and had a pretty good feel for what was admirable about our country versus what was not. In October 1972 he was just thirty and would speak his mind.

I was informed concerning the substance and tenor of the meeting from subsequent discussion with Tran Van Lam. Furthermore a young woman, Nhan Lan, who worked with me in 1971, married Vu Khiem, director of presidency administrative affairs, in December of that year. We met from time to time, and while Vu Khiem was always circumspect and loyal to office and country, he conveyed a sense of the presidency's mood. Gen. Nguyen Van Hieu, although special assistant in Vice President Huong's office, also shared his second-hand, but soundly based, impressions with me.

3. When I expressed sympathetic understanding for Thieu's obduracy, another American was surprised and exclaimed, "But Frank, I thought you didn't like him." I explained that my personal feeling had nothing to do with acknowledging that in this instance Thieu reacted as any Vietnamese should. We ought to have expected that.

4. Ironically, Thieu's own stature improved for thumbing the eye of the importuning Americans. I had often heard him and associates referred to as *liem dit nguy* (ass-kissing puppets), but vulgar references noticeably declined for a couple of months.

5. Immediately after the delayed cease-fire, the small port of De Gi (northeastern Phu Cat district) was taken by communist forces. They raised flags to mark possession. Lt. Col. Nguyen Tuy led RF to retake the town. A few months later he gave me one of the SVNLF flags. That flag is now with the Ngo Van Binh Collection. Sa Huynh, to the north in Quang Ngai province, was the scene of a larger-scale, more protracted conflict that continued until the addition of the 1st Ranger Group to reinforce elements of the 2nd ARVN Division enabled wresting that small harbor back from communist occupation.

6. The reason fewer hamlets were scored in December, I was told at the time, is that some hamlets were administratively folded into others. HES Summary Report, CORDS Reports and Analysis Directorate, 30 November 1972, and my handwritten figures from the December 1972 HES Summary, Binh Collection.

7. The other returnees for whom I had initial contact responsibility were John Fritz, James Newingham, James Rollins, and Richard Waldhaus. I knew Doug, and I had photographs of the others except for Richard Waldhaus.

The helicopter crew was CW2 Stanley Martin, CW2 James Sehl, and SP4 Carl Muse. They were responsive to guidance while we coped with an unanticipated complication.

8. Devious North Korean behavior two decades earlier was cited as the analogy. The different history of the Viet Nam Communist Party was not understood.

9. Operation Homecoming—Escort Officer Instructions, 6 February 1973, Binh Collection.

10. Frank Scotton, Memorandum for the Record, Observations, 12 February at Loc Ninh, 16 February 1973, Binh Collection. My attachment to the memorandum provides quotations from eight interesting persons I encountered at Loc Ninh that day.

11. Richard had been a US Army medic who met a young woman in a market while doing MEDCAP, fell in love, and after finishing his enlistment returned as a civilian to find her.

12. The 3rd Field Hospital was housed in the former American dependent school across from a broad, empty field (used for medevac) adjacent to Tan Son Nhut.

13. Like every other military installation, the 3rd Field Hospital was drawing down rapidly. A few weeks later the facility was signed over to the Seventh Day Adventist medical group, and they committed to maintaining the premises as a high-quality, public-access point of treatment.

14. During those two days the fuse of media interest was lit. There were rumors one of the returnees was still in Saigon, being prepared for a special mission. We were running out of time.

15. Jim Nach informed me by email in October 2011 that Rich, who had received a Bronze Star for his military service, died in 2006 and is buried in a California veterans' cemetery. In a 1975 conversation with Ambassador Whitehouse (as US foreign policy collapsed in Indo-China), he recalled "the case of the POW who didn't want to go home." Charlie said I had been lucky. I replied that there was that, but, most of all, I had the help of Jim Nach and Wayne Peterson, who both knew how to work inside a situation.

16. This is not to imply that DRV/PRG commitment to the agreement was any more than working protocols to their own advantage.

17. Tran Van Tra was transported in a US helicopter from Loc Ninh to Saigon on 29 January. The United States provided a weekly C-130 flight to Hanoi.

Aigle Azur Transport Ariens was a private carrier headquartered in France. The Saigon-based subsidiary branch operated as a distinct entity. It flew Boeing 307 Stratoliners, one flagged as Air Laos and another as Air Cambodge, on a Saigon-Hanoi route with a stopover in Vientiane. The pre–World War II 307 was the first pressurized airliner, and only ten were built before Boeing switched to bombers. After World War II Aigle Azure was able to buy one from Pan Am and four from TWA. I think by 1973 three had crashed, but two were still serviceable and flying. Maintenance (according to GX, who worked for the company part-time) was a constant problem.

The 1954 International Control Commission (ICC) is not to be confused with the International Commission of Control and Supervision (ICCS) set by the 1973 Paris Agreement.

18. I do not mean to suggest that this was determinative in the subsequent collapse of the agreement, but it is indicative of how mistrust and misunderstanding complicated initial implementation. And mine removal continued to be a sticking point. I think in April there was another Task Force 78 hiatus due to problems in DRV–United States talks after the Four-Party Joint Military Commission was dissolved.

19. Jean did not debate the point with General Woodward, but shared his reaction with me that evening.

20. I thought that recapturing FSB Bastogne and other positions between A Shau and Hue, and recovering lost territory in northern and central Binh Dinh, was especially significant.

21. Cao Van Vien was a member of President Diem's bodyguard force; then, after the attempted paratrooper coup in November 1960, he was assigned to airborne training preparatory to being named commander of the Airborne Brigade in March 1961. He refused to participate in the 1963 coup. He formed a strong connection with Nguyen Van Thieu during late 1964 to October 1965 while serving as III Corps commander and went from III Corps to chief of the Joint General Staff. His wife, Tran Thi Tao, made sure the family would be financially secure. Vien was proven brave on the battlefield but not perceptive, and he always deferred to President Thieu.

Le Van Than replaced Pham Van Phu in November 1972.

22. Having an immediately deployable strategic reserve to provide flexibility and respond to critical situations was almost impossible after US and other allied forces withdrew. Vietnamese airborne and Marine elements had played that role but were now almost permanently placed in the field to avoid a vacuum where allied forces had previously operated.

23. Le Van Phoi was my counselor when I affiliated with a Hoa Hao congregation in 1965.

24. Ton That Thien had known all of contemporary Viet Nam's national leaders, from Ho Chi Minh and Ngo Dinh Diem to, and including, Nguyen Cao Ky and Nguyen Van Thieu. Although he could be acerbic, he was overall the most perceptive administrator/scholar of his generation. I was so impressed by his intellect and facility of expression that, when Dick Holbrooke was looking for a contributor to *Foreign Policy* magazine (while Dick was editor) I brought him down the narrow alley off Truong Minh Giang to Thien's house. Ton That Thien eventually left Viet Nam and settled in Canada.

25. Andre Jean Sauvageot was Jean Sauvageot when we worked together in the 1960s and 1970s, but now is better known as Andre.

Reflection 1973

1. Ev was always my most dependable counselor and rear guard, even years later when he retired. In 1992, while I was in China on assignment, my son David had a problem in Pennsylvania. I knew that my earliest possible arrival on

the spot would require a minimum of thirty-six hours. I called Ev, and he was there the next morning, resolved the situation, and gave my son good advice. Of course he was always Uncle Ev for our family.

In 1977 we sold that house before departing for a Burma assignment. We bought another in McLean and left it rent free with Nguyen Be for him to provide assistance to other relocating Vietnamese, among them Nguyen Hung Vuong's family.

2. In the context of the Paris Agreement, the scramble out of Viet Nam, and the opening to the People's Republic of China, it was not easy to be persuasive. The branch post in Taichung was closed for budget reasons, but the branch office in Kaohsiung was retained, and overall the program in Taiwan was active and adequately funded.

3. Bill Colby told me in 1970 that in the previous year a regional assistant DEP-CORDS expressed willingness to do a second tour in Viet Nam, but only as a DEPCORDS, because that would position him for promotion. I do not know who that person was, and Colby did not provide a name, but he said the individual's qualifications did not match his ambition.

4. From President John Kennedy's 1961 inaugural address: "... we shall pay any price, bear any burden, meet any hardship, support any friend. ..."

5. Hostility toward Viet Nam persisted even after the war, to the point that from 1979 to 1992 US policy supported the Khmer Rouge rather than the less despicable replacement government installed by Viet Nam. This was so repulsive that I submitted a formal dissent message from Rangoon.

6. Ev's mention of 1968 duplicity makes it especially ironic that Kissinger was himself rebuffed by President Thieu in 1972.

7. The greatest disservice may have been ending the draft and instituting a volunteer army. Implemented with the intent to gut the antiwar movement (that was actually less antiwar and more anti-possibility that young Americans would be continuously drafted for war in Viet Nam), the policy change altered American history by switching from a citizen-based defense force in time of need to a "centurion" organization that eases expeditionary operations even today.

8. When the Nobel Peace Prize was announced for 1973, Le Duc Tho declined to accept the prize, while Henry Kissinger accepted. That is all one needs to know about each man's character. In 1973 the extent of Kissinger's toadying to the worst instincts of President Nixon, even igniting the president's wrath against others so as to demonstrate his own loyalty, was not known. Availability of tape-recorded conversations has removed that veil. We also know something

about his part in having phones of loyal staff, such as Tony Lake and Winston Lord, illegally tapped. It is incomprehensible that, decades later, presidential candidates would seek a Kissinger benediction.

9. Transcript, William E. Colby Oral History Interview with Ted Gittinger, 2 June 1981, Internet copy, p. 18, LBJ Presidential Library, Austin, TX. The village continues to be used by the contemporary government of Viet Nam to oversee hamlet affairs.

10. Defense Secretary Robert Strange McNamara on a visit to Viet Nam spontaneously clasped hands with Nguyen Khanh as symbolic of American support.

11. I take the point that Cambodian ports played an important role in supply to PAVN, especially for III Corps and IV Corps, but human reinforcement and entire maneuver units came down the trail. Troop ships were not disembarking in Sihanoukville. I also realize there would have been international cries against placing US units as a barrier from Quang Tri to the Mekong, but if that were important to secure an opportunity for RVN independence, then we should have just bitten that bullet and made withdrawal a barter point in exchange for return of PAVN to the DRV.

12. Chasing North Korean remnants beyond the narrow waist of the peninsula just above Pyongyang made a smart war turn painfully dumb.

13. Our only point of societal common bond should not be simply paying taxes.

14. Here I refer to the Second Iraq War. The First Iraq War is one to list in the smart war column, but might not have been necessary if we had unmistakably informed Iraq that we would oppose border alteration and annexation. I do have some thoughts about Afghanistan, but let's not wander far from the Viet Nam that I knew best.

The Last Chapter

1. A Coalition against Corruption, organized in late summer 1974, late effort as it was, basically represented conservative Catholic dismay over favoritism and the accumulation of wealth by persons in power.

2. *Cho chieu* is a countryside expression signifying the period just before a market closes, when pickings are slim but time is running out to make a deal.

   I first met Chau Kim Nhan years earlier, when he was director of the Central Logistics Agency with the Ministry of Defense. In October 1974 President Thieu removed him as minister of finance, not for wrongdoing but to placate popular dissatisfaction with the disintegrating economy.

3. Both officers fought with grim determination until the very end in 1975 and were taken into prison for years before finally being released and authorized travel to the United States.

4. At that time I think Hoang Tung was an alternate member of the Communist Party central committee and editor of *Nhan dan* newspaper. Le Quang Hoa was deputy chief of the Political Warfare Department. It would always be their purpose to promote the party line and be deceptive when that would be in the party's interest.

5. New III Corps commander Du Quoc Dong was disheartened by the lack of JGS support for reinforcement and resigned, replaced by Nguyen Van Toan, who had been removed from II Corps earlier. Nothing more clearly indicated the paucity of capable field commanders at the senior level. Assigning General Hieu would have been a better choice.

6. The supplemental appropriation was $300 million for RVN; $222 million was also requested for Cambodia.

7. I remembered Colby's dictum at the time of Congressman McCloskey's visit in 1971: One should never lie to an elected representative.

8. Besides connecting Frank, I provided other suggestions to representatives, but I also persuaded Representative Abzug not to attend an antigovernment demonstration the evening of departure.

9. I learned months later from Nguyen Be that, in another example of past experience ruling analysis, Pham Van Phu (captured at Dien Bien Phu during the anti-French war) was especially concerned for Kontum and Pleiku because in February 1954 French forces lost Kontum, Mobile Group 100 was annihilated on Route 19, and the whole highlands unraveled. Be's point was that Phu was inclined to fear repetition of the pattern.

10. I am aware that the 22nd was being pressured in Binh Dinh, but hard choices were necessary, and I believe two regiments could have been made available.

11. Route 7B had not been used for years, a key bridge was out, fords were impassable, and time would not allow for the necessary engineering. There was no easy alternative. Only a major effort to open Route 19 (at great cost) or major effort to retake Banmethuot (at great cost) and then evacuate the highlands on Route 14 to 21 could have been considered. And even then it might not have worked.

12. Lionel Rosenblatt and Craig Johnstone, on their own, went from Washington to Saigon and succeeded in assisting many of the PSG cadre to evacuate. Ridiculous guidelines were applied that made it impossible for some to depart. Nay

Luette was tragically abandoned, Nguyen Be escaped on his own on the last day, and Tran Ngoc Chau believes that he was deliberately left behind.

13. I was angry with Jake for years, until one day I saw him on a bench in a small park near the Department of State. He called me over and I sat beside him. His eyes teary, he said, "We had some good years and bad years." I put an arm on his shoulder and knew then that my anger had really been with myself for not doing more.

Index

Abrams, Creighton, 291, 299–300, 305, 311, 323–24

Allitto, Tony, 248–49, 257

Anh, Pham, 23–25, 372nn42–43

An Lao Valley: and Buddhist unrest, 51–52; combined recovery operations in, as model, 45–46, 49–50, 52, 89, 377n40; communist activity in, 45–46; Delta teams in, 172, 174, 403–4n20; destruction in, 282; as favorite place of Scotton, 45, 149; geography of, 45; history of, 45–46; U.S. evacuation of, 162, 376n37

Armed Political Action Teams (APAs), 156–59, 161, 165–66, 189

Army, U.S.: offer of commission in, 178–79

Arnn, Maj., 151–52, 400n11

ARVN/RVNAF: on central Viet Nam, defense of, 60; collapse of support for Diem, 66; Corps commanders, 299, 330–31; corruption and incompetence in, 217, 253, 263, 267, 301; defeats, 1965, 164; desertion rates, 270, 436n9; generals deposing Diem, 76, 101, 145–46, 382n23, 387n14; health of, 269–70, 307, 329–33, 427n39; ineffectiveness of, 59, 106, 119; information programs, 99; isolated bases, vulnerability of, 289; joint command proposals, 141–42, 144, 187; leadership, in 1971, 298–99; morale of, 290; Nguyen Hue Campaign and, 304–5; officers, evasiveness of, 19–20; officers' views on war, 17; Political Warfare Department, 131; poor discipline in, 19; Quang Ngai province operations, 102; rural dislike of, 19; weaponry, 298

Ba (USIS Phu Yen rep.), 23–25, 37–38

Bahnar tribe, 34, 55–56, 77, 89, 164, 288, 378n9

Be, Nguyen: American respect for, 223, 423n14; on Americans, 202, 268; assassination plot against, 179–80; background, 395–96n14; books by, 423n14; and CBS film crew, 174–77; Colby and, 256; co-opting of, 250; as